The Human Rights Dictatorship

Ned Richardson-Little exposes the forgotten history of human rights in the German Democratic Republic, placing the history of the Cold War, Eastern European dissidents and the revolutions of 1989 in a new light. By demonstrating how even a communist dictatorship could imagine itself to be a champion of human rights, this book challenges popular narratives on the fall of the Berlin Wall and illustrates how notions of human rights evolved in the Cold War as they were re-imagined in East Germany by both dissidents and state officials. Ultimately, the fight for human rights in East Germany was part of a global battle in the post-war era over competing conceptions of what human rights meant. Nonetheless, the collapse of dictatorship in East Germany did not end this conflict, as citizens had to choose for themselves what kind of human rights would follow in its wake.

NED RICHARDSON-LITTLE is a Freigeist Fellow at the University of Erfurt, Germany where he leads a project on international crime and globalisation. He received the Fritz Stern Dissertation Prize from the German Historical Institute Washington and a commendation from the Fraenkel Prize committee at the Wiener Library.

Human Rights in History

Edited by
Stefan-Ludwig Hoffmann, *University of California, Berkeley*
Samuel Moyn, *Yale University, Connecticut*

This series showcases new scholarship exploring the backgrounds of human rights today. With an open-ended chronology and international perspective, the series seeks works attentive to the surprises and contingencies in the historical origins and legacies of human rights ideals and interventions. Books in the series will focus not only on the intellectual antecedents and foundations of human rights, but also on the incorporation of the concept by movements, nation-states, international governance, and transnational law.

A full list of titles in the series can be found at:
www.cambridge.org/human-rights-history

The Human Rights Dictatorship

Socialism, Global Solidarity and Revolution in East Germany

Ned Richardson-Little

University of Erfurt

CAMBRIDGE
UNIVERSITY PRESS

University Printing House, Cambridge CB2 8BS, United Kingdom

One Liberty Plaza, 20th Floor, New York, NY 10006, USA

477 Williamstown Road, Port Melbourne, VIC 3207, Australia

314-321, 3rd Floor, Plot 3, Splendor Forum, Jasola District Centre, New Delhi - 110025, India

103 Penang Road, #05-06/07, Visioncrest Commercial, Singapore 238467

Cambridge University Press is part of the University of Cambridge.

It furthers the University's mission by disseminating knowledge in the pursuit of education, learning and research at the highest international levels of excellence.

www.cambridge.org
Information on this title: www.cambridge.org/9781108440783
DOI: 10.1017/9781108341295

First published 2020

A catalogue record for this publication is available from the British Library

ISBN 978-1-108-42467-7 Hardback
ISBN 978-1-108-44078-3 Paperback

Cambridge University Press has no responsibility for the persistence or accuracy of URLs for external or third-party internet websites referred to in this publication, and does not guarantee that any content on such websites is, or will remain, accurate or appropriate.

In memory of
a humanist
Prof. Kurt Sittmann
and
a warrior-scholar
Dr. Prince Kadar White

Contents

Acknowledgements

I was raised in a place that for thousands of years has been the traditional territory of the Huron-Wendat, the Seneca and the Mississaugas of the Credit River, later attending university on unceded Kanien'kehá:ka territory, which has long served as a site of meeting and exchange among indigenous peoples, including the Haudenosaunee and Anishinaabeg nations; and then on the land of the Catawba Nation. I would like to honour and recognise these nations as the custodians of the lands and waters on which I have lived, studied and worked.

In Canada, thank you to Andrea Speltz, Jean-Pierre Hickey, Olivier Jarvis Lavoie, Greg Bouchard, Ryan Bouma, Shinhae Lee, Amy Darwish, Ryan Muscat, Gáspár Csete, Anne Sabourin, Rob Perry and Nikolai Sittmann for everything from the early morning McGill Pizza breakfasts to the late-night attempts to solve the problems of the world. In Toronto, I am grateful to my parents, Ellen and Bruce, my brother Will, sister-in-law Anna, and especially my wee niece Isla for their unflinching support for my hare-brained schemes and for always leaving the light on. To Ruth Gross in Châteauguay, for being a role model through thick and thin – *danke*. In Montréal, my brilliant (in all the ways) cousin Kathleen Perry helped me move into my first and third and fifth apartment and has always been there for me.

In Washington, DC, friendships with Mary McPartland, Andrea O'Brien, Chris Hickman, Natalie Deibel, Elizabeth Charles and Sara Berndt sustained me with both intellectual and culinary fuel – and made America feel like home. I hope to regularly return the favour in Berlin. In North Carolina, I would like to thank Konrad Jarausch, Christopher Browning, Donald Raleigh, Chad Bryant, Cemil Aydin, Susan Pennybacker and Violet Anderson for their generous support and constructive critique. I am also grateful to Jennifer Lynn, Philipp Stelzel, Steven Milder, Jaime Snow, Brittany Lehman, Kristin Dolan, Aaron Hale-Dorell, Julie Ault, Friederike Brühöfener, Daniel Giblin, Sarah Lowry and Derek Holmgren for their insights, solidarity and comradery.

In Exeter (UK), working with James Mark, Raluca Grosescu, Nelly Bekus, Ljubica Spaskovska, Natalie Taylor, Anna Calori, Marc-William

Palen, Rhian Keyse, Tobias Rupprecht, Dóra Vargha and Andrew S. Thompson was an incredibly enriching experience for which I am deeply thankful. I would like to acknowledge the support of the Leverhulme Trust in its funding of "1989 after 1989: Rethinking the Fall of State Socialism" (RL-2012-053). At Cambridge University Press, my gratitude to Michael Watson. Thank you also to a stalwart community of British transplants – Sebastian Gehrig, Jennifer Altehenger, Daniel Steinbach, Thomas Morton and Jameson Tucker.

In Germany, I would like to thank Stefan-Ludwig Hoffmann, Iris Schröder, Stephen Brown and Michal Kopeček for their decisive feedback. Samuel Moyn, Jan Eckel, Paul Betts, Jean Quataert, Marco Duranti and Celia Donert have also been instrumental in crafting this book's arguments – thank you. I am particularly indebted to Lora Wildenthal, whose wisdom and good humour have been indispensable. Through the support of the DAAD, the AHA, the GHI (Washington) and the Berlin Program for Advanced German and European Studies, I was able to complete my research and make lasting connections with Nicole Eaton, Erica Hughes, Jake Smith and Bill Waltz, an invaluable group of engaging scholars. Karin Goihl was a source of constant support and remarkable conversations. In the archives, *ein großes Dankeschön* to Petra Soellner at the Archiv der DDR-Opposition and Christel Brandt at the Stasi Archive, for the tireless efforts. To all the people I have the pleasure of interacting with on Twitter as @historyned – thank you for the insights, the corrections, the humour and for following along all these years. To my colleagues in Erfurt – Christian Methfessel, Iris Schröder, Patrice Poutrus, Franziska Rantzsch, Christiane Kuller, Reiner Prass, Florian Wagner and Silvan Niedermeier – I am grateful for the warm welcome and the true collegiality.

In Berlin, thank you to Sonja Dolinsek, Raluca Grosescu, Andrew Tompkins, Erik Albrecht, Maria Kosboth, Emily Bereskin, Ben Gögge, Luisa Feiersinger, Sage Anderson, Inga Anderson, Ulrich Päßler, Anne McKinney, Adrian Henham, Elizabeth Bonapfel, Janine, Sarah and Timo Fuchs, Anna Delius, Lauren Stokes, Johanna Folland, Lisa Haegele, Erica Weitzman, Alexandra Gruber, Felix Jimenez, David Spreen and Kate Horning – for discussions over coffee at Stabi, Eisern Union at the Alte Försterei, evenings under the trees at Prater, Volkshochschule classes, Spätzle at Schwarze Pumpe, planning conferences over beers at Izzy and Übereck, picnics on Tempelhofer Feld, myriad S-Bahn Ausflüge and exuberant bowls of flaming alcohol in dark, dark German winters.

To the family business that stands behind this book (all errors and omissions are my own): to my neighbour, Ellen Sittmann, for teaching me the dative, and, despite proof-reading every footnote, still coming over with chocolate and tickets for »*KUNST*«. To Julia Sittmann – for the tenacity, ingenuity, critical eye and ability to make everything an adventure. My hope is that they accept recompense in home-cooked meals and occasional(ly) witty banter.

My father-in-law, Kurt Sittmann, read every word of the dissertation upon which this book is based, sometimes several times, and continued to cheer me on anyways. His endless inquisitiveness, scientific rigour and belief in the fundamental place of human dignity and equality in nature continue to inspire me. Dr. Prince White was a brilliant scholar, mentor and social justice activist who returned to his ancestors far too soon. His loss is incalculable, but what he has built will be felt for generations. His determination, oratory and revolutionary ideals should serve as a guiding light for us all. It is to them I dedicate this book.

Abbreviations

BEK	Bund der Evangelischen Kirchen in der DDR
CDU	Christlich Demokratische Union Deutschlands
CSU	Christlich-Soziale Union (Bavaria)
FRG	Federal Republic of Germany
GDR	German Democratic Republic
GfM	Gesellschaft für Menschenrechte – Society for the Protection of Human Rights
ICCPR	International Covenant on Civil and Political Rights
IFM	Initiative für Frieden und Menschenrechte (Initiative for Peace and Human Rights)
KMR	DDR-Komitee für Menschenrechte (GDR-Committee for Human Rights, successor to KSM)
KPD	Kommunistische Partei Deutschlands (Communist Party of Germany)
KSM	Komitee zum Schutze der Menschenrechte (Committee for the Protection of Human Rights)
NATO	North Atlantic Treaty Organization
SDP	Sozialdemokratische Partei (Social Democratic Party, GDR)
SED	Sozialistische Einheitspartei Deutschlands (Socialist Unity Party)
SPD	Sozialdemokratische Partei Deutschlands (Social Democratic Party, FRG)
UDHR	Universal Declaration of Human Rights
USSR	Union of Soviet Socialist Republics
WCC	World Council of Churches

Introduction
The Exploitation of Man by Man Has Been Abolished!

On a cold evening in November 1989, human rights triumphed, and the Berlin Wall disintegrated. Ninety-nine red balloons vanquishing the evil empire.... Or at least that is how the story is usually told: the dictatorship of the Socialist Unity Party (SED) crumbled in the face of several thousand citizens demanding their innate and natural rights. Once the Berlin Wall opened, elections were held, and the state-socialist German Democratic Republic (GDR) vanished, absorbed into the Federal Republic of Germany (FRG). The artificial division of the German nation was overcome, and 18 million people regained their human rights, all of them now "former" citizens of the GDR, a state thrown onto the trash heap of history. Writing in 1978, the East German intellectual Hermann Klenner seemed to have predicted all of this: "Illusion and hypocrisy may be able to delay recognition of truth in the question of human rights, but progress is inevitable. [...] The people will see to this."[1] Surprisingly, this late 1970s testament to the enduring power of human rights was not about a burgeoning circle of dissidents challenging SED rule, but was in fact about the glories of "real existing socialism" in the GDR. The "illusion and hypocrisy" whose days were numbered were those of the capitalist West. For Klenner, the rapid rise of Western human rights activism in the 1970s represented a reactionary attack on progress, an attempt to undermine the valiant work of the natural leaders in the field of human rights: East Germany and the rest of the Socialist Bloc led by the Soviet Union.

Few today would name the German Democratic Republic among the historical pillars of modern human rights. The core tenet of the modern international human rights movement, as it has been propagated since the 1970s, maintains that all human beings possess individual rights that both exist above and beyond the state, and that limit the power of governments to constrain the freedom of their citizens. By this definition,

---

[1] Hermann Klenner, "Human Rights – Hypocrisy and Truth," *Bulletin – GDR Committee for Human Rights* 3, no.1 (1978), 15.

East German citizens were severely lacking in rights. From the founding of the GDR in 1949 to its collapse 40 years later, East Germans had no legal means to claim rights against the state. Under SED rule, political and civil rights – such as freedom of speech and assembly – were strictly limited and policed for ideological content. Popular elections were not competitive and served only to confirm SED rule. The Ministry of State Security – the *Stasi* – conducted mass surveillance, held political prisoners in arbitrary detention, and engaged in psychological torture to suppress dissent and quash opposition.[2] While the Christian church did exist behind the Berlin Wall, the state pressured citizens to renounce their religious affiliation by withholding social and career opportunities and conscientious objectors to mandatory military service faced a harsh alternative as uniformed labourers.[3] To control the movement of its citizens, the SED built a complex of deadly border fortifications, including a 140 km long *wall* around West Berlin, an island located in the heart of the GDR. To get to the West without the requisite permissions, one had to pass through the "death strip" and face a gauntlet of dogs, mines, self-firing weapons and armed guards authorised to use lethal force to stop those intent on committing the crime of "fleeing the Republic." A total of 101 victims were attempting to cross the border, 30 had no intention of crossing, 8 were GDR border guards killed on duty, and one was a Soviet soldier killed by accident.[4]

Since German reunification in 1990, the Stasi and the Berlin Wall have become popular metaphors, symbols of oppressive secret police and inhuman border regimes; the GDR has become synonymous with the abuse of human rights.[5] According to the SED, however, the GDR was a leader in the field of human rights. Almost from its inception in 1946, the

---

[2] Gary Bruce, *The Firm: The Inside Story of the Stasi* (Oxford: Oxford University Press, 2012); Jens Gieseke, *The History of the Stasi: East Germany's Secret Police, 1945–1990* (New York: Berghahn, 2014).

[3] On conscientious objectors, see Bernd Eisenfeld and Peter Schicketanz, *Bausoldaten in der DDR: Die "Zusammenführung feindlich-negativer Kräfte" in der NVA* (Berlin: Ch. Links, 2012).

[4] A total of 101 victims were attempting to cross the border, 30 had no intention of crossing (including a Soviet soldier), and 8 were GDR border guards killed on duty. Hans-Hermann Hertle and Maria Nooke, *Die Todesopfer an der Berliner Mauer 1961–1989: Ergebnisse eines Forschungsprojektes des ZZF Potsdam und der Stiftung Berliner Mauer* (August 2017) (www.berliner-mauer-gedenkstaette.de).

[5] On popular representations of Stasi oppression as the epitome of the GDR, see the film *The Lives of Others* (2006), or Anna Funder's bestseller *Stasiland: Stories from behind the Berlin Wall* (London: Granta Books, 2011). On East Germany and the Berlin Wall as symbols of human rights abuses, see Nick Hodgin and Caroline Pearce, *The GDR Remembered: Representations of the East German State since 1989* (Rochester, NY: Camden House, 2011), 2; Manfred Wilke, *The Path to the Berlin Wall: Critical Stages in the History of Divided Germany* (New York: Berghahn, 2014), 1.

SED claimed to be at the vanguard of human rights, and in 1959 – two years *before* the founding of Amnesty International – the Party created the first human rights organisation in the Eastern Bloc. The SED claimed that the realisation of socialism on German soil had eradicated the roots of fascism and had forever prevented the resurgence of Nazism, which represented the very antithesis of human rights. The end of capitalist class conflict had ushered in a true form of democracy, both politically and in the workplace. Social and economic rights were provided through the state subsidisation or the direct provision of basic needs, which extended to transportation, education, jobs, recreation and cultural opportunities. Only under socialism – where "the exploitation of man by man has been abolished!" – could one truly experience human rights.

The SED also saw itself as a steadfast champion of human rights beyond the borders of the GDR: it fought for the rights of oppressed antifascists, communists and peace activists in West Germany, which they claimed (not entirely without merit) was run by former Nazis, many of whom sought to suppress the Left and remilitarise the German nation. On the world stage, the SED supported the rights of women; attacked imperialist racism in Africa and Asia; campaigned against military regimes in Southern Europe and Latin America; and offered humanitarian aid to fellow socialists around the world.[6] For the SED, this was more than just sloganeering and propaganda: the GDR legally committed itself to multiple UN covenants and treaties – often several years before Western nations – and agreed to the human rights provisions contained in the Helsinki Accords in 1975 on the basis that East Germany was already in full compliance with the norms of international human rights law.

Such claims of socialist superiority in the field of human rights are – clearly – at odds with the way the history of human rights in the Cold War is usually told. The standard narrative emphasises those Western activists, diplomats and statespeople, who successfully campaigned to impose the values of liberal democratic individualism onto recalcitrant socialist states through human rights treaties.[7] In this retelling, the Eastern Bloc

---

[6] On women's rights and state socialism, see Celia Donert, "Whose Utopia? Gender, Ideology and Human Rights at the 1975 World Congress of Women in East Berlin," in Jan Eckel and Samuel Moyn, *The Breakthrough: Human Rights in the 1970s* (Philadelphia: University of Pennsylvania Press, 2014); On solidarity with the Global South and black liberation, see Quinn Slobodian, *Comrades of Color: East Germany in the Cold War World* (New York: Berghahn, 2015). On GDR humanitarianism, see Young-Sun Hong, *Cold War Germany, the Third World, and the Global Humanitarian Regime* (Cambridge: Cambridge University Press, 2015).

[7] Rosemary Foot, "The Cold War and Human Rights," in *The Cambridge History of the Cold War. Vol. III.*, eds. Melvyn Leffler and Odd Arne Westad (Cambridge: Cambridge

defied human rights in all of its forms by abstaining on the Universal Declaration of Human Rights (UDHR) in 1948, and only relenting under duress in 1975 with the Final Act of the Conference on Security and Co-operation in Europe (CSCE) signed in Helsinki by 35 countries in Eastern and Western Europe and which included provisions recognising the validity of international human rights.[8] The Helsinki Accords ostensibly marked the beginning of the end of state socialism as the Eastern Bloc was hit by a "boomerang effect" wherein their citizens suddenly recognised the hypocrisy and cynicism of state socialist promises and rose up to demand their human rights.[9] Under pressure from domestic dissident, foreign diplomats and international NGOs, Soviet General Secretary Mikhail Gorbachev relented and began to implement the human rights he already committed to in the Accords and this spread across the Eastern Bloc toppling countries like dominos in 1989.[10] The end of the Cold War and the victory of human rights were one and the same.

But there was no inherent "bulldozer logic" of human rights that drove East Germans towards revolution, and this book is not a history of the innate power of human rights to spark democracy, freedom and justice in the face of tyranny.[11] Rather, this is a history of how human rights acted to legitimise a socialist dictatorship, before playing a crucial role in its downfall. The SED advanced its own vision of socialist human rights, and East German elites were active participants in the creation of human rights politics within Europe – and later on the world stage. From below,

University Press, 2010), 445–65. Works arguing that human rights were absent from East German politics before 1975 include Christian Joppke, *East German Dissidents and the Revolution of 1989: Social Movement in a Leninist Regime* (New York: New York University Press, 1995), 116; Jürgen Wüst, *Menschenrechtsarbeit im Zwielicht: zwischen Staatssicherheit und Antifaschismus* (Bonn: Bouvier, 1999), 32; Steven Pfaff, "The Politics Of Peace in the GDR: The Independent Peace Movement, the Church, and the Origins of the East German Opposition," *Peace and Change* 26, no. 3 (2001), 287.

[8] The main work asserting that the Helsinki Accords had a revolutionary impact in the Eastern Bloc is Daniel Thomas, *The Helsinki Effect: International Norms, Human Rights, and the Demise of Communism* (Princeton, NJ: Princeton University Press, 2001). Michael Ignatieff argues that the Eastern Bloc had already accepted social and economic rights, but denied the validity of political and civil human rights prior to Helsinki, see *Human Rights as Politics and Idolatry* (Princeton, NJ: Princeton University Press, 2001), 19. Sarah Snyder provides a more nuanced interpretation by examining Helsinki through the lens of transnational social movements, *Human Rights Activism and the End of the Cold War: A Transnational History of the Helsinki Network* (Cambridge: Cambridge University Press, 2011).

[9] Thomas Risse, Stephen Ropp and Kathryn Sikkink, eds., *The Power of Human Rights: International Norms and Domestic Change* (Cambridge: Cambridge University Press, 1999).

[10] Daniel Thomas, "Human Rights Ideas, the Demise of Communism, and the End of the Cold War," *Journal of Cold War Studies* 7, no. 2 (2005), 110–41.

[11] Lynn Hunt, *Inventing Human Rights* (New York: Norton, 2008), 160.

East Germans were not simply passive recipients of a liberal democratic human rights politics delivered to them, prepackaged, by Western activists. On the path to 1989, the people of the GDR had to first reimagine human rights from a domestic perspective to fight for religious freedoms within the socialist system, for the right to emigrate from East Germany or for a new version of socialism that would fulfil the promise of real democratic emancipation. This book is a history of how East Germans, over the four decades of the GDR's existence, imagined, propagandised and instrumentalised human rights in the name of a multitude of shifting ideals: socialism, antifascism, anti-imperialism, Christianity, peace, the environment, democracy and ultimately – the creation of a unified German state.

Human rights, as an idea, had no political or social power without human actors; the abstract rights listed in treaties and covenants only gained meaning in everyday life when they were translated into the cultural and political language of local environments.[12] The question thus becomes how and why a variety of actors within East Germany chose to engage with the growing global human rights system to advance their own particular, and often conflicting, agendas. For most of the actors in this story, human rights were not a lofty concern divorced from the messiness of politics and society, but a moral, legal and rhetorical lens through which to understand the problems of justice and equality both at home and abroad. This book explores how various East Germans adopted global human rights ideas from UN treaties and international activists and imbued this language with local cultural and political meaning to legitimise a state socialist dictatorship under the SED, to demand the reform of the socialist status quo and eventually to justify a revolution and the dissolution of the GDR.

A central theme here is how the SED and East German elites came to understand human rights as a fundamental element of state socialist ideology and the global Cold War. Historians have often struggled to explain how the leaders of the SED could have been so foolish and reckless as to sign on to treaties that contained human rights provisions that were so self-evidently contrary to all fundamental aspects of the East

---

[12] For a classic critique of "ideas [that] get up and do battle on their own behalf," see Quentin Skinner, "Meaning and Understanding in the History of Ideas," *History and Theory* 8, no. 1 (1969), 11. On translation and "vernacularization," see Sally Engle Merry, "Transnational Human Rights and Local Activism: Mapping the Middle," *American Anthropologist* 108, no. 1 (2006), 38–51. On the importance of centering people – and not norms – in human rights history, see Lora Wildenthal, *The Language of Human Rights in West Germany* (Philadelphia: University of Pennsylvania Press, 2012), 169.

German political system. One theory is that the GDR and other Eastern Bloc countries were outmanoeuvred by canny Western diplomats who managed to insert the language of human rights into the Helsinki agreement against the will of communist negotiators unprepared to engage with this issue.[13] Some argue that the SED did recognise human rights as a political danger, but was coerced into signing the Accords out of economic desperation.[14] Others claim that SED chief Erich Honecker dismissed human rights as a triviality, or cynically agreed to the Accords as a ploy to gain international prestige without any intention of living up to its contents.[15] Or they allege the SED wanted to demonstrate its strength and to sadistically prove that they, the people, held no power.[16] Others still remain perplexed as to how senior members of the SED could not see that their entire system of rule violated international human rights.[17]

By presuming that the SED viewed human rights as a threatening and alien notion, scholars have been at a loss to explain its actions and, in turn, missed the implications of socialist human rights politics in the evolution of East German diplomacy and the rise of a domestic opposition. From the perspective of the SED leadership and GDR elites, it was self-evident that human rights legitimised the cause of socialism, and that UN human rights treaties intended to secure the right to self-determination and state sovereignty for all in the face of (and most definitely not in the service of) Western imperialism. According to the view of the SED, there were bourgeois forces within the GDR and in the West that sought to corrupt the concept of human rights and use it as a tool for foreign interventionism. But such forces were in a minority

---

[13] Ferraris claims that "once having accepted – at the preparatory stage in Helsinki – that the principle of human rights should appear in the list, the USSR and the other Socialist countries found that it was more appropriate not to contest too strongly the legitimacy of the principle, but to formulate instead their own interpretation of it." Luigi Ferraris and Mario Alessi, *Report on a Negotiation, Helsinki-Geneva-Helsinki, 1972–1975* (Geneva: Sijthoff & Noordhoff, 1979), 106.

[14] Imanuel Geiss, *The Question of German Unification: 1806–1996* (London: Routledge, 1997), 102; John Schmeidel, *Stasi: Sword and Shield of the Party* (London: Taylor & Francis, 2007), 61.

[15] On the side of triviality, see Mary Elise Sarotte, *The Collapse: The Accidental Opening of the Berlin Wall* (New York: Basic Books, 2014), 18. For cynicism, see Charles Maier, *Dissolution: The Crisis of Communism and the End of East Germany* (Princeton, NJ: Princeton University Press, 1997), 127.

[16] Anthony Glees, "Social Transformation Studies and Human Rights Abuses in East Germany after 1945," in *Recasting East Germany: Social Transformation after the GDR*, eds. Christopher Flockton and Eva Kolinsky (Portland: Frank Cass, 1999), 175.

[17] Frederick Taylor, *The Berlin Wall: A World Divided, 1961–1989* (New York: Harper Collins, 2008), 381.

position, and they faced a united opposition by the rest of the Socialist Bloc, as well as by the growing power of the Afro-Asian Bloc.

The SED developed this perspective through a long-standing engagement with the concept of human rights, beginning in 1946, as they defended their newborn party against attacks from the more established Social Democrats (SPD). From there, the SED both founded the Eastern Bloc's first human rights organisation in 1959 and developed an academic field of "socialist human rights," led by GDR-trained legal experts. The SED integrated the idea of human rights into its discourse, ideology and diplomacy in an era – the 1960s – when the recently decolonised states of Africa and Asia were dominant in international affairs and had put self-determination and economic sovereignty at the centre of the UN human rights agenda.[18] In the years leading up to the Helsinki Accords, anti-colonialism was a much more powerful force in comparison to the fledgling Western liberal non-governmental organisation (NGO) movement, providing an international structure that bolstered the SED's confidence in signing onto the Helsinki Accords.[19] In place of a narrative in which liberal norms originated in the West and spread to the rest of the world, the evolution of human rights in the GDR can only be understood in the context of the Socialist Bloc's engagement with a global system in which multiple ideological conceptions of human rights competed for legitimacy, influence over international institutions and the hearts and minds of people around the globe.

Just as the concept of human rights was not inherently threatening to the SED, it was also not always seen by East Germans as a means of overthrowing state socialism. In challenging the dictatorship of the SED, East Germans often borrowed from the language of the state to

---

[18] Martin Sabrow, "Dictatorship as Discourse: Cultural Perspectives on SED Legitimacy," in *Dictatorship as Experience: Towards a Socio-Cultural History of the GDR*, ed. Conrad Jarausch (New York: Berghahn, 1999), 195–212; Roland Burke, *Decolonization and the Evolution of International Human Rights* (Philadelphia: University of Pennsylvania Press, 2010); Steven Jensen, *The Making of International Human Rights: The 1960s, Decolonization, and the Reconstruction of Global Values* (Cambridge: Cambridge University Press, 2016).

[19] Some have noted the SED's willingness to agree to human rights provisions, but without contextualising its prior engagement with human rights ideology: Hermann Wentker, "Pursuing Specific Interests within the Warsaw Pact: The GDR and the CSCE-Process," in *The Helsinki Process: A Historical Reappraisal*, ed. Carla Meneguzzi Rostagni (Padova: CEDAM, 2005), 45–61; Oliver Bange, "The GDR in the Era of Détente: Conflicting Perceptions and Strategies, 1965–1975," in *Perforating the Iron Curtain : European Détente, Transatlantic Relations, and the Cold War, 1965–1985*, eds. Poul Villaume and Odd Arne Westad (Copenhagen: Tusculanum Press, 2010); Anja Hanisch, *Die DDR im KSZE-Prozess 1972–1985: Zwischen Ostabhängigkeit, Westabgrenzung und Ausreisebewegung* (Munich: Oldenbourg, 2012).

press for freedoms at the margins or for greater rights within the system, rather than demanding revolutionary change outright. Thus, long before human rights became a popular rallying cry for democratisation in 1989, East Germans used the language of international human rights as a tool for negotiating their place within the SED dictatorship. Indeed, GDR human rights protests only began in 1968, when the SED introduced a new constitution to coincide with the UN International Year for Human Rights and asked citizens to submit feedback on the draft, prior to a national referendum on its adoption. The new constitution greatly reduced formal protections for religious freedom, and East German Christians wrote to the state by the thousands – referencing UN human rights treaties – to demand the preservation of their religious freedom. Rather than challenging SED authority, however, the Christian community argued that these rights were necessary so that they could be good socialist citizens. The language of human rights thus served as a tool of negotiation for greater freedom within socialism – not as a means to destroy it.

Despite the explosion of international NGO activism in 1970s (not only in the West, but also in Eastern Europe), the use of human rights as a tool for democratisation and political reform in the GDR only began in the mid-1980s, with the founding of the Initiative for Peace and Human Rights (Initiative Frieden und Menschenrechte, or IFM). The GDR human rights movement emerged from existing movements for peace, the environment, and anti-imperial solidarity and it sought to democratise East German socialism rather than end it entirely.[20] For the IFM and many other East German dissidents and reformers, human rights was seen as a means of saving the ideals of socialism from its current state of bureaucratic stagnation and abuse as realised in the Eastern Bloc.[21] As the SED struggled to cope with a steadily escalating economic crisis and a massive outflow of citizens in the late 1980s, many East German elites became disillusioned with the realities of SED-led state socialism. Hard-line SED leaders alienated lower-level state officials, who watched in dismay as the system around them collapsed through inaction and ideological rigidity. With dissident groups demanding democratised

---

[20] On the rise of human rights dissidents demanding democratisation, see Wolfgang Rüddenklau, *Störenfried: DDR-Opposition 1986–1989* (Berlin: BasisDruck, 1992); Marianne Schulz, *Von der Illegalität ins Parlament: Werdegang und Konzepte der neuen Bürgerbewegungen* (Berlin: Ch. Links, 1992); Thomas Klein, *"Frieden und Gerechtigkeit!": die Politisierung der Unabhängigen Friedensbewegung in Ost-Berlin während der 80er Jahre* (Cologne: Böhlau, 2007).

[21] On human rights as a minimalist post-socialist utopian movement, see Samuel Moyn, *Last Utopia: Human Rights in History* (Cambridge, MA: Belknap, 2010).

socialism from below, human rights acted as shared language between protestors and those state officials who now saw the need for reform. This sense of common purpose helped to forestall a violent crackdown on mass demonstrations and prepared the path to the peaceful transition of power. Human rights did not spark the revolution of 1989, but the idea did help mobilise a broad cross-section of East German society against the dictatorship. The multivalent capacity of human rights to hold a wide variety of meanings and to represent a diversity of political and social aspirations allowed for the creation of a heterodox coalition of interest groups, ranging from radical environmentalists, disaffected artists, conservative Christians and reform communists.

The irony of human rights in East Germany is that the same human rights propaganda and ideology that acted to stabilise and legitimise the SED for decades ultimately contributed to its rapid downfall, as even party members lost faith in the righteousness of the party's dictatorship.[22] In the hands of the state, the idea of human rights was one more tool of legitimisation, but once successfully wrested from the SED by dissident groups, human rights began to serve as a unifying ideal for peaceful revolution. For many lower-tier state functionaries, the meaning of human rights radically shifted as the Party proved itself both incapable of addressing the ongoing crisis and brutal in its response to those who seemed to be presenting constructive criticism.[23] The example of the GDR reveals how, in the words of Costas Douzinas, "human rights are Janus-like, they carry the dual ability to emancipate and dominate, to protect and discipline."[24] The SED's monopolisation of the human rights discourse forestalled the opposition that bubbled up in the 1970s, but its long-term enthusiasm for the concept also meant that when mass protests did erupt in 1989, dissident human rights demands were devastatingly effective in co-opting mid-level elites who sympathised with this message.

In the end, the opening of the Berlin Wall was not the final triumph for East German human rights dissidents, but instead led to the shattering of

---

[22] On the "paradox of stability and revolution," see Sigrid Meuschel, *Legitimation und Parteiherrschaft: zum Paradox von Stabilität und Revolution in der DDR, 1945–1989* (Frankfurt am Main: Suhrkamp, 1992); Detlef Pollack, "Modernization and Modernization Blockages in GDR Society," in *Dictatorship as Experience*, 27–46; Andrew Port, *Conflict and Stability in the GDR* (Cambridge: Cambridge University Press, 2007).

[23] On the rapid shifts in meaning within the discursive world of late socialism, see Alexei Yurchak, *Everything Was Forever, Until It Was No More: The Last Soviet Generation* (Princeton, NJ: Princeton University Press, 2006).

[24] Costas Douzinas, *The End of Human Rights: Critical Legal Thought at the Turn of the Century* (Portland, OR: Hart Publishing, 2000), 175.

the broad coalition that had formed through their opposition to SED rule. Not only did the end of the SED eliminate the focal point that united the mass protests, it raised new questions about how these multivalent visions of human rights would be realised in practice. Only after November 1989 was the idea of human rights widely deployed within the GDR to legitimise economic and political liberalisation through unification with West Germany. While the dissident movement sought to work with reform communists to create a renewed democratised socialism, they were crushed in elections held in March 1990, heralding the end of an independent GDR. Without an independent East Germany, the idea of legitimising a socialist dictatorship in the name of human rights became absurd and led to the erasure of socialist human rights from historical memory and scholarship – a process so complete that the traces that remain are written off as mere propaganda produced by a cynical state. Along with socialist human rights, the diversity of dissident thought has also been subsumed into grand historical narratives of liberal (or neoliberal) human rights sweeping through the Eastern Bloc. The example of the GDR shows, however, that human rights are far from timeless or self-evident, but are always in a state of perpetual reinvention, and that hegemonic regimes of human rights can fall apart with remarkable speed.

Until recently, the history of human rights was written as a linear narrative of progress – from ancient times to the French and American Revolutions – culminating in the postwar creation of the UDHR and the late twentieth-century rise of international NGO activism.[25] Rather than trying to trace the evolution of human rights as a singular universal ideal, the scholarship has turned towards a focus on discontinuities in the meaning of rights between different eras. While historical actors from the American Revolution, 1960s anti-colonial activists and Western human rights NGO workers in the 1990s all spoke about inherent human rights, the political and social agenda they were describing was often radically different, even contradictory.[26] In the past decade, a new wave of scholarship has argued, in the words of Jean Quataert, that "rights are

---

[25] Paul Gordon Lauren, *The Evolution of International Human Rights: Visions Seen* (Philadelphia: University of Pennsylvania Press, 2003); Micheline Ishay, *The History of Human Rights: From Ancient Times to the Globalization Era* (Berkeley: University of California Press, 2008).

[26] Moyn argues that the contemporary human rights movement can be traced back to the proliferation of NGO activism in the 1970s, while Hoffmann argues that it is more accurately a product of the post–Cold War era with the turn in the 1990s towards military interventionism in the name of protecting human rights. Moyn, *Last Utopia*; Stefan-Ludwig Hoffmann, "Human Rights and History," *Past & Present* 232, no. 1 (2016), 279–310.

not self-evident, self-policing, or ethically monolithic; they are historical constructs rooted in struggle and are even at odds with one another."[27] Rather than positioning the modern human rights system – including the international legal structures of the United Nations and the global activist networks of NGOs – as the natural endpoint of a millennium-long struggle for justice, it is simply the latest translation of human rights into political action.

The turn towards a more critical historical perspective has produced a broader exploration of the competing genealogies of human rights. Instead of viewing the history of human rights solely as the universal struggle for individual freedom, historians have begun to rediscover the social and political movements that have challenged or contradicted liberal conceptions of rights. If human rights acted as the "lingua franca of global moral thought" in the late twentieth century, it was a language with many dialects – not all of which were mutually intelligible.[28] Prior to the 1970s, human rights were much more closely associated with the establishment of national power and the assertion of state sovereignty as part of Afro-Asian demands for decolonialisation and self-determination.[29]

Despite the widening of perspectives on human rights, scholars have only glancingly engaged with the legacy of how socialists have understood human rights.[30] In most historical accounts, the Eastern Bloc plays the role of antagonist in the grand narrative of eventual Western triumph: state socialism acts as the totalitarian heavy denying freedoms in the name of complete state control in contrast to the modern international human rights movement with its focus on the legal protection of the individual.[31] When a socialist contribution to rights is recognised, it is

---

[27] Jean Quataert, *Advocating Dignity: Human Rights Mobilizations in Global Politics* (Philadelphia: University of Pennsylvania Press, 2011), 4.

[28] On human rights as a *lingua franca* see Ignatieff, *Human Rights as Politics and Idolatry*, 53. On the plurality of human rights conceptions in the immediate postwar period, see Mark Goodale, "The Myth of Universality: The UNESCO 'Philosophers' Committee' and the Making of Human Rights," *Law & Social Inquiry* 43, no. 3 (2018), 596–617. On "polycentrism" and human rights history, see Jan Eckel, *Die Ambivalenz des Guten: Menschenrechte in der internationalen Politik seit den 1940ern* (Göttingen: Vandenhoeck & Ruprecht, 2015).

[29] Stefan-Ludwig Hoffmann, "Genealogies of Human Rights," in *Human Rights in the Twentieth Century*, ed. Stefan-Ludwig Hoffmann (Cambridge: Cambridge University Press, 2010), 4.

[30] An exception in the earlier generation of scholarship is Micheline Ishay, "The Socialist Contributions to Human Rights: An Overlooked Legacy," *The International Journal of Human Rights* 9, no. 2 (2005), 225–45.

[31] Accounts of US advocacy of postwar human rights often use Soviet opposition as a foil, see Mary Ann Glendon, *A World Made New: Eleanor Roosevelt and the Universal Declaration of Human Rights* (New York: Random House, 2001). Other scholars have

presumed to be limited in scope to social and economic rights – again in contrast to the West, where political and civil rights were the priority.[32] In the scholarship on human rights in Eastern Europe, the emphasis has been placed on dissident activists and their role in dismantling state socialism from the 1970s onwards, in conjunction with their international allies in the West.[33] In recent years, however, socialist conceptions of human rights have been rediscovered, with Benjamin Nathans writing on the role of rights language in the domestic politics of the USSR, and Jennifer Amos and Elizabeth Kerley exploring the role of human rights in Soviet diplomacy.[34] In the case of East Germany, Paul Betts has examined the relationship between social rights policy and international human rights; Anja Hanisch has investigated the complexities of East German participation in the Helsinki Accords; and Katharina Kunter has delved into the overlapping conceptions of human rights between East German Protestants, the World Council of Churches and the SED.[35]

Rather than seeing the history of human rights as one of revolution alone, it is also part of the rich history of complaint, negotiation and

demonstrated that Eastern Bloc criticism of racial inequality shaped US state responses to civil rights activism. Carol Anderson, *Eyes off the Prize: The United Nations and the African American Struggle for Human Rights, 1944–1955* (Cambridge: Cambridge University Press, 2003); Mary Dudziak, *Cold War Civil Rights: Race and the Image of American Democracy* (Princeton, NJ: Princeton University Press, 2011).

[32] The idea that the West offered political rights, the East offered social rights, and the Third World offered solidarity rights, stems from Karel Vasek's flawed Three Generations model. Steven Jensen, "Putting to Rest the Three Generations Theory of Human Rights," *Open Global Rights* (blog), November 2017 (www.openglobalrights.org).

[33] Snyder, *Human Rights Activism and the End of the Cold War*; Robert Horvath, "Breaking the Totalitarian Ice: The Initiative Group for the Defense of Human Rights in the USSR," *Human Rights Quarterly* 36, no. 1 (2014), 147–75; Robert Brier, "Broadening the Cultural History of the Cold War: The Emergence of the Polish Workers' Defense Committee and the Rise of Human Rights," *Journal of Cold War Studies* 15, no. 4 (2014), 104–27; Jonathan Bolton, *Worlds of Dissent: Charter 77, the Plastic People of the Universe, and Czech Culture under Communism* (Cambridge, MA: Harvard University Press, 2012).

[34] Benjamin Nathans, "Soviet Rights-Talk in the Post-Stalin Era," in *Human Rights in the Twentieth Century*, 166–90; Jennifer Amos, "Embracing and Contesting: The Soviet Union and the Universal Declaration of Human Rights, 1948–1958," in *Human Rights in the Twentieth Century*, 147–65; Elizabeth Kerley, "The Contest for Human Rights: Soviet Soft Power through Détente, Reform, and Collapse, 1973–1991." PhD diss., Harvard University, 2016.

[35] Paul Betts, "Socialism, Social Rights, and Human Rights: The Case of East Germany," *Humanity* 3, no. 3 (2012), 407–26; Anja Hanisch, *Die DDR im KSZE-Prozess 1972–1985*; Katharina Kunter, "Human Rights as a Theological and Political Controversy among East German and Czech Protestants," in *Christianity and Modernity in Eastern Europe*, eds. Bruce Berglund and Brian Porter (New York: Central European University Press, 2010), 217–43.

protest in everyday life in the GDR.[36] East Germans protested, complained about and critiqued SED policy through accepted legal means; dissented by challenging the state illegally, both individually and at times *en masse*; finally, formed opposition groups aimed at directly taking power from the SED in 1989. Conversely, East Germany was a dictatorship, but SED officials were forced to engage in a constant process of compromise and negotiation to implement its plans and gain the cooperation of the population.[37] As Konrad Jarausch has argued, East Germany was a "welfare dictatorship" – a classification that "recalls the ideological goals of socialism, and the vision of an egalitarian social reform that it hoped to achieve for the benefit of the lower classes," while still underscoring "the forced nature of the GDR's socialist utopia and coercive methods used to achieve its goals."[38] The SED secured stability with social engagement and economic benefits, not just mass surveillance and the repression of the state security apparatus.

To build upon this existing scholarship, this book intertwines the history of human rights as ideology, discourse, law, diplomacy and domestic politics, with a focus on how concepts of human rights were generated, publicised, instrumentalised and internalised. In so doing, the history of human rights in the GDR must also be situated in a dynamic system of international politics and processes of globalisation. The division of Germany created an arena of competition for international legitimacy that drove the SED to contend with human rights criticism, more so than any other socialist state.[39] Generating its language of rights

---

[36] These definitions of critique, protest, dissent and opposition are adapted from Ehrhart Neubert, *Geschichte der Opposition in der DDR: 1949–1989* (Berlin: Ch. Links, 1998), 29–33.

[37] On the GDR as a totalitarian state and criticisms of this framing, see Andrew Port, "The Banalities of East German Historiography," in *Becoming East German: Socialist Structures and Sensibilities after Hitler*, eds. Mary Fulbrook and Andrew Port (New York: Berghahn, 2013), 2–9. On the everyday negotiation of power and conflict, see Mark Allinson, *Politics and Popular Opinion in East Germany 1945–1968* (Manchester: Manchester University Press, 2000); Jeannette Madarász, *Conflict and Compromise in East Germany, 1971–1989: A Precarious Stability* (Houndmills: Palgrave Macmilan, 2003); Port, *Conflict and Stability in the GDR*; Sandrine Kott, *Communism Day-to-Day: State Enterprises in East German Society* (Ann Arbor: University of Michigan Press, 2014). On the GDR as a "participatory dictatorship," see Mary Fulbrook, *The People's State: East German Society from Hitler to Honecker* (New Haven, CT: Yale University Press, 2008).

[38] Konrad Jarausch, "Care and Coercion: The GDR as Welfare Dictatorship," in *Dictatorship as Experience*, 60.

[39] On the diplomatic competition between the two Germanies, see William Gray, *Germany's Cold War: The Global Campaign to Isolate East Germany, 1949–1969* (Chapel Hill: University of North Carolina Press, 2003); Hermann Wentker, *Außenpolitik in engen Grenzen: Die DDR im Internationalen System, 1949–1989* (Munich: Oldenbourg, 2007); Mathias Stein, *Der Konflikt um Alleinvertretung und Anerkennung in der UNO: Die*

in dialogue with Western critics and domestic dissidents meant that the SED also had to align this translation with that of its Eastern Bloc allies and simultaneously appeal to the Global South. East German Christians formed their own language of protest not only in reaction to the SED but also inspired by contacts with global ecumenical Christianity. Dissidents in the GDR were both aligned with transnational activist movements that bridged the European East-West divide and linked to organisations in the Global South. The human rights movement of the 1980s triangulated between the everyday problems of East Germans, the ideology of the SED and the transnational human rights movement, to strike a balance between constructive citizenship and anti-state opposition. While 1989 was the most dramatic highpoint of human rights politics within the GDR, it was a final chapter in a long history of translation, competition and reimagination.

Chapter 1 begins with the establishment of the SED and its turn towards human rights in 1946 and examines the 1949 creation of the German Democratic Republic as a dictatorship in the name of human rights. Chapter 2 charts the evolution of the SED's human rights politics, from the creation of the Committee for the Protection of Human Rights in 1959 to the turn towards engagement with global human rights politics and the embrace of postcolonial discourses of self-determination, through the legal theories of Hermann Klenner. In the late 1960s, as examined in Chapter 3, the SED took its human rights politics to the world stage, first with the UN International Year for Human Rights and then through a series of major treaties with the West, which secured near-universal diplomatic recognition for the GDR. Chapter 4 examines the ambiguous rise of human rights as a language of protest beginning in 1968 for Christians and those seeking to exit the country, ending with its failure to produce a full-fledged human rights movement in the late 1970s. In Chapter 5, the simultaneous shift of the peace movement towards politicisation through human rights and the collapse of a socialist human rights ideology among East German elites in the 1980s are elucidated. Finally, Chapter 6 details the role of human rights in the events at the Berlin Wall, and throughout East Germany, in November 1989. Ultimately, this book is about how the fight for human rights in

---

Deutsch-deutschen Beziehungen zu den Vereinten Nationen von 1949 bis 1973 (Göttingen: V&R Unipress, 2011). North Korea also adopted human rights language in the immediate postwar period, though without the intensity of the GDR, see Robert Weatherley and Song Jiyoung, "The Evolution of Human Rights Thinking in North Korea," *Journal of Communist Studies and Transition Politics* 24, no. 2 (2008), 272–96.

East Germany was a battle over competing conceptions of what human rights meant, as the idea moved to the centre stage of global politics in the postwar era. The end of dictatorship in East Germany was not the end of this conflict as citizens had to choose for themselves what kind of human rights would follow in the wake of the collapse of state socialism.

1 Creating a Human Rights Dictatorship, 1945–1956

In the wake of the Second World War, human rights stood as the antithesis to the horrors of the Third Reich, becoming synonymous with postwar liberal and social democratic idealism in the West. But these were not the only visions for a new postwar order founded on human rights and others saw the need for more radical measures. In occupied Germany, legal scholar Karl Polak argued that neither social democracy nor liberalism were the solution to fascism. The failure of the Weimar Republic's parliamentary democracy and its descent into fascism was the natural end point of the capitalist system. Any form of restored democracy that allowed for the return of capitalism risked plunging the world back into war and thereby could never realise human rights. According to Polak, only a socialist revolution could truly extinguish the threat of fascism so there could be "no human rights without socialism!"[1]

Polak was no fringe thinker, but a leading theorist for the Socialist Unity Party (SED), and his slogan would form the basis of East German human rights doctrine for the next forty years. His turn to the language of human rights, and its embrace by communists in the Soviet Zone of Occupation, represented an important turning point. Until the postwar period, human rights had a poor reputation among German socialists who tended to view it – as Karl Marx did – as a hypocritical slogan of bourgeois liberalism. While the socialist anthem *Die Internationale* promised to "fight for human rights" (*erkämpft das Menschenrecht*), this line was unique to the German version and likely only included because it rhymed.[2]

The postwar turn to human rights by the Left in Germany – both Social Democrats and Communists – emerged from the peculiarities of

---

[1] Karl Polak, "Gewaltteilung, Menschenrechte, Rechtsstaat: Begriffsformalismus und Demokratie," (1946), reprinted in Karl Polak: Zur Entwicklung der Arbeiter- und Bauern-Macht (Berlin: Staatsverlag der DDR, 1968), 126–44.

[2] Emil Luckhardt furnished the German translation in 1910. Leszek Kolakowski, "Marxism and Human Rights," *Daedalus* 112, no. 4 (1983), 81.

political competition in Occupied Germany. In 1946, elections were scheduled across the Soviet Zone of Occupation to confirm the legitimacy of the Socialist Unity Party, created from a forced merger of the Communist (KPD) and the Social Democratic (SPD) parties earlier that year. In Berlin, however, they would have to face off against the still independent Social Democrats operating in the occupied sectors in the West of the city. During the campaign, the SED claimed to represent a moderate path to socialism through democratic means, in partnership with all those who opposed fascism. Their rival Social Democrats ran on a platform explicitly attacking the SED as totalitarians seeking to implement a new dictatorship after the Soviet model, unveiling the slogan "No Socialism without Human Rights!"[3] The Berlin elections quickly became a bitterly fought proxy battle over the future of German socialism: Would the people opt for Soviet-aligned antifascism or anti-communist Social Democracy? The Berlin election proved to be a humiliating defeat for the SED, which trailed behind the Social Democrats with the support of less than a third of the voting public.[4]

The SED came to two important conclusions after the Berlin fiasco: first, so soon after the end of the Nazi dictatorship, the German people could not be trusted to embrace antifascism and socialism through democratic means. The party's early posture of moderation and gradualism was quickly replaced by an emphasis on revolutionary change and strict party control.[5] Second, the SED would never again cede the high ground of human rights to its enemies. Instead of running from the idea, the SED instead assimilated it into its ideological worldview, even as it shed its support of electoral democracy and embraced authoritarian methods of rule. When the Soviet Zone became the German Democratic Republic under SED rule in 1949, the political system reflected this new logic: according to the SED, the cause of socialism and human rights were now one and the same. The newly founded GDR would be a dictatorship, but it would be a dictatorship in the name of human rights.

Human Rights, Basic Rights or Class Rights

The conflict over the meaning of human rights emerged from competing visions of how to establish democracy in postwar occupied Germany.

---

[3] Friedrich-Ebert-Stiftung, *Archiv der sozialen Demokratie* (AdsD), 6/PLKA000150, "Kein Sozialismus ohne Menschenrechte" (20.10.1946).

[4] Dirk Spilker, *The East German Leadership and the Division of Germany: Patriotism and Propaganda 1945–1953* (Oxford: Oxford University Press, 2006), 101.

[5] On the "Stalinization" of the SED, see Gareth Pritchard, *The Making of the GDR, 1945–53: From Antifascism to Stalinism* (Manchester: St. Martin's Press, 2000), ch. 7.

The year 1945 was seen as a decisive turning point at which the errors of the past could be corrected, and a repeat of Nazism prevented. While the Allies agreed at the Potsdam Conference that they would work together "for the eventual reconstruction of [German] life on a democratic and peaceful basis," what this democratisation would mean in practice was still an open question and one that would be shaped by Germans.[6] For the Left, there were three generally recognised historical models of rights informing these debates: first, human rights (*Menschenrechte*), grounded in the universalist Enlightenment thought of the American and French revolutions; second, basic rights (*Grundrechte*), based on the liberal constitutionalism of the German nationalists of 1848 and the Weimar Republic; and third, class rights, wherein political status determined eligibility for political participation, as in Russia after the October Revolution of 1917.

Although the idea of human rights can be traced back through numerous moral, political and religious traditions, the revolutions of the late eighteenth century popularised a vision of rights that can be viewed as the starting point for the modern concept. Drawing from the radical Enlightenment and earlier discourses about natural rights, the American Declaration of Independence written by Thomas Jefferson 1776 stated, "We hold these truths to be self-evident: that all men are created equal; that they are endowed by their Creator with certain unalienable rights; that among these are life, liberty, and the pursuit of happiness."[7] Similarly, the National Constituent Assembly of France produced the Declaration of the Rights of Man and Citizen in 1789, which proclaimed, "Men are born and remain free and equal in rights," and that "liberty, property, safety and resistance against oppression" were "the natural and imprescriptible rights of man."[8] Although both documents asserted the "equality, universality, and naturalness" of the rights that they proclaimed, the supposedly universalist regimes created by the American and French revolutions excluded women, propertyless men and the enslaved from full citizenship and equal rights. Already in the eighteenth century, activists demanded equal rights for women; the Haitian Revolution

---

[6] On the competing process and philosophies of democratization, see Konrad Jarausch, *After Hitler: Recivilizing Germans, 1945–1995* (Oxford: Oxford University Press, 2006), 130–39.

[7] Michael Zuckert, "Natural Rights in the American Revolution: The American Amalgam," in *Human Rights and Revolutions*, ed. Jeffrey Wasserstrom (New York: Rowman & Littlefield, 2007), 65–82.

[8] On the shift from the "ancient rights" invoked during the 1688 English Revolution to the human rights rhetoric of the late eighteenth century, see Lynn Hunt, *Inventing Human Rights* (London: W.W. Norton, 2008), 21.

contested the exclusion of black colonial subjects; and enslaved people in the United States demanded their own emancipation.[9] In spite of these shortcomings, the "Rights of Man" advocated by American and French revolutionaries created a model for demanding certain inalienable rights, to be realised through political means in the name of universal human equality.[10]

In the German lands of the mid-nineteenth century, however, liberals did not employ this precedent when they sought to foment their own democratic and national revolution.[11] German philosophers, such as Immanuel Kant and Johann Gottlieb Fichte, had developed the concept of natural and human rights and the composer Ludwig van Beethoven denounced Napoleon Bonaparte for "trampling human rights under foot," but this language did not trickle into mass politics.[12] Rather than speaking in universal terms during the upheavals of 1848, however, the Frankfurt National Assembly proclaimed instead the "Basic Rights of the German People."[13] It proposed a liberal constitution to provide Germans with rights and liberties including freedom of thought and expression, freedom of religious belief and practice, freedom of movement and – the ultimate of all bourgeois concerns – the right to property. This catalogue of rights was to be part of a new constitution for a state that would unify the German people (*Volk*), provide them with a political system under the rule of law (*Rechtsstaat*) and eliminate old feudal

---

[9] On contemporary challenges to eighteenth-century human rights declarations, see Joan Scott, "French Feminists and the Rights of 'Man': Olympe de Gouges's Declarations," *History Workshop* 28 (1989), 1–21; Richard Brown, *Self-Evident Truths: Contesting Equal Rights from the Revolution to the Civil War* (New Haven, CT: Yale University Press, 2017).

[10] On the discontinuities between the eighteenth-century "rights of man" and modern human rights, Samuel Moyn, *Last Utopia: Human Rights in History* (Cambridge: Belknap, 2010), 85–86.

[11] "Rights of man" did briefly penetrate into Prussian state discourse after the French Revolution. Under § 83, "The general rights of man are based on the natural freedom to seek and promote one's own well-being without offending one another's rights." Einleitung, *Allgemeines Landrecht für die Preußischen Staaten* (1.06.1794).

[12] Kant is foundational to modern rights theory, but he only used the term "human rights" in passing. Luigi Caranti, "Kant's Theory of Human Rights," in *Handbook of Human Rights*, ed. Thomas Cushman (London: Routledge, 2012), 35. Jean-Christophe Merle "Fichte and Human Rights," *Fichte's Foundations of Natural Right*, ed. Gabriel Gottlieb (Cambridge: Cambridge University Press, 2016), 239–58. "Nun wird er auch alle Menschenrechte mit Füßen treten, nur seinem Ehrgeize frönen; er wird sich nun höher als alle andern stellen, ein Tyrann werden!" quoted in Franz Gerhard Wegeler and Ferdinand Ries, *Biographische Notizen über Ludwig van Beethoven* (Koblenz: Bädeker, 1838), 78.

[13] Some radical democrats including Gustav von Struve did speak of human rights, but they were excluded from the National Assembly. Hans Jörg Sandkühler, *Menschenwürde und Menschenrechte: Über die Verletzbarkeit und den Schutz der Menschen* (Freiburg: Karl Alber, 2016), 280–81.

privileges in favour of equal rights for all citizens of the *Reich*. Citizenship based on membership in the German nation would be the basis of the new nation-state, not universal humanity.[14]

The implementation of this vision was slow in coming after the political failure of the 1848 revolution: Germany was only unified in 1871, and the aim of a constitutional order on the basis of equal German citizenship was not realised until 1918 with the collapse of the German Empire and the creation of the democratic Weimar Republic.[15] The 1919 Constitution included a section on "Basic Rights and Duties," which reflected the divided nature of Weimar Germany by including classical liberal freedoms such as freedom of speech, protections for the right to property, as well as social and economic rights to reflect the importance of Social Democracy. The Weimar Republic's entire constitutional order, including these rights, was based on popular sovereignty, as Article 1 declared, "all state authority emanates from the people."[16] Although Germany was now a democratic republic, this did not mean that citizens could invoke basic rights to overturn the laws of parliament: because the power of the legislature came from the people, the rights of the constitution could not stand above it.[17] Conflicts over the implementation of basic rights were to be resolved through the democratic process in the *Reichstag*, not through the judiciary. The Far Right and the Far Left fiercely contested the constitutional order of the Weimar Republic and the meaning of rights in the years before the Nazi rise to power, but the idea of universal human rights was absent from such conflict.[18]

In 1917, the Bolsheviks rejected both the universalist rhetoric of human rights and the nationally demarcated language of basic rights, presenting instead a vision of class-based rights. The 1918 Constitution promised the right to vote to all "toilers," regardless sex or nationality, but denied it to those from the exploiter classes or known enemies of the revolution, including "employers of hired labour, persons living on

---

[14] On debates over the boundaries of the German *Volk* and citizenship, see Mark Hewitson, *Nationalism in Germany, 1848–1866: Revolutionary Nation* (Basingstoke: Palgrave Macmillan, 2010), 48–49.

[15] In Imperial German law, basic rights existed, but they were limits that the state created on its own power, not subjective rights that could be used by citizens to restrain state action. Peter Caldwell, *Popular Sovereignty and the Crisis of German Constitutional Law: The Theory and Practice of Weimar Constitutionalism* (Durham, NC: Duke University Press, 1997), 31.

[16] Ibid., 66.   [17] Ibid., 78.

[18] For example, prolific liberal scholar Hans Kelsen does not mention it at all in his work on individual rights. Alexander Schwitanski, *Die Freiheit des Volksstaats: die Entwicklung der Grund- und Menschenrechte und die deutsche Sozialdemokratie bis zum Ende der Weimarer Republik* (Essen: Klartext, 2008), 297.

unearned income or from rent, kulaks, priests, former gendarmes [,] other categories of Tsarist official, and officers in the White Armies."[19] The Soviet constitution was at once "neo-corporate" as it assigned rights based on class and position, but also egalitarian as it made access to Soviet citizenship available to all nationalities. As one historian has argued, "Party leaders believed that they were leading a transnational social class, not a state."[20] Because class, not universal humanity, was the organising basis of society, the problem of human rights was of no interest to the Bolsheviks; the term is wholly absent from the writings of Vladimir Lenin.

The one universal right that Lenin did promote was that of self-determination as a tool in the overthrow of the imperialist and capitalist oppression and exploitation.[21] His emphasis on this right was made manifest in the "Declaration of Rights of the Working and Exploited People" (passed in January 1918), which explicitly named only one right: self-determination.[22] Although ostensibly modelled on the French Declaration of the Rights of Man and Citizen, in the place of a catalogue of universal rights, the Declaration presented plans to abolish private ownership of land and convert banks into state property as a means of emancipating "the working people from the yoke of capital."[23] This linkage of the right to self-determination with socialist revolution would later prove crucial to Soviet and East German politics in the postwar era.[24]

These revolutionary moments provided contrasting templates for reform, but the postwar German Left was also shaped by the multifaceted history of German socialism's engagement with the meaning of rights, from Karl Marx in the mid-nineteenth century, through the Social Democratic Party of Germany (SPD, founded 1863) and, finally, the

---

[19] Sheila Fitzpatrick, *The Russian Revolution* (Oxford: Oxford University Press, 2008), 91.

[20] Golfo Alexopoulos, "Soviet Citizenship, More or Less: Rights, Emotions, and States of Civic Belonging," *Kritika: Explorations in Russian and Eurasian History* 7, no. 3 (2006), 491.

[21] Jürgen Kuczynski, *Menschenrechte und Klassenrechte* (Berlin: Akademie-Verlag, 1978), 20.

[22] On the drafting of the 1918 Declaration, see Alexander Rabinowitch, *The Bolsheviks in Power: The First Year of Soviet Rule in Petrograd* (Bloomington: Indiana University Press, 2008), 116–23.

[23] Christopher Read, *War and Revolution in Russia, 1914–22: The Collapse of Tsarism and the Establishment of Soviet Power* (Basingstoke: Palgrave Macmillan, 2012), 137. Vladimir Lenin, Declaration of Rights of the Working and Exploited People (3.1.1918) (www.marxists.org).

[24] Lauri Mälksoo, "The Soviet Approach to the Right of Peoples to Self-Determination: Russia's Farewell to *Jus Publicum Europaeum*," *Journal of the History of International Law* 19, no. 2 (2017), 200–18.

Communist Party of Germany (KPD, founded 1919). Karl Marx himself dismissed enthusiasm for the "Rights of Man" as a rhetorical trick of the bourgeoisie to equate their class interests with the rights of all humanity. The realisation of a system of individual rights positioned against the power of the state was little more than "the rights of egoistic man, of man as a member of bourgeois society, that is to say an individual separated from his community and solely concerned with his self-interest."[25] At the same time, Marx did endorse the realisation of political democratic rights as a crucial step on the path to socialism. Because he viewed the idea of human rights as little more than a bourgeois affectation, Marx never developed, in his many writings, any kind of theory of how rights would function after the revolutionary abolition of capitalism.[26]

While Marx was dismissive of universalist human rights rhetoric, the worker and socialist movements that followed had a more ambivalent relationship with the concept. Radical workers sometimes employed the rhetoric of human rights in the mid-nineteenth century, but the rise of the Social Democrats led to a greater focus on access to political rights, rather than on universalistic ideals.[27] According to the "evolutionary socialism" of the SPD, political and economic rights for workers were crucial tools in the lawful struggle for a classless society. The 1891 Erfurt Program argued that "the working class cannot lead its economic struggles or develop its economic organization without political rights."[28] The SPD only sporadically and inconsistently spoke of human rights and it remained a marginal aspect of socialist thought for the SPD, never fully theorised or central to the party's politics. For some, like party theorist Eduard Bernstein, human rights were not a matter of political democracy, but of basic economic rights: because everyone had a human right

---

[25] Karl Marx, "On the Jewish Question," in *The Marx-Engels Reader*, ed. Robert Tucker (New York: Norton, 1972), 38–40. Earlier, Fichte highlighted the distinction between civic rights and human rights in arguing that while Jews were entitled to the latter, their refusal to join the Christian community barred them from the former. Anthony LaVopa, *Fichte: The Self and the Calling of Philosophy, 1762–1799* (Cambridge: Cambridge University Press, 2001), 147.

[26] On the rejection of human rights language in the eighteenth and nineteenth centuries, see Jeremy Waldron, *Nonsense upon Stilts: Bentham, Burke and Marx on the Rights of Man* (New York: Routledge, 2014). Buchanan argues that Marx is silent – rather than inherently hostile – on human rights after the revolution, Allen Buchanan, *Marx and Justice: The Radical Critique of Liberalism* (Totowa, NJ: Rowman & Littlefield, 1982), 68.

[27] On human rights language and labour radicalism, see Schwitanski, *Die Freiheit des Volksstaats*, 46–48.

[28] Karl Kautsky, *Bernstein und das sozialdemokratische Programm: eine Antikritik* (Berlin: Dietz, 1899), 162.

to life, there was a natural right to subsistence through the right to work.[29] For others, like party leader August Bebel, the fight for the "Rights of Man" was synonymous with the general aims of Social Democracy, but he also denounced the oppression of non-Europeans in German colonies as violations of human rights.[30]

At the close of 1918, the Communist Party emerged from the splintering of the SPD, and – at least initially – followed a very different path on the question of rights from that of the Bolsheviks. Rosa Luxemburg, one of the KPD's founders, echoed earlier SPD demands for political rights as an integral part of socialist democracy. She wrote that "democracy is indispensable to the working class, because only through the exercise of its democratic rights, in the struggle for democracy, can the proletariat become aware of its class interests and its historic task."[31] After the October Revolution, Luxemburg openly attacked Lenin and the need for a proletarian dictatorship, writing "freedom only for the supporters of the government, only for the members of one party – however numerous they may be – is no freedom at all. Freedom is always and exclusively freedom for those who think differently."[32] In January 1919, however, SPD Chancellor Friedrich Ebert gave order to suppress the Far Left Spartacist Uprising and worked with Far Right *Freikorps* mercenaries to assassinate Luxemburg and KPD co-founder Karl Liebknecht.[33] Their murders not only created a deep rift between Social Democrats and Communists but also erased Luxemburg's alternative vision of a rights-oriented communism.

The new KPD leadership aligned itself with the USSR and followed the party line set out in Moscow, which – eventually, by the postwar era – led German Communists to (somewhat ironically) embrace the 1848 Revolution as a model. Throughout the Weimar Republic, the KPD sought to use the democratic rights stipulated by the 1919 Constitution to implement its agenda of revolutionary socialism to defeat not only the bourgeois parties but also the hated Social Democrats. This led to "the uneasy coexistence of two political languages – of gradualism and

---

[29] Schwitanski, *Die Freiheit des Volksstaats*, 100.
[30] Bebel reprinted in Carl Schorske, *German Social Democracy, 1905–1917: The Development of the Great Schism* (Cambridge, MA: Harvard University Press, 1955), 43; on Bebel, human rights and colonialism, see Gerhard A. Ritter, "August Bebel, Freiheit und Emanzipaton. Menschenrechte und Arbeiterbewegung im Kaiserreich," *Moving the Social* 18 (1997), 21–22.
[31] "Reform or Revolution," in Rosa Luxemburg, *Reform or Revolution and Other Writings* (Mineola, NY: Dover, 2012), 61–62.
[32] Luxemburg, "The Russian Revolution," 214.
[33] Mark Jones, *Founding Weimar: Violence and the German Revolution of 1918–1919* (Cambridge: Cambridge University Press, 2016), 233–37.

intransigence," as the party actively exploited the democratic rights of a system it aimed to destroy.[34] For both the SPD and the KPD during the Weimar era, when human rights were mentioned, they were a matter of gaining and using state power, not the elevation of the individual above state power.[35] After the Nazi rise to power in 1933, however, the KPD leadership went into exile in the USSR. The rise of fascism led the Soviets to change tactics: at the 7th Congress of the Communist International (Comintern), they endorsed the creation of popular fronts between communists and antifascist bourgeois forces, and as such, the KPD was forced to make peace with the Social Democrats. Under the leadership of Walter Ulbricht and Wilhelm Pieck, a new rhetorical moderation took hold as the KPD reached out to their political rivals who were in exile in Prague.[36] At the KPD's conference in 1935, Pieck argued that Germany was not yet ready for a socialist revolution and that the party needed to appeal to the ideals of 1848 so that Germany could finally experience a bourgeois revolution as a first step on the path to communism. Their cause was now the "struggle for democratic freedoms," such as the right to free speech, a free press and electoral democracy.[37] This message was echoed by the Committee for the Creation of a German Popular Front, which issued the Manifesto of 118, from Paris, written predominantly by novelist Heinrich Mann, calling for "a Germany characterized by peace, freedom […] and energetic democracy."[38]

This turn to basic rights by the KPD in exile mirrored developments within the USSR. In 1936, Joseph Stalin introduced a new Soviet Constitution, supposedly "the most democratic in the world."[39] The class and identity aspects of the 1918 Constitution were rolled back so that political rights were officially granted to all citizens "regardless of racial or national membership, faith, educational level, residence, social origin, property status, and past activities." Rights to be exercised in "the

---

[34] Eric Weitz, *Creating German Communism, 1890–1990: From Popular Protests to Socialist State* (Princeton, NJ: Princeton University Press, 1997), 320.

[35] Schwitanski, *Die Freiheit des Volksstaats*, 454–55.

[36] Jean-Michel Palmier, *Weimar in Exile: The Antifascist Emigration in Europe and America* (London: Verso, 2006), 176.

[37] Gregory Sandford, *From Hitler to Ulbricht: The Communist Reconstruction of East Germany, 1945–1946* (Princeton, NJ: Princeton University Press, 2017), 5.

[38] Andreas Agocs, *Antifascist Humanism and the Politics of Cultural Renewal in Germany* (Cambridge: Cambridge University Press, 2017), 29.

[39] Benjamin Nathans, "Soviet Rights-Talk in the Post-Stalin Era," in *Human Rights in the Twentieth Century*, ed. Stefan-Ludwig Hoffmann (Cambridge: Cambridge University Press, 2010), 171–73. On the decline of legal nihilism and the rise of socialist legality under Stalin, see Inga Markovits, "The Death of Socialist Law?" *Annual Review of Law and Social Science* 3 (2007), 236–37.

interests of toilers and the strengthening of the socialist system" were matched with duties to the state and to the cause of socialism. The Constitution promised Soviet citizens an extensive catalogue of social and economic rights including the right to work, leisure and education. Rather than leading to the realisation of these rights, the so-called Stalin Constitution was instead a prelude to the Great Terror of 1937: "The civil rights, personal freedom" and democracy promised by the Constitution "were trampled almost immediately and remained dead letters until long after Stalin's death."[40] Although Stalin did not develop a socialist theory of human rights, his methods offered a preview to how the SED would later synthesise the rhetoric of rights and constitutionalism with the practices of dictatorship.

The Soviets initially viewed KPD exiles with suspicion and then persecuted them after the Nazi invasion in 1941, but by the end of the war, Stalin came to see the Germans as a tool to secure Soviet interests.[41] According to Stalin, Germany had not yet reached the correct stage of historical development for the transition to socialism, remarking in 1944 that "communism fits Germany like a saddle fits a cow."[42] In keeping with the moderating calls for a popular front in the 1930s, the KPD was expected to return to Germany and create a bloc to fight for democracy with other antifascist forces. The immediate task was not to enact a radical socialist agenda, but to complete the unsuccessful revolution of 1848 and realise a bourgeois democracy on the path to an eventual socialist revolution.[43] When the Red Army advanced into Berlin, the Soviets did not yet have a plan to create a separate socialist German state but they did assume that the de-Nazification of Germany would require years of occupation. In the immediate years after the end of hostilities, the Soviets purposefully kept their options open to prevent the resurgence of fascism by any means necessary.[44]

[40] J. Arch Getty, "State and Society under Stalin: Constitutions and Elections in the 1930s," *Slavic Review* 50, no. 1 (1991), 18.

[41] Around 60 percent of the 2,000 German Communists in exile in the USSR were killed during the Great Terror, and KPD exiles were interned at the beginning of the war. Eric Weitz, "German Communism," in *The Cambridge History of Communism*, eds. Silvio Pons and Stephen Smith (Cambridge: Cambridge University Press, 2017), 591.

[42] Peter Grieder, *The East German Leadership, 1946–73: Conflict and Crisis* (Manchester: Manchester University Press, 1999), 13.

[43] Weitz, *Creating German Communism, 1890–1990*, 308.

[44] Spilker convincingly argues that the USSR did not immediately seek creation of a separate socialist Germany, but Loth's argument that the SED sabotaged the Soviet to force the creation of the GDR is exaggerated. Spilker, *The East German Leadership and the Division of Germany*, 5 and Wilfried Loth, *Die Sowjetunion und die Deutsche Frage: Studien zur Sowjetischen Deutschlandpolitik von Stalin bis Chruschtschow* (Göttingen: Vandenhoeck & Ruprecht, 2007).

Basic Rights and Socialism in Occupied Germany

In June 1945, Germany stood defeated, occupied and divided. The United States, the United Kingdom, France and the Soviet Union each administered a separate region of the fallen Third Reich with the city of Berlin under the joint control of all four. The Soviet Zone, the largest of the four, stretched from the Elbe in the west to the Oder and Neisse rivers, beyond which formerly German territories were now under the control of Poland or the USSR. The Zone contained the Prussian agricultural estates of Brandenburg, sparsely populated Mecklenburg on the Baltic coast, the foothills of Thuringia in the interior, as well as Saxony with the great trading city of Leipzig and the firebombed remains of Dresden. In the heart of the Soviet Zone lay the ruins of Berlin, laid to waste by Allied aerial bombardment and the guns of the advancing Red Army. On 9 June, little more than a month after the unconditional surrender of the German armed forces, the Soviet Military Administration, headquartered in the Berlin suburb of Karlshorst, officially took control over the Eastern Occupied Zone and its more than 18 million inhabitants. Shortly thereafter, the Communist Party of Germany was resurrected to serve as a proxy for the USSR, declaring its support for a broad antifascist coalition that would include bourgeois parties and guarantee liberal democratic rights and freedoms.[45]

For the KPD to gain support from the population in the Soviet Zone, it not only had to appeal to the significant minority who supported the communist cause (either for idealistic or self-serving reasons) but also engage with the passive majority who had until recently embraced National Socialism.[46] Declaring its principles in the "Appeal to the German People from the Communist Party," the KPD shed its earlier mantle of violent struggle and class warfare, and spoke of democracy, national unity and antifascism. The appeal claimed that the KPD had no interest in imposing a Soviet-style system as Germany would first have to experience a bourgeois revolution, brought about through an "antifascist, democratic regime [;] a parliamentary-democratic republic with all democratic rights and freedoms for the people."[47] Just as a coalition of bourgeois and socialist political forces had joined together to defeat the Nazi war machine, it could work together in peacetime to put the country

---

[45] Norman Naimark, *The Russians in Germany: A History of the Soviet Zone of Occupation, 1945–1949* (Cambridge, MA: Belknap, 1995), 10.

[46] Pritchard, *The Making of the GDR*, 16–18.

[47] "Aufruf des ZK der KPD vom 11. Juni 1945," in *"Nach Hitler kommen wir": Dokumente zur Programmatik der Moskauer KPD-Führung 1944/45 für Nachkriegsdeutschland*, eds. Peter Erler, Horst Laude and Manfred Wilke (Berlin: Akademie Verlag, 1994), 394.

on its proper path towards an eventual socialist future by overcoming the failings of Germany's historical development.

The KPD adopted the language of basic rights and democracy, but what that meant in practice remained contested – even among leading party officials. For Walter Ulbricht, the outward public moderation of the party was little more than a means to an end. Ulbricht was a staunchly orthodox Stalinist, who had joined the KPD in the 1920s and attended the International Lenin School of the Communist International in Moscow before serving as a political officer in the International Brigades in the Spanish Civil War. In 1945, he told a party colleague: "It is quite obvious. It has to look democratic, but we must have everything firmly in our hands."[48] Elections would provide a veneer of bourgeois democracy in the short term to make the eventual socialist revolution more palatable for the masses. To keep up appearances, Ulbricht demanded that party members stop singing Bolshevik songs or wearing red party armbands to publicly demonstrate the KPD's new moderation.[49]

Others within the party leadership, such as Anton Ackermann – chief architect of the Appeal to the German People – were more hopeful that parliamentary means could pave the way for a democratic and peaceful transition to socialism. Ackermann's early biography closely resembled that of Ulbricht's, from a childhood in Saxony through to his political education in Moscow, although he would later serve as a volunteer soldier in the International Brigades, rather than as a political officer overseeing purges. In February 1946, Ackermann wrote the article "Is There a Special Path to German Socialism?" arguing that the KPD need not necessarily follow the route of violent socialist revolution.[50] Unlike in the USSR under Lenin, "in Germany the possibilities not only of coming to power but also of exercising that power are incomparably better than they were in Russia."[51] Because the Soviet Military Administration had already rejected hard-line demands for immediate revolution, and the KPD Central Secretariat had commissioned Ackermann to write the article, such a plan was not a radical departure from the party line. Nonetheless, Ackermann and others remained hopeful that the working classes represented the majority of the German nation and that the KPD could come to power via the ballot box rather than the violent imposition of a "dictatorship of the proletariat."

---

[48] Quoted in J. H. Brinks, "Political Anti-Fascism in the GDR," *Journal of Contemporary History* 32, no. 2 (1997), 209.

[49] Naimark, *The Russians in Germany*, 42.

[50] Catherine Epstein, *The Last Revolutionaries: German Communists and Their Century* (Cambridge, MA: Harvard University Press, 2003), 128.

[51] Grieder, *The East German Leadership, 1946–73*, 11.

Despite this optimism, the first move was to coerce a merger between the KPD and the Social Democrats to create a unified party of the Left in the Soviet Zone. The KPD was the USSR's favoured party in the Zone, but the Soviet Military Administration had also allowed for the creation of several competitor parties, including the SPD, as well as the Liberal Democrats (LDPD) and the Christian Democrats (CDU). The KPD had more than 150,000 members in the summer of 1945, but by the end of that year, SPD membership already exceeded 400,000.[52] While the Soviets prioritised avoiding a split in the working-class vote, both parties comprised members enthusiastic about a merger, as well as factions that were bitterly opposed. Many rank-and-file SPD members feared the dictatorial inclination of the Soviets, while many KPD members – already frustrated by the restrictions on radical action – opposed the further dilution of revolutionary fervour by including Social Democrats. When persuasion alone failed to bring about unity, Soviet authorities bought off leaders with promises of continued power and influence, and brought the rest in line with threats, blackmail and violence.[53] Finally, at a joint conference on 21 April 1946, Otto Grotewohl, leader of the Soviet Zone SPD, and Wilhelm Pieck, head of the KPD, formally agreed to the merger of their parties. The photograph of their handshake on that day became the symbol of the new Socialist Unity Party. Although Pieck and Grotewohl served as co-chairs of the party until 1950, it was Walter Ulbricht who emerged behind the scenes as the actual locus of power in the SED.

The first test of the new party came when the Soviets called elections across the Zone for October 1946.[54] Already in June of that year, a referendum on the expropriation of war criminals and active Nazis successfully passed in Soviet-occupied Saxony with 77 percent in favour, so popular voting appeared to be a viable path forward. The SED leadership anticipated that elections would secure the Party's democratic legitimacy and demonstrate the popularity of a unified Left. At a planning meeting, Grotewohl declared, "This first election is a highly political event of great significance not only for the Eastern and other zones of Germany, but throughout the world."[55] The one complication was the city of Berlin, where the Soviets had to allow for voting across the whole

[52] Andreas Malycha and Peter Jochen Winters, *Die Geschichte der SED: von der Gründung bis zur Linkspartei* (Berlin: Bundeszentrale für politische Bildung, 2009), 16 and 21.

[53] On the KPD-SPD merger as both coercion and idealism, see Pritchard, *The Making of the GDR*, 108–32.

[54] Norbert Podewin, *20. Oktober 1946: die erste Nachkriegswahl in Berlin* (Berlin: Helle Panke, 2006).

[55] BArch, DY30/IV 2/1/4 Protokoll, 3. Tagung des Parteivorstandes (18–20.6.1946), 56.

city as it was under occupation by all four Allied Powers. The Berlin election, the first and only one to include both East and West until 1990, forced the SED to compete against the still independent Social Democrats, active in the American, French and British sectors. While the Berlin election was a gamble for the Soviets, it was also an opportunity to demonstrate that the united front presented by the newly merged SED in the East – rather than the still independent and stridently anti-communist SPD – was the choice of the German people. For the Western Allies and the SPD, however, this was a chance to show that the SED was a puppet of the Soviets that did not have genuine support from the German people.

During the election campaign, party leaders legitimised both the existence of the new SED and its right to rule by appealing to antifascism rather than socialism. Antifascism for the SED was less an ideology than a collection of legitimising narratives founded on the traumas of recent German history and centred on the notion that "the SED, its state, and, ultimately, the citizens of its state are heirs to those who fought *for* socialism and *against* fascism and won the battle of history."[56] The credibility of the SED leadership rested on their public opposition to Nazism, their personal experiences of combating fascism and their individual suffering during World War II. By drawing on the experiences of catastrophe and defeat that East Germans had suffered, antifascism – through loyalty to the SED – offered citizens the opportunity to become one of the "victors of history," even if they had previously supported the Nazis.

The SED bolstered the grand narrative of antifascism with a substantial program for reform in its electoral manifesto: "The Basic Rights of the German People: The Path to German Unity." Drafted by legal scholar Karl Polak in cooperation with Otto Grotewohl and the Soviet authorities, the Basic Rights Manifesto echoed the liberal-nationalist language of 1848 and the Weimar Constitution of 1919, presenting the SED not just as an opponent of Nazism but also as the natural successor to the German progressive tradition.[57] Published on the front page of the

---

[56] Julia Hell, "At the Center an Absence: Foundationalist Narratives of the GDR and the Legitimatory Discourse of Antifascism," *Monatshefte* 84, no. 1 (1992), 24–25; Konrad Jarausch, "The Failure of East German Antifascism: Some Ironies of History as Politics," *German Studies Review* 14, no. 1 (1991), 85–102; Epstein, *The Last Revolutionaries*; Josie McLellan, *Antifascism and Memory in East Germany: Remembering the International Brigades, 1945–1989* (Oxford: Oxford University Press, 2004).

[57] On the drafting of the Manifesto, see Erich Gniffke, *Jahre mit Ulbricht* (Cologne: Verlag Wissenschaft und Politik, 1966), 209; Heike Amos, *Die Entstehung der Verfassung in der Sowjetischen Besatzungszone/DDR, 1946–1949* (Münster: LIT Verlag, 2006), 42–49.

SED's national newspaper *Neues Deutschland* a month before the election, it promised that the SED welcomed an open exchange of views with all "antifascist and democratic parties and organizations," and would bring about a system of parliamentary supremacy, equality before the law and rights to free expression, religion and property. Polak claimed that the Manifesto was "the most progressive document that has ever been printed in the German language on the basic question of our existence as a state," which was so democratic that Germans from all political parties could accept it.[58]

There were, however, some allusions to the SED's more radical agenda. The Manifesto adopted the rhetoric of the liberal tradition of equal rights, democracy and national unity, but it also laid the ideological groundwork for a dictatorship in the name of antifascism by emphasising the continuing guilt of individual Germans. The people of Germany were not portrayed as a captive population that had been freed, but implicitly treated as possible threats to a new democratic order due to their recent proclivities towards fascism.[59] It also implied that those who were not sufficiently antifascist could have their rights severely curtailed to protect the cause of democracy without fully embracing the class rights rhetoric of the early Soviet era. It also included provisions for the breakup of "private corporations, major banks, cartels and syndicates," and a legal system in which "the will of the people is the highest law!"[60]

In the month leading up to the election, the Basic Rights Manifesto was distributed widely in Berlin and across the Soviet Zone in an intense campaign by the SED. According to Wilhelm Pieck, the campaign's main message was that "the SED sees the realization of basic rights as the foundation on the path to the respect and safeguarding of German Unity."[61] Pieck personally promoted this at numerous public events, calling on "all democratic and peace-loving forces" to support the SED to ensure "the right to free expression, freedom of organization, the freedom of art and science, the inviolability of the home and the right to work, education and leisure and full freedom of belief and thought."[62] In addition to the efforts of SED members, the Cultural Association (*Kulturbund*) – an ostensibly non-partisan, but SED-aligned intelligentsia organisation – promoted the Manifesto as a visionary founding

---

[58] Amos, *Die Entstehung der Verfassung*, 56.

[59] Jeffrey Herf, *Divided Memory: The Nazi Past in the Two Germanys* (Cambridge, MA: Harvard University Press, 1997), 30.

[60] "Die Grundrechte des deutschen Volkes," *Neues Deutschland* (22.9.1946), 1.

[61] BArch, DY30/IV 2/1/10 Bericht des Zentralsekretariats von Wilhelm Pieck, 3.

[62] Wilhelm Pieck, "Öffentliche Diskussion: Über die Grundrechte unseres Volkes," *Neues Deutschland* (25.9.1946), 2.

document for the new democratic Germany.[63] In spite of an extreme shortage of paper, the SED produced extra editions of *Neues Deutschland* in the weeks leading up to the vote, printing numerous features on the Manifesto and its contents.[64]

The election was a decisive moment for the SED, but also for the still independent Social Democrats. SPD leader Kurt Schumacher – a long-time party member who had spent most of the Third Reich in concentration camps – had led the Western Zone opposition against the creation of the SED, denouncing the Communists as "red-painted Nazis."[65] Once the election campaign began, he declared, "on 20 October, Berliners must decide, if they will be governed by a dictatorship [...] as they have been for the past 12 years or whether they want a new future on the basis of democracy and socialism through Social Democracy."[66] In that vein, a new slogan was unveiled: "No Socialism without Human Rights!"[67] It built the rhetoric of the campaign against the creation of the SED, during which one anti-merger pamphlet warned, "dictatorships know no tolerance: human rights and cultural humanity perish. [...] Homogenized state parties are a plague of our social era."[68] Schumacher expanded on this in his public speeches arguing that human rights were not simply the rights of citizens in a bourgeois society or the special rights of workers, but the universal rights shared by all: "While we will fight with great passion and dedication for social benefits, one is only prepared to die for the great idea of freedom."[69] According to Schumacher, all the economic and social rights that social democracy stood for would flow from the creation of a genuinely democratic society that guaranteed political and civil rights.

The appeal of the SPD's message stemmed not just from its commitment to the ideals of pluralism and liberal democracy but also because it spoke to Germans as victims of Nazism rather than co-perpetrators. Whereas the SED placed the blame at the feet of the

---

[63] David Pike, *The Politics of Culture in Soviet-Occupied Germany, 1945–1949* (Stanford, CA: Stanford University Press, 1992), 214–15.

[64] Paul Steege, *Black Market, Cold War: Everyday Life in Berlin, 1946–1949* (Cambridge: Cambridge University Press, 2007), 78.

[65] Patrick Major, *The Death of the KPD: Communism and Anti-Communism in West Germany, 1945–1956* (Oxford: Oxford University Press, 1997), 43.

[66] Quoted in Podewin, *20. Oktober 1946*, 14.

[67] AdsD, 6/PLKA000150 "Kein Sozialismus ohne Menschenrechte" (20.10.1946).

[68] AdsD, 6/FLBL001536 "An die Mitglieder der SPD!" (31.3.1946).

[69] Kurt Schumacher, *Reden, Schriften, Korrespondenzen 1945–1952* (Berlin: Dietz, 1985), 414.

German people, the SPD appealed to popular resentment towards the occupation.[70] The SPD tied their SED rivals to the mass rapes perpetrated by the Red Army and the ruinous reparations and confiscations carried out by the Soviets across the Zone.[71] Throughout the election campaign, the SPD also linked the idea of human rights to promises of relief for the suffering civilian population who saw themselves as victims of unspeakable horrors, first through the mass bombings of the Allies and then through the hardships of the Soviet occupation.[72] As one campaign leaflet read, "If the future of Berlin is to be secured, two major tasks of the present must be solved: ensuring the material needs of the population of Berlin and securing human rights for all."[73]

When the election results were finally tallied on 20 October 1946, the SED was blindsided by an abysmal defeat.[74] In spite of the intense propaganda campaign and the heavy voter suppression, the SED failed to gain an absolute majority anywhere in the Soviet Occupied Zone.[75] Worst of all, in Berlin, it was routed by the SPD, which won a decisive plurality of 48.7 percent in the city as a whole. The SED finished third, with a paltry 20 percent, behind the Christian Democrats.[76] Even in the Soviet Sector, the SPD managed to win 43.6 percent of the vote with the SED limping behind at less than 30 percent.[77] *Neues Deutschland* covered for the embarrassment with a front page declaring, "Great Electoral Victory of the SED in the Zone," which focused on the results from outside Berlin where Soviet influence and the absence of SPD competition had at least produced a plurality of support for the SED.[78] Instead of legitimising the SED, the election was a fiasco, revealing how shallow the party's support truly was.

---

[70] On public resentment of Soviet occupation, see Donna Harsch, *Revenge of the Domestic: Women, the Family, and Communism in the GDR* (Princeton, NJ: Princeton University Press, 2007), 38; Naimark, *The Russians in Germany*, 120.

[71] Naimark, *The Russians in Germany*, 121, 181.

[72] On human rights in German victimhood narratives, see Lora Wildenthal, "Rudolf Laun and the Human Rights of Germans in Occupied and Early West Germany," in *Human Rights in the Twentieth Century*, ed. Stefan-Ludwig Hoffmann (Cambridge: Cambridge University Press, 2010), 125–46.

[73] AdsD, 6/FLBL001419 "Berliner!" (20.10.1946).

[74] Harold Hurwitz, *Die Stalinisierung der SED: Zum Verlust von Freiräumen und sozialdemokratischer Identität in den Vorständen 1946–1949* (Opladen: Springer-Verlag, 2013), 148.

[75] Jürgen Falter and Cornelia Weins, "Die Wahlen in der sowjetisch besetzten Zone von 1946," *Historical Social Research/Historische Sozialforschung*, Supplement 25 (2013), 337–39.

[76] Arthur Schlegelmilch, *Hauptstadt in Zonendeutschland: Die Entstehung der Berliner Nachkriegsdemokratie, 1945–1949* (Berlin: Haude and Spener, 1993), 393.

[77] Spilker, *The East German Leadership and the Division of Germany*, 101.

[78] "Großer Wahlsieg der SED in der Zone," *Neues Deutschland*, (22.10.1946), 1.

The SED's self-diagnosis of their failure to garner popular support would ultimately determine the path forward for the party, as the election post-mortem descended into factionalism.[79] For Otto Grotewohl, the unpopularity of the SED was to be blamed on the public perception that the party was merely a puppet of the Soviet occupiers: "Under no circumstances can we appear to be Quislings. This is not the party. It does not need to be and it is desired by no one."[80] For hard-liner Hermann Matern, the problem was not public perception, but the electorate: he blamed the high turnout of "former members of the [Nazi Party] and the degenerate bourgeoisie of the Kurfürstendamm [Western Berlin's famous boulevard]" for the election result.[81] Another party member blamed the party's failure to tap into nationalist sentiment and the promise of basic rights and democracy under the SED as the path to German unity.[82]

Anton Ackermann rejected these arguments and instead blamed the SPD's successful campaigning on the themes of rights and democracy: "It was no coincidence that one of the strongest arguments of the Social Democrats in Berlin against us and [against] the fundamental rights promoted by our party was this: why do you not go back to the original source, to the civil liberties of Britain or the Constitution of France? [Why not go back to] the freedom of personality and the basic rights of man rather than the basic rights of the people [*Volk*]."[83] Ackerman still believed that – in contrast to Russia in 1917 – there was still the opportunity for the SED "to come to power by democratic means, and not just that, but also to exercise power by democratic means."[84] Standing with Ackermann, Richard Weimann, one of the founders of the Soviet Zone SPD, attributed the loss to SED hard-liner rhetoric: "The Social Democrats won the masses because they had the general postulates of humanity, human rights, and democracy in the foreground, and placed them in opposition to dictatorship."[85]

In the analysis of Walter Ulbricht, however, the problem was neither rhetorical nor strategic, but rather ideological. The SED needed to develop a new conception of democracy instead of dredging up a model from the past: "Some reject the system of Weimar democracy as a matter of principle, and some still fancy the traditions of the English, the French

---

[79] Hurwitz, *Die Stalinisierung der SED*, 205.
[80] Vidkun Quisling led the Nazi-collaborationist regime in Norway and became synonymous with traitorous proxies of foreign occupiers. BArch, DY30/IV 2/1/10 Protokoll, 6. Tagung des Parteivorstandes (24./25.10.1946), 1/33.
[81] Ibid., 1/40.   [82] Ibid., 1/64–5.   [83] Ibid., 2/33.
[84] Ibid., 2/16–7 and /23. Quote from Hurwitz, *Die Stalinisierung der SED*, 210.
[85] Ibid. 2/41.

or other democracies," argued Ulbricht, "but we are going a new way, and therefore the problem of democracy must now also be theoretically underpinned." While the Basic Rights Manifesto was a good start, it "requires a deeper justification."[86] What he neglected to mention was that he would soon lead the Party away from Ackermann's "Special Path to German Socialism" towards total SED control, centred on his own personal leadership. When Ulbricht spoke of improving the party's understanding of democracy, it was as a means of legitimising the rejection of open elections in favour of "democratic centralism" along Soviet lines. The SED would no longer allow competitive elections to threaten its hold on power.

Ending Democracy, Embracing Human Rights

Not even a month after the disastrous Berlin election, the SED moved ahead by presenting the first draft of a Constitution for a "German Democratic Republic."[87] Building from the Basic Rights Manifesto, it declared that all citizens – men and women – were equal before the law; guaranteed the right of free expression, assembly and organization; and promised free and secret parliamentary elections. On the social and economic side, it enshrined the principle of equal pay for equal work, and the right to social security, holidays, and time for recreation. There were even eight articles providing for freedom of religious thought, education, and practice. While the draft in many ways resembled the liberal democratic 1919 Weimar constitution, Ulbricht declared that it went "far beyond" its predecessor by eliminating the separation of powers between the executive and the legislative branches.[88] In the new German Democratic Republic, all power would be held by the parliament, which would seat all antifascist parties alongside representatives from mass organisations such as the trade unions, the Democratic Women's League of Germany, and the Free German Youth (FDJ).

The draft Constitution did not mention human rights explicitly, but a separate ideological response to the SPD prepared by Karl Polak did. When Ulbricht enunciated the need for a "deeper justification" for the SED's version of democracy, the party turned to Polak to reconcile the new popularity of human rights with unified party control and the cause of the socialist revolution. Having previously taken the lead on shaping

---

[86] BArch, DY30/IV 2/1/10 Protokoll, 6. Tagung des Parteivorstandes (24./25.10.1946). 2/74.
[87] "Entwurf der Verfassung für die DDR," *Neues Deutschland* (15.11.1946), 1.
[88] Spilker, *The East German Leadership and the Division of Germany*, 107.

the Basic Rights Manifesto and the draft Constitution, Polak was immensely influential, and his scholarly work formed the basis for the theory and practice of law in the GDR.[89] He also acted as the first of many translators of the concept of human rights in East German history.[90] A devoted Marxist who saw the idea of the "dictatorship of the proletariat" as the crucial historical insight of modernity, Polak's worldview was deeply affected by his time spent in exile in the USSR after his dismissal from the German civil service in 1933 due to his Jewish ancestry.[91] While Polak was an ideologue, he was also a skilled propagandist and political operator who could present hard-line communist policy in the language of moderation.

The Soviet Occupation Authority played an important role in shaping the new Constitution, but there was no socialist human rights doctrine that could be borrowed from the Soviet ideological repertoire, so Polak was forced to invent his own. In December 1946, he took to the pages of the SED's theoretical journal *Einheit* to map out an overarching philosophical foundation for the creation of a socialist state on German soil.[92] He argued that Germans lacked a historical tradition of constitutional rights and freedoms needed to rectify the crimes of Nazi Germany and forestall a recurrence of fascism. The Weimar Constitution provided no guidance because fascists had once already exploited its flaws to seize control of the German state, and there was no reason to think it would not happen again. While he supported the revolutionary character of earlier bourgeois constitutions, Polak ruled out a return to the French Revolution's "Rights of Man and Citizen" or the "Basic Rights" of 1848 as anachronistic and anti-democratic. He argued, "What gave 'human rights' the powerful aura that it today still retains, is not their content but their proclamation and implementation. [...] They were revolutionary slogans and therein lies their meaning, not the idea that they were final, eternal truths announced independently of their historical situation."[93] A declaration of rights for 1946 needed be rooted in the present conditions of historical development, not in nostalgia for the past or the tired rhetoric of bygone eras.

If past human rights declarations were merely vessels for the revolutionary ideology of their era, then Polak argued, in the postwar moment

---

[89] Marcus Howe, *Karl Polak: Parteijurist unter Ulbricht* (Frankfurt: Klostermann, 2002).
[90] On the concept of translation, see Sally Engle Merry, "Transnational Human Rights and Local Activism: Mapping the Middle," *American Anthropologist*, 108, no. 1 (2006), 38–51.
[91] Peter Caldwell, *Dictatorship, State Planning, and Social Theory in the GDR* (Cambridge: Cambridge University Press, 2003), 93–95.
[92] Polak, "Gewaltteilung, Menschenrechte, Rechtsstaat."   [93] Ibid., 138.

socialism was the natural heir to the human rights traditions of the past: "The struggle for the realization of socialism is the struggle for human rights; the path to human rights is the path to socialism; the content of human rights is the liberation from the chains and the prejudices of the capitalist social order."[94] In making this argument, Polak did not contradict Marx's critique of the Rights of Man, but instead moved it in a new direction. Human rights, according to Polak, were part of the "superstructure" of society, which merely reflected the socioeconomic "base." As such, human rights could not exist outside of their relationship to the stage of historical development achieved by a society. While an exploitative capitalist economic order would inevitably produce a hypocritical form of bourgeois human rights, a socialist society would foster real human rights for all. For Polak, "Socialism is by definition the realization of human rights; and human rights are, if they are not to remain an empty principle, only realized insofar as socialism has been made a reality."[95] Just as the true democracy of socialism was self-evidently superior to bourgeois parliamentary democracy, the socialist era would usher in a new form of human rights that would outshine its inferior predecessors.

Polak did not confine his thoughts to an abstract theory of human rights but applied these insights to contemporary political practice. Addressing the slogan of the SPD – "No Socialism without Human Rights" – he simply declared the exact opposite to be true: there could be "No Human Rights without Socialism!" Polak denounced efforts to scare the German public with the "bogeyman" of "socialism without human rights" and dismissed such attacks as part of a campaign of "wilful defamation of the Soviet Union."[96] Whereas the SPD sought to turn back the clock to the failed human rights of the bourgeois past, the SED was moving towards a superior socialist future. For Polak, this meant bringing about, "the expropriation of the expropriators, the overthrow of the capitalist social order and its system of the exploitation of man by man and overcoming capitalist oppression and rule through the free association of people."[97] By integrating the language of human rights into the ideology and historical narrative of the SED, Polak shifted the focus of the human rights discourse away from the crimes of the occupying Soviet forces towards the necessity of socialism as a unifying political program. In 1945, the KPD declared its support for antifascist democracy to assuage fears of revolutionary socialism; a year later, the

---

[94] Ibid., 139.   [95] Ibid., 139–40.   [96] Ibid., 140.   [97] Ibid., 138.

SED claimed instead to be the great champion of human rights and that socialism was the only path towards their realisation.

After the elections of 1946, the SED steadily became more authoritarian and its public commitment to democracy melted away. Without a guarantee of victory, the party leadership resolved to no longer hold competitive elections to bolster its legitimacy.[98] Anton Ackermann initially held onto the idea of a democratic transition to socialism, but by 1948 he was compelled by the Party to denounce the idea of a "special path" as "false and dangerous ... through which nationalism and anti-Bolshevism could penetrate even the ranks of our party."[99] Impediments to SED control within the Soviet Zone were removed: Jakob Kaiser, the independent-minded leader of the local Christian Democrats, was first forced out of his position then compelled to emigrate to West Berlin.[100] In 1948, the SED officially became a "Party of the New Type," modelled on the Communist Party of the Soviet Union and Stalin's works were introduced as key teaching texts for Party members.[101]

Counterintuitively, as the SED abandoned pluralism, its use of human rights language became more prominent, not less. While Polak had provided the translation of human rights into an acceptably socialist form, it was Otto Grotewohl, who would popularise it within the party. As a former Social Democrat, he could speak to the disaffected elements of the party who were most concerned by the party's authoritarian turn. At SED events, he repeated the slogan "No Human Rights without Socialism."[102] He publicly vowed that the rights enshrined in the new East German constitution were "so much more than mere 'individual rights' or judicial claims which the individual has against the state...they are the fundamental principles of the future of German state politics."[103] In a book on the subject, he repeated passages from Polak's *Einheit* article verbatim: "socialism is by definition the realization of human rights; and

---

[98] Malycha and Winters, *Die Geschichte der SED*, 57–58.
[99] Grieder, *The East German Leadership, 1946–73*, 11–16.
[100] Sean Philip Brennan, *The Politics of Religion in Soviet-Occupied Germany: The Case of Berlin-Brandenburg, 1945–1949* (Lanham, MD: Lexington Books, 2011), ch. 3.
[101] Pritchard, *The Making of the GDR*, 163.
[102] Otto Grotewohl, *Im Kampf um Deutschland. Rede auf dem 2. Parteitag der SED*, 1947, 33. Victor Klemperer also mentions Grotewohl using this phrase in 1948, *So sitze ich denn zwischen allen Stühlen: Tagebücher 1945–1959* (Berlin: Aufbau-Verlag, 1999), 513 Polak's original article was also reprinted in a book on the democratization of the justice system edited by future Minister of Justice, Max Fechner ed., *Beiträge zur Demokratisierung der Justiz* (Berlin: Dietz, 1948).
[103] Otto Grotewohl, *Deutsche Verfassungspläne* (Berlin: Dietz, 1947), 68.

human rights are, if they are not to remain an empty principle, only realized insofar as socialism has been made a reality."[104]

When the SPD attempted to use the language of human rights against the SED again in 1948, this time the Party was prepared to respond in kind. From the Western Occupation Zones, the SPD launched a campaign called "In Defence of the Basic Rights and Human Rights in the East," which documented the persecution of former Social Democrats in the Soviet Zone.[105] The SED responded by jailing those who had leaked information on internal party activities to Western activists. This heavy-handed approach both cut off the supply of information and sent a harsh message to those within the Party interested in airing their grievances beyond internal channels. At the same time, senior SED officials, primarily ex-Social Democrats, turned to human rights rhetoric in their counter-propaganda. Grotewohl denounced the Western SPD for its claim that human rights could be possible without the triumph of socialism.[106] He was joined in these efforts by Central Secretariat member Erich Gniffke who spoke out against the Western SPD in an interview with the newsmagazine *Der Spiegel*, based in the British Zone. He argued, "only in a socialist state are there true human rights. Thus, the goal of my struggle can only be: Socialism."[107] Ironically, only a year later, Gniffke was himself expelled from the SED and forced to leave the Zone after publicly promising British occupation authorities that no party would hold a monopoly on power in the new Germany and that all citizens would be guaranteed their rights to vote, assemble, and freely associate.[108] While the SED at least had a retort to Social Democratic human rights attacks now, there were definitely still kinks in the system.

Rights in the German Democratic Republic

Several months after the Western Occupied Zones were merged to become the Federal Republic of Germany, the German Democratic Republic was formed from the Soviet Zone on 7 October 1949. The new GDR was a strange hybrid: it was officially an antifascist democratic state with a Constitution resembling that of the Weimar Republic, but in its actual everyday functions it was modelled on the one-party rule of the Soviet Union. The rights promised in the Constitution echoed the

---

[104] Ibid., 73–74.
[105] Thomas Klein, *"Für die Einheit und Reinheit der Partei": die innerparteilichen Kontrollorgane der SED in der Ära Ulbricht* (Cologne: Böhlau, 2002), 36.
[106] Grotewohl, *Deutsche Verfassungspläne*, 68.
[107] Erich Gniffke, "Gedanken eines Deutschen," *Der Spiegel* 44 (1.11.1947), 15.
[108] Grieder, *The East German Leadership, 1946–73*, 20–21.

language of liberal democracy, but in practice they were used by the state as tools of social control.[109] Political power ostensibly rested in the hands of the National Front (an alliance of antifascist parties and mass organisations led by the SED), with Wilhelm Pieck and Otto Grotewohl acting as president and prime minister respectively, maintaining the symbolic partnership of the Communists and Social Democrats. While the GDR constitution provided a simulacrum of democratic rule and pluralism in which the parliament – the *Volkskammer* – debated legislation, in reality, the docile "bloc parties" of the National Front never deviated from the SED line. Within the SED, Grotewohl was one of the few remaining ex-SPD figures to retain any power: by 1954, seven of the nine members of the Politburo were ex-KPD.[110] Not only were former Communists dominating the party, Walter Ulbricht personified the centralised power structure, displacing Wilhelm Pieck as General Secretary of the SED in 1950. The political system of the GDR was now a dictatorship in all but name.

By contrast, the Federal Republic of Germany's Basic Law created a system of rights that superseded the laws produced by the legislature and allowed citizens to challenge the state through the courts. Written by a Parliamentary Council of 61 men and 4 women, mostly Christian Democrats and Social Democrats, but also two Communists, the Basic Law was grounded in the principles of bourgeois liberalism.[111] The Basic Law was also the first constitution to cite the Universal Declaration of Human Rights and it began in Article 1 with: "Human dignity shall be inviolable. To respect it and protect it is the duty of all state authority. The German people therefore acknowledge the inviolable and inalienable human rights as the basis of every community, of peace, and of justice in the world."[112] These rights were available to all Germans (defined by ethnicity or having lived within the Reich's 1937 borders), including those living in the GDR, but only once they were in the territory of the FRG. The Basic Law included provisions for the future accession of other German territories and the preamble also called upon "the entire German people," to realise "the unity and freedom of Germany in free self-determination," which would later be interpreted by the

---

[109] On the confused nature of the founding Constitution, see Inga Markovits, "Constitution Making after National Catastrophes: Germany in 1949 and 1990," *William and Mary Law Review* 49, no. 4 (2008), 1317–18.

[110] Epstein, *The Last Revolutionaries*, 107.

[111] Markovits, "Constitution Making after National Catastrophes," 1309.

[112] Lora Wildenthal, *The Language of Human Rights in West Germany* (Philadelphia: University of Pennsylvania Press, 2012), 6.

courts along with other articles as a duty of the state to strive towards reunification.[113]

In contrast to West Germany, rights in the GDR were broad statement of ideals that would be implemented according to the principles of Marxism-Leninism and democratic centralism. Just as in earlier German legal regimes, these rights did not bind the policies or decisions of the SED; they were also not subjective rights, in the sense that citizens could use them against the state in a dispute.[114] While Grotewohl and others promoted human rights under socialism as more than mere "individual rights," it was clear from the SED's constitutional deliberations that legally guaranteed individual autonomy would play a microscopic role in the new political order. For citizens in this system, rights functioned as designations of benefits that would be gained in exchange for the fulfilment of duties.[115] In practice, this meant that rights served more as tools and mechanisms of rule than as protections, immunities or guarantees for the individual.[116]

Many sections of the Constitution were simply dead letters in everyday life. As one historian concluded, the "constitution, more than any other body of law in the GDR, exemplified the contradiction between law and political fact."[117] All sections dealing with "parliamentary-democratic or liberal rule of law (*Rechtsstaat*)" were either ignored or fulfilled only in the most superficial manner.[118] Other crucial political and civil rights included in the 1949 Constitution that were blatantly and habitually disregarded included the inviolability of the home, postal secrecy, the choice of where to live, right to free expression, right to a free press, and of the freedom of assembly and association. Crucial for human rights protests in later years, the eight sections of the constitution on freedom of religion were regularly disregarded, and the section guaranteeing a right to emigrate was categorically ignored by the SED.[119] At the same time,

---

[113] Peter Quint, *The Imperfect Union: Constitutional Structures of German Unification* (Princeton, NJ: Princeton University Press, 2012), 11–12.

[114] The legal norms of the "people's democracy" resembled the "organic popular state" as theorized by Laband in the Imperial Era. Caldwell, *Popular Sovereignty and the Crisis of German Constitutional Law*, 31.

[115] Conflicts between citizens were handled by legally grounded, if also ideological, courts even though the GDR did not have a bourgeois legal system with the rule of law. Inga Markovits, *Justice in Luritz: Experiencing Socialist Law in East Germany* (Princeton, NJ: Princeton University Press, 2010).

[116] Hermann Wentker, *Justiz in der SBZ/DDR 1945–1953: Transformation und Rolle ihrer zentralen Institutionen* (Munich: Oldenbourg, 2001).

[117] Caldwell, *Dictatorship, State Planning, and Social Theory*, 63.

[118] Amos, *Die Entstehung der Verfassung in der Sowjetischen Besatzungszone/DDR, 1946–1949*, 329.

[119] On the contrast between constitutional promises and political realities, see Amos, 321–23.

Article 6, which prohibited *Boykotthetze* – the "incitement to warfare and boycott" of democratic institutions – was primarily used by the state to prosecute those who criticised SED rule too harshly.[120]

Political participation in the national affairs was both a right and a duty in the GDR Constitution, but this did not apply to those who sought to return fascism to power.[121] As Otto Grotewohl explained, there would be "no basic rights for those who seek to destroy basic rights themselves, who pursue a policy of undermining the political, social, and governmental foundations of the state."[122] Political pluralism was retained in form, if not in content through the antifascist bloc parties of the National Front, which served to integrate otherwise reluctant groups into the fold. Each was oriented towards a specific demographic: In addition to the two parties formed in 1945 – the Christian Democrats (CDU) for conservative Christians and the Liberal Democrats (LDPD) for small business owners – East Germans could also join the Democratic Farmers' Party aimed at rural communities and the National Democratic Party for the remnants of the conservative middle class and former Nazi party members. Because the Soviet authorities had already systematically forced out any bloc party leaders who bucked the SED line, by 1949 there were few left who would think to challenge the new status quo using party politics.[123] A CDU member, Georg Dertinger, was named Foreign Minister to keep up the appearance that the "bourgeois parties" were included in governing, but he operated under the supervision of Anton Ackermann, officially his deputy.[124] The SED retained the formal trappings of democracy, but voting was neither free nor secret and the first *Volkskammer* election held in 1950 resulted in a count of 99.7 percent voting for the pre-prepared list of National Front candidates.[125] The exceptionally high percentage initially sparked outrage from citizens who saw this as an obvious fraud, but by the end of the 1950s, few bothered to even write to the SED anonymously to complain.[126]

---

[120] On the state's use of *Boykotthetze*, see Markovits, *Justice in Luritz*, 103–4; Brigitte Hoeft, *Der Prozess gegen Walter Janka und andere* (Reinbek: Rowohlt, 1990).

[121] Article 3, Section 2, *Die Verfassung der DDR* (1949) (www.documentArchiv.de).

[122] Grotewohl, *Deutsche Verfassungspläne*, 69.

[123] Caldwell, *Dictatorship, State Planning, and Social Theory*, 64.

[124] Naimark, *The Russians in Germany*, 59.

[125] On voting as a social and political ritual, see Jan Palmowski, "Citizenship, Identity and Community in the GDR," in *Citizenship and National Identity in Twentieth-Century Germany*, eds. Geoff Eley and Jan Palmowski (Palo Alto, CA: Stanford University Press, 2007), 73–91. Hedwig Richter, "Mass Obedience: Practices and Functions of Elections in the GDR," in *Voting for Hitler and Stalin: Elections under 20th Century Dictatorships*, eds. Ralph Jessen and Hedwig Richter (Chicago: University of Chicago Press, 2011), 103–25.

[126] Richter, "Mass Obedience," 112–13.

Social, economic and cultural rights were not guaranteed benefits so much as promises of a quid pro quo with specific rights aimed at gaining loyalty from key demographic groups in exchange for fulfilling certain state prerogatives. One's right to food rations, housing, and day-care was always conditioned on compliance with state authority and participation in the labour market. Young people were promised the "right to recreation, the right to education, and the right to joy and happiness," but these rights were to be realised through joining in the state-run FDJ.[127] The SED emphasised the rights that it offered to women, as they were expected to both produce in the workplace and to reproduce at home and in 1950 it passed the "Law for the Protection of Mother and Child and the Rights of Women," detailing the social services that would be provided by the state.[128] The SED also advanced the "rights of the Sorbian national minority," an approximately 100,000 strong Slavic minority group. Following the lead of Soviet policy on minority nations, the SED viewed Sorbian culture as backwards and premodern and thus vulnerable to reactionary ideologies.[129] To guarantee their participation in the larger project of socialist modernisation, the SED provided targeted benefits, includeding Sorbian-language theatre in the city of Bautzen and Sorbian radio programming on Radio Dresden, as well as the establishment of bilingual schools and workplaces in regions with a large minority population.[130]

The limits of these rights became apparent when they clashed with the imperatives of the SED. The conflict over the right to abortion access in the postwar period is one such moment. While the GDR Constitution proclaimed total gender equality and the rights of women, the imperative to rebuild the working population in the wake of wartime deaths and

---

[127] BArch, NY4090/643 Deutscher Volksrat, Informationsdienst. Hermann Gericgk (FDJ), 19.

[128] Harsch, *Revenge of the Domestic*, 133.

[129] On Eastern Bloc minority policy, see Francine Hirsch, *Empire of Nations: Ethnographic Knowledge and the Making of the Soviet Union* (Ithaca, NY: Cornell University Press, 2005); Celia Donert, *The Rights of the Roma: The Struggle for Citizenship in Post-War Czechoslovakia* (Cambridge: Cambridge University Press, 2017).

[130] Cora Granata, "The Ethnic 'Straight Jacket': Bilingual Education and Grassroots Agency in the Soviet Occupied Zone and GDR, 1945–1964," *German Studies Review* 29, no. 2 (2006), 331–46. One report from a Dresden union representative, charged with implementing a bilingual Sorbian language program at a factory, argued that such efforts were necessary despite the negative reactions from German workers because "the realization of equal rights is above all a political-ideological task." Sächsisches Staatsarchiv, Hauptstaatsarchiv Dresden, 12465 FDGB-Bezirksvorstand Dresden 0629 Maßnahmen des FDGB Bezirksvorstandes (18.11.57).

ongoing emigration trumped women's rights to bodily autonomy in the estimation of the SED.[131] While the Weimar KPD ran on the slogan "Your Body Belongs to You!" in opposition to legal controls on access to abortion, the postwar SED deemed it "vulgar," "anarchistic and individualistic."[132] After the conclusion of hostilities, many doctors in occupied Germany initially chose to ignore the prohibition on abortion – legally banned by Paragraph 218, which dated back to 1871 – to cope with the demand shaped by mass rape, but the KPD, and Walter Ulbricht personally, demanded the re-implementation of a total abortion ban. After a catastrophic number of deaths of women seeking illicit or at-home abortions (more than 6,000 in Berlin in 1946 alone), this was relaxed for cases involving special social circumstances, medical conditions, rape or incest.[133]

These exceptions did not, however, mean that the SED recognised a right to abortion access. Maxim Zetkin, the SED's chief medical officer and son of the feminist pioneer Clara Zetkin, explained that under socialism there could be no such thing as a right to an abortion: "We do not believe in natural rights: the law is a social category. And we recognise the right of society to determine the fate of mother and child, but under *one* condition: that society guarantees them at least the minimum tolerable conditions for existence."[134] Because the KPD had always justified abortion rights as a defence against the exploitation of the capitalist system, in which a working woman could not "combine her economic role as producer with her biological function as reproducer," the triumph of socialism in the GDR had finally relieved women of this contradiction and thus the need for abortion access.[135]

---

[131] Naimark, *The Russians in Germany*, 123.

[132] On the Weimar-era KPD's use of this slogan, see Julia Sneeringer, *Winning Women's Votes: Propaganda and Politics in Weimar Germany* (Chapel Hill: University of North Carolina, 2002), 149. Quotes from SED officials rejecting a return to Weimar policy in Harsch, *Revenge of the Domestic*, 145; Atina Grossmann, "Pronatalism, Nationalism and Socialism," in *Between Reform and Revolution: German Socialism and Communism from 1840 to 1990*, eds. David Barclay and Eric Weitz (New York: Berghahn Books, 1998), 451.

[133] Naimark, *The Russians in Germany*, 123.

[134] BArch, DY30/IV 2/17/28 Zetkin to Vorstand der SED (2.10.1946).

[135] Cornelie Usborne, *Cultures of Abortion in Weimar Germany* (New York: Berghahn Books, 2007), 58. Continued emphasis on "social indicators" as the basis for justifying abortions also aimed to elide Red Army rape as the motivation for many seeking terminations. Kirsten Poutrus, "(K)eine Frauensache: Das Abtreibungsphänomen im sowjetisch besetzten Nachkriegsdeutschland (1945–1950)," in *Ohne Frauen ist kein Leben: der 218 und moderne Reproduktionstechnologien* (Berlin: Hoffmann, 1994), 99.

Protest without Human Rights in the 1950s

To gain the loyalty – or at least compliance – of the citizens of the GDR, the SED offered a combination of carrots (incentives through rights) and sticks (the threat of state security). Despite this, East Germans persistently protested SED policy and, at times, mounted acts of collective resistance.[136] The people of the GDR lived under a dictatorship, but they did not mindlessly submit to state directives. In everyday life, conflict and negotiation between the population and the authorities was commonplace: from the very beginning of the GDR's existence, citizens complained openly about "low bonuses and high production quotas, harsh working conditions and long hours, poor planning and rampant bureaucracy, scant production materials and unavailable consumer goods, elevated prices and burdensome rationing, inadequate social benefits and scarce housing."[137] Similarly, the Protestant and Catholic churches in East Germany fought to maintain their public position in the face of marginalisation in a now officially atheistic state. SED ideology was also a point of contestation for some intellectuals, who sought to create more space for open exchange, legality and democracy within the socialist system.

Across the various forms of protest in the new GDR, the language of human rights was almost entirely absent. Although the SED consistently claimed to represent the ideals of human rights, this was practically never seized upon by citizens to protest state policy or challenge the power of the Party. In contrast to the SED, East Germans did not try to translate the abstraction of human rights into localised demands for change in the early years of the GDR. Citizens leveraged their own positions as skilled workers or mothers or devoted Marxists fulfilling the aims of the state to gain privileges and benefits.[138] Because the state required their productive and/or reproductive labour, East Germans had some means of negotiation with managers and bureaucrats who needed to fulfil the plan. When these methods failed, some chose to emigrate to the West in protest against political and economic conditions while

---

[136] On the centrality of civic engagement and critique for the GDR's longevity and stability, see Mary Fulbrook, *The People's State: East German Society from Hitler to Honecker* (New Haven, CT: Yale University Press, 2008), 250–51.

[137] Andrew Port, *Conflict and Stability in the GDR* (Cambridge: Cambridge University Press, 2007), 115.

[138] On strategies of engagement and negotiation in the everyday, see Port, *Conflict and Stability in the GDR*; Sandrine Kott, *Communism Day-to-Day: State Enterprises in East German Society* (Ann Arbor: University of Michigan Press, 2014); Harsch, *Revenge of the Domestic*.

others challenged authority more passively, by submitting invalid ballots in factory elections, telling political jokes or engaging in purposefully sloppy and disruptive working practices.[139] In everyday life, it was easier to make demands rooted in one's identity, than to invoke the far-off promises of the UDHR. For its part, the SED created institutional means for East Germans to express their discontent in ways that would effectively, but surreptitiously, reinforce the legitimacy of the party rather than undermine it while carefully policing public discourse to ensure that ideas and language that could delegitimise its rule were rapidly suppressed.

Even when GDR protests escalated into open conflict with the SED, human rights were virtually never mentioned. On 16 June 1953, construction workers in East Berlin began protesting rationing and work quotas and by the next day this transformed into mass demonstrations numbering in the tens of thousands in the capital with hundreds of smaller protests across the country. On the 17th, the Soviets deployed tanks to suppress the demonstrations, killing hundreds in the process. The 1953 Uprising is often described as a fight for human rights, with some observers comparing it to 1989 saying both events reflected "a desire for a united democratic Germany, and the restoration of basic human rights."[140] While protestor demands rapidly expanded from improved working conditions to free elections and the release from prison of the politically persecuted, there is only a single documented example of East Germans using the term *human rights* in connection with the uprising in 1953:[141] On 18 June,

---

[139] Port, *Conflict and Stability in the GDR*, 120–21. On *Eigen-Sinn*, protest through nonconformity and "self-will," see Alf Lüdtke, *Herrschaft als soziale Praxis: historische und sozial-anthropologische Studien* (Göttingen: Vandenhoeck & Ruprecht, 1991); Thomas Lindenberger, *Herrschaft und Eigen-Sinn in der Diktatur: Studien zur Gesellschaftsgeschichte der DDR* (Cologne: Böhlau, 1999).

[140] Quotation from Gary Bruce, *Resistance with the People: Repression and Resistance in Eastern Germany, 1945–1955* (Lanham, MD: Rowman & Littlefield, 2003), 3. The 1953 Uprising is deemed "an uprising for freedom and human rights" by Karl Wilhelm Fricke; "'17. Juni 1953' – Vorgeschichte und Verlauf" in *Volkserhebung gegen den SED-Staat: eine Bestandsaufnahme zum 17. Juni 1953*, eds. Roger Engelmann and Ilko-Sascha Kowalczuk (Göttingen: Vandenhoeck & Ruprecht, 2005), 57. Dietrich describes the aim of the uprising as the "restoration of basic and human rights after the model of the free and democratic constitutional state." Torsten Diedrich, *Waffen gegen das Volk: Der 17. Juni 1953 in der DDR* (Munich: Oldenbourg, 2003), 139.

[141] There are no references to *Menschenrechte* in Stasi reports on the uprisings. Roger Engelmann and Daniela Münkel, *Die DDR im Blick der Stasi 1953: Die geheimen Berichte an die SED-Führung* (Göttingen: Vandenhoeck & Ruprecht, 2013). There is also no mention of human rights claims in the primary sources cited in numerous studies of 1953 including Engelmann and Kowalczuk, *Volkserhebung gegen den SED-Staat*; Ilko-Sascha Kowalczuk, Armin Mitter and Stefan Wolle, *Der Tag X, 17. Juni 1953: die "Innere Staatsgründung" der DDR als Ergebnis der Krise 1952–54*

a group of workers from Magdeburg laid a wreath at a war memorial with a ribbon stating, "17 June 1953 – To the Victims for Freedom and Human Rights."[142] Solidarity protests in West Berlin described it as a fight for "the human rights of everyone in the Eastern Zone," but this did not reflect the slogans of the protesters.[143]

The SED responded to organised opposition and dissent with brutal suppression and show trials, but it also allowed for carefully controlled forms of complaint, which permitted citizens to let off steam and provided unofficial public opinion polling.[144] Article 3 of the 1949 Constitution guaranteed the right of every GDR citizen to submit *Eingaben* – petitions – to state officials, and, surprisingly, this right was largely respected in practice.[145] Common in state socialist countries dating back to the Soviet Revolution (when Lenin argued that it was an essential link between the workers and the state), GDR citizens showered state officials with *Eingaben* regarding the lack of consumer goods, poor housing conditions and ineffective local functionaries. The lost art of writing effective *Eingaben* has become a central aspect of the memory of everyday life in the GDR: the film *Goodbye Lenin!* (2003) features an ardent SED-member and skilled *Eingaben* writer, who, after missing the fall of the GDR while in a coma, continues to assist her neighbours in writing complaint letters, not realising they are for use in the new capitalist system. More than 12,000 *Eingaben* were sent just to the *Volkskammer* between 1949 and 1958 and by the 1960s, the State Council, the highest political organ of the GDR, received more than 100,000 *Eingaben* every year.[146] Many citizens sent their petitions straight to the top, so that

(Berlin: Ch. Links Verlag, 1995); Ulrich Mählert, *Der 17. Juni 1953: ein Aufstand für Einheit, Recht und Freiheit* (Berlin: Dietz, 2003).

[142] Quoted in Bruce, *Resistance with the People*, 222.

[143] West German union leader Ernst Scharnowski quoted in Christian Ostermann and Malcolm Byrne, *Uprising in East Germany 1953: The Cold War, the German Question, and the First Major Upheaval behind the Iron Curtain* (Budapest: Central European University Press, 2001), 174.

[144] Bruce, *Resistance with the People*. Franz-Josef Kos, "Politische Justiz in der DDR. Der Dessauer Schauprozeß vom April 1950," *Vierteljahrshefte Für Zeitgeschichte* 44, no. 3 (1996), 395–429 and Petra Weber, *Justiz und Diktatur: Justizverwaltung und politische Strafjustiz in Thüringen 1945–1961* (Munich: Oldenbourg, 2000). On expression of discontent as "steam valve" and valuable source of information, see Port, *Conflict and Stability in the GDR*, 103.

[145] Peter Becker, *Akten, Eingaben, Schaufenster – die DDR und ihre Texte: Erkundungen zu Herrschaft und Alltag* (Berlin: Akademie Verlag, 1997); Felix Mühlberg, *Bürger, Bitten und Behörden: Geschichte der Eingabe in der DDR* (Berlin: Dietz, 2004); Jonathan Zatlin, *The Currency of Socialism: Money and Political Culture in East Germany* (Cambridge: Cambridge University Press, 2007), ch. 7.

[146] Werner Patzelt and Roland Schirmer, *Die Volkskammer der DDR: Sozialistischer Parlamentarismus in Theorie und Praxis* (Opladen: Springer-Verlag, 2013), 416; Paul

Walter Ulbricht and after him Erich Honecker received daily post on matters ranging from desiccated oranges and poorly fitting clothing to lazy building managers. So long as citizens phrased these petitions as constructive criticism to further the cause of socialism, they were legally guaranteed a reply, although responses were habitually late and often unsatisfactory.[147] For important works of legislation, the SED also organised "discussions" where state officials could explain draft bills to gauge public reaction and to determine points of resistance, after which propaganda was adjusted accordingly. Periodically, these were organised on a mass scale: in 1954, 300,000 East Germans took part in a six-month consultation over a proposed new Family Code, which was ultimately postponed due to often raucous objections at public events.[148]

The Protestant and Catholic churches would both play an important role in popularising the language of human rights, but most of the conflict over the place of Christianity in the early GDR revolved instead around constitutional rights. Under Articles 41–48 of the GDR Constitution, the right to free religious belief and practice was ostensibly protected and the use of state schools for the provision of religious instruction guaranteed. Despite these promises, the SED steadily suppressed Church activities through the 1950s. The SED considered the Christian faith to be a "dying remnant of bourgeois society," but with 80 percent of the East German population adhering to the Protestant faith and another 12 percent identifying as Catholic, it had been expedient to include these protections in the Constitution to appeal to sceptical Christians.[149] As such, rights for Christians and their churches were steadily rolled back, and new institutional measures were put in place so that membership would be eroded in the long term.

The first major fight with the churches over constitutional rights began in 1951 when the SED decreed that Marxism-Leninism would be taught in schools. As a result, Christians were removed from the teaching profession, and the limited space initially provided to the church within schools for after-hours religious instruction was increasingly curtailed.[150] Complaints citing constitutional rights were ignored. The next major conflict came in 1954 when the SED officially made the

Betts, *Within Walls: Private Life in the GDR* (Oxford: Oxford University Press, 2010), 174–75.

[147] Jeremy Straughn, "'Taking the State at Its Word': The Arts of Consentful Contention in the GDR," *American Journal of Sociology* 110, no. 6 (2005), 1598–1650.

[148] Harsch, *Revenge of the Domestic*, 284–85.

[149] Robert Goeckel, *The Lutheran Church and the East German State: Political Conflict and Change under Ulbricht and Honecker* (Ithaca, NY: Cornell University Press, 1990), 3.

[150] Betts, *Within Walls*, 55.

Jugendweihe – a secular youth initiation ceremony invented by nineteenth-century freethinkers – into a socialist institution.[151] GDR youths would not be forced to take part in the Jugendweihe, but participation was necessary for privileges such as higher education. German churches had previously banned congregants from partaking in both confirmation and the Jugendweihe and the SED's actions were interpreted as an effort to reduce the power of the Church through attrition. When the churches claimed this violated the constitutional rights of Christians, the SED argued that it was upholding the right to freedom of religion: "The state and the Party are dedicated to protecting the freedom of belief and conscience. It is the free and democratic right of parents to decide with their children, whether the child goes to the Jugendweihe or confirmation or both. This right is protected by the constitution."[152]

In its various attempts to defend religious freedom in East Germany, the Catholic Church only sporadically included references to human rights. In July 1953, Bishop of Berlin Wilhelm Weskamm wrote to Otto Grotewohl calling for greater respect for religious rights and freedoms as well as increased adherence to the rule of law in the wake of the 1953 Uprising. While Bishop Weskamm primarily cited the GDR Constitution to underpin his case, he also cited the so-called Stalin Note of 1952 which had publicly outlined a Soviet peace proposal for Germany and had referenced the need of the people to "enjoy human rights and basic freedoms," regardless of race, sex, language or religion.[153] Again in 1958, a pastoral letter decried the "disregard for human rights," in connection with Christians losing their positions over a refusal to leave the church.[154] These appeals were not successful.

Many East German intellectuals chafed under the increasingly dogmatic strictures of the SED, but they did not invoke human rights to push back against the centralisation of power under Ulbricht.[155] During the 1953 Uprising, the intelligentsia was notably absent from those striking and demonstrating in the streets – the scientist Robert Havemann, who

---

[151] On the protests against the *Jugendweihe*, see Ehrhart Neubert, *Geschichte der Opposition in der DDR: 1949–1989* (Berlin: Ch. Links, 1998), 118.

[152] Betts, *Within Walls*, 61.

[153] "Memorandum des Bischofs von Berlin, Wilhelm Weskamm," (11.7.1953) in Gerhard Lange, *Katholische Kirche - sozialistischer Staat DDR: Dokumente und öffentliche Äußerungen 1945–1990* (Berlin: Bischöfliches Ordinariat, 1993), 67; Peter Ruggenthaler, *Stalins großer Bluff: Die Geschichte der Stalin-Note in Dokumenten der sowjetischen Führung* (Munich: de Gruyter, 2007), 112.

[154] "Hirtenwort der Bischöfe und Bischöflichen Kommissare in der DDR," (15.4.1958) in Lange, *Katholische Kirche – sozialistischer Staat DDR*, 122.

[155] Guntolf Herzberg, *Anpassung und Aufbegehren: die Intelligenz der DDR in den Krisenjahren 1956/58* (Berlin: Ch. Links Verlag, 2006).

would later become one of the GDR's most prominent dissidents, went to the crowds and unsuccessfully tried to calm tensions and disperse the demonstrators.[156] The philologist Viktor Klemperer, who had been persecuted by the Nazis for his Jewish heritage, was sceptical of the SED, but he also feared a resurgence of fascism, and therefore joined the party and even served as a *Volkskammer* representative. While Klemperer wrote a book on the corruption of language by dictatorship during the Third Reich (his diary often noted a similar process in the GDR), he accepted and promoted the SED's human rights discourse.[157] In 1948, he had encouraged teachers to not just repeat the slogan "no human rights without socialism," but to demonstrate "step by step, first how they are linked; then how there can be no human rights without socialism, finally: that only within Marxism can one successfully develop one's personality."[158]

Ernst Bloch, one of East Germany's most prominent philosophers, did incorporate the idea of human rights into a conception for a better socialism, but his ideas remained on the page.[159] In 1953, Bloch argued that, rather than abandoning them wholesale, socialist society needed to salvage what it could from the bourgeois and natural rights traditions: "In consideration of human rights, [the revolution] seeks bourgeois freedom without the bourgeois citizen." Paraphrasing both Lenin and *Die Internationale*, he went on to say, "Marxism is all-powerful because it is true, just as it is all-powerful because [in the words of] the *Internationale*, it fights for human rights in depth and breadth."[160] But Bloch did not promote this idea through his teaching at the University of Leipzig, and was forcibly retired before he could publish on the subject again. By the mid-1950s, Bloch's colleagues – threatened by what they deemed to be his ideological unreliability and hopeless utopianism – stripped him of his position in Leipzig and removed his works from university curricula.[161] When the Berlin Wall was erected in August 1961, Bloch was

---

[156] Bernd Florath, *Annäherungen an Robert Havemann* (Göttingen: Vandenhoeck & Ruprecht, 2016), 288.

[157] John Wesley Young, "From LTI to LQI: Victor Klemperer on Totalitarian Language," *German Studies Review* 28, no. 1 (2005), 45–64.

[158] Klemperer, *So sitze ich denn zwischen allen Stühlen*, 513.

[159] On Bloch's place in Marxist human rights thinking, see Costas Douzinas, "Adikia: On Communism and Rights," *Critical Legal Thinking*, 20.11.2010 (www.criticallegalthinking.com).

[160] The original saying from Lenin is, "The theory of Marx is all-powerful, because it is true," and the lyric is "the Internationale, it fights for human rights" (*erkämpft das Menschenrecht*). Ernst Bloch, "Marx und Bürgerliche Menschenrechte" *Aufbau* 9, no. 5 (1953), 405.

[161] Caldwell, *Dictatorship, State Planning, and Social Theory in the GDR*, 99. Neubert, *Geschichte der Opposition in der DDR*, 109–11.

visiting the FRG and chose not to return to the GDR. Although he did eventually develop his ideas on human rights, socialism, and utopia in *Natural Rights and Human Dignity*, it was only published in West Germany.[162]

In 1956, when Soviet leader Nikita Khrushchev's denunciations of Stalin's crimes began an era of "thaw," some East German intellectuals began to organise for a more "humanistic" socialism in the GDR, but they turned to Marx rather than to human rights as a guide for renewal. The philosopher Wolfgang Harich presented his ideas for a democratised utopian socialism to Walter Ulbricht in 1956, which led directly to his arrest as a "counterrevolutionary."[163] He was imprisoned until 1964. A similar fate befell philosopher Walter Janka, also accused of counter-revolutionary conspiracy, after he formulated a Marxist critique of SED rule. Janka and his co-defendants' were convicted in a show trial, prosecuted under the infamous Article 6 of the Constitution – *Boykotthetze* – and imprisoned until 1960.[164] While both challenged how the SED ruled the GDR, neither Harich nor Janka advanced the idea of human rights as a solution to East Germany's democratic failings.

Systemic critiques of power were met with harsh punishment, but the SED also closely policed any use of rights language that challenged the principle of Party control. One victim of this was, of all people, the minister of justice, Max Fechner. Imprisoned by the Nazis for his membership in a Social Democratic resistance group during the Third Reich, Fechner joined the SED after the war, serving as president of the International Association of Democratic Lawyers and as first minister of justice in the GDR. In response to the 1953 Uprising, Fechner told *Neues Deutschland* that violations of the law would be punished, but "the right to strike is guaranteed by the constitution. The leaders of the strikes will not be punished for being members of a strike leadership committee."[165] In response, the Politburo denounced Fechner as an enemy of the state, stripped him of his party membership, and he was sentenced to eight years imprisonment. His successor as minister of justice was Hilde Benjamin, who had presided over many of the earliest show trials and was now placed in charge of the legal crackdown

---

[162] Ernst Bloch, *Naturrecht und menschliche Würde* (Frankfurt: Suhrkamp, 1961).
[163] Alexander Amberger, *Bahro – Harich – Havemann: Marxistische Systemkritik und politische Utopie in der DDR* (Paderborn: Verlag Ferdinand Schöningh, 2014).
[164] On Janka and Harich's persecution, see Neubert, *Geschichte der Opposition in der DDR*, 106–9 and Sven Sieber, *Walter Janka und Wolfgang Harich: zwei DDR-Intellektuelle im Konflikt mit der Macht* (Berlin: Lit, 2008); Hoeft, *Der Prozess gegen Walter Janka und andere*. On the use of these legal tools, see Markovits, *Justice in Luritz*, 103–4.
[165] Quoted in Klein, *Für die Einheit und Reinheit der Partei*, 202.

following the Uprising. Fechner was released from prison in 1956, and his party membership was later reinstated, but the message that even top ministers would be punished harshly for undermining the position of the SED in the language of rights was crystal clear.[166]

The SED also sought to suppress West German human rights activism, fearing its potential to undermine the internal legitimacy of the GDR. The Stasi not only created front organisations in the Federal Republic to campaign against the democratic failings of the FRG, they also took direct action against West German NGOs.[167] To disrupt the activities of the Association of Free German Jurists (UFJ), which documented violations of the rule of law in the GDR, the Stasi kidnapped its head, Walter Linse, from West Berlin in 1952 and he was executed in Moscow the following year.[168] The Stasi also insinuated themselves into Western groups as a means of intelligence gathering and one such target was the Liga für Menschenrechte (League for Human Rights). The League collected information on human rights violations in East Germany and acted as a conduit for dissident literature. In 1956, the Stasi sent Wolfram von Hanstein to infiltrate the League. Arrested by the Soviet authorities and sentenced to death for espionage, von Hanstein had been released and recruited by the Stasi.[169] After emigrating to West Berlin, he quickly rose through the ranks of the local branch of the League for Human Rights, as well as several other anti-communist organisations.[170] Von Hanstein then used his positions to funnel information to his Stasi handlers on incoming refugees and planned escapes

---

[166] Caldwell, *Dictatorship, State Planning, and Social Theory in the GDR*, 65–66.

[167] For example, the *Zentralrat zum Schutz demokratischer Rechte und zur Verteidigung Deutscher Patrioten*, published several pamphlets on political repression and peace in the early 1950s.

[168] During the Nazi era, Linse was in charge of the Aryanization of Jewish property in Chemnitz, one of several to make the transition from Nazism to anti-communist human rights activism in 1950s West Germany. Susanne Muhle, *Auftrag Menschenraub: Entführungen von Westberlinern und Bundesbürgern durch das Ministerium für Staatssicherheit der DDR* (Vandenhoeck & Ruprecht, 2015), 137–38.

[169] Von Hanstein had tried to establish a branch of the League in Dresden in 1948 but later claimed Colonel Sergei Tiul'panov of the Soviet Military Authority offered him clemency so long as he ceased all public human rights activities in the Soviet Zone. BArch, Z35/351 Deutsches Büro für Friedensfragen, Vermerk (27.1.1948); Lora Wildenthal, "Human Rights Activism in Occupied and Early West Germany: The Case of the German League for Human Rights," *The Journal of Modern History* 80, no. 3 (2008), 550.

[170] Von Hanstein appears to have founded the "Research Institute for Human Rights Questions" – one of many such SED-funded organizations to criticize the rights-record of West Germany under Adenauer. Aside from one pamphlet, there is no other available documentation on the organization's activities or other evidence of its existence. Wolfram von Hanstein, *Forschungsinstitut für Fragen der Menschenrechte* (Cologne: Dt. Liga für Menschenrechte, 1958).

from the GDR.[171] In 1959, after years of unconfirmed suspicions, he was exposed as a spy and imprisoned for espionage once more – this time by West German authorities.[172] While the human rights organisations of West Germany were riven by internal disputes and largely ineffective to begin with, the Stasi managed to also co-opt them in the service of their own intelligence gathering.

Conclusion

In the immediate postwar era, the SED rapidly adapted to the new popularity of human rights ideas among Social Democrats by co-opting the concept of human rights, rather than running from it. In spite of the long-standing disinterest or even outright scorn for human rights among German socialists, the ideological flexibility demanded of the KPD during its time in Soviet exile during the Nazi era prepared them to reconcile radical goals with moderate rhetoric. Already in 1946, the SED was able to adopt the language of human rights and adapt it to increasingly illiberal and authoritarian systems of rule, to police the use of this language by party elites and regular citizens alike, and thus to ensure that it would not be used to undermine the authority of its leadership. Establishing a pattern that would prove to be effective for the next 40 years, the SED responded to human rights criticism not by liberalising, but by developing new ideological approaches and reformulating its propaganda to appropriate the language of its critics.

The problem the SED would soon face was that the world of human rights politics was rapidly becoming far more complicated than a fight between socialist factions inside Germany. The passage of the UDHR in 1948 established a new site of contestation in a time of rising Cold War tensions. Beyond the conflict between East and West, human rights were rapidly becoming a central element of the anti-imperialist decolonisation movements from the global south. The SED had learned how to deflect attacks on its legitimacy from the Social Democrats with a slogan, but in the coming years, adapting East German ideology and propaganda to the emerging global system of human rights would prove to be a far more difficult process.

---

[171] Wildenthal, "Human Rights Activism in Occupied and Early West Germany," 551.
[172] Von Hanstein eventually escaped to the GDR in 1964 but died soon thereafter. Ibid., 552.

2 Inventing Socialist Human Rights, 1953–1966

Human rights initially entered the SED lexicon in the immediate post-war period through its rivalry with the Social Democrats, but by the late 1950s, the question of human rights had become vastly more complex than a competition over who legitimately represented the German working class. The establishment of two German states in 1949 transformed this conflict into a battle between West Germany and the German Democratic Republic – now accused of being an illegitimate dictatorship, guilty of systemic human rights violations and under the thumb of the continued Soviet occupation. The competition between these two countries moved the conflict from the local to the global stage, where the recently created Universal Declaration of Human Rights (UDHR) now served as an international point of reference. Complicating matters further was the rising Non-Aligned Movement, which also wanted a say in the meaning of human rights, refusing to allow the Cold War superpowers to define the terms of debate on their own.

Under Walter Ulbricht's leadership, the SED spent the 1950s consolidating its political power within the GDR, but it could do little to overcome East Germany's global ostracism. In 1955, the Soviet Union unilaterally granted sovereignty to the GDR and it ostensibly became an independent nation, allied to the USSR and the rest of the Eastern Bloc through the Warsaw Pact. Yet outside this alliance, only the People's Republic of China and Yugoslavia diplomatically recognised the existence of the GDR. West Germany had proclaimed to the world that there was only one German state, and that state was the FRG. According to this policy – the so-called Hallstein Doctrine – West Germany vowed to cut diplomatic ties and foreign aid to any country (outside the socialist bloc) that entertained relations with the GDR. For newly independent states in Africa and Asia, West German offers of

53

monetary aid and technical assistance were enough to shun the comparatively poorer and less influential GDR.[1]

In response to this campaign of global isolation, the SED sought to fight back ideologically. From the pressures of this German-German competition was born the *Komitee zum Schutze der Menschenrechte* (Committee for the Protection of Human Rights, or KSM). Founded by the SED in 1959, the KSM predated Amnesty International and was the only state-directed human rights organisation in the socialist world and would remain so until the late 1980s. Initially tasked with campaigning for the release of imprisoned communists in the Federal Republic, the KSM organised letter-writing campaigns and charity concerts, and produced pamphlets on human rights abuses for mass consumption abroad and international diplomatic pressure. Over the course of the 1960s, however, the KSM evolved into the human rights think tank for the GDR, providing expertise and propaganda for the struggle against apartheid, the Vietnam War and the Greek military dictatorship.

Beyond the KSM, a new generation of East German intellectuals also developed a full-fledged ideological conception of "socialist human rights." In response to the rise of a non-Western majority at the United Nations, they adopted the anti-colonialist concept of self-determination as a human right. East German intellectuals tied together the SED's quest to gain international recognition with postcolonial aspirations and evolving global human rights politics of the emerging Non-Aligned Movement. This hybrid concept of human rights allowed the GDR a voice on the international stage loud enough to demand recognition as a champion of international values and anti-imperialism, distinct from its West German rival, which backed oppressive (neo-)colonial regimes in Africa and Asia.

As this chapter will show, the evolution of human rights in the GDR in this period was, nonetheless, a chaotic and uncoordinated process driven by improvisation from the middle rather than planning from above. With little direction from SED leadership, the KSM developed its discourse of protest by drawing upon existing cultural narratives of antifascism as it initially lacked expertise on international human rights. Within the universities, the development of human rights theory was hampered by ideological rivalries and a purge of the legal profession at the Babelsberg

[1] William Gray, *Germany's Cold War: The Global Campaign to Isolate East Germany, 1949–1969* (Chapel Hill: University of North Carolina Press, 2003); Mathias Stein, *Der Konflikt um Alleinvertretung und Anerkennung in der UNO: Die deutsch-deutschen Beziehungen zu den Vereinten Nationen von 1949 bis 1973* (Göttingen: V&R Unipress, 2011); Hermann Wentker, *Außenpolitik in engen Grenzen: Die DDR im Internationalen System, 1949–1989* (Munich: Oldenbourg, 2007), 170–79.

Conference in 1958. In the mid-1960s, when SED party leaders did attempt to use human rights rhetoric in a conflict over citizenship with West Germany, they failed to consult their own experts and blundered into an embarrassing legal fiasco. Despite these difficulties and missteps, there was practically no domestic backlash challenging state policy in the name of human rights. As we shall see, while the SED continued to face human rights criticism from the West, the party had no reason to fear such action from its own citizens.

Human Rights as Antifascism

The formal division of Germany in 1949 created new demarcation lines in the battle over human rights. West German Christian Democrats (CDU) now joined with the SPD in deploying human rights in their denunciation of state socialism as a form of tyranny. For the first time, human rights became part of a shared language of anti-communism across political lines. The CDU's turn to human rights paralleled a broader movement among Western European conservatives, *laissez-faire* liberals and communitarian Catholics, centred around the European Convention on Human Rights (1950). In contrast to the UDHR, the European Convention contained no provisions for social or economic rights and concentrated instead on the right to life, the rule of law, freedom of religion and liberal freedoms such as expression and association.[2] This rapidly became part of the cultural landscape of the early Cold War, and as Marco Duranti has argued, "to be properly European meant to be free to exercise one's human rights," while "the peoples in the Soviet Bloc had fallen under the shadow of a new Oriental despotism."[3] Human rights were thus redefined as a core value of Western Europe in contrast to the absence of human rights under the totalitarian "other" of Eastern Europe.

Over the course of the 1950s, the rhetoric of both the West German government and a host of NGOs increasingly used the idea of human rights to attack the legitimacy of the GDR. Although neither Germany was a member of the United Nations, the FRG began to officially commemorate International Human Rights Day in 1951, celebrating

---

[2] On the importance of conservatives, see Marco Duranti, *The Conservative Human Rights Revolution: European Identity, Transnational Politics, and the Origins of the European Convention* (Oxford: Oxford University Press, 2017). On the importance of Catholic Personalism, see Samuel Moyn, "Personalism, Community, and the Origins of Human Rights," in *Human Rights in the Twentieth Century*, ed. Stefan-Ludwig Hoffmann (Cambridge: Cambridge University Press, 2010), 85–106.

[3] Duranti, *The Conservative Human Rights Revolution*, 350.

the passage of the UDHR every year on 10 December.[4] The Commission for an Indivisible Germany (*Kuratorium Unteilbares Deutschland*), a nationalist organisation backed by political notables from the Left and Right, began to submit complaints to the United Nations accusing the GDR of violating rights as outlined in the UDHR.[5] The UN human rights organs refused to accept such petitions, even from member nations, so these missives prompted neither investigations nor condemnation.[6] Yet, the mere fact that they were sent to the UN set off a flurry of press activity in West Germany about human rights abuses in "the Zone."[7]

In 1952, a request from the United Nations to the Soviet Control Commission, still officially in charge of the not-fully sovereign GDR, forced the SED to once again compete with Western rivals over the meaning of human rights. The letter requested information for the annual *Yearbook on Human Rights*, which documented laws relating to the implementation of the UDHR.[8] Soviet Political Counsellor Vladimir Semyonov relayed the request to Prime Minister Grotewohl, suggesting that they highlight the achievements of the Five-Year Plan and constitutionally guaranteed social rights such as the right to work, to education and to health care.[9] He surmised that the SED needed to proactively submit a response to forestall West German efforts to use the publication for propaganda purposes. Semyonov's instincts were correct: the FRG not only planned to contribute to the volume but also sought to prevent the GDR's inclusion, so as to deny it any form of diplomatic recognition.[10]

The GDR bureaucracy went far beyond this suggestion and sent the information on almost 90 laws passed since 1949 to the UN. Soliciting submissions from various state agencies, the Ministry for Foreign Affairs simply asked for all material relating to any human right listed in the UDHR. As a result, the final report contained information on policy

[4] BArch, B136/3003 Bundeskanzleramt, "Tag der Menschenrechte," (10.12.1951).
[5] Markus Gloe, *Planung für die deutsche Einheit: der Forschungsbeirat für Fragen der Wiedervereinigung Deutschlands, 1952–1975* (Wiesbaden: VS Verlag, 2005), 181.
[6] Samuel Moyn, *Last Utopia: Human Rights in History* (Cambridge, MA: Belknap, 2010), 100–1.
[7] The East German foreign ministry carefully tracked Western media coverage of these petitions. PA AA, MfAA, A18271.
[8] BArch, NY4090/467 UN Secretary General Lie to the Chairman of the Soviet Control Commission (9.5.1952). The Soviet Union officially granted the GDR's sovereignty on 20 September 1955.
[9] BArch, NY4090/467 Semyonov to Grotewohl (3.7.1952).
[10] Stein, *Der Konflikt um Alleinvertretung und Anerkennung in der UNO*, 71 n. 403.

ranging from day-care spaces to workplace gender equality to coal pro-duction.[11] Any improvement of human welfare related to any right in the UDHR was deemed to be a triumph of human rights for the GDR. If, as Karl Polak had argued, human rights were the product of socialism, then all improvements to society and the economy that came about from socialist rule were relevant. Because the United Nations uncritically published all submissions to the *Yearbook*, the GDR's contribution was included, though significantly shortened.[12]

The skirmish over the UN *Yearbook* was only a prelude to the escal-ation in tensions between East and West over GDR sovereignty and legitimacy. In 1958, Soviet leader Nikita Khrushchev announced his goal to remove the Western allies and their armed forces from Berlin, which remained under four-power occupation, claiming that the city belonged wholly to East Germany.[13] That same year, General Secretary Walter Ulbricht promised at the SED's Fifth Party Congress, held under the slogan "Socialism Is Victorious," that East Germany would overtake West Germany economically within three years. The SED replaced an earlier five-year plan with a new, more ambitious, seven-year plan that radically accelerated agricultural collectivisation in the countryside, increased production goals for industry and pushed for a massive increase in the number of women in the workplace.[14] As part of the initiative to overtake the West, and to stem the ever-increasing emigration to the FRG, the SED launched a major propaganda effort against West Germany, all under the banner of antifascism.

The antifascism campaign – directed by head of the Politburo's Agita-tion Committee Albert Norden – portrayed the Federal Republic as returning to Nazism and threatening to plunge the world once again into war.[15] The campaign contrasted how former Nazis now held positions of power in West Germany while socialists and supporters of peace were being systematically suppressed by the state. In postwar West Germany,

---

[11] PA AA, MfAA, A5829 Beitrag der DDR zum UN-Jahrbuch für Menschenrechte 1953.
[12] GDR entry, *Yearbook for Human Rights for 1953* (New York: United Nations, 1955), 89–91.
[13] Hope Harrison, *Driving the Soviets up the Wall: Soviet-East German Relations, 1953–1961* (Princeton, NJ: Princeton University Press, 2003), 105.
[14] André Steiner, *The Plans That Failed: An Economic History of East Germany, 1945–1989* (New York: Berghahn, 2010), 91; Donna Harsch, *Revenge of the Domestic: Women, the Family, and Communism in the GDR* (Princeton, NJ: Princeton University Press, 2007), 236–37.
[15] Michael Lemke, *Einheit oder Sozialismus? Die Deutschlandpolitik der SED 1949–1961* (Cologne: Böhlau, 2001), 435; Michael Lemke, "Kampagnen gegen Bonn: Die Systemkrise der DDR und die West-Propaganda der SED 1960–1963," *Vierteljahrshefte für Zeitgeschichte* 41, no. 2 (1993), 4.

the government argued that Weimar had fallen because antidemocratic forces had been allowed to flourish under the protection of the liberal order. To prevent such a reoccurrence, the FRG first banned the Far Right Socialist Reich Party in 1952 and the following year, the Communist Party (KPD) was put on trial as a threat to democracy. In 1956, the courts found that the KPD was incompatible with the "free democratic basic order" of the Federal Republic and the party along with more than 80 other affiliated groups were all officially banned.[16] According to Norden and the SED, this echoed the Nazi persecution of the Left and only the GDR represented a true opposition to this resurgent threat: if Nazism was the endpoint of the crisis of capitalism in the Weimar Republic, then the restoration of capitalism in West Germany would cause history to repeat itself until a socialist revolution finally eradicated fascism at its very roots.[17]

The SED's accusations of West German illiberalism and renewed military armament were not baseless, even if they were exaggerated. Between 1953 and 1958, West German authorities conducted 46,476 political investigations leading to charges against 1,905 individuals, most of whom were communists. As Patrick Major writes "there were so many judges of Nazi vintage still passing sentence in the FRG that it is very difficult to talk of an unprejudiced judiciary in the 1950s and 1960s." It took liberal reforms in 1968 to end "a period of political justice which did not reflect credit on the Federal Republic's legal system."[18] The FRG had also joined the North Atlantic Treaty Organization (NATO) and refounded a national military – the *Bundeswehr* – in 1955. The following year, universal conscription was reintroduced for a military still primarily led by veterans of the Nazi-era *Wehrmacht*.[19] West Germany may not

---

[16] Patrick Major, *The Death of the KPD: Communism and Anti-Communism in West Germany, 1945–1956* (Oxford: Oxford University Press, 1997), 292. Norbert Frei, *Adenauer's Germany and the Nazi Past: The Politics of Amnesty and Integration* (New York: Columbia University Press, 2002), 251–76.

[17] Official East German memory of Nazis crimes did not specifically recognize antisemitism or the centrality of the Holocaust, see Jeffrey Herf, *Divided Memory: The Nazi Past in the Two Germanys* (Cambridge, MA: Harvard University Press, 1997). In Western Europe, however, those drafting the European Convention on Human Rights also failed to connect their work to the Final Solution, see G. Daniel Cohen, "The Holocaust and the 'Human Rights Revolution,'" in *The Human Rights Revolution: An International History*, eds. Akira Iriye, Petra Goedde and William Hitchcock (New York: Oxford University Press, 2012), 63.

[18] Major, *The Death of the KPD*, 282.

[19] On West German rearmament, see David Clay Large, *Germans to the Front: West German Rearmament in the Adenauer Era* (Chapel Hill: University of North Carolina Press, 2000). The East German National People's Army (NVA) was also dependent on former Wehrmacht officers, see Peter Lapp, *Ulbrichts Helfer: Wehrmachtsoffiziere im Dienste der DDR* (Bonn: Bernard & Graefe, 2000).

have been on a sure path to renewed fascism, but the SED was correct in its description of a government riddled with former Nazis, courts used to suppress left-wing political opposition and a rapid remilitarisation led by soldiers who had recently served the Third Reich.

The campaign aimed to embarrass the FRG in the eyes of the international community, but the SED also wanted to build support from the West German people.[20] East German elites fervently believed that the working masses of West Germany naturally longed for a socialist revolution and were on the verge of throwing off the shackles of bourgeois tyranny. On the party level, the Social Democrats had officially renounced both Marxism and the goal of ending capitalism in the party's Godesberg Program of 1959, which also accused the SED of "radically suppressing freedom" and "violating human rights," making reconciliation with the SED an impossibility.[21] Because the path to unity "from above" was closed, the SED turned to unity "from below" by trying to appeal directly to the SPD's rank and file.[22] Convinced that the conservative SPD leadership was out of touch with its radical base, the SED's Department of Western Affairs confidently declared, "*objectively* the peace-loving forces in all of Germany have their home in the GDR, even if *subjectively* they are not yet aware of this."[23] The masses only needed to be properly educated before they would naturally demand unification on SED terms.

Norden's antifascism campaign built upon existing propaganda against the "bloody judges" who had served under the Nazis, expanding it to also target other figures in Chancellor Konrad Adenauer's government who were complicit in the crimes of the Third Reich.[24] The SED held show trials in absentia for leading Western political figures: Minister for Displaced Persons Theodor Oberländer was convicted in absentia for his role in the 1941 Lviv Massacre; under pressure from his own party, Oberländer resigned from the government in 1960. The SED held another show trial in 1963, this time for Hans Globke, author of the Third Reich's antisemitic legal codes, who had risen to become the

---

[20] Arnd Bauerkämper, *Das umstrittene Gedächtnis: Die Erinnerung an Nationalsozialismus, Faschismus und Krieg in Europa seit 1945* (Paderborn: Ferdinand Schöningh, 2012), 203.

[21] "Godesberger Programm" in Wilhelm Mommsen, ed., *Deutsche Parteiprogramme* (Munich: Isar Verlag, 1960), 673–91.

[22] Dietrich Orlow, "Between 'Unity of Action' and 'Lackeys of Imperialism': The Contradictory Attitudes of the East German Communists toward the West German Social Democrats, 1959–1989," *German Studies Review* 36, no. 2 (2013), 307–25.

[23] Quoted in ibid., 315.

[24] The campaign against West German judges began in 1957. Bauerkämper, *Das umstrittene Gedächtnis*, 201–2.

right-hand man to Konrad Adenauer.[25] The campaign culminated in 1965 with the publication of *The Brown Book: War and Nazi Criminals in the Federal Republic*, which documented – for the most part, accurately – more than 1,800 former Nazis in positions of power and prominence in West Germany.[26]

In addition to these spectacular cases, on 21 May 1959, the SED created the Committee for the Protection of Human Rights (KSM) to highlight the plight of those imprisoned by the ban on the West German KPD.[27] The group was originally named the *Committee for the Protection of Human Rights against Militaristic Arbitrariness and Class Justice in West Germany*, but it was soon shortened to fit limited newspaper space.[28] There is no recorded explanation for why the Committee chose the mantle of human rights, but it likely came in response to the steady stream of attacks delivered by West German NGOs to the United Nations over the course of the late 1950s.[29] The SED had previously created several ad hoc groups to protest on behalf of specific prisoners (none of which mentioned human rights); now the Committee was tasked with consolidating and institutionalising this work.[30] While earlier

---

[25] Jeffrey Herf, *Divided Memory: The Nazi Past in the Two Germanys* (Cambridge, MA: Harvard University Press, 1997), 183–85; Devin Pendas, *The Frankfurt Auschwitz Trial, 1963–1965: Genocide, History, and the Limits of the Law* (Cambridge: Cambridge University Press, 2006), 18.

[26] National Council of the National Front, *Brown Book: War and Nazi Criminals in West Germany* (Berlin: National Council of the National Front, 1965).

[27] The KSM's existence and its activities are absent from academic histories of the GDR with the exception of Friederike Brinkmeier, *Der Einfluss des Kalten Krieges auf den internationalen Menschenrechtsschutz* (Berlin: Berliner Wissenschafts-Verlag, 2004); Anja Mihr, *Amnesty International in der DDR: der Einsatz für Menschenrechte im Visier der Stasi* (Berlin: Ch. Links, 2002). The former Secretary of the KSM, Siegfried Forberger, has written on the organization's activities and his own role within the group in his self-published memoir, *Das DDR-Komitee für Menschenrechte: Erinnerungen an den Sozialismus-Versuch im 20. Jahrhundert; Einsichten und Irrtümer des Siegfried Forberger, Sekretär des DDR-Komitees für Menschenrechte von 1959 bis 1989* (Self-pub., 2000), and in Forberger, "Das DDR-Menschenrechtskomitee," *ICARUS: Zeitschrift für soziale Theorie, Menschenrechte und Kultur* 15, no. 1 (2009), 26–28.

[28] The group's original title was, *Das Komitee zum Schutz der Menschenrechte, gegen militaristische Willkür und Klassenjustiz in Westdeutschland.*

[29] While most of KSM archives have survived, there is no documentation on the rationale for the organization's creation. Minutes from SED meetings at the time provide no evidence and, in his memoir, Forberger notes that he was never informed why the SED decided to form an organization devoted to human rights or where the idea originated. Forberger, *Das DDR-Komitee für Menschenrechte*, 27. On West German activities, see Gloe, *Planung für die deutsche Einheit*, 181. The East German foreign ministry carefully tracked West German media coverage of these petitions. PA AA, MfAA, A18271.

[30] For example, in 1949, the "National Committee for the Freeing of Max Reimann" was created to campaign for the release of the imprisoned KPD Chairman from the British Occupied Zone. "Nationalkomitee zur Befreiung Max Reimanns: Appell," *Neues Deutschland* (23.6.1949), 1.

committees had protested on behalf of socialists globally, including a campaign to support imprisoned Greek anti-fascist Manolis Glezos, the KSM limited its activism to West Germany alone.[31]

The founders of the KSM saw the organisation as the heir to two Weimar era organisations: the German League for Human Rights and Red Aid (*Rote Hilfe*).[32] The League had grown out of the anti-war movement and campaigned for peace and international cooperation in the interwar period with a membership consisting mostly of leftists who saw human rights as a problem of realising international peace through domestic demilitarisation.[33] In comparison, Red Aid was an explicitly socialist organisation that raised funds for imprisoned activists, helped the children of communists when parents were ill or too busy working to raise them and demanded an end to the use of the justice system as a tool for class warfare.[34] The KSM presented itself as a nonpartisan and antifascist social organisation, as the League for Human Rights had been, but the focus on direct action in support of prisoners more closely resembled the practices of Red Aid. In fact, the Committee adopted much of Red Aid's rhetoric, including its attacks on "class justice" and its slogan: Practice Solidarity!

Although the initial focus of the KSM was ostensibly prisoner advocacy, the opening meeting of the Committee already delineated its mission of fighting for human rights within the broader goals of peace and antifascism:

Militarism and the policy of aggressive war will inevitably encounter the resistance of all peace-loving forces and necessarily extinguish human rights [such] as the right to advocate for peace and [...] for the most basic vital

---

[31] E. Rigas, *Ritter der Akropolis: zur Verteidigung von Manolis Glezos* (Berlin: Dietz, 1959).

[32] Forberger, *Das DDR-Komitee für Menschenrechte*, 26.

[33] In GDR historiography, the League was depicted as a Communist initiative, but it represented a broad swath of the Left and included liberals as well. Alexander Schwitanski, *Die Freiheit des Volksstaats: die Entwicklung der Grund- und Menschenrechte und die deutsche Sozialdemokratie bis zum Ende der Weimarer Republik* (Essen: Klartext, 2008). Lora Wildenthal, "Human Rights Activism in Occupied and Early West Germany: The Case of the German League for Human Rights," *The Journal of Modern History* 80, no. 3 (2008), 515–56.

[34] Heinz Jürgen Schneider, Erika Schwarz and Josef Schwarz, *Die Rechtsanwälte der Roten Hilfe Deutschlands: Politische Strafverteidiger in der Weimarer Republik* (Bonn: Pahl-Rugenstein, 2002); Sabine Hering and Kurt Schilde, *Die rote Hilfe* (Opladen: VS Verlag, 2003); Nikolaus Brauns, *Schafft Rote Hilfe! Geschichte und Aktivitäten der proletarischen Hilfsorganisation für politische Gefangene in Deutschland (1919–1938)* (Bonn: Pahl-Rugenstein, 2003).

interests of all working people. The breach of human rights is therefore an essential part of the militarist system.[35]

The newly elected Chairwoman of the Committee, Friedel Malter, a veteran KPD functionary who had survived the concentration camps, argued that the priorities of the Committee included the ratification of a just peace treaty for Germany that would "include human rights, democratic freedoms for the population in West Germany," to combat the West German judges who "trample upon human rights," to practice solidarity with the families of the victims of class justice and to expose the West German system of "judicial terror" in all areas of civil life.[36]

Despite portraying itself as a non-state organ, the KSM reported directly to SED propaganda chief Albert Norden, accepted requests for specific propaganda material from the Ministry for Foreign Affairs, and allowed Walter Ulbricht to personally edit propaganda that it produced.[37] Nonetheless, the Committee was given a great deal of leeway: the only substantial feedback from SED leaders after the first six months was that their propaganda needed to use the term *human rights* more often, to better appeal to West Germans.[38] While Norden officially supervised the group, the KSM also had the backing of Gotthard Feist – a powerful figure at the Free German Trade Union Federation (FDGB) – who used his influence to secure funding and minimise micromanagement from above.[39]

Aside from Malter, the 20 founding KSM members were almost exclusively intellectuals and academics, with the day-to-day operations of the Committee in the hands of Secretary Siegfried Forberger, a recent graduate from the Walter Ulbricht Academy for Legal and Political Science in Potsdam. Once established, the Committee also recruited prominent East Germans including the actor Erwin Geschonneck and Rosa Thälmann, the widow of the much-mythologised KPD leader Ernst

---

[35] BArch, DZ7/6822 Protokoll über die konstituierende Sitzung des Komitees (21.5.1959), 1.

[36] BArch, DZ7/6822 Protokoll über die konstituierende Sitzung des Komitees, 1–4.

[37] BArch, DY30/IV 2/13/577 Kommissionssitzung (25.1.1960). Although there is little documentation on the supervision of the Committee, Albert Norden's files show that material from the Committee was edited by the Politburo and that its international actions required Ulbricht's personal approval. BArch, DY30/IV A2/2.028/109, Norden to Ulbricht (7.2.1963) and Norden to Ulbricht (18.2.1963). The KSM was one of many organizations created in this era to support GDR foreign policy initiatives including numerous "friendship societies." Wentker, *Außenpolitik in engen Grenzen*, 206–10.

[38] Forberger, *Das DDR-Komitee für Menschenrechte*, 25; BArch, DY30/IV 2/13/577 Kommissionssitzung (25.1.1960) and PA AA, MfAA C1580/76 Verletzungen der Menschenrechte in der BRD 1961–1962.

[39] Feist's daughter Margot was married to Erich Honecker, future SED General Secretary. Forberger, *Das DDR-Komitee für Menschenrechte*, 33–35.

Thälmann, whose death in a concentration camp made him an antifascist martyr.[40] During the 1960s, official number of members in the Committee ranged from 65 to 75, divided between a core set that produced the messaging, and a larger group of representatives from GDR factory and union organisations, tasked with communicating that messaging to a broader audience of workers. Although membership fluctuated over the years, Malter and Forberger were constants, remaining in their respective positions as chairwoman and secretary for more than three decades through the fall of the Berlin Wall in 1989. Although the Committee's membership initially included members of the non-SED bloc parties and unaffiliated notables – including author Stefan Heym – reliable party veterans and intellectuals educated in the GDR defined its agenda. As a result, the SED had nothing to fear from an organisation that saw promoting state socialism and realising human rights as the same goal.

Even though it was an organ of the SED's propaganda machine, the KSM's day-to-day campaign activities closely resembled those of Western NGOs. Senior members worked to build up membership rolls, especially through celebrity recruitment, and set the tenor of the various campaigns. Staff chose specific victims of human rights abuses, publicised their cases and mobilised mass response. Volunteers at the grassroots participated via donations, fundraising events, and letter writing campaigns. All these activities were also learning experiences for Committee staff that had little background in activism or the concept of human rights. Secretary Forberger recalled in his memoirs that almost all involved had heard of human rights only as a lyric in the socialist anthem *The Internationale*.[41] While the KSM was in charge of human rights propaganda for the GDR, it was woefully short of expertise on human rights.

Between 1959 and 1966, the KSM campaigned for the release of dozens of prisoners. Its efforts followed a predictable pattern: when a member of an East German organisation (such as the SED's youth movement, the FDJ, or the GDR's central trade union, the FDGB) was arrested in the FRG for being a threat to the West German democratic order, Secretary Forberger would swing into action and mobilise the organisation. The Committee would draft press releases for the national SED newspaper *Neues Deutschland* and for the East German

---

[40] Invitation letters, Akademie der Künste (AdK), Geschonneck Archiv 71, Malter to Geschonneck (6.1.1960); AdK, Pauls Wiens Archiv, 2349 Malter to Wiens (6.1.1960). AdK, Max Butting Archiv 440 Forberger to Butting (12.8.1960); BArch, DZ7/67 Mitglieder des Komitees.

[41] Forberger, *Das DDR-Komitee für Menschenrechte*, 25.

newswire service ADN, which in turn would carry the message to various regional publications. KSM members and volunteers would then spread the word in their workplaces and worker organisations. In some cases, they coordinated a barrage of protest letters from both friends and colleagues of the imprisoned, and from workers wanting to practice solidarity. The Committee coordinated financial assistance and acted as a liaison between the family of the prisoner and defence lawyers in the West. When prisoners were released, the Committee organised the press coverage of their triumphant return to the GDR.

The campaign for the release of Adolf Metzner, "worker functionary" at a fish processing plant in Sassnitz on the Baltic island of Rügen, is illustrative of the KSM's standard operating procedures. On 5 February 1961, Metzner was apprehended by West German authorities while meeting with representatives of the postal workers union in Frankfurt am Main, and charged with "anti-constitutional intentions."[42] The Committee immediately dispatched the GDR's star attorney Friedrich Karl Kaul to defend him before the West German court. A founding member of the KSM, Kaul had unsuccessfully defended the KPD's constitutionality and he would later act as the lead East German joint-plaintiff in several war crimes prosecutions, including the Frankfurt Auschwitz Trial.[43] In addition to providing his legal representation, the Committee also coordinated communication between Metzner and his family who were unable to travel to the FRG.

The Committee's publicity sought to shock East Germans by showing the mistreatment of a "peace-loving German patriot" by the West German state. According to the Committee's press releases, Metzner was not only imprisoned but also purposely placed in a cell with dangerous criminals suffering from tuberculosis.

The height of discrimination and vulgarity against the upright anti-fascist fighter for peace Adolf Metzner must be that he was sentenced to share a cell with the sex killer Zigli, serving a life-sentence for molesting and then killing an 8-year-old boy. Only with difficulty could he keep at bay this homosexual at night. It was only after vigorous protests that he was transferred to another cell.[44]

The appeal to sympathy based on lurid detail and homophobia in human rights activism was not unique to the KSM in this era and similar rhetoric can be found in a report on East German prisons by Amnesty International: "The ex-prisoners interviewed have been unanimous in

---

[42] BArch, DZ7/40 Anlage zur Presseinformation über Adolf Metzner, 1.
[43] Annette Rosskopf, *Friedrich Karl Kaul: Anwalt im geteilten Deutschland, 1906–1981* (Berlin: Spitz, 2002); Pendas, *The Frankfurt Auschwitz Trial, 1963–1965*, 123–30.
[44] BArch, DZ7/40 Anlage zur Presseinformation über Adolf Metzner, 1.

stating that the worst feature of their imprisonment was the enforced close association with criminals of all kinds, including homosexuals, sex criminals and murderers."[45] In this case, the KSM report went on to speculate that the West German prison doctors who certified Metzner as medically fit to work were conspiring to destroy his health on orders from the state: "Was this treatment of Adolf Metzner on the orders of the Adenauer Bonn Gestapo? Such methods are known to us."[46]

Shortly before his trial in January 1962, the KSM worked with Metzner's fellow workers in Sassnitz to organise a concert to raise awareness of his arrest, and to collect funds for his family. From East Berlin, the Committee encouraged protest letters addressed to the prosecutor's office in Frankfurt. Paul Fabian, a 77-year old retired metal worker who was also a member of the KSM, organised a letter writing campaign on behalf of Metzner. Letters from Metzner, delivered (and possibly ghost written) by the KSM, were also published in the East German press.[47] The youth newspaper *Junge Welt* published one such letter, where Metzner told his supporters from prison, "I can assure you that I have the strength to get through all of this. [...] Not for a moment will I betray the interests of the working class and all peace-loving forces."[48] The same article quoted a report from the Associated Press that the Frankfurt court had received more than 4,000 letters of protest.

Metzner was found guilty, but only sentenced to time already served, and thus he returned to the GDR in February 1962. The *Berliner Zeitung* headline declared "Solidarity Opens the Dungeons" and the paper claimed that the KSM's campaign had resulted in more than 30,000 letters of protest being sent to the Frankfurt prosecutor's office.[49] As much as the individual horrors of the West provided a propaganda focal point, the KSM also recognised the value inherent in success as a means of providing supporters with a sense that their actions had made a difference in the world. At a homecoming event organised for Metzner in Stralsund on the mainland near his hometown, a Committee member announced to the crowd "this disgraceful trial against Adolf Metzner is also a trial against the interests of the German working class." Metzner was

[45] Amnesty International, *Prison Conditions in East Germany: Conditions for Political Prisoners* (London: Amnesty International, 1966), 49.
[46] BArch, DZ7/40 Anlage zur Presseinformation über Adolf Metzner, 2.
[47] BArch, DY46/3944 Fabian to Forberger (9.5.1962).
[48] BArch, DZ7/40 "Ein Brief aus dem Kerker" *Junge Welt* (24.1.1962).
[49] BArch, DZ7/40 "Solidarität öffnete Kerker" *Berliner Zeitung* (12.2.1962). There is no evidence in the KSM archives that show any effects produced by this campaign.

given an opportunity to thank the crowd for their support and call upon them to continue the fight to free others still imprisoned in the West.[50]

In these campaigns, the KSM did not advance any kind of legal conception of human rights, but it did create a new cultural discourse of human rights based on East German antifascist narratives. Relying on existing tropes from films and mass-produced novels, the Committee portrayed those imprisoned in the West in line with the fictional heroes of the resistance, standing up to fascist warmongers. GDR popular culture depicted the world as cleanly divided between "democratic world" and "fascist dictatorship," typically portrayed through family stories with strong father figures, representing the legitimate authority of the state, and mothers and children as the continuation of socialism through the generations.[51] The basic arc in antifascist novels was the active, male-coded, protagonist triumphing over the forces of fascism in the face of the female-coded desire for surrender and submission.[52] These narratives drew on very real experiences of catastrophe and defeat, and offered East German citizens the opportunity to vicariously act as "victors of history" by aligning themselves with the antifascist cause through loyalty to the SED – despite having previously supported the Nazis.

The narrative similarities were explicitly crafted by the Committee, often by members who were themselves central to the making of anti-fascist cultural products. There was a direct overlap in human rights activities and cultural production of antifascist narratives: playwright Hedda Zinner, who wrote *The Ballad of Ravensbrück* on the solidarity of female concentration camp victims, served as a delegate to a meeting of the UN Human Rights Commission in 1965.[53] Otto Gotsche, author of the novel and later film, *The Flag of Kriwoj Rog* (1967) about an antifascist family in a coal-mining town surviving the Second World War also served as secretary of the State Council and represented the GDR at a UN conference on human rights in Budapest in 1966.[54] KSM member Erwin Geschonneck starred in the leading role of the film adaptation.

When one East German wrote to the *Committee* volunteering an account of his arrest and imprisonment in West Germany, Secretary Forberger rejected the submission on the grounds that it lacked thematic

---

[50] BArch, DZ7/40 "Adolf Metzner stürmisch gefeiert" *Tribüne* (13.2.1962).
[51] On the Manichaean character of SED antifascism, see Herf, *Divided Memory*, 13.
[52] On the family and antifascism, see Julia Hell, *Post-Fascist Fantasies: Psychoanalysis, History, and the Literature of East Germany* (Durham, NC: Duke University Press, 1997), ch. 1.
[53] BArch, DY30/5398 Delegation zur 21. Tagung der UN-Menschenrechtskommission in Genf.
[54] BArch, DY30/IV A2/13/58 Internationale Tätigkeit des Staatsrates der DDR.

and ideological coherence. In his reply, he outlined how the story needed to be rewritten to hit a series of key narrative points,

1. Bonn [West Germany] is against all-German understanding, against peace and thus against communication between Germans.
2. Bonn instead approves of the reinforcement of division, rearmament with nuclear weapons, and war.
3. But this is not the will of the West German population. Bonn has therefore reacted with demagoguery (anti-Soviet agitation, anti-communism, now against the GDR, the People's Republics, etc.) and terror (against fighters for peace, patriots, democrats, draft resisters). The effectiveness of this demagoguery is diminished by the growing strength and power of the peace camp and so there is a reinforcement of terror. Terror is a sign of fear and weakness (here there are many possibilities to discuss the facts of your trial).
4. Confidence that understanding and peace will prevail (weakness and fear of imperialists).
5. Necessity of the popular struggle against imperialism and militarism in West Germany, necessity of solidarity with all German patriots and fighters for peace.[55]

These points needed to be clear from the story and not simply relayed to readers as abstract concepts. The Committee acted as a lens through which the specific experiences of East German activists and officials could be focused to produce a cohesive narrative to condemn West Germany and promote the GDR.

KSM campaigns reinforced these narratives through a myriad of details and techniques. At a fundraising drive at the *Schwarze Pumpe* coal processing plant in 1960, the Committee chose to have Ernst Kays speak on behalf of the cause. A vulcaniser at the plant, Kays was not only a veteran of the Spanish Civil War but had also been in the Esterwege Concentration Camp; he told the audience that he "learned to practice solidarity sharing his last piece of bread with fellow anti-fascists" while imprisoned by the Nazis.[56] In KSM profiles of men arrested in West Germany, the damage done to the whole family by the absence of a strong father figure was a recurring theme: in a series of articles in regional newspapers over Christmas 1964 on Georg Jacobi, his role as

---

[55] BArch, DZ7/22 Forberger to Filling (6.12.1960), 1–2.
[56] BArch, DZ7/06 "Hohes Lied der Solidarität im Kombinat Schwarze Pumpe," *Brandenburgische Neuste Nachrichten* (8.12.1961). Josie McLellan, *Antifascism and Memory in East Germany: Remembering the International Brigades 1945–1989* (Oxford: Clarendon Press, 2004).

father took centre stage. The headline in the *Märkische Volksstimme* read "The Third Christmas without Dad," and the newspaper *Freiheit* ran a large photo of his unhappy family reading a letter from prison together.[57] KSM cases invariably concluded with the restoration of the happy family, through the re-establishment of the antifascist authority figure, usually with photos of Chairwoman Friedel Malter looking on at the scene smiling with the satisfaction of another job well done.

It is difficult to assess the popularity of the KSM beyond its core membership. Although the Committee received funding from the state, a significant portion of its budget was raised through fundraising drives at factories and cultural events such as radio concerts. While few financial records remain, in its first year, the Committee received more than 980,000 marks in donations from East Germans.[58] Among several dozen full-time members – as opposed to those who helped with specific campaigns – it appears that there was genuine enthusiasm for the cause. Some took it upon themselves to organise protest letter writing circles or to raise money at their workplace, while others participated more passively by tracking the progress on lists of political prisoners that the Committee issued to members and updated through its newsletter.[59]

With the construction of the Berlin Wall on 13 August 1961, the mandate of the KSM expanded dramatically. Facing an increasing wave of emigration and rising tensions with the West over cross-border traffic, the SED chose to seal the border to the FRG, including a ring of fortifications around West Berlin in the centre of the GDR.[60] The building of the Wall created dozens of complicated child custody disputes and the KSM began providing aid to parents who were now cut off from their children in West Berlin. But the larger problem for the Committee, and the SED, was the backlash against the Wall as a violation of basic human rights. Willy Brandt, the Social Democratic mayor of West Berlin and future Chancellor of West Germany, argued, "above all we must seize the initiative in order to denounce this flagrant violation of international human rights."[61] Brandt also unsuccessfully requested that the United States bring the matter before the United Nations as a

---

[57] "Das Dritte Weihnachtsfest ohne den Vati," *Märkische Volksstimme* (Potsdam) (25.12.1964) "Dem Frieden die Freiheit," *Freiheit* (Halle) (9.12.1964).
[58] BArch, DY30/IV 2/13/577 Vorlage für die Kommissionsitzung (11.6.1960), 2. Records on Committee finances in other years are incomplete.
[59] For examples of member engagement, see BArch, DY46/3944 Fabian to Forberger (9.5.1962); BArch, DY46/3944 Fabian to Malter (10.2.1964); AdK, Pauls Wiens Archiv, 2349.
[60] Harrison, *Driving the Soviets up the Wall.*
[61] "Rede des Regierenden Bürgermeisters von Berlin vor dem Deutschen Bundestag, 18.8.1961." *Das Parlament* (Vol.11. Nr. 35), 3.

violation of the UDHR.[62] The Berlin Wall quickly became the focal point for accusations of human rights abuses levelled at the SED by the Ministry of All-German Affairs in Bonn, the Geneva-based International Commission of Jurists, and the Council for Central German Culture – an organisation that considered the territory ceded to Poland at the end of the war as the "real" Eastern Germany.[63] The KSM was tasked with not only creating counter-propaganda to refute these attacks but also finding ways to reach out to an audience beyond the two Germanies.

The KSM produced a series of pamphlets – technically addressed to the UN Human Rights Commission, but really aimed at West Germans and the international community in general – with the message that Chancellor Konrad Adenauer was a new Hitler who sought to destroy any domestic opposition standing in the way of his goals for international military domination. The UN steadfastly refused to accept petitions from either Germany, but the existence of the Human Rights Commission still served as a symbolic forum for the competing claims as the press reprinted arguments from both sides.[64] In pamphlets with inflammatory titles such as *Under Hitler in the Concentration Camps, under Adenauer in Prison*, the Committee profiled individuals who had been imprisoned in West Germany as well as under the Nazis to demonstrate the continuity between the Third Reich and the Federal Republic.[65] Other publications focused on West Germany as a threat to international peace, arguing that the persecution of socialists and pacifists smoothed the path to war. West Germany sought "to create a graveyard atmosphere in internal politics permitting undisturbed nuclear rearmament, to prevent, if possible, the

[62] Steven Jensen, *The Making of International Human Rights: The 1960s, Decolonization and the Reconstruction of Global Values* (Cambridge: Cambridge University Press, 2016), 48.

[63] Bundesminister für Gesamtdeutsche Fragen, *Verletzungen der Menschenrechte, Unrechtshandlungen und Zwischenfälle an der Berliner Sektorengrenze seit Errichtung der Mauer (13.8.1961–15.8.1962)* (Bonn: Bundesminister für Gesamtdeutsche Fragen, 1962); International Commission of Jurists, *The Berlin Wall: A Defiance of Human Rights* (Geneva: International Commission of Jurists, 1962); Kurt Rabl, *Die Menschenrechte und die SBZ* (Bonn: Mitteldeutscher Kulturrat, 1965). Rabl's membership in the Nazi SS during the Second World War did not preclude a career in human rights activism in postwar West Germany. Lora Wildenthal, *The Language of Human Rights in West Germany* (Philadelphia: University of Pennsylvania Press, 2012), 121.

[64] PA AA, MfAA A18292 Huang to Malter (28.10.1963) and Bruce to Malter (3.4.1963). On the United Nations as a site of symbolic conflict, see Jan Eckel, "Human Rights and Decolonization: New Perspectives and Open Questions," *Humanity* 1, no. 1 (2010), 123.

[65] Komitee zum Schutze der Menschenrechte, *Unter Hitler im KZ, unter Adenauer im Gefängnis*. (Berlin: Komitee zum Schutze der Menschenrechte, 1962)

spreading of truth about its aggressive and revenge-seeking plans, and to cripple the rightful resistance of the people to these plans."[66]

In crafting a response to West German accusations, the Committee was able to piggyback on critiques of Adenauer's government by a growing human rights movement within the Federal Republic. At this time, three major organisations began to challenge the political status quo of life in the FRG: "the International League for Human Rights shined a light on ex-Nazis in public life, West German Amnesty [International] rejected anti-communism as a guide to political action, and the Humanist Union confronted the churches' disproportionate influence in public life."[67] East German propaganda particularly seized on the "Spiegel Affair" of 1962, during which the news magazine *Der Spiegel* ran an article on the lack of readiness of NATO forces in Europe, based on leaked documents, and was subsequently accused of treason by then Defence Minister Franz Josef Strauss. The magazine's offices were raided by the police, the article's author was arrested in the middle of the night while on holiday in Spain, and the magazine's publisher Rudolf Augstein spent 103 days in prison before being cleared of any wrongdoing by the courts. The ensuing public uproar forced Strauss out of Adenauer's cabinet.[68] In response, the KSM released a pamphlet *From Schabrod to Augstein: 22 Months of Terror Justice*, which equated Augstein's treatment with the persecution of the KPD, including its leader Karl Schabrod, arguing that liberals and intellectuals were also a target of Adenauer's mass repression alongside socialists.[69]

Despite the KSM's increased activity, foreign policy elites in the GDR were increasingly concerned that East German human rights propaganda was ineffective. The editor of the foreign affairs journal *Deutsche Außenpolitik*, Hans Aust, wrote to a colleague, "In my opinion, the mere claim that the GDR has fulfilled all of the requirements of the UN's Universal Declaration of Human Rights is not sufficient."[70] Aust believed that the GDR needed a positive, authentic, message about its own human rights record, rather than simply denouncing the crimes of the West. The next month, a report from the East German Ministry for

---

[66] Committee for the Protection of Human Rights, *Memorandum of the Committee for the Protection of Human Rights of the GDR on the Violation of Human Rights in West Germany* (Berlin: Committee for the Protection of Human Rights, 1961), 6.

[67] Wildenthal, *The Language of Human Rights in West Germany*, 65.   [68] Ibid., 80.

[69] Komitee zum Schutze der Menschenrechte, *Von Schabrod bis Augstein: die Bilanz von 22 Monaten Justizterror: 642 Demokraten und Atomkriegsgegner abgeurteilt und eingekerkert* (Berlin: Komitee zum Schutze der Menschenrechte, 1962).

[70] Aust was criticizing a protest by the GDR League for International Cooperation, but the messaging did not significantly differ from the KSM. BArch, DY13/2828 Aust to Daub (7.1.1963).

Foreign Affairs noted that although the idea of human rights was of great importance due to its "broad popularity," the GDR was incapable of competing with the FRG. Of greatest concern was that "our individual arguments remain defensive, because they are merely a response to West German attacks."[71] Just as in 1946, when the SED first faced off against the Social Democrats, a new ideological response was needed to deal with the increasingly complex and globalising politics of human rights.

Decolonisation, Self-Determination and Socialist Human Rights

In contrast to the immediate postwar period, by the time the Berlin Wall was built, the international politics of human rights had evolved to become truly global. The United Nations passed the UDHR on 10 December 1948, and – in spite of the SED's newfound enthusiasm for human rights rhetoric in Germany – the USSR's decision to abstain on the vote to adopt the UDHR meant that the milestone went uncelebrated in the socialist bloc.[72] The SED's national newspaper *Neues Deutschland* delayed reporting on the vote for an extra day, only then to run a short article on the front page proclaiming, "The Struggle for Human Rights is the Struggle against Old and New Fascism."[73] The piece focused on how Soviet delegate Andrei Vyshinski's proposal to strengthen passages on combating fascism was voted down by the colonial powers. The article quickly moved from this affront to the subject of American imperialism and emerging tensions over the status of Berlin. The actual contents of the UDHR were omitted, leaving only the broader narrative of the struggle between East and West, human rights serving only as yet another ideological battleground.

The UDHR had little impact on East Germany at the time, but the problem of self-determination and human rights at the United Nations would soon prove instrumental to SED politics. Self-determination had long been a cornerstone of anti-imperialism, with both American President Woodrow Wilson and Soviet leader Vladimir Lenin employing the term as a rallying cry against colonial subjugation and the oppression of

---

[71] PA AA, MfAA, A9706, Aktivierung der Arbeit auf dem Gebiet der Menschenrechte (7.2.1963), 1.

[72] The socialist abstentions were the USSR, the Ukrainian SSR, the Belorussian SSR, Poland, Czechoslovakia and Yugoslavia.

[73] "Kampf um die Menschenrechte heißt Kampf gegen den alten und neuen Faschismus," *Neues Deutschland* (12.12.1948), 1.

minorities earlier in the century.[74] The concept was revived in international rhetoric with its inclusion in the Atlantic Charter of 1941 (a joint US-British declaration of Allied war aims), but by the time the UN Charter was drafted in 1945, it had been downgraded from a right to a "desirable ideal."[75] Certain drafters, including John Humphrey (Canada) and René Cassin (France), successfully opposed the inclusion of self-determination in the UDHR, characterising it as a threat to the new international order, which would be "misused" to challenge European colonialism.[76] During debate at the United Nations, Soviet delegate Alexei Pavlov unsuccessfully advocated for its inclusion, but he was able to secure support for important sections on non-discrimination, social rights and gender equality.[77]

The eventual abstention by the Soviets and their Eastern European allies – on the grounds that the final draft focused too much on individual rights and excluded provisions for national self-determination – was not an outright rejection of the concept of human rights, but rather a critique of specific aspects of the UDHR as written. Nonetheless, abstaining put the Socialist Bloc in the awkward company of Saudi Arabia, which objected to sections on religious freedom, and Apartheid South Africa, which opposed the extension of rights to colonial subjects and sections on non-discrimination.[78] While this constellation made it appear as though the UDHR was universally embraced outside of a rogue's gallery of oppressive regimes, the Canadian government also abstained on an earlier vote and its attitude towards the UDHR "bordered on hostility," on the grounds that the declaration violated the principles of federalism and parliamentary supremacy. The United States agreed to the Declaration only after it was guaranteed that it would not be legally binding.[79]

---

[74] Although in 1919, Wilson's conception of self-determination was more influential in the colonial world, it was eclipsed by Lenin's. On this transition, see Erez Manela, *The Wilsonian Moment: Self-Determination and the International Origins of Anticolonial Nationalism* (Oxford: Oxford University Press, 2007).

[75] Young-Sun Hong, *Cold War Germany, the Third World, and the Global Humanitarian Regime* (Cambridge: Cambridge University Press, 2015), 18.

[76] Roland Burke, *Decolonization and the Evolution of International Human Rights* (Philadelphia: University of Pennsylvania Press, 2010), 37.

[77] Johannes Morsink, *The Universal Declaration of Human Rights: Origins, Drafting, and Intent* (Philadelphia: University of Pennsylvania Press, 1999), 31.

[78] On the Soviet justifications for its abstention, ibid., 21–25. For a detailed analysis of the Andrei Vyshinsky's arguments on behalf of the USSR, see Anna Lukina, "Soviet Union and the Universal Declaration of Human Rights," Max Planck Institute for European Legal History Research Paper Series No. 2017-01.

[79] Andrew Thompson, *On the Side of the Angels: Canada and the United Nations Commission on Human Rights* (Vancouver: University of British Columbia Press, 2017), 21; Mark

Western delegations were able to omit self-determination from the UDHR, but already in 1950, representatives from the Global South were able to bring the issue of self-determination into the debates over converting the Universal Declaration into a legally binding treaty.[80] Decolonisation began to upend the balance of power at the United Nations as the brutal suppression of uprisings in Kenya, Algeria and Vietnam put the spotlight on the human rights abuses of British and French colonial regimes.[81] At the 1955 Afro-Asian Conference in Bandung, arguably the birthplace of the Non-Aligned Movement, the final document named the human right to self-determination as one of its seven principles.[82] For the newly decolonised states, human rights represented a call for national liberation and the creation of sovereign states, often explicitly citing the American and French revolutions.[83] Human rights were not always central to the politics of self-determination, but anti-colonial activists in Africa, Asia and the Middle East ensured that the global politics of human rights could not circumvent the problem of self-determination.[84]

Although the Soviet Union led the socialist bloc in abstaining on the UDHR, it steadily embraced the language of human rights in international affairs over the coming decade, instrumentalising it to attack racial discrimination in the United States and Western imperialism around the world.[85] By 1952, the British Foreign Office had grown increasingly concerned that the Eastern Bloc was working with Latin American and Arab states at the United Nations to transform human rights into an "anti-colonial" weapon.[86] In deliberations on the transformation of the non-binding UDHR into a pair of international covenants, the USSR continued to play an important role in promoting

---

Mazower, "The Strange Triumph of Human Rights, 1933–1950," *The Historical Journal* 47, no. 2 (2004), 379–98.

[80] Jensen, *The Making of International Human Rights*, 43–44.

[81] Fabian Klose, *Human Rights in the Shadow of Colonial Violence: The Wars of Independence in Kenya and Algeria* (Philadelphia: University of Pennsylvania Press, 2013); Mathilde von Bulow, *West Germany, Cold War Europe and the Algerian War* (Cambridge: Cambridge University Press, 2016).

[82] Roland Burke, "'The Compelling Dialogue of Freedom': Human Rights at the Bandung Conference," *Human Rights Quarterly* 28, no. 4 (2006), 947–65.

[83] Julian Go, "Modeling States and Sovereignty: Postcolonial Constitutions in Asia and Africa," in *Making a World after Empire: The Bandung Moment and Its Political Afterlives*, ed. Christopher Lee (Athens: Ohio University Press, 2010), 107–40.

[84] For African activists, human rights were not central to their anti-colonialism, but always tied to self-determination. Andreas Eckert, "African Nationalists and Human Rights, 1940s–1970s," in *Human Rights in the Twentieth Century*, 283–300.

[85] Jennifer Amos, "Embracing and Contesting: The Soviet Union and the Universal Declaration of Human Rights, 1948–1958," in *Human Rights in the Twentieth Century*.

[86] Fabian Klose, *Menschenrechte im Schatten kolonialer Gewalt: Die Dekolonisierungskriege in Kenia und Algerien 1945–1962* (Munich: Oldenbourg, 2009), 278.

self-determination, demanding the continued inclusion of social and economic rights in the UN human rights system, while also standing in the way of efforts to create international enforcement mechanisms that would interfere in their internal affairs.[87] By the end of the decade, the USSR's abstention was written out of Soviet histories, which now positioned the socialist world as the driving force behind the United Nation's human rights initiatives.[88]

Through the 1950s, the SED's grasp of the symbolic politics of human rights at the global level remained limited, and efforts to use UN commemorations to push back against West German attacks were not terribly successful. In 1956, the GDR League for the United Nations, an organisation dedicated to agitating for East German admission to the United Nations, commissioned the postal service to create a set of commemorative stamps representing self-determination and racial equality: The result was three stamps, each showing a picture of one of the "the white, black and yellow races."[89] League members begrudgingly accepted the design even though the message of racial equality was only comprehensible when all three stamps were viewed together.[90] No one involved appears to have noticed that the stamp portraying the "white race" was given the highest monetary value in the series.[91] The stamps were released in the GDR to little fanfare, but before long a group of anti-communist activists in West Berlin saw an opportunity for mischief.[92] The anonymous group altered the 5 penny stamp reworking the original message, "Human Rights Day – German Democratic Republic" to read, "Day of Humans without Rights – Germans Are Slaves of the Soviets."[93] Even in the realm of commemorative stamps, the discourse and symbolism of human rights was a site of contestation across the German-German border.[94]

By the 10-year anniversary of the UDHR, the SED still struggled to present a coherent and positive vision of human rights. To celebrate

---

[87] On the role of the USSR and other socialist countries in the transformation of the UDHR into the 1966 Human Rights Covenants, see Daniel Whelan, *Indivisible Human Rights* (Philadelphia: University of Pennsylvania Press, 2010).
[88] Amos, "Embracing and Contesting," 164.   [89] BArch, DM3/4054 No. 104–105, 137.
[90] Ibid., Steiniger to Lieber, No. 141.
[91] Quinn Slobodian, "Socialist Chromatism: Race, Racism, and the Racial Rainbow in East Germany," in *Comrades of Color: East Germany in the Cold War World*, ed. Quinn Slobodian (New York: Berghahn, 2015), 23–39.
[92] "Tag Der Menschenrechte," *Junge Welt* (12.12.1956).
[93] "Fälschungen: Die Widerstands-Philatelie," *Der Spiegel* 6 (6.2.1957).
[94] On the broader conflict over symbols of sovereignty, including stamps, see Margarete Myers Feinstein, *State Symbols: The Quest for Legitimacy in the FRG and the GDR, 1949–1959* (Boston: Brill, 2001).

Human Rights Day in 1958, the postal service released another commemorative stamp series: One stamp depicted two men, coded European and African, while the other showed a pair of women, coded
European and Asian. Once again, the connection to human rights and
racial equality was difficult to discern without looking at the whole series.
The Ministry for Foreign Affairs also prepared a message to the General
Assembly commending the UDHR as a "highpoint in the fight of the
nations for democratic rights and freedoms" and "an achievement of the
antifascist and anti-colonialist struggle."[95] Not letting an opportunity to
attack West Germany go to waste, the message also pledged that the
GDR only sought the peaceful and democratic reunification of Germany
in contrast to the "Hitlerite" policy of rearmament pursued by the
FRG.[96] Yet at the last minute, the message was cancelled and there
was no mention of the UDHR's 10th anniversary in East German media,
only half a year before the creation of the Committee for the Protection of
Human Rights.

These weaknesses represented a deeper struggle within the SED to
integrate the idea of self-determination into a conception of human
rights. In the 1940s, the Party had only referred to self-determination
in connection with freedom from American and imperialist intervention,
while human rights were limited to the conflict between their vision of
socialism and that of their Social Democratic rivals.[97] In his original work
on socialism and human rights in 1946, Karl Polak simply did not
address the problem of colonialism or self-determination, but by 1953,
the situation had changed: at an international conference of jurists in
East Berlin, he specifically praised the 1941 Anglo-American Atlantic
Charter as the first "world declaration of human rights" because of its
inclusion of the idea of self-determination – in contrast to the Universal
Declaration, which did not.[98] The next year, writing in the East German
legal journal *Neue Justiz*, Polak declared: "Throughout history, human
rights have been identical with the freedom of peoples, the chief expression of which is state sovereignty and self-determination."[99] But the
adaptation of socialist ideology to the rapidly evolving international

---

[95] BA, DM3/4088 10 Jahre Tag der Menschenrechte. PA AA, MfAA A18273 No. 28.
[96] Ibid., No. 31.
[97] BArch, NY4090/643 Otto Grotewohl Rede vor dem Deutschen Volksrat (22.10.1948),
      14; and Lemke, *Einheit oder Sozialismus?*, 31.
[98] BArch, DY30/IV 2/13/442 Deutsche Konferenz zur Vorbereitung der Internationalen
      Juristenkonferenz 1953, 26. Elizabeth Borgwardt, *A New Deal for the World: America's
      for Human Rights* (Cambridge, MA: Belknap, 207).
[99] Karl Polak, "Menschenrechte und Politischer Freiheitskampf," *Neue Justiz*, no. 2
      (1954), 57.

politics of human rights, unfolding at the United Nations, had come to a halt, and these new ideas did not move from the academic world into political practice. Polak abandoned the topic of human rights, concentrating instead on wiping out ideological revisionism in legal studies until his death in 1963.

While one East German academic, Bernhard Graefrath, did take up the problem of human rights after 1954, his work failed to make an impact on SED ideology. Graefrath had joined the SED in 1946 at the age of 18 and had studied to become a People's Judge (*Volksrichter*) during the immediate postwar period, before graduating law at the Humboldt University in East Berlin in 1951. While working as a lecturer at Humboldt, he was also a leading member of the GDR League for the United Nations and in 1956 he published a slim volume entitled, *The United Nations and Human Rights*. He cited the Soviet Foreign Minister, but built the main thrust of his arguments upon the declarations of the Bandung Conference. In the Afro-Asian call for self-determination and its denunciation of racial discrimination and imperialism in the name of human rights, Graefrath saw a devastating critique of "the core element of fascism," a system that represents imperialism "at its most refined and cruelly developed."[100] As activists in the non-aligned world took up the language of human rights against Western colonialism, Graefrath claimed that there were parallels between this oppression and the "imperialistic" policies of the FRG towards the GDR.[101]

Although Graefrath's work was timely, it had almost no impact.[102] Neither the SED elite nor the socialist scholarly community seized upon the language of Bandung to challenge West Germany on human rights, and the linkage with self-determination failed to enter mainstream discourse. In 1958, the Afro-Asian Bloc scored a major victory at the United Nations by gaining official recognition for Algeria's inherent right to self-determination, but by this time there was no one left in the GDR willing to connect the dots.[103] In that same year, Karl Polak led a purge of the legal profession at the Babelsberg Conference, thinning the ranks of young and ambitious legal thinkers. One of those purged was Bernhard

---

[100] Bernhard Graefrath, *Die Vereinten Nationen und die Menschenrechte* (Berlin: Deutscher Zentralverlag, 1956), 7.

[101] Burke, "The Compelling Dialogue of Freedom"; Quinn Slobodian, "Bandung in Divided Germany: Managing Non-Aligned Politics in East and West, 1955–63," *The Journal of Imperial and Commonwealth History* 41, no. 4 (2013), 644–62.

[102] Forberger, *Das DDR-Komitee für Menschenrechte*, 217. When Graefrath's professional fortunes improved in the GDR, he also gained recognition from other Eastern Bloc scholars. Hanna Bokor, "Human Rights and International Law," in *Socialist Concept of Human Rights*, ed. Imre Szabó (Budapest: Akadémiai Kiadó, 1966), 281 and 288.

[103] Hong, *Cold War Germany, the Third World, and the Global Humanitarian Regime*, 139.

Graefrath. He was dismissed from his lectureship at Humboldt University, and sent to work as an administrator in the small town of Zossen for two years as a form of ideological re-education before being allowed to return to his previous post.[104]

The KSM generated plenty of propaganda after its founding in 1959, but it failed to develop any kind of doctrine or ideology to address the international politics of human rights. There were no reference works that could provide East German functionaries with an authoritative definition of human rights; the *Lexikon A–Z*, published in Leipzig in 1962, still dismissed human rights as serving to "protect the ruling classes of the West," with no mention of a socialist alternative.[105] Human rights consciousness remained low, even among those prisoners who had been the subject of KSM campaigns. When the Committee issued questionnaires to returning prisoners to gain material for their propaganda, most left blank the question regarding the specific human rights violations they had suffered. Of the very few who answered, all simply repeated the key elements of their story: Gerhard Looß, for example, made no mention of rights – constitutional or human – and reiterated that he had entered West Germany legally, thus making his imprisonment unjust.[106] The Committee also had difficulty in coaxing the East German intelligentsia to incorporate human rights language into their political discourse. In 1963, the KSM asked the *Kulturbund* for assistance in a protest action, but only 4 of the 43 letters of support from chapters across the country mentioned human rights, and instead denounced the actions of the FRG as violations of the rule of law, as a great injustice or as an act of arbitrariness (*Willkür*).[107]

The one crack where human rights language penetrated into the discourse of the GDR bureaucracy was at the Berlin Wall where internal security reports described attempts to breach the wall as violations of human rights.[108] Even more explicit was the infamous "shooting order" issued to East German border guards, which justified the use of lethal force at the Berlin Wall as a means to prevent "a crime against the

[104] BStU, MfS, AP 82.7971/92.
[105] Quoted in Mihr, *Amnesty International in der DDR*, 38.
[106] BArch, DZ7/39 Fragebogen Gerhard Looß, question 11.
[107] The protest letters mentioning human rights came from *Kulturbund* chapters in Frankfurt (Oder), Freiburg, Oranienburg and Halle. BArch, DY 27 6331, Koordinierung von Protestaktionen gegen die Inhaftierung des Leiters des Verlages der Nation, Günter Hofé.
[108] BArch, DVH 58/6004 Materialien über die Verletzung der Menschenrechte durch aggressive Anschläge des Gegners an der Staatsgrenze der DDR zu Westberlin (13.8.1961–31.8.1963).

sovereignty of the German Democratic Republic, against peace, humanity, and human rights."[109] According to the SED, the Berlin Wall stood as a barrier against the destruction of socialism by the forces of imperialism and was officially called the "Anti-Fascist Defence Rampart." Since the Wall ensured the continued existence of an antifascist state, its violent protection was folded into the discourse of human rights. To violate the Wall was to contravene the human rights of all East Germans by threatening the revival of fascism.[110]

The purge of the legal profession at Babelsberg also meant that East German academic work on human rights did not progress beyond Karl Polak's earlier formulation. Authors tended to quote SED leaders almost exclusively, thereby insulating themselves from accusations of "revisionism," but also stymieing any development of a discourse of human rights that would be effective outside the GDR. In the end, the ideological stagnation was not solved by an SED leader, but by a young legal academic named Hermann Klenner.[111] Born in 1926, Klenner served in the Second World War and joined the Nazi Party at the age of 18 (which was only revealed in 1986 while Klenner was representing the GDR at the United Nations), but became a dedicated socialist in the postwar period. After gaining his doctorate at the University of Halle in 1951 he began working at Humboldt University in East Berlin, where, by the age of 30, he was made professor of legal theory and the history of law.[112] However, his rapid rise was – like Graefrath's – cut short by the purge at the Babelsberg Conference in 1958.[113] Not only was Klenner removed from his academic position, he was censured by Ulbricht. After

---

[109] A copy of the order from 1962 is reprinted in Bernhard Pollmann, *Lesebuch zur deutschen Geschichte. Band 3* (1984), 245–46.

[110] On desire for international respectability in spite of the violence at the Berlin Wall, see Patrick Major, *Behind the Berlin Wall: East Germany and the Frontiers of Power* (Oxford: Oxford University Press, 2010), 145.

[111] For critical analysis of Klenner's human rights theories, see Klaus Adomeit, "Rechtsphilosophie, Marxismus und Menschenrechte: Zum Erscheinen einer Festschrift für Hermann Klenner," *Juristen Zeitung* 53, no. 4 (1998), 186–91. Tore Lindholm, "Prospects for Research on the Cultural Legitimacy of Human Rights: The Case of Liberalism and Marxism," in *Human Rights in Cross-Cultural Perspectives: A Quest for Consensus*, ed. Abdullahi An-Na'im (Philadelphia: University of Pennsylvania Press, 2011), 387–426; Andreas Fisahn, "Marxismus und Menschenrechte," *Argumente* 4, no. 2 (2011), 22–28. On Klenner's work from a Marxist perspective, see Uwe-Jens Heuer, "Hermann Klenner – ein moderner Enzyklopädist," *Z: Zeitschrift marxistische Erneuerung* 65 (2006).

[112] Henry Leide, *NS-Verbrecher und Staatssicherheit: Die geheime Vergangenheitspolitik der DDR* (Munich: Vandenhoeck & Ruprecht, 2007), 87. BArch, DC20/9417 Information über die Angelegenheit der Professoren Dr. Mollnau und Dr. Klenner (3.12.1968), 4.

[113] Peter Caldwell, *Dictatorship, State Planning, and Social Theory in the GDR* (Cambridge: Cambridge University Press, 2003), 90–92.

serving a short term of "re-education" as the mayor of Letschin, a village on the border with Poland, he began to teach again at the College of Economics in Karlshorst, an East Berlin suburb.[114] There, he turned his attention to the problem of international human rights.

In 1964, Klenner published his groundbreaking work, *Studies on Basic Rights*, which moved past the slogans of Karl Polak, the cultural narratives of the Committee and the international observations of Bernhard Graefrath, to construct a comprehensive new history and philosophy of "socialist human rights." According to Klenner, the history of human rights stretched back to the English *Magna Carta* of 1215, when feudal lords first claimed their rights against the monarchy.[115] The rights stemming from the revolutions of the eighteenth century in the United States and France advanced beyond the feudal rights of the *ancien régime*, but they were – as Marx had argued – no more than the rights of bourgeois citizens disguised as universal human rights and defined by the principles of egotism, exploitation and oppression, that produced alienation and atomisation. According to Klenner, truly universal human rights were only realised through the Russian Revolution in 1917, which ushered in a new historical epoch by eliminating the forces of exploitation and oppression. The abolition of capitalism meant that humankind was "freed from all economic, ideological, and political chains," and as a result, a new form of human rights would also be fulfilled.[116]

Here, Klenner turned to the language of self-determination as the connective tissue linking socialism and the realisation of human rights. Because the socialist revolution abolished capitalism and ended all exploitation, it alone was capable of producing a system that realised self-determination. The victory of the working-class revolution was the triumph of all humanity (unlike the bourgeoisie, who wrongly claimed the same thing) and as a result, the distinctions between state, society and the individual no longer existed. Socialism allowed for real self-determination in which the interests of the individual and society were not in conflict, indeed – they were one and the same. Through such reasoning, the lines between socialism and self-determination became

---

[114] Michael Stolleis, *Geschichte des öffentlichen Rechts in Deutschland Bd. 4: Staats- und Verwaltungsrechtswissenschaft in West und Ost 1945–1990* (Munich: C. H. Beck, 2017), 578.

[115] East German efforts to appropriate the entirety of German history to legitimize SED rule peaked in the 1960s. Stefan Berger, "National Paradigm and Legitimacy: Uses of Academic History Writing in the 1960s," in *The Workers' and Peasants' State: Communism and Society in East Germany under Ulbricht 1945–71*, eds. Patrick Major and Jonathan Osmond (Manchester: Manchester University Press, 2002), 251.

[116] Hermann Klenner, *Studien über die Grundrechte* (Berlin: Staatsverlag der DDR, 1964), 11.

blurred as both came to mean the realisation of a state ruled by the leading party of the working class, on behalf of all.[117] Self-determination was thus the indispensable right of the socialist human rights project, not just one right among many.

When Klenner spoke of self-determination, he was not reaching back in time to the proclamations of Lenin but drawing on the anti-colonial human rights politics playing out at the United Nations. The admission of 17 African nations to the United Nations in 1960 had ended the Western voting majority at the General Assembly paving the way for the passage of the "Declaration on the Granting of Independence to Colonial Countries and Peoples."[118] The first article of the declaration effectively criminalised the colonial system: "subjection of peoples to alien subjugation, domination and exploitation constitutes a denial of fundamental human rights, is contrary to the Charter of the United Nations and is an impediment to the promotion of world peace and co-operation." A further article affirmed "All peoples have the right to self-determination," and the final section demanded that nations observe the principles of the "non-interference in the internal affairs of all States."[119] American diplomats made an effort to redirect the Declaration towards a condemnation of Soviet imperialism, but they were rebuffed. In a reversal of the vote on the UDHR in 1948, the United States now joined the European colonial powers in abstaining.[120]

Klenner hailed the 1960 Declaration as an important step towards the liberation of all peoples through socialism. In a riff on the lyrics of the *Internationale* with some added Hegelian mysticism,[121] Klenner held out hope that human rights would be realised for all when "all the peoples have heard the signal" (through a world united under socialism) and then man would overcome his contradictions, within himself and with nature.

Wherever in the world the people are fighting against the exploitation, ignorance, and oppression brought about by the imperialists, they are fighting a just struggle for their self-determination. Wherever in the world there is the struggle against

---

[117] Ibid., 123–28.
[118] Eckert, "African Nationalists and Human Rights, 1940s–1970s," 300.
[119] UN Declaration on the Granting of Independence to Colonial Countries and Peoples. General Assembly resolution 1514 (XV), 14 December 1960.
[120] Jensen, *The Making of International Human Rights*, 55–56.
[121] The literal translation of the refrain from the German version of *Die Internationale*: "People – hear the signals!/On to the last battle!/The Internationale/Fights for human rights – *Völker, hört die Signale!/Auf zum letzten Gefecht!/Die Internationale/erkämpft das Menschenrecht.*

the threat of war, it is a struggle for the most important human right, the right to a peaceful life![122]

In resisting the neo-fascist imperialism of West Germany and establishing socialism on German soil, the GDR was thus a leading force in the quest for world peace and human rights.

Klenner may have rewritten the history of human rights and integrated the socialist bloc into the grand anti-imperial struggle for self-determination playing out at the United Nations, but what did it mean to have human rights under socialism in the GDR? Klenner argued that, as a member of GDR society, a citizen experienced certain basic rights (*Grundrechte*), all of which were manifestations of broader principles of universal human rights. The self-determination of all East German citizens allowed SED rule to realise human rights within the boundaries of the GDR. The rights that resulted from the revolution were not mere holdovers from the bourgeois epoch of history with a more universalist implementation, but something entirely new. These rights "are not characterised by a sphere free of the state in which the individual can act with private arbitrariness (a petit-bourgeois conception and illusion), but rather through the ever more comprehensive state-organized mastery of lawful social relations of the masses of the people."[123] In the place of the freedom to act out of self-interest, basic rights under socialism functioned as a means for the state to mobilise, orient, and organise "the masses onto the path to their own liberation."[124] Human rights did not exist to allow the individual to separate from society but rather to fulfil the interests of both the individual and society in harmony.

Just as in the 1936 Stalin Constitution, all rights were now balanced by the concurrent duties to employ one's rights to the fullest while realising the greatest benefit for both the individual and society.[125] In a society where a citizen had the right to work or the right to education, they also had the duty to work and the duty to educate themselves for their own sake and for that of the larger community. For Klenner, "[T]o interpret the right to work as the right to be lazy or the right to education as the right to be stupid, belongs to the typical bourgeois basic rights conception of subjective idealism," and was thus wrong.[126] The right to work was not the right to have the state provide you with a job, but to cease being alienated from one's work and to labour on behalf of society and

---

[122] Klenner, *Studien über die Grundrechte*, 127.   [123] Ibid., 53.   [124] Ibid., 54.

[125] Ibid., 78–88. On Soviet rights language and the Stalin Constitution, see Benjamin Nathans, "Soviet Rights-Talk in the Post-Stalin Era," in *Human Rights in the Twentieth Century*.

[126] Klenner, *Studien über die Grundrechte*, 115.

not for the profit of a capitalist. While bourgeois human rights gave equal weight to truth and falsehood, the right to education under socialism was not total freedom of expression but the right to learn the truth and the duty to assist in the "struggle against bourgeois ideology, against revisionism and against dogmatism."[127]

The right to political participation under socialism meant that citizens could now fully participate in the governance of their state through the vehicle of the leading party of the proletariat. It did not mean political pluralism – in the bourgeois sense – which only allowed for citizens to choose from parties that served the interest of capital. According to Klenner, political rights thus consisted of,

the right to free association in social organizations, the right to assembly and the freedom of demonstration, the right to participate in referenda, the right to actively take part in the work of the parliament and its institutions (including the election and removal of representatives by the citizenry), in the right to the armed defence of the workers' and peasants' state and in the right to legality in all actions by the state.[128]

In the place of a false bourgeois politics, one had the right and duty to active citizenship in a society and in institutions of state – both political and military – that truly served one's interests.

Klenner's conception of socialist human rights provided a politically useful double-standard, simultaneously excusing the abuses of the SED dictatorship while still allowing East Germany to criticise the shortcomings of other states through the language of human rights. Because capitalist states were still in the bourgeois phase of history, denial of voting rights or censorship over there could be attacked as a violation of human rights; while these same actions by a communist regime were justifiable in order to protect socialist achievements and realise the interests of the people. Under socialism, it was conceptually impossible to even claim that the rights of the individual were being violated, as the interests of society and citizens were inherently the same. In a system where the state represented the pure expression of the will of all of humanity, how could the rights of the individual *not* be fulfilled? While one could argue that low-level functionaries imperfectly realised the will of the Party, the legitimacy of the system was unimpeachable. The double standard between the socialist world and the capitalist world was politically convenient, but it was nonetheless rooted in an ideological

---

[127] Ibid., 114.   [128] Ibid., 118.

belief that the GDR had crossed a threshold into a stage of historical development that had produced the total emancipation of humanity.[129]

Klenner's theories may have been influenced by contemporaries in the Eastern Bloc, but it was not simply a GDR derivative of Soviet ideology. At this time, the Soviet Union did employ human rights as a rhetorical weapon against Western colonialism, but it did not claim to have realised any kind of distinctly "socialist human rights," but only that the USSR was governed by the principles of "socialist legality."[130] Official Soviet doctrine held that constitutional rights differed significantly from human rights as those rights were derived from being a citizen of the USSR rather than universal humanity.[131] In 1960, when the USSR hosted the "International Meeting of Communist and Workers Parties," the final statement signed by 81 parties from around the world made no mention of human rights, but rather "democratic rights and freedoms."[132] Soviet legal scholarship on human rights only began in earnest in the late 1960s and early 1970s, in response to the domestic activism and the negotiations over the Helsinki Accords. The first comparable work seeking to create a legal conception of how human rights function under socialism in the Soviet Union – I. Farber's *Freedom and Human Rights in the Soviet State* – only appeared in 1974.[133] In the rest of the Eastern Bloc, only one other theorist was working on human rights, namely Imre Szabó, a Hungarian philosopher who had published an orthodox Marxist analysis of human rights in 1948, but his work did not integrate postcolonial rhetoric into socialist human rights doctrine.[134]

The appropriation of anti-imperial human rights rhetoric not only put the GDR ahead of the Soviet Union, but also provided an important advantage against West Germany. Between the two Germanies, the FRG ostensibly had a head start in deploying the idea of self-determination. The preamble to the Basic Law of 1949 called upon "the entire German

---

[129] On Klenner's "total emancipation" thesis, see Lindholm, "Prospects for Research on the Cultural Legitimacy of Human Rights: The Case of Liberalism and Marxism," 412–15.

[130] Amos, "Embracing and Contesting: The Soviet Union and the Universal Declaration of Human Rights, 1948–1958."

[131] Nathans, "Soviet Rights-Talk in the Post-Stalin Era."

[132] *Statement of 81 Communist and Workers Parties: Meeting in Moscow, USSR, 1960* (New York: New Century Publishers, 1961).

[133] I. Farber, *Svoboda i Prava Cheloveka v Sovetskom Gosudarstve* (1974); Christopher Osakwe. "Soviet Human Rights Law under the USSR Constitution of 1977: Theories, Realities and Trends," *Tulane Law Review* 56 (1981–82), 250. On 1970s Eastern Bloc scholarship, see Richard Greenfield, "The Human Rights Literature of Eastern Europe," *Human Rights Quarterly* 3, no. 2 (1981), 136–48.

[134] Imre Szabó, *Az emberi jogok mai értelme* (Budapest: Hungária, 1948); Szabó, *Socialist Concept of Human Rights*.

people," to realise "the unity and freedom of Germany in free self-determination," providing a strong rhetorical parallel to anti-colonial demands. From below, ethnic Germans expelled from Czechoslovakia and the lands annexed to Poland and the Soviet Union at the end of the Second World War cited their right to self-determination in demanding the return of the "lost territories" via a "right to a homeland."[135] At the same time, the radical youth wing of the Social Democrats pressed the national SPD to condemn French policy in Algeria, as it "not only infringed against the right to self-determination of nations and human rights but also constituted a betrayal of the principles of democratic socialism."[136] Among conservatives and social democrats, this was an accessible discourse that was already in use.

Nonetheless, the government of the FRG actively avoided linking self-determination to its demands for human rights in the GDR or for reunification on Western terms. The expellee population provided vital support for the CDU-led government in the 1950s, but their rhetoric was seen as politically unfeasible at the federal level because it would alienate French and British allies.[137] Only in 1959 with decolonisation already underway did the FRG reverse its policy and begin to call on the international community to respect the right of all Germans to self-determination. In 1961, West Berlin mayor (and later Chancellor) Willy Brandt sought help from the Western Allies to denounce the construction of the Berlin Wall in the name of human rights.[138] The UN General Assembly was, however, preoccupied by the French massacre of several hundred individuals during a dispute over the occupation of a Tunisian military base used for operations in Algeria. The initiative was abandoned when the United States, already tepid on the idea of human rights, chose not to press the issue.[139] The West German claim to stand for the right of self-determination was also rejected in the postcolonial countries. At the All-African People's Congress of 1961, the Federal Republic was ranked as one of the "main perpetrators of neo-colonialism," in part due to its close alliance with the imperial powers of Western Europe and warm relations with Apartheid South Africa.[140] Although West Germany first escalated

---

[135] Lora Wildenthal, "Rudolf Laun and the Human Rights of Germans in Occupied and Early West Germany," in *Human Rights in the Twentieth Century*. Andrew Demshuk, *The Lost German East: Forced Migration and the Politics of Memory, 1945–1970* (Cambridge: Cambridge University Press, 2012).

[136] Quoted in von Bulow, *West Germany, Cold War Europe and the Algerian War*, 126.

[137] Gray, *Germany's Cold War*, 101.

[138] Thomas Werneke, *Die Stimme der Vernuft? Menschenrechtssprache als Teil des Politischen während des Ost-West-Konflikts, 1961–1973* (Brussels: Peter Lang, 2016), 255–67.

[139] Jensen, *The Making of International Human Rights*, 48–49.

[140] Gray, *Germany's Cold War*, 122.

the German-German human rights conflict to the global stage, the rise of the Afro-Asian Bloc placed colonialism and not anti-communism at the centre of the UN human rights agenda, putting the Federal Republic at a disadvantage.

The rise of anti-colonial human rights politics also propelled Hermann Klenner's work to a wider audience of elites within the GDR. In contrast to Graefrath's book on the United Nations, Klenner's ideas on socialist human rights were a hit even before they had been published. KSM Secretary Siegfried Forberger attended Klenner's *Habilitation* defence where an early draft of the book's contents was presented and found his work to be "fascinating." He later wrote of the experience: "For the first time, I was hearing a law professor speaking extemporaneously with logical clarity, convincing arguments, and publishable formulations on the essential aspects and problems of Marxist human rights theory."[141] In 1965, Forberger invited Klenner to give a speech to a meeting of the KSM and recruited him as a member. Klenner also found a patron in Hans Schaul, the editor of *Einheit*, the SED's political theory journal, in which Karl Polak's article had originally been published in 1946.[142] While some more conservative members of the SED's publishing bureaucracy expressed concerns over Klenner's work, Schaul's support ensured that *Studies on Basic Rights* was published without extensive revision by the censors.[143]

Influential supporters may have aided Klenner's rise, but just as importantly, he was skilled at presenting his ideas to non-specialists and turning ideology into powerful polemic. In a 1965 address to the KSM, he declared,

On our side [...] are those who fought for human rights during the dark night of fascism. The defendants are now the judges; the persecuted of yesterday are today the rulers; and they have built a *Rechtsstaat* in which human rights are the cornerstone of our democracy. [...] To paraphrase Heinrich Heine: a catalogue of basic rights does not make a man free, just as a cookbook cannot make him full. [...] Because we know that the course of history is inexorable, because we know that the power of the people is immense, and so we know that the age-old longing of man for freedom and peace, for equality, and justice will soon be realised across the world.[144]

---

[141] Forberger, *Das DDR-Komitee für Menschenrechte*, 189.   [142] Ibid., 195.

[143] Ibid., 190. His support was also likely why Klenner was allowed to publish an article-length version of the book in the SED's international affairs journal. Hermann Klenner, "Fünfzehn Jahre Menschenrechtspraxis in Deutschland," *Deutsche Außenpolitik* 9 (1964), 1155–62.

[144] BArch, DZ7/26 Protokoll der Komiteesitzung (26.4.1965) "Zwanzig Jahre Menschenrechtspraxis," 3/15.

For Klenner, the project of socialism in East Germany was part of a grand historical narrative of the progress towards the realisation of human rights around the world. He preserved the earlier appeals to a shared antifascist culture and identity and now embedded them in a new conception of human rights, centred on the norms and texts of the United Nations and international discourses of self-determination.

By the mid-1960s, the combination of Klenner's ideas and the dwindling number of persecuted left-wing prisoners in West Germany paved the way for the KSM to transition from an activist organisation dedicated to freeing communists to a propaganda and ideological machine capable of engaging with the problem of human rights at the United Nations. After Babelsberg, Klenner was a pariah, but only seven years later his work was rapidly becoming orthodoxy. Scholarly articles on rights under socialism now cited his work extensively and used it as the starting point for their arguments. A 1966 article in the legal journal *Staat und Recht* cited Klenner's book six times – compared to three Ulbricht citations and only one of Grotewohl and one of Lenin.[145] In East Germany, Hermann Klenner was now the leading authority on the problem of socialism and human rights.

The Dangerous Mix of Propaganda and Law

Klenner's new discourse of "socialist human rights" was embraced by the academy and several party elites, but it fell short of being fully integrated into the policy-making process. Top officials still lacked a legal understanding of human rights, made manifest in a clumsy and embarrassing propaganda initiative over the definition of German citizenship in 1966.[146] As part of its claim to being the only legitimate German state, the Federal Republic asserted an exclusive mandate (*Alleinvertretungsanspruch*) over all Germans, meaning that all citizens of the GDR were deemed to be citizens of West Germany and subject to its laws, including those banning the KPD and other communist organisations as threats to the democratic order.[147] In anticipation of a summit between the SED

---

[145] Willi Büchner-Uhder, Eberhard Poppe and Rolf Schüssler, "Grundrechte und Grundpflichten der Bürger der DDR: Zur staatstheoretischen und -rechtlichen Grundrechtsforschung," *Staat und Recht* 4 (1966), 563–77.

[146] Jan Palmowski, "Citizenship, Identity, and Community in the GDR," in *Citizenship and National Identity in Twentieth-Century Germany*, ed. Geoff Eley and Jan Palmowski (Stanford, CA: Stanford University Press, 2007), 73–92. Sebastian Gehrig, "Cold War Identities: Citizenship, Constitutional Reform, and International Law between East and West Germany, 1967–75," *Journal of Contemporary History* 49, no. 4 (2014), 794–814.

[147] Gray, *Germany's Cold War*, 12.

and Social Democrats to be held in July 1966 in West Germany, the Federal Republic was forced to grant a limited exception from prosecution to state officials, who otherwise would have been subject to arrest as threats to the constitutional order, for the sake of this one specific meeting.[148]

Seeing this exception as a political act, the SED replied in kind: on 13 October 1966, Walter Ulbricht signed the *Law for the Protection of the Citizenship and Human Rights of Citizens of the GDR*. It stated that anyone who attempted to prosecute East Germans for "the exercise of their constitutional rights" or to enlarge the jurisdiction of the West German state at the expense of an East German citizen could be punished with up to five years in prison. Individual East Germans could launch civil action to be financially compensated for the violation of their rights by filing a complaint with their local state prosecutor's office. It also guaranteed citizens would be provided with financial recompense even if the convicted West German perpetrator failed to pay.[149]

The inclusion of the concept human rights was not seriously debated or discussed by SED officials. The Politburo neglected to consult with human rights experts and the addition of the term appears to have occurred late in the process as earlier drafts omitted it entirely.[150] The preamble of the law claimed that "these measures reflect the commitment of the German Democratic Republic to humanity, to the realization of international law and the protection of legal security," and that it followed from the international legal principles of the "Potsdam Declaration, the United Nations Charter, [and] the London Charter of the International Military Tribunal of Nuremberg." From that list, only the UN Charter mentioned human rights, and it was legally irrelevant given that neither East nor West Germany were members of the United Nations. No specific human rights violations were cited and only a

---

[148] Wentker, *Außenpolitik in engen Grenzen*, 239–43; Ingo von Münch, *Dokumente des geteilten Deutschland: Quellentexte zur Rechtslage des Deutschen Reiches, der BRD und der DDR*, Vol. 1 (Stuttgart: Kröner, 1968), 222.

[149] "Gesetz zum Schutze der Staatsbürger- und Menschenrechte der Bürger der DDR," in *Gesetzblatt der DDR* (Berlin: Staatsverlag der DDR, 1966), 81.

[150] Forberger, *Das DDR-Komitee für Menschenrechte*. 22 BArch, DY30/J IV 2/2/1079 Protokoll Nr. 40/66 Sitzung am 4. Oktober 1966. At the Politburo meeting, it was listed simply as "Gesetz zum Schutze der Bürger der DDR." Palmowski argues that the law was a precursor to the 1967 law defining a separate East German citizenship, which explains why the focus was not on international human rights, Palmowski, "Citizenship, Identity and Community in the GDR," 76.

general reference was made to the "serious violations of citizens contrary to international law."[151]

Although the law was vague about what human rights it would be protecting, the financial compensation it demanded was very clear. A report from the Ministry of the Interior claimed that 3,217 East German citizens had been detained or imprisoned between 1958 and 1966. Additionally, those East German citizens who had been prosecuted as enemies of the West German democratic order – many defended by the KSM – had been sentenced to 1,595 months (133 years) of prison time. According to the detailed remuneration tables accompanying the law, these offences stipulated a payment of slightly more than 4 million marks.[152] This substantial demand was widely publicised, but no actual legal case was ever mounted against the government of the Federal Republic or against any specific officials. In the West German media, the claims were dismissed as a media stunt – one tabloid openly denounced it as a mere distraction from the fifth anniversary of the building of the Berlin Wall. After this initial splash in the media, the law was promptly ignored.[153]

The SED appears to have had no intention of following through on the actual substance of the law, as no bureaucratic preparations were made for eventual lawsuits or claims from citizens.[154] Yet, East Germans took the law seriously and began to file grievances with their local state prosecutor's office. While a handful of cases from average citizens could have been ignored, one of the first complaints came from the president of the *Volkskammer*, Johannes Dieckmann. The day after the law came into effect, he wrote to his local prosecutor in Potsdam about an incident from 1961 when a crowd rushed the stage where he was speaking during a cultural event in West Germany: "What actually happened in Marburg is that I came within a hair of being lynched. [...] The attack on the stage caused me no physical harm. Nevertheless, I believe I have a valid claim to compensation and herewith register my complaint."[155] Nowhere in his story does he mention any efforts by West German officials to

---

[151] "Gesetz zum Schutze der Staatsbürger- und Menschenrechte der Bürger der DDR," 81.

[152] BArch, DO1/10296 Schadenersatz – ein rechtliches und menschliches Gebot.

[153] "Über vier Mill. Mark fordert ein Zonen-Komitee von Bonn als Entschädigung für die Inhaftierung von 'DDR-Bürgern' in der BRD," *Die Welt* (3.8.1966); "Propaganda mit 13. August," *Der Kurier* (3.8.1966).

[154] BArch, DP3/3157, Wendland to Funk (20.10.1966).

[155] In the original, "ich um ein Haar Opfer eines Lynchmordes geworden wäre."; BArch, DP3/3157 Folder 22/67. Dieckmann to Bezirksstaatsanwalt Potsdam (14.10.1966). While Dieckmann's claims are exaggerated, the incident described did occur. Reinhard Hübsch, *"Dieckmann raus: Hängt ihn auf!": Der Besuch des DDR*

prosecute him or expand their judicial jurisdictions. Like the victims of human rights abuse publicised by the Committee, however, Dieckmann's complaint had more to do with a violation of antifascist norms and narratives than any kind of legal offence. His human rights had been violated because his efforts to convey a message of socialism and peace had been foiled by aggressive anti-communists. The legal case was nonexistent, but his story was consistent with the narrative formulations of human rights violations, as presented by the KSM over the past seven years.

SED officials at the Ministry of Justice and the chief prosecutor's office had not anticipated a spontaneous public response to the law, and they now scrambled to minimise bureaucratic chaos. The chief prosecutor's office sent out belated instructions to local offices on criteria for valid complaints under the law and in spite of the propaganda demanding payment for incidents from 1958 to 1966, the Ministry of Justice sought to amend the law so that it would explicitly only apply to incidents that had occurred after the date it was passed (13 October 1966).[156] On 15 November, Minister of Justice Hilde Benjamin officially notified Chief Prosecutor Josef Streit that the law was not retroactively valid and all claims for incidents prior to the passage of the law should be rejected.[157] This, of course, obliterated the existing propaganda campaign claiming 4 million marks in damages, but it would at least forestall a deluge of lawsuits and a huge financial liability for compensation that the Federal Republic would never pay.

It is possible that Benjamin's decision would have stymied further demands for compensation were it not for a minor clerical error two months earlier in West Germany that set off the next bizarre chapter. On 13 September 1966, the Office of the Chief Prosecutor of Cologne sent out a request for the arrest of Kurt Forster, the SED Party Secretary at a miner's lamp factory in Zwickau. Forster was sought in connection with an incident in 1961 when he stayed at the home of a member of the banned KPD while visiting West Germany.[158] The warrant, accusing Forster of representing a threat to the Federal Republic of Germany, was sent out by post from Cologne to the local police station in the small

---

Volkskammerpräsidenten Johannes Dieckmann in Marburg am 13. Januar 1961 (Bonn: Pahl-Rugenstein, 1995).

[156] BArch, DP3/109. Zur Sicherung der einheitlichen Praxis bei der Anwendung des "Gesetzes zum Schutz der Staatsbürger und Menschenrechte der Bürger der DDR" (19.10.1966). BArch, DP3/3157, Folder 22/67. Wendland to Funk (20.10.1966).

[157] BArch, DP3/109, Benjamin to Streit (15.11.1966).

[158] The letter is located at BArch, DP3/3154, Gesetz zum Schutz der Staatsbürger- und Menschenrechte der DDR vom 13. Oktober 1966 – Entschädigungssachen Bd. 1.

town of Lichtenstein. It seems to have escaped Cologne's attention that the town of Lichtenstein was located in the GDR. When the paperwork on Forster's outstanding warrant was photocopied for filing purposes, the photocopier accidentally produced a third copy, which a clerk then assumed was meant to be distributed to the appropriate police authorities. Forster's last known address, gleaned from when he had crossed the border at the time of the incident, was added to the paperwork, before being signed by the chief prosecutor, mechanically working his way through a pile of dozens of documents.[159]

When the request arrived in the GDR in early October, the police department passed it up the chain of command: first to the local prosecutor's office and then the regional prosecutor's office in Karl-Marx-Stadt, and then onto the State Crimes Department in the chief prosecutor's office in East Berlin. On 8 November, nearly two months after it had been originally sent from Cologne, it reached the desk of the GDR's Chief Prosecutor Josef Streit. Although his office had refused to process complaints lodged by East German citizens, and the warrant was mailed before the 13 October effective date, the incident was deemed to be such a clear example of West German judicial overreach that his office immediately swung into action anyway. Launching a full investigation into the incident, Streit's office contacted Kurt Forster for a full account of his run-in with the West German authorities five years earlier. Forster was baffled by the whole situation, recounting how he had visited the home of an acquaintance from Cologne whom he had originally met at a peace festival in the GDR. He received a phone call while still in Cologne, but at a different address, informing him that the police had raided the home of his friend who had been arrested. The authorities had seized Forster's suitcase as evidence. Rather than face possible arrest, he decided to return to East Germany immediately, which he did without incident. In addition to the interview, the arrest warrant was sent to the Stasi for typewriting analysis to determine why two machines appeared to have been used and to decipher the handwriting underneath a scribble. (The Stasi report eventually determined that the text under the scribble listed Forster's employment information from 1961 but had nothing substantial to say about the typewriter.)[160]

Streit then launched a propaganda campaign against this "provocation" by the West, distributing information to media in both West and East Germany. The Cologne letter was reprinted in *Neues Deutschland*.

---

[159] Details of the error were later determined by a West German reporter and published in "Das dritte Blatt," *Der Spiegel* (21.11.1966).
[160] BArch, DP 3/3154 File 1/67.

In West Germany, stories on Forster and the arrest warrant ran in the *Frankfurter Allgemeine Zeitung, Die Welt, Frankfurter Rundschau, Süddeutsche Zeitung* and the (West) *Berliner Morgenpost*. In the version distributed by the SED, Forster's story remained mostly true to his telling, save a few colourful exaggerations, such as a claim that he had evaded capture in Cologne while the raiding police officers were distracted. In response, the Cologne prosecutor's office denied all involvement and described the whole story as "absurd."[161] Finally, on 14 November, Streit filed charges against two officials from Cologne whose names were listed on the arrest warrant on the basis of the 1966 law.[162]

While the incident as a whole was a public embarrassment for the West German legal establishment, the lawsuit went nowhere. The Cologne office and the accused officials never responded to the charges, and by February 1967, Streit's office had given up hope that they ever would.[163] At the same time, the increased publicity for the Law for the Protection of the Citizenship and Human Rights meant that GDR prosecutor's offices were flooded with complaints from East Germans seeking redress for violations of their human rights. Although some local offices did only enough to avoid offending the petitioners, others helped coach claimants on how to phrase their demands, providing suggestions on how to maximise their compensation.[164] The prosecutor's office in Leipzig even created standardised forms to make the process as straightforward as possible.

In spite of this local work, the chief prosecutor's office rejected every application. When the office deigned to respond to applicants at all, petitioners received a terse letter: "This illegal act of persecution has been noted with interest and has been officially registered. The initiation of special proceedings cannot occur as the law cannot be applied retroactively."[165] None of the incidents reported occurred after the law took effect, and many dated back to the 1950s. Claims were often invalid for multiple reasons: several applications came from individuals arrested prior to their emigration to the GDR, making them West German residents (and thus making their claims of judicial overreach moot). One brazen petitioner had been imprisoned in Switzerland while working as a spy for the GDR.[166] Beyond the fact that his activities did not fall

---

[161] "Angeblich Haftbefehl aus Köln nach Zwickau gesandt," *Tagesspiegel* (11.11.1966).
[162] BArch, DP3/3154 File 1/67.
[163] BArch, DP3/3154 File 1/67. Note to Friedrich (10.2.1967).
[164] BArch, DP3/3159 File 6/29.   [165] BArch, DP3/3155 File 13/1967.
[166] BArch, DP3/3159 File 2/69. Apparently, the applicant was quite understanding that the law did not apply to those imprisoned beyond West Germany.

into the normal range of "exercising constitutional rights," he never even came into contact with West German authorities.

The discrepancy between the actual text of the law and the contents of the applications can be explained by East Germans interpreting violations of human rights in narrative rather than legal terms. None of the claims mention any specific violations of human or actual constitutional rights but they all conformed to the antifascist narrative as disseminated by the KSM. Each of the applicants portrayed themselves, or the family member they were applying on behalf of, as innocent victims, seeking only to promote peace or socialism, oppressed by the West German (or in the one case, Swiss) police state. Most of the applications were short on the details of the incidents that led to the arrest but provided extensive lists of their losses. Some asked for lost wages, others for medical bill reimbursements stemming from illnesses contracted in the West, while a few only asked for money to replace personal items confiscated by the West German police, such as a pair of gloves or a jacket. In one case, an SED official arrested while living in Kiel asked for more than 110,000 marks in compensation for his car, house and furnishings that he claimed were seized when he was imprisoned from 1960 to 1962.[167] No claim was ever accepted and none of the applicants received compensation from the state in any form.

In spite of the blanket refusal to go forward with any lawsuits or to provide compensation, many petitioners refused to believe that their claim was invalid. As one functionary noted after meeting with an applicant, Herr W. "could not be convinced that he was not entitled to compensation under the law or that the law has no retroactive force."[168] Several wrote back every year or so, even if they had received a formal notice of rejection, demanding to know when their compensation would arrive. Often, they would write to other organisations such as the Committee for the Protection of Human Rights to ask for assistance with what they presumed to be a bureaucratic omission. In some instances, the chief prosecutor's office had to arrange several meetings with the applicant to explain in person that the law did not apply. One applicant who had been imprisoned in 1950 first filed his complaint in 1975 (which was rejected immediately) but took until 1986 to finally accept that he would not be receiving any recompense.[169]

The drama surrounding the law only came to a close in 1988 when an applicant forged documents to claim a larger pension based on his oppression by West German authorities. While this individual filed his

---

[167] BArch, DP3/3159 File 2/68.   [168] BArch, DP3/3159 File 1/69.
[169] BArch, DP3/3159 File 1/75.

initial complaint in November 1966 (and was rejected), shortly before his 65th birthday in 1987, he wrote to his local prosecutor's office again, hoping to receive a bonus to his monthly pension for the 15 months of his West German imprisonment. When his application was rejected once again, he altered the letter he received in reply from the prosecutor's office to make it appear as though his request had been granted. Although the claimant was clearly unaware of the fact that no one had ever been compensated before, the authorities were not, and they quickly picked up on his forgery. The applicant was imprisoned for fraud in 1988, which marked the only prosecution to be successfully carried out as the result of the 1966 law.[170]

Beyond the nuisance of these applications, however, the citizens of East Germany almost entirely avoided the language of human rights as a tool to protest or make claims against the SED in this era. The KSM received only a handful of complaint letters regarding domestic policy and, of those, few that chose to question the official logic of human rights. One letter that has survived in the archives was sent in 1965 by Frau M. to Paul Wiens, a playwright and member of the Committee's Board. Frau M. demanded to know how the KSM could reconcile its promotion of human rights with the severe restrictions placed on her daughter, who lived in the West, to be able to visit her mother. At the end, she acidly inquired, "Please tell me, Herr Wiens, where can I find the office for human rights for those who are here and cannot safely leave?"[171] Instead of replying, Wiens forwarded the letter to the Ministry of the Interior – as would become standard policy for all such "provocative" correspondence.

The idea of human rights did gain in popularity among East German Christians, but without a coherent focus. For the Catholic Church in the early to mid-1960s, human rights was increasingly a term of choice for attacking various state injustices, including the forced collectivisation of farms and the coercion of doctors into providing abortion services against their conscience.[172] In 1963, Catholic Bishops expressed concern about the draft of a new youth law that could violate the right to religious freedom, by imposing an atheistic Marxist-Leninist worldview. In doing so, they cited the recently published encyclical of Pope John XXIII,

---

[170] BArch, DP3/3159 File 49/67.
[171] AdK, Paul Wiens Archiv 2349 Frau M. to Paul Wiens (3.11.1965).
[172] "Gegen die Verletzung von Menschenrechten bei der Werbung zum Eintritt in die LPG (6.4.1960)," in Gerhard Lange, *Katholische Kirche – sozialistischer Staat DDR: Dokumente und öffentliche Äußerungen 1945–1990* (Berlin: Bischöfliches Ordinariat, 1993), 180; Ute Haese, *Katholische Kirche in der DDR: Geschichte einer politischen Abstinenz* (Düsseldorf: Patmos Verlag, 1998), 72.

Pacem in Terris, that endorsed the concept of human rights and specific-ally cited the UDHR.[173] Conversely, some Protestant pastors showed support for the activities of the Committee for the Protection of Human Rights. One spoke at a KSM fundraiser in 1964, where he denounced the FRG as the "so-called Christian part of our Fatherland" and said, "let us openly demand: give people freedom to fight for justice and peace, because all men have a right to live."[174] But the small number of clergy who embraced the KSM were discouraged from working with the organ-isation by the Church. A different pastor, who became a member of the Committee and even joined a delegation to deliver pamphlets to UN offices in Geneva, was eventually pressured by his superiors into quitting the group entirely.[175]

At the same time, the few East German dissidents showed little interest in human rights. In 1964, the scientist Robert Havemann gave a series of critical lectures on his vision of Marxist utopianism, entitled "Scientific Aspects of Philosophical Problems." Havemann had been imprisoned by the Nazis for his Communist beliefs, and in the postwar period had served as a member of the *Volkskammer.* Building upon other critical Marxist intellectuals of the 1950s, who had argued that the SED was straying from the true path of socialism, Havemann had no interest in promoting a vision of individual human rights, but rather a form of universal liberation by means of Marxist dialecticism.[176] In a version of his lectures published in the West, under the title *Dialectics without Dogma,* he said "freedom is only desirable, it is only moral, when it is not the freedom of individuals, but the freedom of all, the freedom is for every human being, which allows everyone to decide according to his will and his desire."[177] By 1965, Havemann was an inspiration for dissidents within the intellectual and cultural elite of East Germany for speaking out. As a result, the SED kicked him out of the party, removed him from the Academy of Sciences and caused him to be fired from his post at Humboldt University. Although Havemann's dissent was seen as a danger to the SED, this threat did not include reference to the idea of human rights.

---

[173] "Zum Entwurf eines neuen Jugendgesetz," (1.12.1963) in Lange, *Katholische Kirche – sozialistischer Staat DDR,* 203–4. On Catholic engagement with *Pacem in Terris,* see Bernd Schäfer, *The East German State and the Catholic Church, 1945–1989* (New York: Berghahn, 2010), 148.

[174] BArch, DZ7/26 Diskussionsbeiträge (13.11.1964), 22 and 26.

[175] Forberger, *Das DDR-Komitee für Menschenrechte,* 141–42.

[176] Hans-Christoph Rauh and Peter Ruben, *Denkversuche: DDR-Philosophie in den 60er Jahren* (Berlin: Ch. Links, 2005), 350.

[177] Robert Havemann, *Dialektik ohne Dogma? Naturwissenschaft und Weltanschauung* (Reinbek: Rowohlt, 1965), 104.

Western NGOs continued to accuse the GDR of human rights violations, but the SED considered it a containable threat. In 1966, Amnesty
International selected East Germany as a target country for a report on
prison conditions – a socialist country alongside (then) Rhodesia and
Paraguay to provide political "balance" – and wrote to SED officials to
ask for information about the domestic justice system. In keeping with
their existing suspicion of NGO activism, the Stasi concluded that
Amnesty was a front organisation working on behalf of the CIA and
other foreign intelligence agencies under the guise of political neutrality.
The KSM was forbidden from communicating with the representatives
of Amnesty on the grounds that even their formal refusal to participate in
the investigation could be used against the SED. The Stasi argued that
the best course of actions would be to simply ignore the organisation's
requests, which remained SED policy going forward.[178]

Conclusion

By 1966, the conflict that first launched the KSM seven years earlier had
changed significantly. There were no more imprisoned Communists and
peace activists; the antifascist propaganda campaign had run its course;
and the final child custody case was nearing its conclusion.[179] The
belligerence of the West German government also began to ease, as
elections that year ended in a coalition government led by the Christian
Democrats in partnership with the Social Democrats. In contrast to the
militantly anti-communist postwar SPD leader, Kurt Schumacher, who
had opposed all engagement with the SED, the current SPD chairman
and Foreign Minister Willy Brandt favoured engagement with East Germany. By 1968, the FRG even allowed for the refounding of a communist party (now called the *Deutsche Kommunistische Partei*) on West
German soil, despite the 1952 ban on the KPD.

The problem for the Committee moving forward – as for East German
human rights politics as whole – was that the new ideology of socialist
human rights needed to be disseminated and assimilated across the vast
state and party bureaucracies of the GDR. Klenner's new ideas about
human rights were not politically useful if they were only understood by a
select group of intellectuals, none of whom controlled the levers of state
power. The Law for the Protection of the Citizenship and Human Rights

---

[178] Mihr, *Amnesty International in der DDR*, 268–93.
[179] The last of the child custody cases that the KSM assisted with was not resolved until
1967, through a ruling of the European Court of Human Rights, "Angelika Kurtz
wieder in West-Berlin," *Tagesspiegel* (8.2.1967).

of the Citizens of the GDR and the legal chaos that ensued demonstrated the dangers of political actors engaging in human rights politics without the expert knowledge needed to insulate them from such consequences. The eventual, widespread, internalisation of the idea of socialist human rights by Party and state apparatus would not come from the diligence of the Committee, but rather from renewed East German effort to join the United Nations as part of the 1968 International Year for Human Rights.

3   Socialist Human Rights on the
World Stage, 1966–1978

In his New Year's address, SED General Secretary Walter Ulbricht reminded all citizens of the GDR that the United Nations had declared 1968 to be the International Year for Human Rights. East Germany's contribution to the event, commemorating the 20th anniversary of the Universal Declaration of Human Rights (UDHR), was to be a new socialist constitution, which Ulbricht promised would be "based on respect for human rights and that highest of human rights, the right to peace."[1] As both Germanies were excluded from UN membership, and East Germany remained isolated outside of formal relations with fellow socialist nations, the SED leadership seized upon the International Year as an opportunity to demonstrate the GDR's superiority in the field of human rights, in the hope of finally paving the way for widespread international diplomatic recognition. While human rights activism by Western NGOs would explode in the late 1970s, a decade earlier, the international politics of human rights was dominated by recently decolonised countries from the Global South, which promoted a vision of human rights grounded in self-determination and anti-colonialism.

The campaign during the International Year for Human Rights failed to achieve a diplomatic breakthrough for the GDR, but for the SED, it cemented elite belief that East Germany was a rising star in the field of international human rights – not a pariah. The propaganda campaign in 1968 touched all parts of the East German state apparatus and in doing so it normalised the idea of human rights both as a tool of international relations, and as an integral component of state socialism. The theoretical conception of "socialist human rights" developed by Hermann Klenner in 1964 was now adopted and disseminated by East German elites, who began to view human rights as a cause that was deeply intertwined with the principle of self-determination and sovereignty rather than individualism or interventionism.

[1] Walter Ulbricht, "1968 – Jahr wichtiger Entscheidungen," *Neues Deutschland* (1.1.1968), 1.

97

The SED's propaganda campaign in 1968 did not result in recognition, but it did create the conditions necessary for East Germany's human rights diplomacy of the 1970s. In 1975, 35 countries in Europe and North America – representing both sides of the Cold War – signed the Final Act of Conference on Security and Co-operation in Europe (CSCE), better known as the Helsinki Accords. The agreement originated in an Eastern Bloc initiative from the mid-1960s to negotiate Western recognition of the GDR and the new postwar Polish-German border.[2] The agreement ultimately confirmed the existence of East Germany as a separate state, ratified the postwar borders of Europe and provided guarantees for increased free exchange of people and ideas across the Cold War divide.[3] Included in these guarantees were pledges by the signatories to uphold the principles of international human rights. In academic literature, it is taken for granted that the human rights of the Helsinki Accords were oriented towards liberal democracy and thus deeply alien to the SED and the rest of the Eastern Bloc.[4]

In fact, by the time the Helsinki negotiations had begun in earnest in the early 1970s, the leadership of the SED and party elites had already internalised the concept of human rights as an essential part of the socialist project at the peak of post-colonial influence on international politics. For East German elites, this had the effect of freezing in place a seemingly self-evident linkage between anti-imperialism and the ideals contained in UN treaties and covenants. This subjective understanding of human rights as inherently pro-socialist and anti-imperialist was fundamental to East German diplomacy in the 1970s, as the GDR gained

---

[2] Békés Csaba, "The Warsaw Pact, the German Question and the Birth of the CSCE Process 1961–1970," in *Helsinki 1975 and the Transformation of Europe*, ed. Oliver Bange and Gottfried Niedhart (New York: Berghahn, 2011), 113–28.

[3] The text of the Helsinki Accords was split into "baskets": Basket I, European security; Basket II, cooperation in economics, science, technology and the environment; Basket III, humanitarian and cultural cooperation; and Basket IV, conference follow-up.

[4] The main work asserting that the Helsinki Accords represented a rupture for Eastern Bloc in terms of human rights is Daniel Thomas, *The Helsinki Effect: International Norms, Human Rights, and the Demise of Communism* (Princeton, NJ: Princeton University Press, 2001). Ignatieff argues that the Eastern Bloc had already accepted social and economic rights, but that socialists had denied the validity of political and civil human rights prior to Helsinki. Michael Ignatieff, *Human Rights as Politics and Idolatry*, (Princeton, NJ: Princeton University Press, 2001), 19. GDR-specific work arguing that human rights as a concept was absent before 1975 include Christian Joppke, *East German Dissidents and the Revolution of 1989: Social Movement in a Leninist Regime* (New York: New York University Press, 1995), 116; Jürgen Wüst, *Menschenrechtsarbeit im Zwielicht: zwischen Staatssicherheit und Antifaschismus* (Bonn: Bouvier, 1999), 32; Steven Pfaff, "The Politics of Peace in the GDR: The Independent Peace Movement, the Church, and the Origins of the East German Opposition," *Peace & Change* 26, no. 3 (2001), 287.

recognition from West Germany, joined the United Nations, and signed on to the Helsinki Accords – all of which involved endorsing international human rights norms. The SED's campaign during the International Year for Human Rights and the influence of non-aligned nations in creating a global human rights system that appeared to value self-determination and non-intervention above all else was crucial for the creation of an ideological environment where the treaties of the 1970s were possible. For East Berlin, Tehran was a crucial stop on the path to Helsinki.

The GDR and the Year for Human Rights 1966–1968

The mid-1960s were a precarious moment for the concept of human rights in East German ideology. In 1965 and 1966, with the waning of the antifascism campaign and the decline in prisoners that the Committee for the Protection of Human Rights (KSM) could campaign for, the SED even neglected to commemorate International Human Rights Day on 10 December. The cause of imprisoned activists in West Germany was also being pushed aside by a new interest in the global struggle for liberation, backed by a variety of solidarity committees to support African decolonisation, Vietnamese liberation and other revolutionary movements around the world. In contrast to the 1 million mark raised for the KSM in its first year, the Vietnam Solidarity Committee collected aid worth around 75 million East German marks between 1965 and 1968.[5] While, in 1967, the Committee had welcomed legal scholar Bernhard Graefrath as another major intellectual force, the following year, Hermann Klenner, the main theorist of socialist human rights doctrine, was again accused of ideological revisionism and again threatened with the loss of his career and influence.[6] While he was shunned from official events for some time, Klenner's professional life was saved by his decision to accept an offer from the Stasi to become an informant ("informal collaborator" or IM) under the cover name IM Klee.[7]

---

[5] Gregory Witkowski, "Between Fighters and Beggars: Socialist Philanthropy and the Imagery of Solidarity in East Germany," in *Comrades of Color: East Germany in the Cold War World*, ed. Quinn Slobodian (New York: Berghahn, 2015), 76.

[6] On Graefrath joining the committee, see Siegfried Forberger, *Das DDR-Komitee für Menschenrechte: Erinnerungen an den Sozialismus-Versuch im 20. Jahrhundert; Einsichten und Irrtümer des Siegfried Forberger, Sekretär des DDR-Komitees für Menschenrechte von 1959 bis 1989* (Self-pub., 2000), 28.

[7] For more on the fallout for Klenner's career, see ibid., 273 and Hasso Hofmann, "The Development of German-Language Legal Philosophy and Legal Theory in the Second Half of the 20th Century," in *A Treatise of Legal Philosophy and General Jurisprudence:*

It is possible that socialist human rights could have been an ideological trend from the post-Stalin thaw that was snuffed out as a deviation from orthodox Marxism-Leninism.[8] Rather than fade away, however, socialist human rights not only experienced a revival but also were integrated into the core of SED ideology by the end of the 1960s due to the intersection of the GDR's quest for diplomatic recognition and the fortuitous timing of International Year for Human Rights. To maintain its relevance, the KSM turned to global human rights issues and by 1966, the main agenda item at a major KSM event was no longer prisoner solidarity, but the Federal Republic's complicity in American aggression towards Vietnam. Advertising for the Committee's charity radio show in 1967 called for solidarity with "the people of Vietnam, Greece, Spain, the Middle East" in addition to "the democrats of West Germany."[9]

Although the Committee sought to move beyond the scope of the German-German conflict, its survival and that of human rights within SED ideology could not have been guaranteed without the impetus of the United Nations. In the mid-1960s, neither Germany had gained membership to the United Nations because the Great Powers would not accept the formal division of the country. For many international organisations, Germany remained officially united: at the Olympics, East and West Germany were compelled to compete as a single team under a compromise flag of red, black and gold with the Olympic rings in the centre.[10] At the same time, West Germany had manoeuvred itself into observer status representing "Germany" at important UN bodies such as UNESCO.[11] The FRG also continued to claim the right to speak on behalf of all Germans, including those in the GDR and the rest of the Eastern Bloc, while threatening to cut ties with any state that recognised East Germany. For the SED leadership, the affront of West Germany's growing international stature alongside what it viewed as constant

---

Volume 12 – Legal Philosophy in the Twentieth Century: The Civil Law World, Tome 2, ed. Enrico Pattaro and Corrado Roversi (Dordrecht: Springer, 2016), 357–58. Klenner's work as an informant with the Stasi is documented in BStU, MfS, AIM 17340/89 vol. 1–5. Klenner appears to be the only member of the Committee to have acted as a Stasi IM.

[8] Such as cybernetics theory, which rapidly rose and fell in the 1960s, see Peter Caldwell, *Dictatorship, State Planning, and Social Theory in the GDR* (Cambridge: Cambridge University Press, 2003), 141–84.

[9] BArch, DZ7/26 Hedda Zinner speech (2.12.1966) and "Dem Frieden die Freiheit" Handblatt (December 1967).

[10] Erin Redihan, *The Olympics and the Cold War, 1948–1968: Sport as Battleground in the U.S.–Soviet Rivalry* (Jefferson, NC: McFarland, 2017), 197–202.

[11] William Gray, *Germany's Cold War: The Global Campaign to Isolate East Germany, 1949–1969* (Chapel Hill: University of North Carolina Press, 2003), 189.

internal interference in East German affairs by the Western powers was intolerable.

The Soviet Union did not support a unilateral entry of the GDR into the United Nations, but Ulbricht hoped to make an end-run around the Great Powers and appeal directly to the rising Afro-Asian bloc.[12] On 28 February 1966, Ulbricht sent a telegram to UN Secretary General U Thant informing him that East Germany would be formally applying for membership.[13] Although he was known to be personally sympathetic to the GDR's desire to gain equal standing with the FRG, Thant did not support Ulbricht's initiative on the grounds that there was no international consensus. At the UN Security Council (which held the responsibility for accepting or declining the application), the Western powers immediately circulated a note stating that the GDR was not eligible for membership. With failure assured due to American, British and French opposition (each could individually veto the application), the Soviet Union did not even attempt to put the issue on the agenda. In spite of a concurrent "goodwill" tour to non-aligned states, not one neutral country spoke out in favour of the East German application at the General Assembly.[14] In response, Ulbricht wanted to instigate a renewed propaganda campaign against West Germany, but this plan was quickly vetoed by the Soviets, who were in the midst of negotiating a treaty with the Federal Republic.[15]

As an alternative, the SED turned to a plan to normalise the GDR via international human rights. At the instigation of Jamaica, the General Assembly had designated 1968 as the International Year for Human Rights and it invited all members to "intensify their domestic efforts in the field of human rights with the assistance of their appropriate organizations, in order that a fuller and more effective realization of those

---

[12] Scholarship on the East German campaign for Third World recognition has ignored the SED's use of human rights propaganda. Hermann Wentker, *Außenpolitik in engen Grenzen: Die DDR im Internationalen System, 1949–1989* (Munich: Oldenbourg, 2007), 276–315. Stein only mentions human rights in connection to the difficulties for the FRG due to its friendly relations with colonial regimes. Mathias Stein, *Der Konflikt um Alleinvertretung und Anerkennung in der UNO: Die deutsch-deutschen Beziehungen zu den Vereinten Nationen von 1949 bis 1973* (Göttingen: V&R Unipress, 2011), 71.

[13] Stein, *Der Konflikt um Alleinvertretung und Anerkennung in der UNO*, 126.

[14] Gray, *Germany's Cold War*, 189–90.

[15] Oliver Bange, "The GDR in the Era of Détente: Conflicting Perceptions and Strategies, 1965–1975," in *Perforating the Iron Curtain: European Détente, Transatlantic Relations, and the Cold War, 1965–1985*, eds. Poul Villaume and Odd Arne Westad (Copenhagen: Tusculanum Press, 2010), 58.

rights and freedoms might be achieved."[16] Soon afterwards, the United Nations adopted three major treaties that would form the backbone of the international human rights system: the Convention on the Elimination of Racial Discrimination (CERD), which declared segregation and apartheid to be human rights violations; the International Covenant on Civil and Political Rights (ICCPR); and the International Covenant on Economic, Social and Cultural Rights (ICESCR). The covenants were adopted in 1966 and intended to translate the rights contained in the UDHR into legally binding treaty obligations. Reflecting the importance of the Afro-Asian bloc, the first article of both of the Human Rights Covenants affirmed: "All peoples have the right of self-determination."[17] The General Assembly requested that member nations use the International Year for Human Rights as an opportunity to sign onto these key UN human rights treaties, and then demonstrate their support for the International Year through symbolic measures.

Conveniently, the timing of International Human Rights Year coincided not only with Ulbricht's diplomatic goals but also with East Germany's progression to the next phase of history. Having officially begun the "construction of socialism" in 1952, the SED planned to announce that the GDR had completed its transition from an antifascist state to a "socialist people's community" in 1968.[18] To cement this accomplishment, the original GDR Constitution, with its tributes to German unity and bourgeois political structures, was to be replaced by a "Socialist Constitution" that would reaffirm SED rule and East Germany's alliance with the Soviet Union. To secure popular support for the new constitution, the SED first planned a mass consultation – *Volksaussprache* – on its contents and then a national plebiscite.

The SED framed the constitution and the process leading to its adoption as a testament to the realisation of self-determination and other human rights norms in the GDR. This began with Walter Ulbricht's New Year's address, broadcast nationally and published on the front page of the national newspaper *Neues Deutschland*, where he explicitly stated that, "Our new socialist and humanistic constitution, which is based on respect for human rights [...], is also a fine contribution of

---

[16] General Assembly Resolution 1961 (XVIII) (12.12.1963); Steven Jensen, *The Making of International Human Rights: The 1960s, Decolonization, and the Reconstruction of Global Values* (Cambridge: Cambridge University Press, 2016), 78–79.

[17] On the process of drafting the Covenants and the problem of self-determination, see Daniel Whelan, *Indivisible Human Rights* (Philadelphia: University of Pennsylvania Press, 2010), 112–36.

[18] On the "sozialistische Menschengemeinschaft," see Stefan Wolle, *Aufbruch nach Utopia: Alltag und Herrschaft in der DDR 1961–1971* (Berlin: Ch. Links, 2012), 179.

the German Democratic Republic to the objective of this 'International Year [for Human Rights].'" Although the Soviet Union had forbidden an all-out propaganda campaign against West Germany, Ulbricht did not hold back from contrasting the crimes of the FRG with the virtuous behaviour of the GDR.

In West Germany, however, the year of human rights is marked by support by the ruling circles in Bonn for the barbaric US war against the Vietnamese people. It is dedicated to the disenfranchisement and the gagging of the people through the Emergency Decrees, the dismantling of social services, and neo-Nazi propaganda.[19]

The speech marked the first time that Ulbricht had publicly linked the idea of human rights to any specific accomplishments under socialism or particular abuses in the capitalist world.

The SED had a two-pronged strategy to capitalise on the International Year for Human Rights: the GDR would convince the developing world that its domestic politics were in line with international human rights norms, thus legitimising the GDR's claim to membership in the United Nations. At the same time, the International Year would be weaponised against West German claims to represent the whole of the German nation. According to a Politburo directive, it was crucial to show the world that "socialist humanism is the embodiment of human rights and to unmask the misuse of the idea of 'human rights' that drives the implementation of West German imperialist class interests." As such, the GDR would demonstrate its humanistic character through "unrestricted support for the Vietnamese people against the barbaric war of American imperialism," solidarity with the Arab world to "overcome the effects of Israeli imperialist aggression," and support for new nations in "realizing the right to self-determination and the liquidation of all remaining traces of colonialism and neo-colonialism." Simultaneously, the SED would highlight West German support for the American war in Vietnam and the alleged aim of the Federal Republic to acquire nuclear weapons – "an acute danger to peace and thus a permanent attack on human rights" – and Bonn's refusal to renounce its "imperialistic" claims to sovereignty over East German territory.[20]

While Ulbricht promoted the "socialist and humanistic constitution" as a document "based on respect for human rights," the number of

[19] Ulbricht, "1968 – Jahr wichtiger Entscheidungen."
[20] BArch, DY30/J IV 2/3/1404 Protokoll Nr. 43/68 Sitzung am 8.5.1968. Inhaltliche Konzeption – "Internationale Jahr der Menschenrechte," 1–3.

explicitly named rights decreased in comparison with the 1949 Consti-tution.[21] The Citizens Rights section in the original constitution was now renamed Basic Rights and Basic Duties of Citizens. The new document still included numerous liberal-democratic-sounding rights to free expression and political participation, but the right to strike had been removed – to the consternation of many East Germans. Another point of contention was the reduction of enumerated religious freedoms: the 1949 constitution contained eight articles guaranteeing freedom of belief and the independence of the churches, while the new document con-tained only a single article mentioning freedom of religion, but no longer of belief and conscience.[22]

The Socialist Constitution's crucial innovation was not in the rights that it provided to the people, but the legitimacy it bestowed upon the SED. The first article stated,

The German Democratic Republic is the socialist state of the German nation. It is the political organization of the working people of the cities and countryside, who under the leadership of the working class and its Marxist-Leninist Party [the SED], are realizing socialism.[23]

Article 2 continued from this premise, claiming that the end of capitalism in the GDR meant "the exploitation of man by man has been abolished forever."[24] Article 6 also explained that the GDR would abide by the principles of socialist internationalism and would follow the lead of the Soviet Union in these matters. The contribution of the constitution towards international human rights was in the realisation of socialism within the GDR and internationalism under the leadership of the Soviet Union. Because capitalism and imperialism were the source of war and conflict, this partnership with the USSR would in turn contribute to global peace through the spread of self-determination beyond the bound-aries of the socialist world.

---

[21] Ulbricht, "1968– Jahr wichtiger Entscheidungen." Propaganda in the media also linked the realisation of the socialist constitution to the longer history of the German struggle for human rights. Hermann Klenner, "Frei von dreifacher Bürde: Eine Betrachtung über die Menschenrechte in unserer sozialistischen Verfassung," *Neues Deutschland* (30.3.1968).

[22] Mark Allinson, *Politics and Popular Opinion in East Germany 1945–1968* (Manchester: Manchester University Press, 2000), 142–43.

[23] Article 1. Verfassung der DDR vom 6.4.1968 (www.documentarchiv.de/ddr).

[24] The first recorded use of the phrase came in 1828, by the French socialist Amand Bazard, ostensibly citing French theorist Henri Saint-Simon. William Clare Roberts, *Marx's Inferno: The Political Theory of Capital* (Princeton, NJ: Princeton University Press, 2016), 110–19. The phrase was already used in the SED's "Manifesto to the German People" in 1946.

In promoting its human rights achievements, the SED not only touted the social and economic benefits of socialism but also explicitly promised to fulfil the UN Covenant on Political and Civil Rights. The propaganda released by the KSM portrayed the GDR as a true political democracy where all power was held by the people.[25] In the pamphlet on political and civil rights written by Hermann Klenner for the International Year, he argued,

In contrast to an authoritarian state doctrine which actually defines the people as those who do not govern, we maintain that the workers and farmers are not only there to vote but also to govern. Democracy is not that kind of rule in which the forming of the government and legislation depend on periodical elections. Democracy is rather a form of rule in which the people are entitled and in a position creatively to shape their own living conditions. [...] The basic rights of the collective self-government to which every citizen is entitled consists in the fact that every member of our state has the right as a member of a sovereign people to take a creative part in the exercise of power at any time and in every relevant sphere of social guidance.[26]

Rather than hide the contents of the recently passed UN Human Rights Covenants from the public, the full text was presented in an appendix with each article printed beside the corresponding laws of the GDR, which sometimes ran paragraphs longer than the UN text.[27] If readers were not convinced by the quality of human rights in the GDR, they would at least be impressed by the quantity.

Following the mass consultation, the plebiscite in April 1968 was approved with 95 percent in favour of the new constitution.[28] While this was written off in West Germany as a propaganda stunt, the SED used the new constitution and the *Volksaussprache* as the central evidence for the fact that the GDR was a legitimate state in line with the norms of

---

[25] This contradicts the claims that Eastern Bloc countries openly rejected political human rights or only supported economic and social rights. Ignatieff, *Human Rights as Politics and Idolatry*, 19; Aryeh Neier, *The International Human Rights Movement* (Princeton, NJ: Princeton University Press, 2012), 85.

[26] Hermann Klenner, *Civil Rights in the GDR* (Berlin: Committee for the Protection of Human Rights, 1967), 5.

[27] Another pamphlet on the Economic, Social and Cultural Rights Covenant was also published in German, English and French. Willi Büchner-Uhder, *Socialist Human Rights in the GDR, on the Right to Cooperate in the Management of the State, Economy and Culture by All Citizens of the GDR* (Berlin: Committee for the Protection of Human Rights, 1968); Willi Büchner-Uhder, *Les Droits de l'homme du système socialiste en République démocrate allemande* (Berlin: Comité pour la protection des droits de l'homme, 1968); Willi Büchner-Uhder, *Sozialistische Menschenrechte in der DDR* (Berlin: Komitee zum Schutze der Menschenrechte, 1968).

[28] On the results of the plebiscite, see Allinson, *Politics and Popular Opinion in East Germany 1945–1968*, 145.

international human rights.[29] East Germany could not attend as a non-member, but it still issued a declaration to the UN-organised First International Conference on Human Rights, held in Tehran a month after the constitutional plebiscite in May 1968. In Tehran, the primary enemy of human rights for the assembled delegations was not state socialism, but Western imperialism, South African apartheid and Zionism as a colonial project.[30] Hosted by the Shah of Iran, a "development dictator" who had achieved power through a CIA-engineered coup in 1953, more than two-thirds of the 83 countries that sent delegates to the conference were run by non-democratic governments.[31] In addition to an academic colloquium held in East Berlin, the SED issued an official declaration to the participants in Tehran.[32] It argued that,

The decision of the people of the GDR on a new constitution is convincing proof of the realization of the UN Charter and of the right to self-determination as fixed by the human rights covenants, by virtue of which the people freely choose their political status.

To prove its case, the declaration referenced the 12,454 letters received by the GDR constitutional commission with suggestions for changes (which resulted in 118 revisions), and the 11,536,803 citizens who officially voted in favour of the constitution (while also mentioning the 409,733 votes against and the 24,353 spoiled ballots).[33] To demonstrate the centrality of self-determination to East German politics, the SED aimed to highlight not just the overwhelming support of the people but also their universal participation in the political process.

---

[29] See "Für immer beseitigt," *Der Spiegel* 16 (1968), 53.

[30] Whelan, *Indivisible Human Rights*, 151. Recent accounts are divided on the significance of the Tehran Conference: Burke argues that the conference is evidence that anti-colonial human rights had degenerated into cover for authoritarianism, while Jensen is more positive about its role in reviving global human rights. Roland Burke, "From Individual Rights to National Development: The First UN International Conference on Human Rights, Tehran, 1968," *Journal of World History* 19, no. 3 (2008). Jensen, *The Making of International Human Rights.*

[31] Burke, "From Individual Rights to National Development," 283.

[32] The KSM organised a colloquium to run in parallel to Tehran on human rights and self-determination at Humboldt University in East Berlin, which was attended by some from the non-socialist world. Komitee zum Schutze der Menschenrechte in der DDR, *Self-Determination and Human Rights: 1968 Results in the Two German States* (Dresden: Zeit im Bild, 1968); Forberger, *Das DDR-Komitee für Menschenrechte*, 238–40.

[33] BArch, DY30/J IV 2/2/116 Erklärung der Regierung der DDR an die Internationale Konferenz über Menschenrechte vom 22.4. bis 13.5.1968 in Teheran. 2. The statistics presented publicly matched the numbers used by the SED for non-propaganda purposes. Harry Dettenborn and Karl Mollnau, *Rechtsbewußtsein und Rechtserziehung* (Berlin: Staatsverlag der DDR, 1976), 95. For the comments and criticisms of East Germans during the *Volksaussprache*, see Chapter 4.

Although East German propaganda for the International Year for Human Rights fixated on the new constitution, the most transformative actions took place behind the scenes. On 9 October 1968, Foreign Minister Otto Winzer sent a declaration to UN Secretary General U Thant formally announcing the GDR's desire to sign the 1966 UN Human Rights Covenants, the International Convention on the Elimination of All Forms of Racial Discrimination, the Genocide Convention and numerous UNESCO and International Labour Organization and conventions as soon as it became a UN member and was thus eligible to do so.[34] This letter represented the end of a nearly year-long process that began in November 1967, when Foreign Minister Winzer sent a letter to more than a dozen government departments, party organs and organisations asking for a comprehensive review of the Human Rights Covenants and the 1965 International Convention on the Elimination of All Forms of Racial Discrimination.[35] Winzer asked that officials determine whether any of the rights included conflicted with GDR laws, norms or practices and – if so – what reforms would be required for the SED to sign on to them.[36]

Rather than provoking self-criticism, two decades of propaganda had laid the groundwork for East German officials to equate the total realisation of human rights with SED rule. When the various departments reported back to Winzer, the responses were uniformly optimistic and recommended that the GDR sign on to the covenants with only minor reservations.[37] A summary report sent to Walter Ulbricht seven months later claimed, "the problems and questions raised are not so grave, however, that the affirmation by the GDR of the International Covenants would be called into question."[38] The response of Chief Prosecutor Josef Streit is indicative of the general tone of the feedback. While a 1966 report from Amnesty International on the criminal justice system of the GDR concluded: "It is hard to see how a society which guarantees

---

[34] PA AA, MfAA, C487/76 Winzer to U Thant (9.10.1968) File number 1–4.
[35] The internal deliberations are documented in PA AA, MfAA, C487/76 Vorbereitung des Anschlusses und Beitrittserklärung der DDR an die Konventionen über wirt. 1967–1968 UN Konventionen.
[36] These included the League for International Cooperation; the Supreme Court; the Ministries of Justice, Health, Education, Culture, Finance, Higher Education and the Interior; the General State Prosecutor's Office; the State Office for Work; the State Central Administration for Statistics; the KSM; the State Office for Job Training; and the Stasi.
[37] The summary report on the feedback from all departments was collected in PA AA, MfAA, C487/76 Einzelfragen, die aus der unterschiedlichen Regelung bestimmter Komplexe durch das nationale Recht der DDR und durch die Bestimmungen der beiden Menschenrechtskonventionen resultieren.
[38] BArch DA5/660 Kohrt to Ulbricht (22.5.1968).

to its citizens any kind of elementary 'human rights' may be developed in East Germany without some radical changes not only in the penal code but also in the whole concept and organization of the judicial system," Streit did not see any significant potential conflicts between international human rights law and the East German criminal justice system.[39] Streit admitted that some rarely used legal provisions that allowed for work as a form of criminal punishment and the absence of a complex criminal appeals process could be problematic, but fundamentally, "the practice of law enforcement organs in the GDR has for a long time corresponded to the basic rights as determined by the UN General Assembly and in [the ICCPR]." Regarding the convention on racial discrimination, he posited, that "due to the extermination of the social roots of fascism and the subsequent punishment of those in the territory of the GDR responsible for Nazi racial policy, these provisions are hardly an issue."[40]

East German officials did not completely dismiss the risks that the covenants could pose domestically, but they believed them to be manageable through proper public education. Several departments agreed that propaganda efforts would be necessary to address the articles of the covenants that were "no longer relevant "because they had been "overtaken by our social development." Specifically, these officials raised concerns that certain rights could "be exploited by oppositional forces against the GDR" including "the right to emigration, a right to absolute freedom of information, [and] the right to strike."[41] The internal review adopted Hermann Klenner's theory that human rights had evolved in accordance with the historical progress of society as a whole, and as such, rights that had been indispensable in an oppressive bourgeois society were now superfluous, or even harmfully egoistical, in a socialist society. It would be just as irrational for workers to strike against themselves as to emigrate from the workers' and peasants' state.

In contrast to Ulbricht's impulsive application for UN membership in 1966, the internal process of reviewing the covenants had been slow and methodical. The Ministry of Foreign Affairs began reviewing the documents in November 1967 and only at the end of May 1968 did it confirm to Ulbricht that the GDR was already in almost total compliance.[42] Following personal approval from Ulbricht to move forward, the vast

[39] Amnesty International, *Prison Conditions in East Germany: Conditions for Political Prisoners* (London: Amnesty International, 1966), 51.
[40] BArch, DP3/102 Streit to Winzer (4.12.1967).
[41] PA AA, MfAA C 487/76 Abteilung International Organisation "Bemerkungen zur Vorlage über die Erklärung der Bereitschaft der DDR zum Beitritt zu den beiden UN-Menschenrechtskonventionen vom 16.12.1966" (19.9.1968), 3.
[42] BArch, DA5/660 Kohrt to Ulbricht (22.5.1968).

bureaucracy of the GDR swung into action once again. On 19 July, the Council of Ministers drafted a declaration and sent it to the *de jure* highest authority, the Council of State, of which Ulbricht was chair. On 9 September, it was sent back to the Council of Ministers for revisions to deal with ambiguous language.[43] On 20 September, a new draft was approved by the State Council and signed by Ulbricht.[44] Only then was the formal commitment sent to U Thant.

Through this long and winding road, SED officials from the junior levels of the state bureaucracy to the Politburo had examined the problem of human rights and the UN Covenants in great detail with a mind to potential pitfalls. All these officials came to the same conclusion: international human rights, as defined by the United Nations, were not a threat to SED rule. The UN human rights system was assumed to be a natural ally of the socialist cause and the affirmation of the covenants an inherent good. While officials may have had a generally positive inclination towards human rights prior to 1967, the process of approving the UN Human Rights Covenants demanded that these functionaries make a positive connection between a collection of legal articles in the UN treaties and the practices of East German state socialism within their realms of specialisation. At the beginning of 1968, Walter Ulbricht had called the new socialist Constitution a "contribution to the Year for Human Rights" – by the end of 1968, Foreign Minister Winzer confidently declared that the new constitution was "the codification of human rights in the socialist state of the German nation."[45] The SED's motive for affirming the UN Covenants was based on a desire to convince the rest of the world that it stood for human rights, but the very process of codifying this conviction served to reinforce the elite's sense of their own righteousness and the total fidelity of the GDR to the norms of the UN system.

Impact of the International Year for Human Rights

In contrast to the limited impact of the KSM in the early 1960s, the idea of socialist human rights and rights talk in general became much more

---

[43] BArch, DA5/660 Gotsche to Stoph (9.9.1968).

[44] PA AA, MfAA, C487/76 Beschluß des Staatsrates der DDR über die Bereitschaft der DDR zum Beitritt zu den UNO-Menschenrechtskonventionen vom 20.9.1968, File number 9–10.

[45] "Rede des Ministers Otto Winzer, am 9.12.1968 in Berlin anläßlich des 20. Jahrestages der Annahme der 'Allgemeine Deklaration über die Menschenrechte,' durch die UNO," *Dokumente zur Außenpolitik der DDR, 1968.* Band XVI (Berlin: Staatsverlag der DDR, 1971), 482.

prevalent in East German public discourse after 1968. Media coverage of Human Rights Day – 10 December – had previously maintained a narrow focus on imprisoned workers and failures of democracy in West Germany (usually written by members of the KSM), but by the end of the decade, it was used by professional journalists as an opportunity to denounce the global crimes of imperialism. In 1969, the diplomatic correspondent for the *Berliner Zeitung* laid out a picture of Western hypocrisy,

Human Rights Day – the governments of the USA and Israel or the regime in Athens or in Portugal or in Spain have the nerve to solemnly celebrate it? They have the impudence to do so as if there were no [My Lai] and no concentration camps in the Aegean, no colonial war in Angola and no napalm attacks on Arab women and children. And yet all these imperialist regimes have affirmed the Universal Declaration of Human Rights as members of the UN. It just looks different in practice. For imperialism and human rights are mutually exclusive.[46]

The only mention of West Germany came in a passing reference to the Federal Republic's lack of a right to work. The KSM's embrace of socialist human rights as a global struggle against racism, fascism and colonialism had moved beyond select circles to become the norm for state media coverage of world affairs.

A range of reference works and educational texts were also updated to include the new interpretation of human rights. In the widely distributed *Short Political Dictionary* the space devoted to the idea of rights doubled between the 1967 and 1974 editions.[47] Although the 1965 edition of the *Philosophical Dictionary* did not contain an entry on human rights, the 1974 version had an extensive five-page definition.[48] The *Dictionary of the Socialist State*, first published in 1974, included a capsule history of human rights:

After the Second World War – as the result of the struggle against fascism which violated every human right and as part of the struggle for peace – the UN Charter declared the promotion and protection of human rights as the universal task in

---

[46] Klaus Wilczynski, "Menschenrechte," *Berliner Zeitung* (10.12.1969), 1.

[47] The 1967 edition devoted two pages to the Basic Rights and Duties of the Citizen, while the 1974 edition expanded the entry on basic rights and added one on the right to political participation and co-determination for a total of four pages. The entry on the SED was four pages in both editions. Georg König, *Kleines politisches Wörterbuch* (Berlin: Dietz, 1967); Waltraud Böhme, *Kleines politisches Wörterbuch* (Berlin: Dietz, 1973).

[48] Georg Klaus and Manfred Buhr, *Philosophisches Wörterbuch* (Leipzig: Bibliographisches Institut, 1965) and *Philosophisches Wörterbuch. Bd. 2.* (Leipzig: Bibliographisches Institut, 1974), 779–84.

the context of peaceful international cooperation on the basis of the equality of all states and the non-interference in the inner affairs of other states.[49]

School textbooks began to use the absence of human rights in the United States as a pedagogical tool; a lesson on proper comma placement included example sentences about the assassination of Martin Luther King, "a fighter for the human rights of the coloured people in the USA."[50] Officials now had numerous sources that defined the party line, and young people were encouraged to view international injustice through the lens of human rights.

The language of rights also became more prevalent in East German domestic law. A revised Criminal Code, also introduced in 1968, stated that the socialist order "ensures that every citizen can shape his life in full compliance with his dignity, his freedom and human rights in accordance with the rights and interests of the socialist society, the state and its citizens," and that the "dignity of man, his freedom and his rights are protected under the criminal laws of the socialist state."[51] The death penalty in the new code was reserved for those who committed "crimes against the sovereignty of the GDR, peace, humanity and human rights or serious crimes against the GDR."[52] This phrasing echoed the language of the secret "shooting order" issued to Berlin Wall guards that justified the use of lethal force against those attempting to escape to prevent "a crime against the sovereignty of the German Democratic Republic, against peace, humanity, and human rights."[53] Rights also became more prevalent in civil and family law cases, for example, parents who exercised their right (and duty) to work were more likely to gain custody of children in the case of a divorce. In contrast to West Germany, where working mothers were severely discriminated against by the state in regard to child custody, GDR courts often punished non-working parents, male or female alike, by denying or significantly reducing alimony payments and state benefits. The basic rights of a parent could also serve as a mitigating factor in certain circumstances. In a 1971 divorce case, the decision of a mother to move to another city away from her child to attend university was not allowed by the court to

---

[49] Akademie der Wissenschaften, *Wörterbuch zum sozialistischen Staat* (Berlin: Dietz, 1974), 185.

[50] Quoted in John Rodden, *Textbook Reds: Schoolbooks, Ideology, and Eastern German Identity* (University Park: Pennsylvania State Press, 2010), 21, 27.

[51] Chapter 1, Article 2, and Chapter 1, Article 4, in *Strafgesetzbuch der DDR -StGB- vom 12. Januar 1968* (www.verfassungen.de/de/ddr/strafgesetzbuch68.htm).

[52] Moritz Vormbaum, *Das Strafrecht der DDR* (Tübingen: Mohr Siebeck, 2015), 342–44.

[53] Bernhard Pollmann, *Lesebuch zur deutschen Geschichte, Bd. 3* (Dortmund: Chronik Verlag, 1984), 245–46.

prejudice her claims to custody as she was only exercising her right to education. The exercise of one's rights and duties was rewarded, while the failure to do so could result in serious consequences.[54]

State security organs also began to more thoroughly engage with human rights language. In 1969, the charter of the Ministry of State Security outlining its primary tasks and duties now covered the investigation and prevention of crimes that targeted "the sovereignty of the German Democratic Republic, peace, humanity, and human rights."[55] The officials of the GDR state security apparatus not only saw human rights as a core component of their responsibilities but it appears they also had a solid grasp of the ideological terms underlying this new vocabulary. In a report on local church engagement with international human rights issues in the town of Gera, the Interior Ministry differentiated between those who sought to achieve real human rights through international solidarity and those who were simply pawns of the imperialists and employing human rights for anti-communist ends.[56] The language of human rights was not suppressed outright, but carefully policed for its fidelity to socialist ideology.

One part of this dissemination process was the reinvention of the Committee for the Protection of Human Rights as a think tank rather than mass protest organisation. By 1967 there were no more KPD prisoners to advocate for or custody battles to assist in, and (as discussed in Chapter 2) a new communist party, the Deutsche Kommunistische Partei, had established itself in the Federal Republic in 1968, with the tacit permission of the state.[57] Unofficially, the shift began with the KSM producing pamphlets on how the GDR fulfilled the terms of the UN Covenants for the International Year for Human Rights and in 1969, this new role was formalised. Secretary Siegfried Forberger proposed a new set of guidelines for the Committee: first, it would be renamed the DDR-Komitee für Menschenrechte (Committee for Human Rights in the GDR, KMR); second, it would turn its focus towards the fight for

---

[54] Inga Markovits, "Socialist vs. Bourgeois Rights," *University of Chicago Law Review* 45 (1978), 616.

[55] Quoted in Agnès Bensussan, "Einige Charakteristika der Repressionspolitik gegenüber politisch abweichendem Verhalten in der DDR in den 70er und 80er Jahren," in *Die ostdeutsche Gesellschaft: eine transnationale Perspektive*, ed. Sandrine Kott and Emmanuel Droit (Berlin: Ch. Links, 2006), 74.

[56] Thüringisches Staatsarchiv-Rudolstadt (Thuringian State Archives, Rudolstadt) ThSA-R 5-61-1000/7 Bezirkstag und Rat des Bezirkes Gera 17308 "Information zur Diskussion über die Fragen der Menschenrechte in den Kirchen" (1974).

[57] The party was legally founded in Frankfurt, West Germany, on 25 September 1968. Heike Amos, *Die SED-Deutschlandpolitik 1961 bis 1989* (Göttingen: Vandenhoeck & Ruprecht, 2015), 265.

international human rights, self-determination and peace against the forces of imperialism; third, it would work domestically to ensure the realisation of socialist human rights at home by monitoring state agencies and consulting on new laws.[58]

Albert Norden – the chief SED propagandist and supervisor of the KSM since its founding in 1959 – and the SED Central Committee reviewed Forberger's proposal, with a split decision. The new international mandate was approved, but the Committee would have no domestic tasks outside of disseminating information on socialist human rights. Another stipulation required the name to be the GDR-Committee for Human Rights (KMR), rather than the Committee for Human Rights in the GDR. Norden evidently feared that Forberger's suggested name would encourage outsiders to see the organisation as a vehicle for East Germans to demand their human rights against the SED, and that it could become a magnet for complaints from citizens and foreigners alike.[59] Given that in the Soviet Union, in that very same month, a group of dissidents had formed the Initiative Group for the Defence of Human Rights in the USSR, Norden's concerns were not unreasonable.[60]

According to the new – Central Committee approved – guidelines, the KMR had three major goals: first, campaign to "secure peace – the highest of all human rights – against imperialist aggression and intervention"; second, to fight for the "total realization of the right to self-determination" in the face of "Nazism, racism and neo-colonial extortion"; and third, to work for "international cooperation for the furthering of human rights." This work would be conducted in compliance with the GDR Constitution, the UN Charter, the UDHR and the 1966 UN Human Rights Covenants. Alongside these three core objectives, the Committee was also supposed to promote the candidacy of East Germany for membership in the United Nations. The Committee was to accomplish these goals by disseminating information on "the theory and practice of socialist human rights in the GDR" to West Germany and other foreign countries, and by expressing solidarity "through words and

---

[58] Forberger, *Das DDR-Komitee für Menschenrechte*, 282. Aside from Forberger's memoir, there is no evidence to confirm that the committee sought a domestic prerogative in 1969. While his claims could be a self-serving effort to positively portray the committee, Hermann Klenner and other GDR intellectuals did express their support for securing "subjective rights" through "administrative law" within a system of "socialist legality" prior to the 1958 Babelsberg purges. See Chapter 5 for later requests by the committee to deal with domestic claims.

[59] Forberger, *Das DDR-Komitee für Menschenrechte*, 283.

[60] Robert Horvath, "Breaking the Totalitarian Ice: The Initiative Group for the Defense of Human Rights in the USSR," *Human Rights Quarterly* 36, no. 1 (2014): 147–75.

actions" with both the victims of imperialism and all democrats who strive for the realisation of human rights.[61]

Although the committee had been on the verge of dissolution in 1968, it survived to celebrate its 10th anniversary in 1969, albeit with a new name and a new mission. Rather than shuttering the group, Walter Ulbricht and the Central Committee sent the KSM (now the KMR) a letter of congratulations praising its members for acting "in full accordance with the principles and objectives of the Socialist Constitution of our state, the Charter of the United Nations, the UDHR and the UN Human Rights Covenants." According to Ulbricht, the committee "is led, in word and deed, by the supreme of all human rights – to secure peace."[62] Fighting for peace had always been part of the committee's mandate, but now it had shifted from being an outcome of the antifascist propaganda campaigns against West Germany, to becoming vehicle for realising world peace through international solidarity.

The KMR now turned to a variety of foreign causes, many of which were also the subjects of Western human rights campaigning. The committee continued to condemn imperialism and the US war in Vietnam but added new causes as they developed. The committee produced a bulletin on campaign activities – translated into both French and English for international consumption – and published small articles in the East German press expressing their concern, shock and outrage at incidents in Latin America, Greece, Southeast Asia and South Africa.[63] As part of the UN International Year to Combat Racism and Discrimination, the committee launched a major campaign to support the persecuted African-American Communist activist Angela Davis.[64] Writing on her behalf to the judge presiding at her trial, the committee proclaimed that "Angela

---

[61] BArch, DZ7/71 Ziele, Aufgaben und Arbeitsweise des DDR-Komitees für Menschenrechte, 1–5. According to Forberger, the duty to ensure the realisation of socialist human rights within the borders of the GDR was originally a main task of the committee until it was removed by Norden. Forberger, *Das DDR-Komitee für Menschenrechte*, 281–83.

[62] BArch, DZ7/69 Ulbricht to the GDR Committee for Human Rights (21.5.1969).

[63] Press clippings on committee activities (1969–75), BArch, DZ7/14-19.

[64] Sebastian Gehrig, "Reaching Out to the Third World: East Germany's Anti-Apartheid and Socialist Human Rights Campaign," *German History* 36, no. 4 (2018), 574–97. Katrina Hagen, "Ambivalence and Desire in the East German 'Free Angela Davis' Campaign," in *Comrades of Color: East Germany in the Cold War World*, ed. Quinn Slobodian (New York: Berghahn, 2015), 157–87; Sophie Lorenz, "'Heldin des anderen Amerikas' Die DDR-Solidaritätsbewegung für Angela Davis, 1970–1973," *Zeithistorische Forschungen* 10 (2013), 38–60 (www.zeithistorische-forschungen.de); Natalia King Rasmussen, "Friends of Freedom, Allies of Peace: East Germany and the African-American Civil Rights Movement, 1945–1989." PhD diss., Boston College, 2014.

Davis is a symbol for that section of the American population which is coming out against the racist policies of the US Administration both at home, and in Vietnam, out of a sense of loyalty to the principles enunciated in the United Nations Charter and the Universal Declaration of Human Rights."[65] While the committee no longer sought to mobilise workers for specific campaigns, it continued to hold events for its members, which weighed in on the conflict in South Asia, condemned Pakistani efforts to suppress the Bangladeshi right to self-determination and hosted events for visiting Egyptians who denounced Israeli human rights abuses in the wake of the 1972 War.[66] In 1973, the committee focused primarily on human rights abuses in South Africa in coordination with a UN initiative to pass a new convention against apartheid.[67] The following year, it returned to its traditional role of fighting for the release of prisoners, but this time campaigning on behalf of socialists imprisoned by military Juntas in Chile and Uruguay, in particular the head of the Chilean Communist Party, Luis Corvalan.[68] Absent from their campaigns was any discussion of the Biafran War, which was instrumental in launching a new wave of Western humanitarian NGOs, but was likely ignored due to Soviet support for the ruling Nigerian government and its military campaign against the rebellion.[69] Abuses in and by socialist states were never discussed.

The events of 1968 and the proliferation of human rights propaganda and usage by GDR state organs in the years following were all tangible manifestations of a worldview that had securely anchored human rights into its ideology. The SED, loyal intellectuals, educational officials, the judiciary and the security services had assimilated three general ideas: first, that East Germany was a champion of human rights (as defined by the United Nations), especially in comparison to the horrors perpetrated by Western imperialism; second, the socialist world enjoyed a kind of human rights that was qualitatively different and inherently superior to the human rights of the bourgeois world; and third, human rights were intertwined with the principles of self-determination and

---

[65] BArch, DZ7/27 Friedel Malter to Judge Richard Arnason (2.6.1972).

[66] The SED used the Bangladeshi independence movement as leverage to gain recognition from India: Srinath Raghavan, *1971: A Global History of the Creation of Bangladesh* (Cambridge, MA: Harvard University Press, 2013), 157–58.

[67] An indicative statement from the committee is "DDR-Komitee verurteilt Apartheid in Südafrika," *Berliner Zeitung* (11.10.1973).

[68] BArch, DZ7/70 Friedel Malter Rede (21.05.1974). On GDR aid for Chilean refugees, see Sebastian Koch, *Zufluchtsort DDR? Chilenische Flüchtlinge und die Ausländerpolitik der SED* (Paderborn: Verlag Ferdinand Schöningh, 2017).

[69] Lasse Heerten, *The Biafran War and Postcolonial Humanitarianism: Spectacles of Suffering* (Cambridge: Cambridge University Press, 2017).

non-interference in the internal affairs of sovereign nations. By the 1970s, when the SED engaged in an intense period of East-West diplomacy, elites in the GDR saw themselves as protagonists in the long history of human rights, finally fulfilling their promise to the cause, and not – as the West saw them – as hypocrites on the defensive against self-evidently superior democratic values.

From Tehran to the Helsinki Accords

While Ulbricht's plan to use human rights to finally achieve the diplomatic recognition the GDR so desperately craved had failed, the West German diplomatic blockade broke down nonetheless in 1969, when Cambodia established relations with the GDR. The Cambodian refusal to back down from its decision in the face of West German warnings of diplomatic and economic consequences heralded the end of the Federal Republic's Hallstein Doctrine.[70] Two days later, Cambodia was joined by the Ba'thist Revolutionary government in Iraq. Soon thereafter Sudan, Syria, Egypt and South Yemen all broke ties with the FRG to recognise the GDR. While the human rights rhetoric of the previous year had perhaps played a minor role, West Germany's faltering commitment to enforcing the blockade alongside East German promises of extensive loan guarantees were far more important factors. While this small wave of diplomatic exchange was a victory for the SED, it was limited and short-lived. In the same year, when the United Nations voted on the possible admission of the GDR to the World Health Organization only 19 countries supported its entry, with 59 opposing and 27 abstaining.[71] Although the GDR could now count on some support from the Middle East and Asia, the SED's hopes for universal recognition through solidarity with the Afro-Asian Bloc were dashed.

As the global option for UN recognition vanished, the possibilities for partial German reconciliation expanded through political changes in both the FRG and the GDR. The 1969 federal elections in West Germany brought an end to the Grand Coalition of the Christian Democrats (CDU/CSU) and the Social Democrats (SPD), and ushered in the first SPD-led coalition of the postwar era.[72] As mayor of West Berlin, Willy Brandt had vociferously denounced the East German human rights

---

[70] On the end of the Hallstein Doctrine, see Gray, *Germany's Cold War*, 212–19.

[71] Ibid., 204–5.

[72] The Brandt government was a coalition led by the SPD with the support of the liberal Free Democrats (FDP), which had previously served as the junior partner to the CDU/CSU from 1949 to 1966.

record, but as foreign minister in the Grand Coalition, and then as chancellor beginning in 1969, he pursued a more conciliatory policy of engagement with the East under the slogan of "change through rapprochement" (*Wandel durch Annäherung*).[73] The ascendancy of Brandt, and what would become known as the *Neue Ostpolitik*, undermined East Germany's *Westpolitik*, which depended on portraying the FRG as a hive of neo-Nazis, militarists and reactionaries.[74] In contrast to the Grand Coalition, which had been led by ex-Nazi Party member Kurt Georg Kiesinger, Brandt had unimpeachable antifascist credentials as a member of the anti-Nazi resistance during World War II.

The thaw in West Germany was matched by a new willingness to engage in the GDR with the ascendancy of Erich Honecker to the position of General Secretary of the SED in 1971. Walter Ulbricht had increasingly alienated Soviet leader Leonid Brezhnev, and thus Honecker was able to secure support from the USSR in deposing the long-time SED leader. Honecker had been imprisoned by the Nazis as a KPD member and after the war, founded the Free German Youth (FDJ), and rose up in the ranks to become Security Secretary of the Central Committee. Upon taking power, Honecker shifted the focus of East German foreign policy from Ulbricht's offensive posture to a new engagement with West Germany through a policy of "defensive pragmatism."[75] In 1971, the new leadership of the SED laid out three major foreign policy goals: first, the normalisation of relations with the West (and the Federal Republic in particular); second, the admission of the two German states into the United Nations; and third, active participation in the creation of a European peace and security treaty.[76] Each of these steps would require significant public commitments by the SED to the principles of human rights, which became a standard element of treaties, covenants and accords – the signing of which would grant the SED the international

---

[73] On German-German relations and the origins of *Ostpolitik*, see M. E. Sarotte, *Dealing with the Devil: East Germany, Détente, and Ostpolitik, 1969–1973* (Chapel Hill: University of North Carolina Press, 2001); Julia von Dannenberg, *The Foundations of Ostpolitik* (Oxford: Oxford University Press, 2008); Gottfried Niedhart, "Ostpolitik: Transformation through Communication and the Quest for Peaceful Change," *Journal of Cold War Studies* 18, no. 3 (2016), 14–59.

[74] On East German reaction to Brandt's *Ostpolitik*, see Wentker, *Außenpolitik in engen Grenzen*, 320.

[75] Bange, "The GDR in the Era of Détente," 67–70. Honecker was personally at the centre of foreign policy decision making in the GDR from 1971 until 1989. Wentker, *Außenpolitik in engen Grenzen*, 371.

[76] Federica Caciagli, "The GDR's Targets in the Early CSCE Process: Another Missed Opportunity to Freeze the Division of Germany, 1969–73," in *Origins of the European Security System: The Helsinki Process Revisited, 1965–75*, ed. Vojtech Mastny, Christian Nünlist and Andreas Wenger (London: Routledge, 2008), 112.

respectability it needed. In every case, the senior leadership continued to tout its commitment to human rights so long as the language in those provisions remained the same as in key UN treaties, which the SED had already affirmed.

The more flexible and conciliatory approach from both sides soon yielded diplomatic progress. Two agreements loosening travel restrictions set the stage for a treaty of recognition – the Basic Treaty – signed in 1972. While West German negotiators aimed to highlight the problem of human rights in the Basic Treaty, the concept was mentioned only once in the final text. West Germany prioritised family reunification, which many deemed a human rights issue, but this problem was dealt with primarily through private negotiations rather than public diplomacy.[77] In the end, Article 2 stated that both countries would,

be guided by the aims and principles laid down in the United Nations Charter, especially those of the sovereign equality of all States, respect for their independence, autonomy and territorial integrity, the right of self-determination, the protection of human rights, and non-discrimination.[78]

According to Foreign Minister Winzer, "27 years after the end of the Second World War, 23 years after the formation of two independent German states, the socialist GDR and the imperialist FRG, this is a statement not only of international law, but also of historical importance."[79] For the FRG, however, the Basic Treaty signified something entirely different, namely the recognition of German division, but without the full recognition of the legitimacy of the GDR as an independent state under international law.[80]

The diverging interpretations of the treaty extended to the very meaning of rights and self-determination. While the language of the treaty suggested a version of human rights in keeping with the SED's emphasis on state sovereignty (instead of any kind of supernational recognition of individual liberal freedoms), this interpretation was challenged by West German conservatives. The government of Bavaria sought to invalidate the Basic Treaty, arguing that it violated the duty of the state, contained in the West German Basic Law, to pursue reunification and protect the rights of Germans living in the GDR.[81] The West German

---

[77] Sarotte, *Dealing with the Devil*, 153.
[78] The Basic Treaty (21.12.1972) (http://germanhistorydocs.ghi-dc.org).
[79] Quoted in Ingrid Muth, *Die DDR-Außenpolitik 1949–1972: Inhalte, Strukturen, Mechanismen* (Berlin: Ch. Links, 2000), 33 n. 54.
[80] Wentker, *Außenpolitik in engen Grenzen*, 345.
[81] Justin Collings, *Democracy's Guardians: A History of the German Federal Constitutional Court, 1951–2001* (Oxford: Oxford University Press, 2015), 138.

Constitutional Court, however, determined that while the treaty was legal, it did not provide *de jure* recognition of the GDR because to do so would in fact violate the Basic Law. It was the SED, however, not the West German state, which violated the Basic Law by suppressing the rights of Germans within its border.[82] The Constitutional Court thus found that the West German government was legally obliged to interfere in the internal affairs of the GDR and "in fulfilling its constitutional duties, to do everything possible to change and dismantle these inhuman conditions," including "the Wall, the barbed wire, the death strip, and the command to shoot."[83] Where the SED saw an agreement cementing its sovereignty on the ground on non-intervention, the West German court argued for the constitutional necessity of intervention to defend human rights.

Signing the Basic Treaty set off another round of diplomatic recognitions and, by the end of the 1972, 53 countries formally recognised the GDR as a sovereign state including many neutral and non-aligned countries in Europe, such as Sweden, Austria and Cyprus. While the United States delayed formal recognition, in early 1973, most of NATO including France, the United Kingdom, Italy and the Netherlands exchanged ambassadors with the GDR. The passage of the Basic Treaty cleared the final barrier to gaining UN membership and both East and West Germany finally became full members on 18 September 1973. Upon entry, the SED held to their pledge from 1968, and signed on to International Covenant on Economic, Social and Cultural Rights and the International Covenant on Civil and Political Rights.[84] In a statement to the United Nations, the SED proclaimed that "these Covenants promote the world-wide struggle for the enforcement of human rights, which is an integral part of the struggle for the maintenance and strengthening of peace," and that this in turn contributes to, "the joint struggle against their violation by aggressive policies, colonialism and apartheid, racism

---

[82] Ibid., 143.
[83] Quoted in Manfred Wilke, *The Path to the Berlin Wall: Critical Stages in the History of Divided Germany* (New York: Berghahn, 2014), 78. Sebastian Gehrig, "Cold War Identities: Citizenship, Constitutional Reform, and International Law between East and West Germany, 1967–75," *Journal of Contemporary History* 49, no. 4 (2014), 794–814.
[84] Wentker, *Außenpolitik in engen Grenzen*, 444. The GDR commitment to the covenants did not, however, include optional provisions that would allow the UN Human Rights Commission to consider charges brought forward by individuals or other states. Ernest Plock, *The Basic Treaty and the Evolution of East-West German Relations* (Boulder, CO: Westview Press, 1986), 101.

and other forms of assaults on the right of the peoples to self-determination."[85] Having subjected the texts of the covenants to such heavy scrutiny in 1967–1968, the decision to sign on to them in 1973 proceeded without controversy within the SED bureaucracy. The entry into the United Nations encouraged more diplomatic recognition across the world, and in January 1974, Fiji became the 100th nation to establish diplomatic ties with East Germany. Later that year, even the United States recognised East Germany as a sovereign country.

The signing of so many treaties paved the way to mass recognition, but it also prompted some citizens to challenge the government in the language of human rights. A pair of agreements on freer movement signed in 1971 and 1972 initially caused a spike in applications for travel and exit from the GDR.[86] Those early applications to leave made no mention of human rights (which had not been included in the travel agreements). As we shall see in Chapter 4, human rights language only became part of the repertoire of justifications within these applications – the vast majority of which were rejected – after the signing of the Basic Treaty.[87] The number of applications for exit visas once again increased a third time when the GDR joined the United Nations, with some applicants threatening to appeal to the Human Rights Commission. Although the continual rise in applications concerned SED officials, none of the reports entertained these claims as legitimate appeals to human rights, nor did anyone contemplate limiting future human rights commitments to prevent future spikes in emigration applications.

Having finally joined the United Nations, the SED did not let up on its human rights propaganda at home. On the international stage, there was little reason for the SED to perceive human rights politics as inherently antisocialist. East Germany used its platform at the UN to denounce apartheid as a violation of human rights and to support a Soviet-Guinean-Nigerian initiative to pass the International Convention on the Suppression and Punishment of the Crime of Apartheid (ICSPA) in 1973.[88] At the end of the year, the GDR joined with the United Nations in celebrating the 25th anniversary of the passage of the UDHR with a

---

[85] *Treaties and International Agreements Registered or Filed and Recorded with the Secretariat of the United Nations.* Vol. 999 (New York: United Nations, 1983), 294–95.

[86] Patrick Major, *Behind the Berlin Wall: East Germany and the Frontiers of Power* (Oxford: Oxford University Press, 2010), 202.

[87] The third quarter of 1972 saw a 27 percent increase in written applications to travel to the FRG or West Berlin while in-person applications jumped by 55 percent. In the fourth quarter, applications climbed another 60 percent. BArch, DA5/9026 Bericht über den Hauptinhalt der [...] Eingaben im III. Quartal 1972 und im IV. Quartal 1972.

[88] Roland Burke, "Human Rights Day 1973: The 'Liberation' of the Universal Declaration," *Humanitarianism & Human Rights Blog* (http://hhr.hypotheses.org/320).

flood of propaganda in various East German media.[89] Numerous stories ran in East German media in which SED officials proudly expounded on the strengthened position of the GDR in the fight for "peace, international security, the defence of human rights and the abolition of colonialism," through its membership in the United Nations.[90] The television program *The Black Channel*, which showed clips of Western news media followed by socialist commentary from host Karl-Eduard von Schnitzler, ran an episode on human rights in December in conjunction with Human Rights Day. In responding to a West German commemoration of the UDHR that deplored the continued use of torture in many parts of the world, von Schnitzler pointed to the NATO allies of the Federal Republic, such as Turkey or the United Kingdom in Northern Ireland, as practitioners of torture alongside the Chilean Junta and the South Vietnamese military regime.[91]

In West Germany, activists continued to contest the human rights proclamations of the GDR, but with little impact on SED behaviour. A new NGO, the Gesellschaft für Menschenrechte (Society for Human Rights, or GfM), was founded in Frankfurt am Main in 1972 with the mission of campaigning against abuses in the GDR and the socialist bloc. In contrast to Amnesty International, which presented itself as politically neutral (or Amnesty's German chapter, which promoted democracy within West Germany), the GfM explicitly targeted the human rights abuses of state socialism. In the 1950s, nationalist groups demanding reunification sought to delegitimise the GDR through human rights, but now, the protection of human rights had become the core purpose for such organisations, rather than a means to an end.[92] The group made headlines in the Federal Republic, but internationally, anti-imperialism remained the dominant theme of international human rights politics. As one report prepared for the CDU's even more conservative Bavarian sister-party, the Christian Social Union (CSU), lamented, "With the change in majorities in the bodies of world organizations – particularly in the [UN] General Assembly – the socialist states have recognized the possibility of the politicization of human rights, and the free world has almost cleared off the field without a fight.... Above all, the GDR has incorporated from the beginning and with great aggressiveness its

---

[89] Press clippings in BArch, DZ7/18. A commemorative stamp was released, but it prosaically showed only a flame.

[90] "DDR-Mitarbeit in UNO dient dem Frieden: Botschafter Peter Florin gab Interview für 'Horizont,'" *Neues Deutschland* (3.1.1974), 5.

[91] Deutsches Rundfunkarchiv (DRA), Der schwarze Kanal, E084–05-02/0003/051 Nr. 714 "Menschenrechte" und Rechte der Menschen (17.12.1973).

[92] On the founding of the GfM, see Wüst, *Menschenrechtsarbeit im Zwielicht*, 58–71.

concept of human rights in its foreign policy." Due to "the US by its human rights abstinence [and] the Western European countries by their regionalism," the socialist bloc now held the advantage in the field of human rights at the UN – even according to the deeply anti-communist CSU.[93]

Socialist Human Rights and the Helsinki Negotiations

Most accounts of the Helsinki negotiations take it as a given that "the Soviet Union and its allies [...] actively resisted the inclusion of human rights norms," but the Eastern Bloc's stance was more nuanced.[94] The point of contention between East and West was not the inclusion of human rights, but rather what kind of human rights would be included, and for what purpose? There are no transcripts of the actual negotiations, but archival sources allow for the reconstruction of the East German negotiating position through directives sent by the Politburo from 1973 to 1975.[95] For the SED, the goal of the Helsinki negotiations was to cement recognition of East Germany's borders with the Federal Republic and Poland and to ensure that the GDR would still be able to maintain controls over cross-border traffic of people, goods and information. The SED remained wholly dependent on the support of the Soviets in pursuing these goals, and all directives for the East German delegation and their assessments of the negotiations "were the result of previous consultations between the Soviet and the East German chief delegate."[96] At the same time, the GDR did pursue its own agenda while working hand in glove with the USSR.

In the lead-up to the negotiations, the SED leadership did not perceive the inclusion of human rights language as inherently threatening, but rather feared that the agreement could enshrine a "bourgeois" conception of human rights that was ideologically "slanted" towards the West. In 1973, the earliest Politburo directive that explicitly mentioned the problem of human rights instructed the GDR negotiators to

---

[93] BArch, B137/10780 Dieter Blumenwitz, "Selbstbestimmung und Menschenrechte im Geteilten Deutschland aus der Sicht der Konferenz für Sicherheit und Zusammenarbeit in Europa" (November 1974), 11.

[94] Daniel Thomas, "Human Rights Ideas, the Demise of Communism, and the End of the Cold War," *Journal of Cold War Studies* 7, no. 2 (2005), 113.

[95] I am indebted to Anja Hanisch's excellent research, which crucially informs this section. Anja Hanisch, *Die DDR im KSZE-Prozess 1972–1985: Zwischen Ostabhängigkeit, Westabgrenzung und Ausreisebewegung* (Munich: Oldenbourg, 2012).

[96] Hermann Wentker, "Pursuing Specific Interests within the Warsaw Pact: The GDR and the CSCE-Process," in *The Helsinki Process: A Historical Reappraisal*, ed. Carla Meneguzzi Rostagni (Padova: CEDAM, 2005), 45–51.

circumvent the inclusion of human rights in the Statement of Principles, but also told the delegates, that "a reference to respect for human rights and fundamental freedoms in the various states, separate from the Statement of Principles is possible." While they opposed a Vatican proposal to include a section on human rights and "freedom of opinion, conscience and belief," they did authorise the negotiators to embrace language "in accordance with the draft of the UN Declaration on Religious Tolerance."[97]

SED directives throughout 1974 maintained this red line: mentioning human rights in accordance with UN documents was acceptable; human rights language proposed by the West was not. A directive at the beginning of the year laid out the general strategy.

With respect to the principle of respect for human rights and fundamental freedoms, continue to adhere to the narrow formulation of the Soviet draft General Declaration. If the Western states make their agreement on the general declaration dependent on the inclusion of a section on individual rights and freedoms in the Statement of Principles, we could agree to a general mention of the UN Covenants on the Civil and Political Rights and on the Social, Economic and Cultural Rights. The GDR already belongs to the two Covenants.[98]

Three months later, another directive reiterated concerns over human rights statements proposed by the West regarding religious freedom, but specified (again) that references to the two UN Covenants to which the GDR already belonged was a possibility.[99] So long as human rights provisions were limited to the language of existing UN Covenants and principles, the SED would be insulated from danger.[100]

From the perspective of the SED delegation, the main concern was not the Politburo's fears surrounding references to human rights (although they did see certain human rights proposals as possible traps), but rather

---

[97] BArch, DY30/J IV 2/2/1444 Direktive für das weitere Auftreten der Delegation der DDR in der multilateralen Konsultation zur Vorbereitung der Sicherheitskonferenz in Helsinki (17.4.1973), 155–56.

[98] BArch, DY30/J IV 2/2/1486 Protokoll Nr. 2/74 Sitzung des Politbüros am 15.1.1974, Bericht, 56.

[99] BArch, DY30/J IV 2/2/1501 Bericht über die zweite Phase der Konferenz für Sicherheit und Zusammenarbeit in Europa und Direktive für das weitere Auftreten der Delegation der DDR, 3.

[100] Scholtyseck claims that this document shows how "human rights and fundamental freedoms were not to be included in the Final Act," even though the GDR negotiators were explicitly authorised to include mention of human rights if the terms conformed to UN norms. Joachim Scholtyseck, "GDR Dissidents and Human Rights Issues," in *From Helsinki to Belgrade: The First CSCE Follow-Up Meeting and the Crisis of Détente*, ed. Vladimir Bilandžić, Dittmar Dahlmann and Milan Kosanović (Göttingen: V&R Unipress, 2012), 287 n. 14.

the Basket III section of the agreement that concerned the increased flow of information and people across borders. While Basket III is often referred to as the "human rights section,"[101] at the time, its provisions were framed in terms of increased contact and "human relief," and as such the SED viewed the matters as separate. Siegfried Bock, the chief East German negotiator, reported in 1973 that the Western states were trying to undermine the SED's authority: "According to the West's assumption, the socialist states have to pay the 'price' of so-called 'human relief' in return for a multilateral recognition of frontiers."[102] Human rights in the Statement of Principles in Basket I and the Basket III provisions for reuniting families and allowing greater ease of travel and communication were not perceived as the same point of contention by the negotiating team or the Politburo, even if in later years these distinctions would become blurred by grassroots activists.

In the context of the SED's previous commitments, the human rights referenced in the Helsinki Accords appeared to be merely a repetition of earlier commitments made by the GDR. The final version of the Statement of Principles of the Accords included a very explicit guarantee of international human rights norms through "Principle VII: Respect for human rights and fundamental freedoms, including the freedom of thought, conscience, religion or belief," which held that the signatories would "act in conformity with" the UN Charter, the UDHR and the UN Human Rights Covenants. The specific location of this principle in the list of ten, sandwiched between "Principle VI Non-intervention in internal affairs" and "Principle VIII Equal rights and self-determination of peoples"– both of which contained prohibitions on interference in domestic affairs of the signatories – reinforced the seeming lack of danger.[103] In an interview after the fall of the GDR, Politburo member Hermann Axen, who had been intensely involved in the negotiations, noted that "it was important for us that the question of human rights came after the question of non-intervention, equality and sovereignty, the borders [...] in the catalogue of principles."[104] In this way, the text of

---

[101] The characterisation of Basket III as the human rights section, rather than the Statement of Principles in Basket I, is common in the historiography, based on the later use of Basket III provisions on travel and information by human rights activists. Richard Davy, "Helsinki Myths: Setting the Record Straight on the Final Act of the CSCE, 1975," *Cold War History* 9, no. 1 (2009), 1–22.

[102] Bange, "The GDR in the Era of Détente," 70.

[103] The Final Act of the Conference on Security and Cooperation in Europe, 1.8.1975, 14 I.L.M. 1292 (Helsinki Declaration) (www1.umn.edu/humanrts/osce/basics/finact75 .htm).

[104] Hermann Axen and Harald Neubert, *Ich war ein Diener der Partei: autobiographische Gespräche mit Harald Neubert* (Berlin: Edition Ost, 1996), 361.

the Helsinki Final Act echoed the "Declaration on Principles of International Law concerning Friendly Relations and Co-operation among States," adopted by the UN in 1970, which linked respect for human rights to the principles of non-interference in the affairs of sovereign nations, harkening back to the 1960 Declaration, which outlawed colonialism as a violation of human rights.[105] The order of the text and its wording seemed to firmly root the Helsinki Accords in the anti-colonial human rights diplomacy of the previous decade and a half, which put a strong emphasis on the inviolability of state sovereignty.

The SED's interpretation of human rights was supported by its socialist allies as well as many other Western adversaries. On the socialist side, the USSR, Bulgaria, Belarus, Ukraine, Hungary and Romania had all ratified the 1966 UN Human Rights Covenants prior to the conclusion of the Helsinki negotiations, in contrast to Western holdouts including France and the United States, which did not do so until afterwards.[106] Transcripts of conversations between Soviet leader Leonid Brezhnev and Erich Honecker from this period make clear that neither was terribly concerned about the human rights aspects of the Helsinki negotiations, and both presumed that the agreement would strengthen East German sovereignty.[107] Because Brezhnev had personally received assurances from US President Richard Nixon and Secretary of State Henry Kissinger that the agreement would not be used to foment domestic dissent and discord, the Soviet delegation firmly believed that the Western participants would respect the principle of non-interference in internal affairs.[108]

While negotiations were underway, some Western diplomats saw human rights as a means to "win" the Cold War, but the majority actually sought a workable agreement that would facilitate stability and cooperation rather than foment radical change.[109] Western negotiators did not disagree with the SED understanding that the phrasing of the Statement

---

[105] Jensen, *The Making of International Human Rights*, 217, 235–36.
[106] West Germany ratified the ICCPR in 1973; France in 1980; the United States not until 1992, having signed it in 1977.
[107] Hans-Hermann Hertle and Konrad Jarausch, *Risse im Bruderbund: Die Gespräche Honecker–Breshnew 1974 bis 1982* (Berlin: Ch. Links, 2006), 24.
[108] Svetlana Savranskaya, "Human Rights Movements in the USSR after the Signing of the Helsinki Final Act, and the Reaction of the Soviet Authorities," in *The Crisis of Détente in Europe: From Helsinki to Gorbachev 1975–1985*, ed. Leopoldo Nuti (London: Routledge, 2008).
[109] On offensive efforts, particularly by the Dutch, see Floribert Baudet, "'It Was Cold War and We Wanted to Win': Human Rights, 'Détente', and the CSCE," in *Origins of the European Security System: The Helsinki Process Revisited, 1965–75*, ed. Vojtech Mastny, Christian Nünlist and Andreas Wenger (London: Routledge, 2008), 183–98. On Helsinki as a vehicle for the status quo, see Jeremi Suri, "Détente and Human Rights:

of Principles weakened the possibilities for enforcing human rights provisions, which led the West German Christian Democrats to oppose the Helsinki Accords, making them the only major political party in Western Europe to do so.[110] Years later, a CDU politician recalled, "we saw things exactly as the Soviet Union did. Neither of us believed it [Basket III and human rights provisions] would lead anywhere."[111] In exile in the United States, the Soviet dissident Alexander Solzhenitsyn denounced the Helsinki Accords as "the funeral of Eastern Europe" because they included provisions guaranteeing non-intervention.[112] If SED leaders were fooled into thinking they were on safe ground in asserting the GDR's right to non-interference in the name of human rights, there were also many in the West who feared that they were correct.

Although the explicit references to human rights were not terribly threatening, the sections from Basket III of the treaty, on the free flow of information and people across borders, caused real reservations for high-ranking SED members. Minister of Ideology Kurt Hager, Secretary for Security Paul Verner and Stasi chief Erich Mielke, all voiced concerns that Basket III would be misused by the West. The SED would now face even more "misinformation" from Western television and radio and increased individual contacts with visitors would allow the infiltration of foreign provocateurs and intelligence agents.[113] In the end, Erich Honecker judged the security risks to be acceptable given the diplomatic payoff. Not only was he under immense Soviet pressure to sign, but Honecker also thought that the propaganda effects of a major foreign policy success and the international recognition for himself, as a head of state, was worth the risk of possibly increasing Western infiltration.[114] As

American and West European Perspectives on International Change," *Cold War History* 8, no. 4 (2008), 529.

[110] The specific wording of Principle VII was also weakened by using terms such as "respect" rather than "guarantee." Angela Romano, *From Détente in Europe to European Détente: How the West Shaped the Helsinki CSCE* (Brussels: P.I.E., 2009), 38, 42. The only Eastern Europeans to oppose the treaty were the Albanian Communist Party, which consistently refused to take part in the negotiations. US conservatives feared that the agreement represented a triumph for communism in Europe. China saw the Accords as a threatening improvement in US-Soviet relations. Bernd Schaefer, "'Europe Must Not Become Greater Finland,' Opponents of the CSCE – the German CDU/CSU and China," in *Origins of the European Security System*.

[111] Quoted in A. James McAdams, *Germany Divided: From the Wall to Reunification* (Princeton, NJ: Princeton University Press, 1994), 120.

[112] Quoted in Thomas, *The Helsinki Effect*, 124.

[113] Anja Hanisch, "Trügerische Sicherheit: Die KSZE und die Ausreisebewegung in der DDR 1975–1977," in *Der KSZE-Prozess: Vom Kalten Krieg Zu Einem Neuen Europa 1975 Bis 1990*, ed. Helmut Altrichter and Hermann Wentker (Munich: Oldenburg, 2011), 78.

[114] Wentker, "Pursuing Specific Interests within the Warsaw Pact," 55.

he told Brezhnev before signing the Accords, should the West illegally overstep the bounds of the treaty, "there will always be the *Staatssicherheit* [Stasi]."[115]

Charles Maier has argued that "Honecker's interpretation of Helsinki emphasized recognition, not human rights," but when we look closely at the internal documents, we can see that the SED saw the idea of human rights precisely as a means to advancing recognition.[116] Official East German doctrine on human rights, as first formulated by Hermann Klenner in 1964 and disseminated through the International Year for Human Rights in 1968, held that the GDR was a sovereign state based on the principles of self-determination, and thus all efforts to interfere in its internal affairs were a violation of international law and the United Nations-promoted principles of human rights. This conception of human rights allowed SED leaders to see the Helsinki Final Act as a compromise between ideological systems, one that included sufficient safeguards against a one-sided interpretation by the West to protect the GDR from significant diplomatic consequences. The SED's acceptance of the human rights provisions in the Helsinki Accords was not the product of coercion, bullying or desperation, but rather the continuation of a decade long ideological and political trajectory.

Triumph Amid Backlash

Just as Erich Honecker had hoped, his signature cemented the GDR's place in the international community and Helsinki proved to be the final step in achieving universal diplomatic recognition. Immediately following the agreement, East German sovereignty was recognised by Canada – the last NATO holdout – and by 1978, 123 countries formally established relations with the GDR.[117] In the SED's official postmortem analysis, officials described human rights as an area of compromise in which the socialist bloc had carefully out-negotiated the West. The Helsinki Accords' human rights provisions were described as a concession, but the negotiators also claimed that they had "foiled" efforts to prioritise "bourgeois" freedoms through an emphasis on self-determination and cooperation. According to the report, the East German negotiating team had formulated the section on human rights so that "the Western states

---

[115] Bange, "The GDR in the Era of Détente," 71.
[116] Charles Maier, *Dissolution: The Crisis of Communism and the End of East Germany* (Princeton, NJ: Princeton University Press, 1997), 127.
[117] Winkler, *Germany*, 287.

have no basis for interference in or defamation of the internal order of socialist countries."[118] Internal analysis argued that the Statement of Principles on human rights (structured to emphasise the primacy of sovereignty) was anchored in international law, while the Basket III sections on the free exchange of ideas and human contacts were not fully binding – giving the GDR necessary room to manoeuvre.[119] The SED leadership believed that they had signed a document that would uphold their sovereignty and a socialist vision of human rights, while conceding nothing to the principles of liberal democracy in the process.[120]

In spite of the SED's confidence when signing the Accords, it did lead to a backlash in the name of human rights within the GDR and to increased international pressure on the SED. As East German negotiator Siegfried Bock said after the fall of the GDR, "It had been underestimated that the international trend was towards an increasingly effective enforcement of human rights, that the Final Act would acquire a dynamic which made domestic policy adjustments inevitable, and that the international public would not care so much about formulas, however balanced they might be, as they would be inspired by catchwords like freedom of movement and freedom of information."[121] In East Germany, the Helsinki Accords finally produced a significant reaction in the name of human rights loud enough for the SED to notice. A wave of citizens applied to exit the GDR in the wake of the Accords and elements within the Protestant Church seized upon human rights as a rallying cry for greater political engagement and dissent by Christians (as examined in Chapter 4).

The SED also came under renewed international pressure from Western governments and international NGOs. By the late 1970s, anti-colonialism had ceased to be the focal point of UN human rights politics as a new individualistic, cosmopolitan and activist-oriented politics rose up to displace it. The campaign against apartheid did not disappear, but NGOs such as Amnesty International (Nobel Peace Prize winner, 1977) now moved to centre stage by emphasising violations of individual rights and acts of torture over anti-colonialism and self-determination. The United States turned to human rights diplomacy under the presidency

---

[118] BArch, DY 30/ IV B 2/20/ 614 Einschätzungen der Schlußdokumente der KSZE. 7.

[119] Hanisch, *Die DDR im KSZE-Prozess 1972–1985*, 146.

[120] An almost identical evaluation of the meaning of human rights in the Helsinki Accords can also be found in BArch, DY 30/IV 2/1/504 Niederschrift der 15. Tagung des Zentralkomitees (2./3.10.1975), 104.

[121] Siegfried Bock, "The CSCE – An Era of Dissent and Consensus," in CWIHP *E-Dossier* No. 17 (www.wilsoncenter.org).

of Jimmy Carter, supported by new anti-communist human rights NGOs such as Freedom House, as a means of reasserting moral superiority over communism.[122] In West Germany, the CDU took up the banner of human rights activism from opposition to attack the Social-Liberal government under Chancellor Helmut Schmidt (SPD) for its public inaction. The CDU introduced a White Paper at the Bundestag detailing human rights abuses in the GDR, as well as against all ethnic Germans behind the Iron Curtain.[123] This criticism was bolstered by the GfM, Amnesty International and the West Berlin–based Working Group for Human Rights, which launched campaigns to assist East Germans seeking to exit the GDR based on the provisions contained in the Helsinki Accords.[124]

The SED responded to growing pressure in the name of human rights – from abroad and from within – with even more aggressive rhetoric on socialist human rights and increased policing of how this language was used in the GDR. Already in October 1975, Erich Honecker condemned the "campaign of systematic falsification," and demanded monthly reports on how the Party was fighting back against the misconceptions surrounding the content of the Helsinki Accords.[125] In 1976, as the number of applications to exit once again increased, Honecker sent word to party officials across the GDR that "in the recent past, revanchist powers of the FRG have been desperately trying to establish a so-called human rights movement in the GDR." It was necessary to prevent these attempts and "to reject any petitions calling for the denaturalization and departure, as well as those referring to the [Helsinki Accords]."[126] Heinz Geggel, successor to Albert Norden as the chief propagandist of the SED, coached his subordinates on how human rights claims from the West only sought to "conceal the brutality and inhumanity," of imperialist capitalism in contrast to the GDR where "socialist ownership

---

[122] Carl Bon Tempo, "From the Center-Right: Freedom House and Human Rights in the 1970s and 1980s," in *The Human Rights Revolution: An International History*, ed. Akira Iriye, Petra Goedde and William Hitchcock (New York: Oxford University Press, 2012), 223–44; Barbara Keys, *Reclaiming American Virtue: The Human Rights Revolution of the 1970s* (Cambridge, MA: Harvard University Press, 2014).

[123] CDU/CSU in the German Bundestag, *White Paper: On the Human Rights Situation in Germany and of the Germans in Eastern Europe* (Bonn: CDU/CSU Group in the German Bundestag, 1977).

[124] The Arbeitsgruppe für Menschenrechte e.V. was founded in 1978. Bernd Eisenfeld, *Die Zentrale Koordinierungsgruppe: Bekämpfung von Flucht und Übersiedlung* (Berlin: BStU, 1996), 27; Anja Mihr, *Amnesty International in der DDR* (Berlin: Ch. Links, 2002), 123–27.

[125] Hanisch, *Die DDR im KSZE-Prozess 1972–1985*, 98.

[126] Scholtyseck, "GDR Dissidents and Human Rights Issues," 296.

and power relationships" meant that human rights had been achieved.[127] Publicly, SED leader Erich Honecker maintained that the GDR had fully realised human rights and denied that there could be such a thing as genuine civil rights activism in the East Germany by depicting dissidents as Western provocateurs.[128]

Diplomatically, the SED also maintained its earlier position on human rights and refused to give an inch, ideologically, to foreign pressure. In 1977, the first follow-up meeting on the implementation of the Helsinki Accords was held in Belgrade, where the delegation of the United States aimed to put Jimmy Carter's new human rights-oriented foreign policy into action against the Eastern Bloc. In spite of the shift in American policy, West German Chancellor Helmut Schmidt did not follow Carter's lead in aggressively pushing a human rights agenda against the Socialist Bloc. While human rights was once a unifying anti-communist ideal for the Right and Left in West Germany, the rise of *Ostpolitik* and Cold War détente had reduced its appeal for Schmidt, who believed that more could be accomplished through behind the scenes negotiations to pay for the freedom of those who sought to emigrate.[129] By the time of the Belgrade meeting, West Germany had purchased permission for 80,000 ethnic Germans from the GDR and across the Eastern Bloc to move to the West. American efforts to coordinate a hard line with the whole of the Western alliance worried Bonn. Schmidt told US Secretary of State Cyrus Vance, "we cannot talk in abstract terms about human rights, because we have several hundreds of thousands of ethnic Germans in the East, whom we do not want to put in danger."[130]

When the American government sought to apply direct pressure on human rights through bilateral relations, the GDR did not budge. In 1978, American Assistant Secretary for Human Rights Patricia Derian

---

[127] Heinz Geggel, "Closely Tied to the Masses," *Agitatoren Initiatoren. Agitationskonferenz der Bezirksleitung Frankfurt (Oder) der SED am 6. Dezember 1976* (http://research.calvin.edu/german-propaganda-archive/geggel.htm).

[128] Karl Wilhelm Fricke, *Opposition und Widerstand in der DDR: ein politischer Report* (Cologne: Verlag Wissenschaft und Politik, 1984), 162.

[129] West Germany paid the GDR for the release and emigration of prisoners as well as for the right of emigration for ethnic Germans in the rest of the Eastern Bloc, particularly from Romania. Jan Philipp Wölbern, *Der Häftlingsfreikauf aus der DDR 1962/63–1989: Zwischen Menschenhandel und humanitären Aktionen* (Göttingen: Vandenhoeck & Ruprecht, 2014); Dennis Deletant, *Ceauşescu and the Securitate: Coercion and Dissent in Romania, 1965–1989* (Florence: Taylor & Francis, 1995), 117.

[130] On West German reluctance to use human rights against the Eastern Bloc under Schmidt, Bange, "'The Greatest Happiness of the Greatest Number ...'. The FRG and the GDR and the Belgrade CSCE Conference (1977–78)," in *From Helsinki to Belgrade*, 232; Avril Pittman, *From Ostpolitik to Reunification: West German-Soviet Political Relations since 1974* (Cambridge: Cambridge University Press, 2002), 149.

visited East Berlin to meet with the Deputy Foreign Minister Kurt Nier and she was unable to gain even the acknowledgement that the United States had a legitimate right to discuss human rights problems within the borders of the GDR. Nier acknowledged that massive violations of human rights, such as those taking place in South Africa, Chile and Central America, made internal affairs an international issue, but criticising state socialist nations would violate the spirit of détente and Helsinki. Derian then sought to convey her point by way of analogy: in a neighbourhood where everyone kept neat gardens it would become a matter for community discussion if someone began to keep goats in their front yard. Nier coldly responded that if someone were to have problems with goats going where they should not, they could always build a wall to maintain order.[131] With that, the topic of human rights was quickly dropped. In a report from the following year, Derian concluded that while the United States might support dissidents such as Robert Havemann, we should "be modest in our assessment of what we can do in the short run."[132]

Not only did the SED have to contend with the ongoing Helsinki process and a new aggressive posture from the United States on human rights but it also had to answer to the United Nations. The GDR had signed on to both Human Rights Covenants upon joining the United Nations in 1973, and they came into full legal force in 1976. Now the SED would have to report on progress and answer to a committee that would oversee compliance.[133] At the United Nations, West Germany was willing to apply more pressure than at the Belgrade conference, but this was not a serious problem for the GDR. While the first report on the GDR's compliance with the ICCPR went poorly as the representative from the Ministry of Justice was not prepared for Western attacks, this was soon corrected.[134] When renowned legal scholar Christian Tomuschat gained a seat on the UN Human Rights Committee – a panel of 18 experts tasked with reporting on compliance with the ICCPR – the SED responded by getting an appointment for Bernhard Graefrath, a longtime member of the GDR Committee for Human Rights. Even to Western diplomats, Graefrath was seen as having the "highest intellectual

---

[131] Hoover Institution Archive, David Benjamin Bolen papers, Box 13, Folder 7, Derian Telegramm (10.7.1978), 6–7.
[132] Ibid., Derian to Vest (9.7.1979), 4.
[133] Friederike Brinkmeier, *Der Einfluss des Kalten Krieges auf den internationalen Menschenrechtsschutz* (Berlin: Berliner Wissenschafts-Verlag, 2004).
[134] Wentker, *Außenpolitik in engen Grenzen*, 442–45.

rigor," if one took into account his ideological precepts.[135] Graefrath and others dealing with human rights were instructed to go on the offensive against the Federal Republic and other Western countries and to aggressively respond to all criticism.

Because human rights had become a subject of study for socialist academics years earlier, the SED had a wide variety of experts now available from GDR universities and other institutions who could handle the complex problems of UN human rights.[136] In 1975, the GDR Committee for Human Rights had created a bilingual quarterly journal – *Schriften und Informationen* in German and more prosaically *Bulletin* in English[137] – that would provide information on socialist human rights theory concerning contemporary problems, commemorate important events in human rights history and document human rights victories in the socialist bloc and atrocities in the West and the developing world. The first issue went to press only two weeks before the Helsinki Accords were signed and was devoted to the UN International Women's Year including the upcoming World Congress of Women that would be held in East Berlin.[138] Articles provided up-to-date ideological interpretations of international law, offered updates on legal developments at the United Nations from a socialist perspective and gave readers the official line on what events around the world constituted human rights abuses. The journal provided experts within the GDR a forum for exchanging ideas on human rights theory and promoted socialist human rights theory in the West, especially after Forberger sent subscription cards to major libraries across the Eastern Bloc and the West. The journal was soon distributed in dozens of countries, including to one subscriber in Canada, jurist Walter Tarnopolsky, who sat as a member of the UN

---

[135] Dietrich von Kyaw, *Auf der Suche nach Deutschland: Erlebnisse und Begegnungen eines deutschen Diplomaten und Europäers* (Berlin: BWV Verlag, 2012), 152.

[136] In 1978, the Academy of Sciences in Halle held a conference on "Democracy, Freedom, and Human Rights and their Realization in Developed Socialist Society and in the GDR," that included contributions from five East German universities, three Party research and training institutes, the State Secretary of the Ministry of Justice and a Supreme Court judge. "Demokratie, Freiheit und Menschenrechte und ihre Verwirklichung in der entwickelten sozialistischen Gesellschaft," *Staat und Recht* (11/1978), 1033–39.

[137] *Schriften und Informationen* replaced an earlier, more rudimentary, newsletter called *Information* produced by the committee in English, French and German between 1960 and 1974.

[138] *Schriften und Informationen* 1, no. 1 (1975). See also Celia Donert, "Whose Utopia? Gender, Ideology and Human Rights at the 1975 World Congress of Women in East Berlin," in Eckel and Moyn, *The Breakthrough*.

Human Rights Committee where he often faced off against Bernhard Graefrath.[139]

The news coverage of human rights issues expanded in the SED press to match the degree of dissent that was expressed from below. Committee protests regarding human rights abuses in West Germany (mostly on joblessness and the *Radikalenerlass* – the ban on "radicals" working in the civil service) and the rest of the capitalist world filled the pages of the East German press. In 1976, there were around 250 articles on human rights in the national SED newspaper *Neues Deutschland* and in 1977, this shot up to 793 in response to the increasing number of applications to exit. Of those articles, there were 173 articles just on human rights abuses in Chile under the Junta and another 55 on human rights violations in Apartheid South Africa.[140] The East German news agency ADN prepared guidelines on human rights reporting, telling editors that reporting should take the offensive to the West, emphasise emotions and make sure to cite the UDHR and the 1966 Human Rights Covenants.[141] In the late 1970s, the weekly television program *The Black Channel* regularly covered human rights issues from poverty under capitalism, human rights abuses in Chile and Israel, self-determination in Zimbabwe, the Helsinki Accords, the UN Human Rights Covenants and Jimmy Carter's human rights diplomacy.[142] Rather than try to hide from the problem, the SED instead doubled down on its message that the socialist world was the global champion of human rights in solidarity with postcolonial states fighting against the hypocrisy of the imperialist West.

In dealing with human rights activism, Honecker had said at the signing of the Helsinki Accords that the SED could also rely on the Ministry of State Security. The Stasi interpreted the increase in demands to exit as the product of a widening "enemy human rights campaign," to create a political underground against the SED.[143] To suppress the rising number of applications to exit, the Stasi created the Central

---

[139] BArch, DZ7/52 Tarnopolsky subscription card.

[140] Statistics on *Neues Deutschland* compiled through the ZEFYS Zeitungsinformationssystem of the Staatsbibliothek zu Berlin (http://zefys.staatsbibliothek-berlin.de/ddr-presse/).

[141] BArch, DC900/853 Ruth Kallman, Konzeption zur Behandlung der Menschenrechtsproblematik (7.2.1977)

[142] DRA-Der schwarze Kanal, E084–05-02/0003/214 Nr. 878 "Wo die Menschenrechte zu Hause sind..." (28.02.1977); E084–05-02/0003/196 Nr. 860 "Menschenrechte und Menschlichkeit" (25.10.1976); E084–05-02/0003/216 Nr. 880 "Selbstbestimmungsrecht gehört zu den Menschenrechten" (14.3.1977); E084–05-02/0003/211 Nr. 875 20 Minuten "Informationen" (07.02.1977); E084–05-02/0003/302 Nr. 966 "Pharisäer im Dezember" (11.12.1978); E084–05-02/0003/290 Nr. 954 "Carters Wunderland – oder: Das häßliche Amerika" (18.9.1978).

[143] Hanisch, *Die DDR im KSZE-Prozess 1972–1985*, 109.

Coordination Group (*Zentrale Koordinierungsgruppe*, or ZKG) in 1976 that was tasked with intervening with those planning to emigrate and to suppress an initiative by citizens to collaborate with each other to do so.[144] The Stasi turned to a strategy of direct suppression and *Zersetzung* – a tactic of psychological pressure to distract and dissuade citizens from seeking to emigrate.[145] Punishments for those applying to emigrate were increased and included unemployment or imprisonment. International human rights organisations were branded as fronts for Western intelligence organisations and contact with them was deemed an act of espionage.[146] When a West German human rights organisation publicised the names of GDR citizens seeking to exit on the grounds of the Helsinki Accords in 1977, almost everyone listed was subsequently prosecuted for treason.[147] While the Stasi was effective in arresting East Germans who made public demands to exit using Western media and those in the church who sought to use human rights for political change at home, it had far less unrest to deal with than most of its Eastern European counterparts. The Stasi took credit for the comparative lack of human rights activism in contrast to East Germany's more restive socialist neighbours, particularly in Poland and Czechoslovakia, but these countries also had effective secret police forces.[148] As will be examined further in the next chapter, the difference lay in the relative absence of human rights dissent rather than its effective suppression.

While the SED was fully committed to an aggressive human rights policy towards the West, coordination by the Socialist Bloc as a whole was almost nonexistent. Already in the early 1970s, Siegfried Forberger had found it almost impossible to cooperate with the USSR on human rights, describing it as more closed off than the West.[149] When Eastern Bloc Ideology Ministers met in 1977, the GDR representative Kurt

---

[144] Bernd Eisenfeld, "Die Zentrale Koordinierungsgruppe: Bekämpfung von Flucht und Übersiedlung," *Anatomie der Staatssicherheit: Geschichte, Struktur und Methoden: MfS-Handbuch*, Teil 3, 17 (Berlin: BStU, 1996).

[145] The use of *Zersetzung* originated from Stasi directive Nr. 1/76 zur Entwicklung und Bearbeitung Operativer Vorgänge (January 1976) (www.bstu.bund.de/DE/Wissen/MfS-Dokumente).

[146] Archiv der DDR-Opposition, AM 31 Analyse über die gegnerischen Aktivitäten zur Organisierung der politischen Untergrundtätigkeit Hauptabteilung XX (10.1.1978) 2; Bange, "The Greatest Happiness of the Greatest Number," 243.

[147] Oliver Bange, "The Greatest Happiness of the Greatest Number," 245.

[148] The Stasi's self-promotion for defeating a near to nonexistent human rights movement is explained in Douglas Selvage, "'Human Rights Demagoguery Hostile to Détente' The GDR and the Conference on Security and Cooperation in Europe, 1975–1989," in *Human Rights in Europe during the Cold War*, ed. Rasmus Mariager, Karl Molin and Kjersti Brathagen (London: Routledge, 2014), 142.

[149] Forberger, *Das DDR-Komitee für Menschenrechte*, 332.

Hager declared, "to expose this demagoguery and hypocrisy to our people and to the world as a whole, to open the eyes of those who have fallen for this racket about human rights, is a task that requires great activity and conviction, and a quick, coordinated, offensive and effective course of action."[150] But there was no concrete follow-up. The rise of democracy-oriented communist parties in Western Europe – the so-called Eurocommunists – posed a new threat from within the socialist camp. In 1976, at the Conference of European Communist and Workers' Parties held in East Berlin, the Western delegations, particularly from France and Italy, had caused a split by calling for greater attention to the human rights provisions of the Helsinki Accords in the Eastern Bloc.[151] In one Stasi report on foreign "enemy-negative" forces that were misusing Helsinki, Western antisocialists were lumped together with "certain Communist Parties in the capitalists states," as equally dangerous influences.[152] Within the Warsaw Pact states, ideological cooperation on human rights proved difficult. A joint GDR-Polish conference on human rights theory held in Poznan in 1978 did little to foster solidarity. In his memoirs, Forberger reports being "shocked by the political ideological pluralism on the Polish side," and that some of the scholars invited spoke of "unrestricted political rights to freedom of expression, and freedom of assembly and association."[153] The SED had successfully held the line against Western attacks, but the ideological rifts emerging within the socialist world would ultimately prove to be an even greater threat.

At the end of the 1970s, the SED remained confident in its human rights ideology and diplomacy in spite of the pressure from Western diplomats and NGOs. East Germany had become a member of the United Nations, its borders were assured by the terms of the Helsinki Accords, and it now had near-universal diplomatic recognition. While the GDR Foreign Minister was concerned that the West sought to "revise the Final Act, further strain the Détente process, and interfere with the internal affairs of the socialist states," he remained convinced that any claim to an absolute right of free movement and travel was a

---

[150] BArch, DY30/IV 2/1/535 Bericht über die Beratung der Sekretäre für ideologische und internationale Fragen, 11.

[151] Thomas, *The Helsinki Effect*, 108. Laura Fasanaro, "Eurocommunism: An East German Perspective," in *The Crisis of Détente in Europe*, 245–49.

[152] BStU, MfS, BdL Nr. 6040 Zusammenfassung von […] Aktivitäten antisozialistischer, feindlich-negativer Kräfte in einigen Staaten der sozialistischen Gemeinschaft (March 1977).

[153] Forberger, *Das DDR-Komitee für Menschenrechte*, 470.

violation of the Helsinki Accords as it was written.[154] The number of East Germans applying to exit in the name of realising their human rights finally dropped off after aggressive state persecution of applicants, especially those who worked with foreign NGOs. In 1978, the SED came to an accommodation with the Protestant Church – the so-called Church in Socialism arrangement – that provided greater rights for Christians, but at the cost of the Church suppressing internal political dissent. In contrast to most Eastern European states, no human rights organisations arose in the GDR and prominent intellectual and cultural dissidents shied away from international human rights politics. While Western NGOs continued to campaign aggressively on behalf of East Germans, the domestic threat of human rights appeared to be thoroughly quelled.

Conclusion

For East German officials, agreeing to human rights in 1975 was not a breakthrough or some kind of hard-fought admission, but rather a reiteration of SED claims that had been made years earlier. The leaders of the SED were not bullied, hoodwinked or coerced into agreeing to the principles of human rights nor did they simply sleepwalk mindlessly into agreeing to inherently antisocialist ideals that immediately undermined their own legitimacy. Erich Honecker and the GDR negotiators saw some danger in an agreement that included human rights that was structured as to privilege a one-sidedly bourgeois interpretation, but they were convinced that careful negotiation had resulted in a balanced agreement that would reinforce East German sovereignty and prevent intervention in the internal affairs of the GDR. This belief was, perhaps, overly optimistic, but it was based on the internalisation of a socialist human rights doctrine by the East German elite over the past decade of international diplomacy.

The full potential of human rights as a language of dissent and a tool for opposing state socialism was not apparent even after the signing of the Helsinki Accords although several warning signs were there. A new international human rights movement emphasising individual rights over the rights of peoples and participatory democracy over developmental dictatorships was emerging across the West as well as in pockets of Eastern Europe. The primacy of self-determination on the international stage soon entered into eclipse as politicians and activists in Africa and Asia turned their focus from formal imperialism towards problems such

[154] BArch, DY30/11642 Fischer and Winkelmann to the Central Committee (12.3.1980).

as the right to development and the preservation of cultural and traditional rights. But these global trends would only pose a threat to SED rule when East Germans began to challenge the now dominant socialist human rights discourse of the GDR. The idea of human rights was publicly known to East Germans, but what was missing was a translation that could connect these abstract concepts to the everyday problems of the GDR and the social means for these ideas to spread and take root. As the SED had learned through many difficult years of experimentation and muddling about, claiming human rights in theory was very different from successfully engaging in the politics of human rights.

For more than 20 years, the Socialist Unity Party (SED) managed to promote itself as a champion of human rights – without any significant blowback on the domestic front. By 1968, however, it appeared as though the GDR had accidentally sparked a wave of mass human rights activism. When the SED introduced a new constitution and asked East Germans to take part in a mass discussion of its contents, thousands wrote to SED officials to demand changes citing international human rights. They advocated primarily for their religious rights, but also for the right to travel and speak more freely. Both the Catholic and Protestant churches launched campaigns in defence of religious freedom, and young theologians began to see human rights as a means of legitimising their demands for major change. As the SED began to sign on to major international human rights treaties, East Germans responded by using the text of these agreements to demand the right to emigrate. Finally, the passage of the Helsinki Accords in 1975 at a moment of growing human rights consciousness from below and around the world created the possibility for a real movement for political change.

Yet by the end of the decade, the threat to the SED posed by human rights appeared to have dissipated. In contrast to much of the Eastern Bloc, where disaffected intellectuals and elites took up the banner of human rights and created civil society groups like Czechoslovakia's Charter 77 and Poland's Worker's Defence League (KOR), there was not a single independent human rights organisation in the GDR at the beginning of the 1980s.[1] The intellectual and cultural elites of the GDR rejected human rights as too closely tied to Western liberalism and Cold

---

[1] Robert Brier, *Entangled Protest: Transnational Approaches to the History of Dissent in Eastern Europe and the Soviet Union* (Osnabrück: Fibre, 2013), 104–27; Jonathan Bolton, *Worlds of Dissent: Charter 77, the Plastic People of the Universe, and Czech Culture under Communism* (Cambridge, MA: Harvard University Press, 2012); Robert Brier, "Broadening the Cultural History of the Cold War: The Emergence of the Polish Workers' Defense Committee and the Rise of Human Rights," *Journal of Cold War Studies* 15, no. 4 (2013). On the rise of the network of Helsinki monitoring groups, see Sarah Snyder,

War anti-communism. Although Christians began to take up the mantle of human rights to defend religious freedoms, in the 1970s, the Catholic Church ceased to engage politically and went into a form of internal exile, and the Protestant Church came to terms with the SED in 1978 and began to suppress its own political dissidents in exchange for greater political recognition from the state.[2] The burst of petitions demanding a right to exit following the Helsinki Accords died down quickly, and those who did try to mobilise against human rights abuses by the SED and Stasi were quickly arrested.[3] While new forms of activism for peace and the environment emerged during this decade, neither movement connected those ideals to a human rights politics that might threaten the SED's monopoly on power.

The 1970s have rightly been described as a breakthrough decade for a new kind of human rights from below, focused on individualism and transnational activism. The failure of the 1968 Prague Spring and its vision of "socialism with a human face" along with the bloody aftermath of the 1973 Chilean military coup worked together to spark a new kind of transnational human rights politics from below in both East and West.[4] But East Germany was one of many places around the world in which this turning point failed to turn. Ultimately, within the GDR, the Helsinki Accords and the rise of international human rights activism lacked the transformative and revolutionary character that is often attributed to them.[5] There was no single "logic of rights" that compelled the people to revolt against the SED or demand liberal democracy. Instead, there was

---

Human Rights Activism and the End of the Cold War: A Transnational History of the Helsinki Network (Cambridge: Cambridge University Press, 2011).

[2] Bernd Schäfer, *The East German State and the Catholic Church, 1945–1989* (New York: Berghahn, 2010); Katharina Kunter, *Die Kirchen im KSZE-Prozess, 1968–1978* (Stuttgart: Kohlhammer, 2000).

[3] Studies on earlier waves of human rights–based applications to exit and the effective suppression of demands to exit after Helsinki include Patrick Major, *Behind the Berlin Wall: East Germany and the Frontiers of Power* (Oxford: Oxford University Press, 2010) and Anja Hanisch, *Die DDR im KSZE-Prozess 1972–1985: Zwischen Ostabhängigkeit, Westabgrenzung und Ausreisebewegung* (Munich: Oldenbourg, 2012).

[4] On the theory that human rights acted as "a language to replace Marxism," see Marci Shore, *The Taste of Ashes* (New York: Random House, 2013), 11. That it was triggered by the failure of the Prague Spring, see Samuel Moyn, *Last Utopia: Human Rights in History* (Cambridge, MA: Belknap, 2010), 136–38.

[5] On the need for a differentiated understanding of the Helsinki Accords' impact, see Hanisch, *Die DDR im KSZE-Prozess*, 6. The special issue of *Journal of Cold War Studies* 18, no. 3 (2016) argues for the transformative nature of Helsinki. In the "Editor's Note," of the issue, Kramer argues that human rights activism had effectively fizzled out by the early 1980s. Hermann Wentker and Matthias Peter, "'Helsinki-Mythos' oder 'Helsinki-Effekt'?," in *Die KSZE im Ost-West-Konflikt: Internationale Politik und gesellschaftliche Transformation 1975–1990*, ed. Matthias Peter and Hermann Wentker (Berlin: De Gruyter, 2013), 1–14.

an active competition over what human rights meant, both in theory and practice, based on the beliefs and practices of East Germans in their everyday lives.

Human Rights Protest and the 1968 *Volksaussprache*

The first significant human rights protest in East Germany emerged from the intersection of SED propaganda aimed at the United Nations, a wave of modernisation within the Christian churches, and a series of mass consultations – the *Volksaussprache* – held to shepherd along the creation of the new socialist constitution. As such, this protest did not take the form of political demonstrations, but of polite letters written during the *Volksaussprache*. Rather than use human rights to reject the status quo in its entirety, East Germans sought to bend the official discourse of social- ist human rights to fit their own aims and to secure specific freedoms within the legal system of the GDR. East Germans did not use this new language to appeal to a foreign, Western audience to bring international pressure to bear on the state. Instead, East Germans tried to convince the state to provide greater freedoms by co-opting of rhetoric of SED leaders and using officially sanctioned methods of criticism.[6] When much of the world was engulfed in domestic unrest in 1968 – from student uprisings and the anti–Vietnam War movement in the West, to the Prague Spring in the East – in East Germany, human rights were part of a calm and orderly process of domestic reform almost wholly devoid of public disturbances.

When the SED touted East German participation in domestic reforms as part of the International Year for Human Rights, it was more than pure propaganda, and citizens were encouraged to engage and criticize the draft of the socialist constitution. Ulbricht had announced that the new constitution would not be imposed from above, but rather through popular assent. "Now the people will have their say," he promised, calling on all GDR citizens to review the draft "from top to bottom"[7] to form an opinion of its contents and to provide suggestions to the constitutional commission.[8] Between the printing of a draft of the new constitution in the East German media on 2 February and the plebiscite

---

[6] On the politics of the audience, see Bolton, *Worlds of Dissent*, ch. 6. On the performance of loyalty by citizens while criticising the state, see Jeremy Straughn, "'Taking the State at Its Word': The Arts of Consentful Contention in the GDR," *American Journal of Sociology* 110, no. 6 (2005), 1598–1650.

[7] In German "auf Herz und Nieren prüfen" – literally checking something's heart and kidneys.

[8] "Kernsätze aus der Rede Walter Ulbrichts," *Neues Deutschland* (1.2.1968), 1.

on its adoption on 6 April, East Germans deluged the constitutional commission with 12,454 letters and postcards. Every response was catalogued, and the feedback was extensively analysed by state officials. During that time, nearly one million events – mostly small discussions in factories, workplaces and homes – were held around the GDR to present the contents of the proposed constitution and to counter any questions or critiques raised.[9] With approximately 12 million citizens taking part in the final plebiscite, the *Volksaussprache* in 1968 was the largest mass consultation in East German history.[10]

The discussions held during the *Volksaussprache* were neither wholly orchestrated nor wholly free. East Germans could already criticise state policy in petitions or workplace meetings, but the boundaries of constructive engagement and hostility to socialism were relaxed in 1968.[11] While the Stasi carefully tracked those who refused to sign on to collective statements of support for the constitution at factories or among student groups, the functionaries running the public meetings sought to portray criticism and dissent as constructive. An official from Cottbus reported that negative comments were "not always hostile opinions, but much more often the result of uncertainties and speculations about the contents of the new constitution."[12] So long as citizens spoke in the appropriate way, officials could categorise even harsh criticism as benign ignorance. When a citizen did step over the line, SED functionaries sought to shift responsibility for impolitic comments onto systemic failures or foreign influence. In Neubrandenburg, when a teacher asked how the new constitution could be so "magical" that citizens should have to see and hear about nothing else all the time, this outburst was written off as a failure of the military to provide proper political education during

---

[9] BArch, DY30/IV 2/1/373 Bericht der Kommission über die Verfassung der DDR von Klaus Sorgenicht, 108.

[10] A total of 300,000 East Germans took part in a six-month consultation over a proposed Family Code in 1954, ultimately postponed due to raucous public meetings. In 1965, a second effort at reforming Family Law kept meeting sizes smaller and more controlled. Over six months, 750,000 took part in 34,000 events. Donna Harsch, *Revenge of the Domestic: Women, the Family, and Communism in the GDR* (Princeton, NJ: Princeton University Press, 2007), 284–85. Subsequent consultations regarding the Youth Code (1974), the Civil Code (1975) and the Labour Code (1977) – the last mass consultation – also involved between a quarter of a million and nearly six million citizens. See Peter Sperlich, *The East German Social Courts: Law and Popular Justice in a Marxist-Leninist Society* (Westport: Praeger, 2007), 108.

[11] Allinson argues that speech restrictions were eased during the *Volksaussprache*. Mark Allinson, *Politics and Popular Opinion in East Germany 1945–1968* (Manchester: Manchester University Press, 2000), 145.

[12] BArch, DY6/4816 Informationsbericht (15.1.1968), 3.

compulsory service.[13] Western television was blamed when one citizen from the Pößneck district said "the whole discussion about the constitution can't change the contents of the constitution since it's already finished and a done deal."[14] Although it is impossible to determine the degree of sincerity in the letters and comments during this process, there is extensive evidence that many offered frank criticism of the process and the draft constitution.

In the lead-up to the *Volksaussprache*, East German media made human rights a major theme in its coverage of the new constitution and the realisation of East German sovereignty on the international stage. In addition to Walter Ulbricht's New Year's Address (discussed in Chapter 3), in which he tied the constitutional reforms to the International Year for Human Rights, East German state media was awash with human rights stories in early 1968.[15] In January alone, the SED's national newspaper *Neues Deutschland* published 32 articles mentioning human rights. One article on the new constitution argued that while human rights could not be achieved under the "dictatorship of the monopolies" in West Germany, in the GDR where "human rights are the law," true social harmony was possible. Under such a system, East German citizens experienced the "fundamental rights of citizens, such as the right to work, the right to education, the equality of men and women, not just promises on paper."[16] The human rights achieved in East Germany were, however, only possible due to GDR sovereignty, the affirmation of which was central to the SED's message and to the *Volksaussprache*.

Although the SED spoke of the realisation of human rights through the new constitution, the document reduced the number of rights that East Germans formally held, in particular religious freedoms. While the rights in the 1949 Constitution were rarely observed in practice, the new constitutional draft reduced the number of articles protecting freedom of conscience and religious practice from eight (Art. 41 to 48) to one (Art. 38). Up to this point, church officials in the GDR had only occasionally used the term *human rights* in their denunciations of various state

---

[13] MLHA-Schwerin 10.34-7/2182 Meinungen zum Beschluß der Volkskammer über die Durchführung des Volksentscheids, Neubrandenburg (5.4.1968), 2.

[14] Quote from ThSA-R 5-95-1005 Bezirksleitung Gera IV/B-2/13/682. Einschätzung über den Stand der Volksaussprache im Kreis Pößneck (21.3.1968). Officials also blamed the influence of Western propaganda to excuse extreme criticism from citizens during the 1954 Family Code discussions, see Harsch, *Revenge of the Domestic*, 208.

[15] Walter Ulbricht, "1968 – Jahr wichtiger Entscheidungen," *Neues Deutschland* (1.1.1968), 1. This was also printed on the front page of the CDU-Ost Bloc Party's newspaper *Neue Zeit*.

[16] "Verfassung sozialistischer Gemeinschaft," *Neues Deutschland* (5.1.1968), 1.

policies including land reform and the suppression of church privileges, but this language was usually incidental and did not form the backbone of any kind of sustained or coherent attack on state power.[17] In 1968, however, the Catholic and Protestant churches both mobilised to defend their rights, turning to the UDHR to make their case.

Although Christians had long been suspicious of the language of human rights, this had begun to shift in the 1940s, as conservative Christians, primarily Catholics, ceased to link human rights to the revolutionary atheism of the French Revolution and began to claim the concept for the cause of morality and anti-communism.[18] In 1963, Pope John XXIII officially endorsed the Universal Declaration in his encyclical *Pacem In Terris*.[19] From the other end of the political spectrum, the World Council of Churches (WCC) – an organisation dedicated to global ecumenical cooperation – sought to link faith to the cause of decolonisation and justice for the Global South, where many of its participating churches were located. In 1968, the Fourth Assembly of the WCC moved human rights to the forefront of its agenda, and created an antiracism campaign to support decolonisation and protest apartheid.[20] German Protestants had long opposed the concept of human rights, viewing it as "synonymous with chaos, anarchy, and anti-clericalism," but the international ecumenical movement provided a means of engaging with this emerging political movement without embracing secular liberalism.[21]

The Christian response to the *Volksaussprache* began with Cardinal Alfred Bengsch, the Catholic Archbishop of Berlin, who wrote to the constitutional commission on 5 February arguing that "the redesign of

[17] Joachim Goertz, "Kirche und Menschenrechte in der DDR," *Horch und Guck* 14 (1995), 68–70. For Catholic Church declarations mentioning human rights prior to 1968, Gerhard Lange, *Katholische Kirche – sozialistischer Staat DDR: Dokumente und öffentliche Äußerungen 1945–1990* (Berlin: Bischöfliches Ordinariat, 1993), 122, 160, 181.

[18] Samuel Moyn, *Christian Human Rights* (Philadelphia: University of Pennsylvania Press, 2015).

[19] Pope John XXIII, *Pacem in Terris: Encyclical Letter of Pope John XXIII on Human Rights and Duties* (London: Catholic Truth Society, 1980).

[20] Christian Albers, "Der ÖRK und die Menschenrechte im Kontext von Kaltem Krieg und Dekolonisierung," in *Globalisierung der Kirchen: Der Ökumenische Rat der Kirchen und die Entdeckung der Dritten Welt in den 1960er und 1970er Jahren*, ed. Katharina Kunter and Annegreth Schilling (Göttingen: Vandenhoeck & Ruprecht, 2014), 189. Bastiaan Bouwman, "From Religious Freedom to Social Justice: The Human Rights Engagement of the Ecumenical Movement from the 1940s to the 1970s," *Journal of Global History* 13, no. 2 (2018), 252–73.

[21] Katharina Kunter, "Human Rights as a Theological and Political Controversy among East German and Czech Protestants," in *Christianity and Modernity in Eastern Europe*, ed. Bruce Berglund and Brian Porter (New York: Central European University Press, 2010), 219–22.

the Constitution is neither consistent with universal human rights nor an advance from the Constitution of 1949." Bengsch prominently cited Ulbricht's New Year's Address and claimed that eliminating the guarantees of religious freedom from the old constitution was a direct attack on the Church's ability to function. Moreover, the emphasis on creating a socialist state discriminated against those with a Christian worldview (*Weltanschauung*) and as such "calls into question whether all citizens are equal before the law." He demanded the restoration of guarantees for religious practice and belief because "only under these conditions can the Church carry out its activities in true freedom and serve the common good. And only under these conditions can the basic rights as expressed in Article 18 of the Universal Declaration of Human Rights of the United Nations be realized in our new Constitution."[22] On the one hand, offering these rights to citizens and the Church would improve East German society as a whole, and on the other, failing to do so would violate the norms of the UDHR.

On 15 February, the Protestant bishops of East Germany echoed Bengsch's argument in terms of human rights. They asked that the new constitution be created so that Christians and those citizens who do not share the worldview of the ruling party can share in the responsibility for our political system with a clear conscience. The draft emphasises that man and human dignity should be the focus of the new constitution. For the International Year for Human Rights, the draft includes the statement that the rules of international law occupy an important place in the Constitution.[23] Protestant church leaders urged all parishioners and church officials to study the draft constitution carefully, and Bishop Hans-Joachim Fränkel of Görlitz distributed a detailed seven-page analysis of the new constitution with direct comparisons to international human rights documents to show its deficits.[24]

The SED tried to publicly reassure Christians that the new constitution was not a threat to their faith. In a speech printed in *Neues Deutschland*, Walter Ulbricht said, "I can only repeat that religious freedom as it currently exists, will continue to exist and there is no intention to change that."[25] Out of view of the public, however, SED officials denounced the Church's intervention in the *Volksaussprache* as an attack

---

[22] BArch, DY30/IV A2/13/46 Bengsch to Ulbricht (5.2.1968), 1–4.
[23] Evangelisches Zentralarchiv EZA104/687 Noth et al. to Ulbricht (15.2.1968), 1.
[24] EZA104/687 Abschrift Evangelischer Nachrichtdienst in der DDR Nr. XXI/7 (14.2.1968) and Fränkel to the Evangelisches Konsistorium (21.2.1968).
[25] "Walter Ulbricht beantwortet Fragen," *Neues Deutschland* (16.2.1968), 4.

on the sovereignty and democratic processes of the GDR. In a private response to Cardinal Bengsch, officials argued that Christians were already represented on the constitutional commission and in the *Volkskammer* through the Christian Democratic bloc party, making the actions of the Church both parochial and redundant. The SED did not accept that the new constitution reduced religious freedom as the new, slimmed down, single article on religious freedom fully conformed with Article 18 of the UDHR. In a formal response to Bengsch, the party explained that those articles from the UDHR, which were self-evidently not at issue in the GDR, need not be explicitly included in the new constitution. In that vein, the Constitution also did not include formal prohibitions on forced labour and torture because they were unthinkable.[26] Neither persuaded nor intimidated by this response, Bengsch distributed an edited version of his original letter across the country to be read out at Mass on 3 March, more than four weeks before the final vote.[27]

Despite Ulbricht's reassurances, East German Christians flooded the constitutional commission with letters demanding the restoration of the 1949 constitutional protections for religion. Nearly half of the more than 12,000 pieces of mail received by the commission concerned religious freedom, with several hundred more advocating for educational rights also dealing with religious schooling.[28] This number underplays the extent of the public outcry, as many of the letters were signed by multiple individuals, or several members of church organisations, or even entire parishes. One submission from a Catholic community in the town of Lenterode had 218 signatures spread over two letters.[29] At public meetings and in SED reports, the issue of religious rights – to practice freely, to access religious education and to be a good socialist citizen while maintaining a Christian worldview – often dominated proceedings. The human rights language contained in most of these petitions repeated the key phrases of the bishops, and SED officials noted that many of the letters regarding religious freedom were copied from each other – down to identical typographical errors.[30]

---

[26] BArch, DY30/IV A2/13/46 Stellungnahme zum Schreiben des Kardinal Bengsch (5.2.1968), 3–4.
[27] Lange, *Katholische Kirche – sozialistischer Staat DDR*, 235–36.
[28] BArch, NY4192/111 Gliederung der Vorschläge nach Artikeln des Verfassungentwurfs.
[29] BArch, DA1/4157 Letters no. 9669 and 9670. The same letter was sent twice on the same date to accommodate the number of signatures. Church groups had first begun sending group petitions during the failed 1954 Family Code consultations. Harsch, *Revenge of the Domestic*, 207.
[30] BArch, DY30/IV2/1/373 Bericht der Kommission über die Verfassung der DDR von Klaus Sorgenicht, 118.

By employing the language of human rights, East Germans sought to legitimise a Christian worldview within the socialist system without challenging the SED's right to rule. Most letter writers pointed out that they supported socialism as an economic system or as a "way of life" (*Lebensform*), but they feared that without guarantees for religious freedoms, the new Constitution excluded those with a Christian worldview from the socialist community. These letters framed human rights as fully compatible with state socialism, so long as the SED did not decide to arbitrarily and unnecessarily reject Christians and Christianity. Only when the SED rejected its own Christian citizens, would they be forced to vote against the constitution in the upcoming vote.[31] Suddenly, it was individual East Germans offering a carrot and a stick to the SED: if we Christians are provided with rights, we will be good citizens and support the constitution, but if not, we will be forced to become unruly.

A letter from Michael G. of the city of Halle is typical of letters from Christians using human rights language during the *Volksaussprache*.[32] He opens by saying he was an "informed citizen of the socialist GDR," and was greatly concerned by the discrepancies between Ulbricht's New Year's address and his other speeches, in which he assured East Germans that religious freedom would not be diminished.

As a Christian, I must also state that the right to freedom of conscience (which concerns not only Christians), as well as crucial basic rights of churches and religious communities have been eliminated. Freedom of conscience is granted in our present Constitution in Article 41 and in the "Universal Declaration of Human Rights" in Article 18. Since conscience belongs to the heart of every person, I consider it essential to explicitly state this right to freedom of conscience again.

Having established first his bona fides as a good citizen and helpfully pointing out the omissions of the draft, he then made a plea for a socialist GDR in which Christians could continue to play an active role.

It is not enough for me that these rights are still granted, but not mentioned in discussions and presentations of the draft Constitution. It is clear to me that a socialist state also needs a socialist constitution. But I also think that nevertheless the attribute – socialist – should not in this sense be absolute and constant, so that nothing else counts.

---

[31] There were still a handful of Christians who did argue for religious rights as natural and timeless. A couple from Templin demanded the inclusion of rights to religious practice and freedom of belief based on the principle that "these human rights cannot be changed through law," BArch, DA1/4076 Letter no. 1569.

[32] BArch, DA1/4116 Letter no. 5573.

In his conclusion, he continued to walk the line between being helpful and demanding, writing, "I consider that the removal of rights through the limitation of the above Articles, cannot be deemed an advance from the basic rights of the current Constitution and I expect a response or changes."

Some citizens directly linked their demands to the East German campaign for diplomatic recognition and membership in the United Nations. In a letter deemed by the constitutional commission "typical of working Christians and Catholics," a man from Dresden asked, "since the GDR is striving for membership in the UN, shouldn't the human rights that are binding for all UN members be included without restrictions in the new Constitution?"[33] In another example, a letter signed by four professionals from Erfurt asking for the inclusion of greater religious freedoms, cautioned that the GDR's good work would be put at risk by the absence of human rights in the constitution.

The German Democratic Republic aspires towards membership in the United Nations. We support this effort wholeheartedly. Through this our Republic would have the opportunity on a global platform in the forum of all peoples to show that the idea of humanism is universally possible. This means, however, that we need to make the positive aspects and conditions of UN [membership] our own.[34]

Such arguments connecting human rights to foreign policy goals were not limited to educated professionals: At a public meeting of workers in Frankfurt/Oder, some asked whether it would create problems for the GDR when it eventually joined the United Nations if the constitution did not include all the rights of the UDHR, specifically the right to leave the country.[35]

As the result of the Church campaign, human rights language appeared not only across the whole of the GDR but it was also employed by a broad cross-section of society. Even Dresden, which was unable to receive Western TV signals (known colloquially as the Valley of the Clueless), produced a high concentration of letters on religious freedom – a strong indicator for the success of Church campaigns over the influence of foreign media.[36] While individual letter writers using the language of human rights were often male, group letters from small communities and

---

[33] BArch, DA1/4126 Letter no. 6544.   [34] BArch, DA1/4202 Letter no. 4718.

[35] BArch, DY6/4544 3/68 Sonderinformation über die Diskussion der Werktätigen zur Ausarbeitung einer sozialistischen Verfassung in der DDR (15.2.1968), 10.

[36] Officials noted high concentrations of letters from Cottbus and Dresden on religious freedom. BArch, DY30/IV2/1/373 Bericht der Kommission über die Verfassung der DDR, 118.

religious groups included large numbers of female signatories.[37] In class terms, educated professionals were more likely to invoke human rights, but here as well, group letters contained a wide cross-section of society. One group petition with 15 signatories from Erfurt, which cited the UDHR in demanding greater religious freedom and the right to travel, included six high school students, three university students, three office clerks, a pipefitter, an electrician and an apprentice.[38] East Germans did not universally use the language of human rights, but when human rights were translated into the everyday problems and concerns of GDR citizens, no particular region, gender or class averred from using this language to make demands.

While the Church-organised campaign for religious rights provided the script for the vast majority of human rights-based claims by East Germans, some citizens came up with their own arguments, bolstered by various sources.[39] Most media coverage of human rights remained vague as to the exact contents of the Universal Declaration and the UN Human Rights Covenants, but East Germans could – with a little effort – find the full texts in domestically printed sources. The UDHR was reprinted in the widely available 1966 reference book *The UN*, and the UN Covenants could be found in the mass-produced publications of the Committee for the Protection of Human Rights (KSM).[40] In two pamphlets specially prepared for International Year for Human Rights, the KSM helpfully printed the entire text of both covenants, so every citizen could easily compare and contrast how each article had been achieved through specific East German laws.[41] One article in the Christian Democratic newspaper *Neue Zeit* directed readers to the East German journal on the United Nations – *UNO-Bilanz* – for the full text of the International Covenant on Political and Civil Rights, if they were interested in confirming the fidelity of the new criminal code to

---

[37] On the predominance of men as the public face of Eastern European human rights, see Bolton, *Worlds of Dissent*, 43.

[38] BArch, DA1/4126 Letter no. 6507.

[39] Around half of the letters sent to the Constitution Commission concerned religion, whereas the right to travel (Article 28) was the subject of 3 percent of the letters received and the right to freedom of opinion and expression (Article 23) represented almost 2 percent. BArch, NY4192/111 Gliederung der Vorschläge nach Artikeln des Verfassungsentwurfs.

[40] Peter Klein, *Die UNO* (Berlin: Dietz, 1966), 166–72. Cited in BArch, DA1/4076 Letter no. 1533. This same book was also cited by dissidents in the late 1980s. Archiv der DDR-Opposition, Samizdat PS 013/05 Aufbruch: Informationsmaterial des Ökumenischen Friedenskreises (26.7.1988), 7.

[41] Hermann Klenner, *Die politischen Bürgerrechte in der DDR* (Berlin: Komitee zum Schutze der Menschenrechte, 1967). Willi Büchner-Uhder, *Sozialistische Menschenrechte in der DDR* (Berlin: Komitee zum Schutze der Menschenrechte, 1968).

international law.[42] A wide variety of popular publications also printed detailed information about the rights contained in these international documents: one man from Cottbus noted in his letter to the constitutional commission that he learned about the Universal Declaration from his wife's copy of the GDR women's magazine *Für Dich*.[43]

Without the unifying effect of the Church, responses on other issues were eclectic in argumentation and style. Lothar M. from the village of Dobberkau said that while the living standard in the GDR was high and the right to work was clearly realised, the failure to include the right to travel could give the unfortunate impression, both at home and in the West, that the GDR was "similar to a prison that one cannot leave."[44] Dieter A. from Seifersdorf expressed his worry that without the inclusion of a right to travel, the constitution – and with it the GDR as a whole – would be seen as falling behind the goals of the UDHR.[45] A chemist from the northern city of Rostock bluntly asserted that everyone had certain basic rights and that the right to travel could not be restricted to a mere right to choose a place of residence within a country: "The right to free expression is an inalienable right and a hallmark of human dignity," and "a partial right of free movement is none at all."[46]

East Germans contested many more issues than just religion, travel and free expression, but these were the only rights they portrayed as human rights. When GDR citizens challenged the SED's monopoly on political power or dealt with problems of gender inequality and women's rights, or economic rights, they did not connect these issues to human rights. These citizens eschewed universalism and chose instead to ground their criticism in established discourses, identities and local traditions. When it came to political rights, East Germans most often criticised the new Art. 1 (which enshrined SED political dominance) as a violation of socialist democracy or by provocatively pointing to the Prague Spring as a positive example for the GDR to follow.[47] While East German protests about abortion shifted dramatically in the late 1960s from a discourse of alleviating social harm towards an emphasis on personal rights, women did not connect their demands for bodily self-determination to international human rights rhetoric during the *Volksaussprache*.[48] Many workers complained that they did not have the right to form their own union, or choose their place of employment, and they

---

[42] Walter Trebs, "Mit Völkerrecht im Einklang," *Neue Zeit* (4.2.1968).
[43] BArch, DA1/4077 Letter no. 1606.   [44] BArch, DA1/4079 Letter no. 1839.
[45] BArch, DA1/4173 Letter no. 11227.   [46] BArch, DA1/4162 Letter no. 10193.
[47] BArch, DA1/4126 Letter no. 6516 and Letter no. 10089 for respective examples.
[48] Donna Harsch, "Society, the State, and Abortion in East Germany, 1950–1972," *American Historical Review* 102, no. 1 (1997), 53–84.

even protested the formal loss of the right to strike (even if it had never been a reality) causing a significant backlash. One SED official described the letters demanding a right to strike as "spiteful" – with some citizens proclaiming it as the "basic democratic right of the worker."[49] When these GDR citizens spoke of "democratic rights," they did so from within a tradition of class struggle and their identities as workers, without aspiring to any vision of international human rights.

Those who sought to actively disrupt the *Volksaussprache* by distributing leaflets attacking the process or writing anti-SED graffiti on public buildings, sometimes invoked specific freedoms they wanted to be instated but, here again, they did not make claims in the human rights terms. The most common form of attack, as documented by the Stasi, was slogans such as "Have Courage, Vote No!" or leaflets that read "We Berliners big and small say no to the constitution."[50] While some leaflets dealt with political and civil freedoms – one sent out in Weimar called for "free and secret elections, and press and information freedom" – these did not use the vocabulary of rights, let alone human rights. Dissenting leaflets more directly denounced the SED for, as one put it, creating the "Human Prison of the GDR."[51] When outright defying the SED, East Germans chose brevity over appeals to abstract ideals and international law.

In response to the huge outpouring of concern from East German Christians, the SED did in fact increase the number of Articles in the Constitution on freedom of religion and belief from one to two. In announcing this change, alongside 118 other minor revisions, the constitutional commission pronounced: "Our constitution documents before all the world that the rights of citizens are in full accordance with the human rights declaration of the United Nations." The commission went on to declare that the GDR had realised the very UN ideals that had originally birthed the UDHR in 1948 in the face of the "thousand-fold injustice in many capitalist states."[52] When voting day finally came on 6 April 1968, the SED leadership received the mass approval they had wanted from the *Volksentscheid* (plebiscite). After weeks of education,

---

[49] BArch, DA1/ 4201 7. Bericht über die bei dem Verfassungskomitee eingegangenen Zustimmungen und Vorschläge (8.3.-14.3.), 8. Democratic rights quotation from BArch, DA1/4157 Letter no. 9650.

[50] It rhymed in the original: "Wir Berliner groß und klein, sagen zur Verfassung Nein."

[51] All quotes from BStU, MfS, Bericht der HA XX/2 zur Aktion "Optimismus" (11.4.1968).

[52] "Bericht über die Ergebnisse der Volksaussprache zum Entwurf der neuen, sozialistischen Verfassung der DDR und die Änderungen zum Verfassungsentwurf," *Berliner Zeitung* (28.3.1968), 5.

negotiations, threats and coercion, nearly 95 percent of the eligible East German population voted in favour of the new constitution. Electoral participation by the clergy, usually around 60 percent, even increased to around 90 percent.[53] The officially tally counted 11,536,803 votes for yes, 409,733 for no, and 24,353 spoiled ballots.[54]

In the USSR, 1968 opened with a major trial of prominent dissidents; in neighbouring Czechoslovakia, the Prague Spring would soon lead to an armed Soviet intervention to end the effort at creating "socialism with a human face."[55] By contrast, the GDR had managed to conduct a nationwide process of political reform – formally granting even greater power to the SED – and, outside of a few dozen pamphleteers and a large quantity of polite letters from the populace, it had avoided significant disruption or unrest. While SED officials saw the bishops as a nuisance, a report by the constitutional commission spoke proudly of the massive response from Christians because it demonstrated their political engagement. Although some priests and pastors had spoken out against the Constitution on religious grounds, thankfully none had called for a return to a "bourgeois parliamentary" system, as was happening in Czechoslovakia.[56] In spite of Ulbricht tempting fate with the *Volksaussprache*, and a few sympathetic protests in solidarity with the events in Prague later that year, the GDR was one of the few countries in the world not rocked by mass protest and dissent in 1968.[57]

Ultimately, religious leaders had successfully mobilised the Christian community within the existing structure of the Marxist-Leninist state and their limited call for pluralism in terms of worldview did not extend to political pluralism as well. Thousands of East Germans had either taken up the language of human rights to protest a state policy, or at least signed their names to letters that did so, but those who most radically

---

[53] Robert Goeckel, *The Lutheran Church and the East German State: Political Conflict and Change under Ulbricht and Honecker* (Ithaca, NY: Cornell University Press, 1990), 179.

[54] Final statistics cited in BArch, DY30/J IV 2/2/116 Erklärung der Regierung der DDR an die Internationale Konferenz über Menschenrechte vom 22.4. bis 13.5.1968 in Teheran, 2.

[55] Steven Jensen, *The Making of International Human Rights: The 1960s, Decolonization and the Reconstruction of Global Values* (Cambridge: Cambridge University Press, 2016), 180.

[56] BArch, DY30/IV 2/1/373 Bericht der Kommission über die Verfassung der DDR von Klaus Sorgenicht, 118–21.

[57] Ilko-Sascha Kowalczuk, "'Wer sich nicht in Gefahr begibt …' Protestaktionen gegen Die Intervention in Prag und die Folgen von 1968 für die DDR-Opposition," in *Widerstand und Opposition in der DDR*, ed. Klaus-Dietmar Henke, Peter Steinbach and Johannes Tuchel (Cologne: Böhlau, 1999), 260. The SED faced more popular protest over the decision to tear down the historic University Church in Leipzig that summer. Andrew Demshuk, *Demolition on Karl Marx Square: Cultural Barbarism and the People's State in 1968* (Oxford: Oxford University Press, 2017).

challenge the SED did not press forward with these demands when their complaints went unheeded. The year 1968 did not foster a movement for democratic change, nor did those who spoke out about human rights at the *Volksaussprache* (aside from a handful of exceptions) expand on this protest by demanding systemic political reform. Nonetheless, the demands made in 1968 represented a precursor to new kinds of protest that would emerge in the 1970s as the problems of freedom of travel, expression and religion became increasingly intertwined with the language of human rights, both domestically and globally.

A Church for Human Rights and a Church in Socialism

Although the Protestant and Catholic churches put up a real fight in 1968 against the loss of their constitutional rights, in the following decade, the leadership of both institutions refrained from using human rights to directly confront SED power.[58] The demands during the *Volksaussprache* were not the beginning of more confrontational Church politics, but the forerunner to the SED's accommodation of Christianity within the socialist system. In the early 1970s, the SED shifted tactics away from encouraging a steady decline in religious observance to demanding its integration as a "Church for Socialism," so that organised Christianity would "not be a foreign body" in the system.[59] To avoid openly endorsing state socialism, the Catholic Church withdrew from political life in the GDR, not resurfacing until 1989. For Protestants, however, human rights became part of an internal struggle for the soul of the Church. Those seeking to fight against state power found in human rights a new vocabulary to legitimise opposition to SED abuses. Others aimed to secure the position of the Church as a recognised institution in the GDR by working with the SED by finding common ground through shared solidarity with the Global South. Rather than empowering dissent against the state, the human rights provisions contained in the Helsinki Accords of 1975 presented an opportunity for some Protestant leaders to demonstrate their willingness to work with the SED and their rejection of open political dissent to protect Church autonomy.[60]

---

[58] On the political neutralisation of human rights in the church, see Ehrhart Neubert, *Geschichte der Opposition in der DDR: 1949–1989* (Berlin: Ch. Links, 1998), 356.

[59] Goeckel, *The Lutheran Church and the East German State*, 172–75.

[60] Historical accounts, as well as memoirs from church officials, have often portrayed the use of human rights language in this era as inherently oppositional, but omit the Church's 1968 campaign as well as the accommodations to SED human rights ideology in the 1970s. Daniel Thomas, *The Helsinki Effect: International Norms, Human*

In the early 1970s, the Catholic Church in the GDR continued to occasionally use the language of human rights as a means of protest. When the SED liberalised the GDR's abortion law in 1972, making the procedure freely available in the first trimester of pregnancy, Catholic bishops used the UDHR and the 1968 Constitution to demand that doctors have a right to refuse to perform abortions.[61] In the same year, the SED reacted poorly to Archbishop of Berlin Alfred Bengsch invoking human rights, linking demands for more Church autonomy to the GDR's admission into the United Nations.[62] In 1974, Catholic Bishops also argued that the UDHR protected parents' right to choose how their children were educated.[63] While SED officials were often frustrated by the Church's use of "bourgeois human rights" (and by Archbishop Bengsch in particular), Catholic officials understood human rights only in terms of freedom of religious practice and conscience as Catholics against the atheistic forces of state socialism.[64]

By contrast the Protestant Church looked to the activism of the ecumenical WCC as a guide to human rights engagement both at home and globally. In 1969, East German Protestants were formally split from their Western counterparts, forming the Federation of *Protestant Churches in the GDR* (Bund Evangelischen Kirchen in der DDR, or BEK). In contrast to West German Protestants who saw human rights as a vehicle for anti-communism, the BEK became a strong supporter of the WCC's antiracism campaign, which sought to use the politics of human rights to aid the Global South.[65] From the perspective of the Protestant Church

---

Rights, and the Demise of Communism (Princeton, NJ: Princeton University Press, 2001), 102; Paul Betts, *Within Walls: Private Life in the German Democratic Republic* (Oxford: Oxford University Press, 2010). Manfred Stolpe omits his praise for SED compliance with international human rights norms in "Kirchliche Menschenrechtsarbeit muß weitergehen," in ed. Manfred Stolpe and Iring Fetscher, *Demokratie wagen: Aufbruch in Brandenburg: Reden, Beiträge, Interviews 1990–1993* (Berlin: Schüren, 1994), 193. For the self-serving claim that the very term human rights was taboo in the early 1970s: Albrecht Schönherr, *Gratwanderung: Gedanken über den Weg des Bundes der Evangelischen Kirchen in der DDR* (Leipzig: Evangelische Verlagsanstalt, 1992), 28–29. Particularly self-serving is Günter Krusche's account, an active informant for the Stasi and an opponent of the dissident movement as a Protestant Church leader. Günter Krusche "Menschenrechte in christlicher Verantwortung. Die Kirchen in der DDR und die Menschenrechte," *Ökumenische Rundschau* 49 (2000), 26–42.

[61] Ute Haese, *Katholische Kirche in der DDR: Geschichte einer politischen Abstinenz* (Düsseldorf: Patmos Verlag, 1998), 72.

[62] Ibid., 89.

[63] "Zur Christlichen Erziehung: Hirtenwort der in der Berliner Ordinarienkonferenz versammelten Bischöfe," in Lange, *Katholische Kirche – sozialistischer Staat DDR*, 257.

[64] Schäfer, *The East German State and the Catholic Church, 1945–1989*, 130, 280.

[65] On East German Christian involvement with international antiracism and human rights, see Horst Dähn, *Konfrontation oder Kooperation? das Verhältnis von Staat und Kirche in der*

leaders in the GDR, human rights transcended the political animus of the East-West ideological divide.[66] This meant walking a path that rejected both the crushing atheistic collectivism of socialism and the secular individualism of Western liberalism. As such, support for universal human rights needed to focus on ending the suffering of the poorest and most desperate in the Global South, rather than demanding political rights for relatively prosperous Europeans. Within the BEK, a human rights working group was formed, which elaborated on this vision of Christian human rights by arguing that "if we as Christians or as a Church advocate for human rights, we cannot simply aim to fulfil our own individual demands but must rather see human rights first as the rights of others."[67]

This transcendent conception of human rights proved to be compatible with SED ideology as it rejected Western individualism, emphasised the importance of fulfilling basic needs, and supported international solidarity with postcolonial states. At one extreme, this led some East German Protestant institutions to reproduce many of the tenets of socialist human rights but coloured by a Christian outlook. A newsletter published by the Ecumenical Youth Service, specifically on the subject of the WCC and human rights, focused on abuses in Apartheid South Africa and the crimes of the military Junta in Chile. One article, written by the "UN Study Group of the GDR Christian Peace Conference," perfectly reproduced the theories of East German legal theorist Hermann Klenner as it explained how human rights were originally part of a system of bourgeois exploitation brought down by the October Revolution, which finally ushered in a truly liberating vision of human rights. The UDHR was presented as the continuation of the socialist ideal – the abstention of the Soviet bloc in 1948 naturally omitted – and the socialist world was depicted as valiantly fighting for real human rights in the face of capitalist obstruction at the United Nations. Within the GDR, "the building of a socialist society can be understood as a comprehensive attempt to create social conditions for the realization of human rights," and an editorial cautioned that even churches are "not free from the prejudices, emotions and commitments that are visible in the secular

---

SBZ/DDR 1945–1980 (Opladen: Westdeutscher Verlag, 1982); Hedwig Richter, *Pietismus im Sozialismus: Die Herrnhuter Brüdergemeine in der DDR* (Göttingen: Vandenhoeck & Ruprecht, 2009), 245–55. On the politics of the WCC, see Albers, "Der ÖRK und die Menschenrechte im Kontext von Kaltem Krieg und Dekolonisierung," 189.

[66] This view was echoed by the Moravian Church of East Germany, which was not a part of the BEK. Richter, *Pietismus im Sozialismus*, 247.

[67] Neubert, *Geschichte der Opposition in der DDR*, 260.

discussion [of human rights]."[68] Problems within the socialist world were trivial in comparison to the real human rights abuses experienced by those oppressed by imperialism or living under military regimes, where starvation, poverty and torture were the norm.

Others within the Church, however, saw human rights as a means to both mobilise East German Christians for anti-imperial solidarity *and* to challenge injustices perpetrated at home. In 1973, the GDR branch of the Lutheran World Federation – another organisation aiming to link together Christians on a global scale – produced a study that blended Protestant theology with socialist human rights theory, but nevertheless critiqued the SED's failure to respect the rights of the individual.[69] *Concerns for a Human World: The Normativity and Relativity of Human Rights* praised both socialism and human rights as forces for progress, but at the same time saw real existing socialism in the GDR as terribly flawed. The authors acknowledged that SED human rights theory legitimised GDR policy in terms that would technically satisfy the legal standards of the United Nations, but believed that "[the SED] interpretation is, however, not in accord with reality."[70] Human rights were not only a matter of pressing moral importance, but also a political opportunity because "advocacy for humanity and human rights will provide legitimacy for our activities ... even if efforts to implement human rights are inherently illegal."[71] While more conciliatory Christians believed that the Church should not take sides politically, these authors argued that "the struggle for the dignity and rights of man is ongoing. Our churches cannot remain neutral in this struggle."[72] The SED secretary of state for church affairs prevented the publication of the study, but copies circulated underground in Church circles, as would increasingly become the case with human rights texts in the ensuing years.[73]

While much of the BEK leadership aimed at conciliation with the SED through human rights, Hans-Joachim Fränkel, Bishop of Görlitz, saw the concept as a tool to fight back against state abuses of power.[74] During the *Volksaussprache* in 1968, Fränkel had prepared the theological case for

---

[68] The text also specifically refers to Lenin's "Declaration of the Rights of the Working and Exploited Peoples" as the watershed moment in human rights history. Archiv der DDR-Opposition, HL 204/9 "Zur Bedeutung und Problematik der Menschenrechte," *Information: Ökumenischer Jugenddienst* 11 (1974), 1–6.

[69] Kunter, "Human Rights as a Theological and Political Controversy among East German and Czech Protestants," 224.

[70] EZA 687/46 "Sorge um eine menschliche Welt: Normativität und Relativität der Menschenrechte" (1973), 5.

[71] Ibid., 42–43.   [72] Ibid., 65.

[73] Kunter, *Die Kirchen im KSZE-Prozess, 1968–1978*, 119–20.

[74] Neubert, *Geschichte der Opposition in der DDR*, 262–66.

human rights for general distribution to congregants; in 1972, he began to openly criticise SED power and socialist rights theory. In one address, he attacked the interconnection of rights and duties, saying "the essence of human worth and basic rights is misjudged if they are tied to the measure of performance for socialism. [...] Human rights only have meaning if they are recognized as natural rights and do not presume a certain [ideological] conviction."[75] In early 1975, he publicly argued that no society could fully realise all human rights equally, but "action in the struggle against racism cannot be an alibi for refraining from standing up for human rights at home."[76] Fränkel did not fully embrace Western anti-communism and he continued to acknowledge the need for collective economic rights, but he maintained that rights were natural and rooted in God, not merely a by-product of historical development.

The SED and state security tolerated Christian human rights activism – even encouraged it – but only so long as it remained limited to antiracism and international solidarity. A report noted, without criticism, that there were elements within the GDR that "sought through human rights arguments to further the tolerance of religion and the activities of the Church." The danger did not lie with these Christians, but rather "the reactionary representatives of the Church in the GDR who go farther and insinuate that the socialist state violates human rights and use this to go after the sovereignty and legitimacy of the state and the leading role of the party, and to reject education based on class consciousness."[77] The red line that the churches could not cross when it came to human rights was to challenge the legitimacy of the Party or to directly undermine the ideological preparation of future generations. The SED now accepted that a Christian worldview was acceptable within the socialist state, so long as it posed no threat to socialism.

When Erich Honecker signed the Helsinki Accords on 1 August 1975, it failed to spark a new outburst of Christian human rights activism, and instead led to its co-optation and marginalisation. The Catholic Church in the GDR largely withdrew from politics altogether: after the 1974 protest on education, the next official mention of human rights by Catholic officials East Germany did not come until autumn 1989.[78] The Protestant Church, however, welcomed the signing of the Helsinki Accords in 1975, but its members were split as to why. On the one hand, there were

---

[75] Goeckel, *The Lutheran Church and the East German State*, 216.

[76] EZA 687/46 "Das Zeugnis der Bibel in seiner Bedeutung für die Menschenrechte" (April 1975). Neubert, *Geschichte der Opposition in der DDR*, 262.

[77] ThSA-R 5-61-1000/7 Bezirkstag und Rat des Bezirkes Gera 17308 "Information zur Diskussion über die Fragen der Menschenrechte in den Kirchen" (1974), 2.

[78] Haese, *Katholische Kirche in der DDR*, 92–93.

radical elements that continued to see human rights as a tool for legitimising resistance and strengthening the resolve of dissident Christians. On
the other hand, the leaders of the BEK saw Helsinki as an opportunity to
speed along their larger project of normalising church-state relations.[79]
By endorsing the SED's line on international human rights, the BEK
leadership believed that they could promote peace and combat racism
abroad, while protecting religious believers and conscientious objectors
to conscription at home at the cost of symbolically endorsing certain
aspects of SED human rights rhetoric.

Soon after the signing of the Accords, a group of senior BEK leaders
publicly affirmed the SED's position on the meaning of human rights
and Helsinki. In a 1976 paper, Manfred Stolpe, head of the secretariat of
the BEK, argued that the GDR had already fulfilled all human rights
obligations demanded by international law, and that criticisms of the
SED "usually come from a one-sided individualistic understanding of
human rights."[80] The document signalled the Church's interest in a
greater role in East German society, but also reassured the SED that –
as an institution – it did not aim to undermine the power of the state and
that it did not plan to ally with outsiders in their attacks on the GDR.
While in the early 1970s, anti-imperialism and solidarity with the Global
South had formed a point of commonality between East German Protestants and the SED, by the late 1970s, it was the cause of peace that
brought together the two sides. The GDR Synod stated "Helsinki
showed us: One cannot talk about peace without mentioning human
rights. One cannot want human rights for the individual without standing
up for peace for all."[81]

While the Protestant Church as an institution had previously held
competing positions on human rights, after Helsinki, the leadership
strived to present a united front to both the state and its own adherents.
The previously combative Bishop Fränkel soon ceased his politicised
human rights sermons; instead, he spoke out against those who used
Helsinki to legitimise emigration.[82] In 1976, he declaimed: "as a Church,
we can only work for the full achievement of the goals set out in Helsinki,

---

[79] Ehrhart Neubert, *Geschichte der Opposition in der DDR: 1949–1989* (Berlin: Ch. Links
Verlag, 1998), 356–59.

[80] EZA 687/46 Manfred Stolpe, "Universale Menschenrechte" (27.6.1976), 13. Stolpe was
supported by Christa Lewek, his subordinate in the Secretariat, and by East Berlin
Superintendent Günter Krusche (a Stasi informant, IM Günter). On Krusche and the
Stasi, see Wendy Tyndale, *Protestants in Communist East Germany: In the Storm of the
World* (Burlington, VT: Ashgate, 2010), 159.

[81] Quoted in Kunter, "Human Rights as a Theological and Political Controversy among
East German and Czech Protestants," 225.

[82] Neubert, *Geschichte der Opposition in der DDR*, 265–66.

if we also work to ensure that greater opportunities for communication do not lead to the emptying out of important workplaces through the abuse of this trust."[83] The BEK distributed copies of the Accords and other international human rights documents across the GDR, and held organised educational seminars to teach pastors how to integrate human rights with protestant theology in a manner that would not antagonise the state.[84] Church leadership also suppressed grassroots efforts to use human rights to criticise the SED. In 1977, a group of theology students from Naumburg produced and publicly distributed the "Querfurt Paper," which rejected the idea of class conflict and called for pluralism and human rights. Although they did not even explicitly attack the SED, such talk was enough to bring about disciplinary action by the church hierarchy (and close surveillance by the Stasi).[85] The BEK also actively rejected any work with Western NGOs, including Amnesty International, refusing to share information with them, let alone assist in their campaigns.[86]

This policy of conciliation towards the state paid off in 1978, when the BEK came to an agreement with the SED in which they would be recognised as a "Church in Socialism," rather than a "Church for Socialism." After nearly three decades, the SED no longer actively sought the decline and eventual dissolution of Christianity within the borders of the GDR. This agreement stipulated that the Church would not become a "disguised opposition party," but there were many in the grassroots who continued to agitate for political change including Ulrich Woronowicz, a pastor who founded the "Working Group on Human Rights" in the Brandenburg town of Wittenberge.[87] As a young theology student in the early 1950s, Woronowicz fled to West Germany, but later returned to continue working for the church in the GDR.[88] The Working Group sought to transform human rights into a means of mobilising Christians to fight injustice and to legitimise criticism of SED abuses by translating the abstract language of international treaties with the everyday vocabulary of Christian worship. One sample prayer written in 1978 read,

---

[83] Quoted in ibid., 258.
[84] EZA 687/47 Niederschrift über die Sitzung der ad hoc Gruppe Menschenrechte (14.10.1976)
[85] Neubert, *Geschichte der Opposition in der DDR*, 316. Lothar Tautz, ed., *Friede und Gerechtigkeit heute: das "Querfurter Papier" – ein politisches Manifest für die Einhaltung der Menschenrechte in der DDR* (Magdeburg: Sachsen-Anhalt LStU, 2002); Hanisch, *Die DDR im KSZE-Prozess*, 140–41.
[86] EZA 101/683 Arbeitsgruppe Menschenrechte beim BEK, Auszug aus dem Protokoll der 55. Sitzung des Vorstandes der Konferenz der Ev. Kirchenleitungen (30.6.1975).
[87] Neubert, *Geschichte der Opposition in der DDR*, 355.   [88] Ibid., 97.

Lord, Thou God of justice and peace,
You call on us to be the voice of the voiceless.
That is why we lament to you the disregard of human dignity in
many countries.
We lament the violation of guaranteed human rights in our own
country.
We think about ... (individuals, groups and issues can be called
here.)[89]

For the 30th anniversary of the UDHR, the group openly challenged the
BEK line in prayer, saying "we lament to you [God] the violation and
contempt for human rights in many countries around the world and in
our own," and asked for divine help to find the courage to "defend
against injustice within the church and in the world."[90] Such critical
initiative from below was not appreciated by Church leaders and when
Woronowicz sent material on human rights directly to the BEK that had
not been pre-approved by his local superiors, it was simply returned
without comment.[91] In 1979, the Working Group was disbanded under
intense pressure from both Church leadership and the Stasi.[92]

In the years following the signing of the Helsinki Accords, the SED
and the Stasi were, however, consistently positive about the Church's
institutional engagement with human rights. The SED bureaucracy positively noted that Church activities on the Helsinki process were free of
imperialist propaganda. In October 1975, when the BEK held an event
on the Accords and human rights in the town of Buckow, one state
official happily observed that the "consciousness of the [Helsinki
Accords] in socialist countries was praised," and that the discussion
exhibited "no anti-communist tendencies."[93] When the BEK produced
the short book "Human Rights and Christian Responsibility" in 1981, a
reviewer for the ministry responsible for church oversight found it to be
"an explicit rejection of the imperialist forces and enemies of Détente
that seek to incorporate the Churches of the GDR into the anti-
communist and interventionist conception of human rights."[94] So long

---

[89] Archiv der DDR-Opposition, Ki 02/03 Evangelische Kirche in Berlin-Brandenburg,
Arbeitsgruppe Menschenrechte. Meeting at Hirschluch (26./27.5.1978).
[90] Archiv der DDR-Opposition, Ki 02/03 Evangelische Kirche in Berlin-Brandenburg,
Arbeitsgruppe Menschenrechte (27.11.1978)
[91] EZA 101/686 Schönherr to Stolpe (16.1.1978).
[92] Archiv der DDR-Opposition, Ki 02/03 Evangelische Kirche in Berlin-Brandenburg,
Arbeitsgruppe Menschenrechte. Linn to Woronowicz (13.7.1979); Neubert, *Geschichte
der Opposition in der DDR*, 315.
[93] BArch, DO4/4727 Information Nr. 2/1976 zur KSZE-Konsulation der Konferenz
Europäischer Kirchen vom 27. bis 31.10.1975 in Buckow/DDR vom (19.1.1976), 5–6.
[94] Christa Lewek et al., *Menschenrechte in christlicher Verantwortung* (Berlin: Evangelische
Verlagsanstalt, 1981). BArch, DO4/495 Zu einigen Problemen der gegenwärtigen

as Christians criticised abuses in the capitalist world, and publicly down-played violations in the GDR, the SED had no objections.[95] To avoid the marginalisation of the Catholic Church, the BEK accepted SED rhetoric internationally and disciplined those within its own ranks who would upset the political order, to more freely work to achieve its spiritual, moral and institutional goals at home and abroad. The acceptance of SED human rights framing had paid off for the Churches once before, in 1968, when they were given additional formal legal recognition in the new Constitution. Continued collaboration on human rights issues appeared to offer a more conciliatory path forward.

But for many East German Christians, these theological debates were irrelevant to what they viewed was the central problem of human rights: emigration. The case of Rainer Bäurich, an engineer from Dresden and devout Christian, is one example of those who embraced the idea of becoming West German rather than seeking to realise his rights as a Christian within the GDR. Bäurich served five years in prison after his letter to Bavarian Minister-President Franz Josef Strauß, "Manifesto of a Christian under Socialism," was intercepted by the Stasi. In making his case to emigrate, which was eventually allowed, he stated, "I unre-servedly declare my allegiance to the Federal Republic of Germany, which I regard as my fatherland, now that the territory of the GDR has obviously been lost to Germany. [...] I am tormented by this yearning for the Federal Republic, because this free, pluralistic welfare state is my intellectual and political home."[96] Although the leadership of the Prot-estant Church engaged with human rights as a theological challenge, emigration rather than apartheid was far more present in the everyday life of GDR Christians.

Human Rights and the Emigrationists

After the Second World War, Hannah Arendt argued that there was a paradox at the heart of the idea of human rights: their existence and their loss "coincides with the instant a person becomes a human being in general – without profession, without a citizenship, without an opinion,

---

Auseinandersetzung um die Menschenrechte unter besonderer Berücksichtigung der Haltung der Kirchen, 18.
[95] Hanisch, *Die DDR im KSZE-Prozess*, 134–35.
[96] Ibid. and Rainer Bäurich, "Manifest eines Christen im Sozialismus," in Roger Woods, *Opposition in the GDR under Honecker, 1971–85* (Basingstoke: Macmillan, 1986), 177; Eberhard Kuhrt, Hannsjörg Buck and Gunter Holzweissig, *Am Ende des realen Sozialismus 3. Opposition in der DDR von den 70er Jahren bis zum Zusammenbruch der SED-Herrschaft* (Opladen: Leske & Budrich, 1999), 87–88.

without a deed by which to identify and specify himself."[97] In the case of the GDR, this explains how citizens seeking to emigrate turned to the language of human rights once appeals to all other forms of civic identity had failed, and why human rights demands to exit did not produce a broader movement for political change. The SED responded to exit-applications, especially those made public, by means of coercion and psychological intimidation.[98] Through the loss of benefits, employment and education, the SED effectively broke the social bonds between those individuals asking to leave and their friends, co-workers and acquaintances. On the one hand, this discouraged others from following in their footsteps, but on the other hand, it radicalised citizens who were pushed to the margins of society as they tried to leave. As a result, most of those who internalised a belief that they had inherent human rights against the state were severely isolated and sought to depart the GDR altogether rather than change it from within.[99]

As with Christian human rights protests, those seeking to emigrate also began to make their demands well before the signing of the Helsinki Accords. Requests to travel and emigrate dropped sharply after the building of the Berlin Wall in 1961, but in 1972, the number of applications once again began to rise.[100] For many East Germans, travel to the West had been a constant desire (if only because every other family had relatives in the Federal Republic), but the early 1970s brought a double blow of declining social mobility and global price shocks for raw goods causing a drop in standards of living, which prompted a renewed impulse to emigrate permanently.[101] On the level of international diplomacy, it was not human rights promises that drove applications to travel and exit, but rather the normalisation of relations between East and West, and the relaxation of Cold War tensions under détente. When the Four-Power Agreement on Berlin reaffirming the post-war rights and responsibilities of the United States, the United Kingdom, France and

---

[97] Roger Berkowitz, "Hannah Arendt on Human Rights," in *Handbook of Human Rights*, ed. Thomas Cushman (London: Routledge, 2012), 63.

[98] Manfred Gehrmann, *Die Überwindung des "Eisernen Vorhangs": Die Abwanderung aus der DDR in die BRD/West-Berlin 1949–1989 als innerdeutsches Migranten-Netzwerk* (Berlin: Ch. Links, 2009), 148–59.

[99] On the "shift in subjectivity" from instrumentalisation to internalisation, Mark Goodale and Sally Engle Merry, *The Practice of Human Rights: Tracking Law between the Global and the Local* (Cambridge: Cambridge University Press, 2007), 43–44.

[100] Major, *Behind the Berlin Wall*, 198.

[101] On family connections, ibid., 199. On declining social mobility, see Detlef Pollack, "Modernization and Modernization Blockages in GDR Society," in *Dictatorship as Experience: Towards a Socio-Cultural History of the GDR*, ed. Konrad Jarausch (New York: Berghahn, 1999), 27–46. On price shocks, see Gareth Dale, *Popular Protest in East Germany* (London: Routledge, 2004), 72.

the USSR as occupying powers was signed in 1971, the main question GDR citizens asked at public meetings was how this would make their own personal travel to the West easier.[102] Reports noted that there were "citizens who are little prepared to bring themselves to understand the politically necessary measures in regards to travel and the reasons for their rejection are not recognized."[103] While the agreement did not mention human rights, signs of reconciliation between East and West nonetheless caused expectations for easier travel. When East and West Germany signed a Transit Treaty in May 1972, which again made no mention of human rights, applications to travel or emigrate to West Germany spiked.[104] By the end of the year, the total number of travel applications rose to more than 2,600.[105]

At first, the language of these requests was similar to that of the *Volksaussprache*: writers affirmed their support for the SED and portrayed their requests as a simple extension of state policy. Citizens soon became more assertive in claiming they had a human right to leave.[106] After the signing of the Basic Treaty and the entry of the GDR into the United Nations, East Germans began to use human rights language to directly challenge the SED, rather than make polite requests. One report noted that,

The accession of the GDR to various UN covenants prompted an increasing number of citizens to justify their complaints regarding rejected requests for emigration and travel to West Germany and the rejection of GDR citizenship with the fact that the ratification of the Covenant on Political and Civil Human Rights conferred upon them the right of free choice of citizenship and determining their place of residence and the rejection of their applications was therefore unlawful.[107]

---

[102] BArch, DY6/4878 Eingehende Informationsberichte aus dem Bezirk Halle, Meinungen zum Vierseitigen Abkommen über Westberlin (9.9.1971); BArch, DY6/5023 Eingehende Informationsberichte aus dem Bezirk Dresden (10.-14.9.1971).

[103] BArch, DA5/11379 Bericht über den Hauptinhalt [...] Eingaben 1971, 19.

[104] In 1972, travel applications jumped 20 percent from the first to the second quarter; in the third quarter of that year written applications rose again another 27 percent, while in-person applications jumped by 55 percent. BArch, DA5/9026 Bericht über den Hauptinhalt der [...] Eingaben im II. Quartal 1972, 11. Bericht über den Hauptinhalt der Eingaben im III. Quartal 1972, 6. In the third and fourth quarter, applications shot up another 60 percent; applications to permanently emigrate to West Germany doubled. BArch, DA5/9026 Bericht über den Hauptinhalt der Eingaben im IV. Quartal 1972, 4–5.

[105] Hanisch, *Die DDR im KSZE-Prozess*, 405.

[106] BArch, DA5/9026 Bericht über den Hauptinhalt der Eingaben im II. Quartal 1972, 11.

[107] BArch, DA5/9026 Bericht über den Hauptinhalt der Eingaben im IV. Quartal 1973, 7–8.

In the town of Pirna, 41 people signed a mass letter supporting the petition to exit of four local residents.[108] The letter maintained the style of an officially tolerated loyal criticism, but the act of having multiple signatures was a provocation because petitions were meant to be individual appeals not an organised protest. Frustrations with official intransigence ran high, with a growing number of petitions including threats to appeal to the United Nations directly. One-fifth of applicants told state authorities that if they were not issued an exit visa they would be forced to depart the GDR illegally.[109] The following year, the number of applications declined, but some of the petitioners continued to employ the language of human rights. In April 1974, Karin and Werner Karl Nuthmann, a working-class couple from Brandenburg, came to Alexanderplatz in East Berlin and set up signs demanding the right to free movement, citing UN human rights covenants and the GDR constitution. Both were arrested, and Werner Karl was put in a psychiatric hospital for a short time before both were deported to West Germany.[110]

Just as earlier treaties normalising relations with the West had sparked demands to travel, East Germans immediately anticipated an easing of travel restrictions when the signing of the Helsinki Accords was announced– even before anyone had read its final terms or knew it included provisions on human rights. Officials in Leipzig complained that people had "illusions" regarding how it would impact travel policy.[111] SED functionaries in the towns of Oranienburg, Zossen, Rathenow and Brandenburg an der Havel sent similar reports on how citizens were expecting a liberalisation of border policy.[112] Once the full text of the Accords was published in the national newspaper *Neues Deutschland* and other daily newspapers, such as the *Berliner Zeitung* and the Christian Democratic newspaper *Neue Zeit* on 2 August 1975, it set off a wave of applications to depart, with citizens now specifically citing the human rights sections contained in the treaty.

The immediate effect of the Helsinki Accords has also been wildly exaggerated in historical accounts working from contemporary Western press reports. Some have claimed that 100,000 East Germans demanded the right to exit in the wake of the SED's signature, while others say that

---

[108] Siegmar Faust, *Ich will hier raus...* (Berlin: Guhl, 1983), 114–15.
[109] BArch, DA5/9026 Bericht über den Hauptinhalt der [...] Eingaben im IV. Quartal 1973, 8.
[110] Karl Wilhelm Fricke, *Der Wahrheit verpflichtet: Texte aus fünf Jahrzehnten zur Geschichte der DDR* (Berlin: Ch. Links, 2000), 405.
[111] BArch, DY6/5058 Information über Meinungsäußerungen unserer Bürger zu aktuell-politischen Fragen, Bezirk Leipzig (12.7.1975) and (31.7.1975).
[112] BArch, DY30/IV B 2/5/1382 Information (31.7.1975).

numbers peaked at more than 300,000 by 1978.[113] Based on a population of approximately 16 million, such a wave of would-be emigrants
would have been dramatically destabilising. Multiple studies of the archival record have, however, found the numbers to be far smaller: in 1975,
there were approximately 13,000 exit applications, increasing to around
20,000 the following year.[114] The number of exit applications would not
reach 100,000 annually until 1987. While the numbers have been exaggerated, the turn to human rights by those applying to exit was clear.
According to an internal SED report, in the fall of 1975, the number of
applications jumped by 40 percent and every fourth letter explicitly
mentioned the Helsinki Accords.[115] The demands to leave in the name
of human rights continued to grow in numbers and intensity over the
next three years. In 1977, the Ministry of the Interior reported that the
majority of the applications to exit claimed a "right to free movement"
based on "one-sided interpretations" of international documents, treaties and East German law. Such claims bore the "unmistakably increased
ideological influence of imperialist mass media."[116] By 1978, this had
escalated to a condemnation of SED rule: "the centrepiece of their
arguments is the slander of the politics of the GDR in regard to the
guarantee of human rights. The approval of their emigration is evaluated
as a criterion of democracy, of personal freedom, and the humanity of the
social order."[117]

---

[113] The 100,000 figure is cited in Thomas, *The Helsinki Effect*, 107–9. Rosemary Foot,
"The Cold War and Human Rights," in *The Cambridge History of the Cold War. Vol. III*,
ed. Melvyn Leffler and Odd Arne Westad (Cambridge: Cambridge University Press,
2010), 460; Snyder, *Human Rights Activism and the End of the Cold War*, 71; A. James
McAdams, *Germany Divided: From the Wall to Reunification* (Princeton, NJ: Princeton
University Press, 1994), 130; Tyndale, *Protestants in Communist East Germany*, 78; R. J.
Crampton, *Eastern Europe in the Twentieth Century* (London: Routledge, 1994), 358;
Karl Wilhelm Fricke, *Opposition und Widerstand in der DDR: ein politischer Report*
(Cologne: Verlag Wissenschaft und Politik, 1984), 163. The 300,000 peak is from
Tufton Beamish, *The Kremlin's Dilemma: The Struggle for Human Rights in Eastern
Europe* (San Rafael, CA: Presidio, 1979), 184–85.
[114] Bernd Eisenfeld, "Die Ausreisebewegung – eine Erscheinungsform widerständigen
Verhaltens," in *Zwischen Selbstbehauptung und Anpassung: Formen des Widerstandes und
der Opposition in der DDR*, ed. Ulrike Poppe, Rainer Eckert and Ilko-Sascha Kowalczuk
(Berlin: Ch. Links, 1995), 192–223; Manfred Gehrmann, *Die Überwindung des
"Eisernen Vorhangs": Die Abwanderung aus der DDR in die BRD/West-Berlin 1949–1989
als innerdeutsches Migranten-Netzwerk* (Berlin: Ch. Links, 2009); Major, *Behind the Berlin
Wall*.
[115] BArch, DA5/9026 Bericht über den Hauptinhalt der Eingaben im III. Quartal 1975.
[116] BArch, DO1/16488 Einschätzung über die Entwicklung und den Inhalt rechtswidriger
Ersuchen auf Übersiedlung nach der BRD (1977), 3.
[117] BArch, DO1/16488 Information über Erscheinungen und Entwicklungstendenzen bei
der Unterbindung rechtswidriger Versuche von Übersiedlungen nach der BRD
(1972–1978), 10.

During the *Volksaussprache*, East Germans had politely hinted that violating human rights could cause diplomatic problems, but now they flatly pointed out the gulf between the SED's international rhetoric and its domestic reality. In a letter to the SED's department responsible for church affairs, Barbara and Lutz S. from Sömmerda cited the activism of the GDR-Committee for Human Rights, and after berating the relevant official that "human rights begin at home," they requested his assistance in procuring a permit to exit to "allow our family to realize our right to self-determination."[118] Others not only appropriated the language of the SED but also the whole catalogue of human rights causes that they touted in the media, to press their case forward. Siegmar Faust argued that SED propaganda on imperialist interventionism and right-wing dictatorships in Chile, Uruguay, Vietnam, Laos and Portugal was "laughable" considering the many political prisoners in the GDR. He questioned why the SED became "suddenly allergic to any mention of the Universal Declaration of Human Rights and the Helsinki Final Act," when it was directed at themselves.[119] Those demanding their right to leave also quickly figured out how to use Western media and the burgeoning international NGO scene to increase their leverage. In 1975, the brother of a prisoner in East Germany organised a campaign, in collaboration with Amnesty International, demanding his release based on UN human rights provisions, which resulted in 40,000 letters sent to the SED.[120] Two years later, another would-be emigrant staged a one-man demonstration at the Palace of the Republic with a sign "Freedom and Human Rights – Let Me Leave!" He made sure to notify Western journalists to get maximum publicity.[121]

The best publicised case of post-Helsinki emigrants was that of Dr. Karl-Heinz Nitschke from the town of Riesa. Nitschke had previously applied to emigrate in 1973 to be reunited with a sister who lived in West Germany, but when this request was denied, he opted for a more public approach, drafting a letter accusing the SED of systematic violations of human rights and invoking his right to leave the country based on the UDHR, the UN Human Rights Covenants and the Helsinki Accords.[122]

---

[118] BArch, DY30/IV B 2/14/31 Barbara and Lutz S. to Bellmann (14.8.1977).
[119] Faust, *Ich will hier raus ...*, 148.
[120] Joachim Scholtyseck, "GDR Dissidents and Human Rights Issues," in *From Helsinki to Belgrade: The First CSCE Follow-Up Meeting and the Crisis of Détente*, ed. Vladimir Bilandžić, Dittmar Dahlmann and Milan Kosanović (Göttingen: V&R Unipress, 2012), 295.
[121] Jacqueline Boysen, *Das "weiße Haus" in Ost-Berlin: die Ständige Vertretung der Bundesrepublik bei der DDR* (Berlin: Ch. Links, 2010), 162.
[122] Fricke, *Opposition und Widerstand in der DDR*, 169–70.

This letter was then sent to the United Nations, West German media and a number of other NGOs in West Germany devoted to assisting emigrants from the GDR.[123] Nitschke was arrested along with others who co-signed the letter, but international pressure and the existing West German procedures for purchasing the freedom of imprisoned would-be emigrants resulted in most being released to the Federal Republic within a year.[124]

While in some Eastern Bloc countries, human rights claims appealed primarily to the educated and the intelligentsia, a Stasi investigation showed that Nitschke's petition had support from a cross-section of East German citizenry.[125] When he decided to leave the GDR, Nitschke posted the unsent letter in his office in Riesa so that others could sign in support. With this method, he garnered 33 signatures, and then later a list of another 20 supporters from the same town, 12 more in Karl-Marx-Stadt and 2 more from the district of Meißen. The 33 initial signatories included 22 workers (most from the local pipe-making factory), 7 office workers, 1 doctor, 1 engineer (both classified as members of the intelligentsia), as well as a housewife and a pensioner.

The emigration process radicalised citizens on the issue of human rights, but the SED's response also removed citizens from the very social structures that could foster a movement for political change. One example of this was the aforementioned Siegmar Faust, a writer who had been expelled from multiple universities in the 1960s for his "politically unreliable" opinions. Placed under Stasi surveillance in 1968, he was subsequently imprisoned for contacts with West Germany, where he had sought to publish some of his banned writings. In 1972, he was released as part of an amnesty in honour of the 23rd anniversary of the founding of the GDR, and soon thereafter began the process of trying to leave the country altogether.[126] In August 1973, he wrote letters to local officials and the attorney general, renouncing his citizenship and requesting to leave the GDR based on the UDHR of 1948, the UN Human Rights Covenants of 1966, the Constitution of 1968 and East German

---

[123] The GfM published Nitschke's letter in Gesellschaft für Menschenrechte, *Petition Riesa: zur vollen Erlangung der Menschenrechte* (Frankfurt am Main: Gesellschaft für Menschenrechte, 1977). For the Stasi analysis of Nitschke's petition, see Information Nr. 624/76 (7.9.1976) in Siegfried Suckut, *Die DDR im Blick der Stasi 1976: die geheimen Berichte an die SED-Führung* (Göttingen: Vandenhoeck & Ruprecht, 2009), 209–12.

[124] Fricke, *Opposition und Widerstand in der DDR*, 170.

[125] On the appeal of human rights activism to the Eastern European intelligentsia, see Bolton, *Worlds of Dissent*, 28.

[126] Anne-Sophie Nold, "Widerstand mit allen Konsequenzen: Ein faustisches Leben in der DDR am Beispiel des Schriftstellers Siegmar Faust," *Horch und Guck* 13 (1994), 18–20.

citizenship law.[127] In Faust's early letters to SED authorities, he employed the idea of human rights in two ways: first, by contrasting SED statements in support of human rights with his own unjust treatment and desire to leave, and second, by referencing specifically violated human rights norms as part of his own narrative of suffering. Human rights served as an external and objective authority that validated his grievances against the state, from his unfair dismissal from work to his imprisonment. By 1976, when he was jailed yet again for his criticism, Faust's discourse shifted. From his prison cell in Cottbus, he produced a handwritten newsletter called *Armes Deutschland* (Poor Germany), a parody of the SED's national newspaper *Neues Deutschland* that was to be an "organ of those fighting for civil and human rights."[128] His everyday demands had been fused with the abstract norms of international treaties so that he was a "fighter for human rights," and his personal interests were now integrated into a narrative of global justice. Abandoning claims to civil rights as a social actor, Faust had turned to the idea of human rights as Arendt had once characterised them: "a right of exception for those who had nothing better to fall back on."[129]

The Helsinki Accords sparked a burst of militant demands to leave the GDR, but by 1978, state suppression of applicants and the low rate of success meant that the number of petitions from East Germans to emigrate dropped off. Although the SED was now being bombarded with letters from Western European and North American NGOs, human rights claims from within waned.[130] East Germans did take advantage of international human rights documents and treaties to support their claims to exit, but they were also willing to use a wide variety of languages and tactics to protest the rejection of their applications, as well as deploying the various materials provided by the SED to legitimise their demands.[131] In the immediate wake of Helsinki, methods of protest against travel restrictions included suicide threats, hunger strikes and public protests during which East Germans waved homemade signs,

---

[127] Faust, *Ich will hier raus*, 44–64.
[128] Anne-Sophie Nold, "Widerstand mit allen Konsequenzen," 22 and Faust, *Ich will hier raus*, 277 n. 36.
[129] Quoted in Roger Berkowitz, "Hannah Arendt on Human Rights," 62.
[130] Letters from abroad in support of petitions to exit the GDR jumped 176 percent between 1977 and 1978. BArch, DA5/11385 Bericht über den Hauptinhalt der an den Staatsrat gerichteten Eingaben, 1978, Anlage 1.
[131] Hanisch, *Die DDR im KSZE-Prozess*, 148.

burned their official documents and chained themselves to objects and buildings.[132] Beyond appealing to human rights, a 1981 report mentioned that East Germans also cited passages from,

the autobiography of Comrade Erich Honecker, "From My Life", the textbook "Constitutional Law," the brochure "Nationality - German citizenship GDR," as well as the interviews of Comrade Honecker with the chief editor of the *Saarbrücker Zeitung* and the British publisher Robert Maxwell.[133]

East Germans were omnivorous when it came to repurposing SED rhetoric in their applications; human rights were one set of tools among many. The Helsinki process added to the list of international documents that citizens could cite, as well as creating an ongoing diplomatic process that GDR citizens could use to their advantage, but it did not cause a human rights revolution.[134]

Protest statements by emigrants strained solidarity with other dissidents and distanced those still loyal to the ideals of socialism from those who most vociferously employed the discourse of human rights. Wolfgang Templin, who later founded the Initiative for Peace and Human Rights (IFM) in the 1980s, attributes the delay in the emergence of a human rights movement in the GDR to the widespread use of human rights language for the purposes of emigration.

It was hard enough to say, "I don't just want to complain, I don't want to just accept things as they are, I want to do something," – then someone else's decision, the decision of a friend, who has had just as many critical experiences, and then says, "There's no point in staying, you can't change anything here," that was very difficult.[135]

While those seeking to exit the GDR took up the discourse of human rights as a means of resistance, the ideological and social implication of their demands to leave East Germany rather than change it from within was to neutralise human rights as a discourse of opposition. As citizens engaged with the idea of human rights to legitimise their departure from East Germany, they discouraged those who sought to stay from

---

[132] Bernd Eisenfeld, "Die Abstimmung mit dem Ausreiseantrag – ein Untergangsbazillus der DDR," in *Bleiben oder Gehen? – Ein deutsches Problem* (Berlin: Gesellschaft zur Förderung Vergleichender Staat-Kirche-Forschung, 2005), 30.

[133] BArch, DO1/16488. Information über die Unterbindung und Zurückdrängung rechtswidriger Ersuchen auf Übersiedlung nach der BRD, 1981.

[134] On Helsinki as an ongoing process, see Hanisch, *Die DDR im KSZE-Prozess*, 148.

[135] Quoted in John Torpey, *Intellectuals, Socialism, and Dissent: The East German Opposition and Its Legacy* (Minneapolis: University of Minnesota Press, 1995), 73.

employing the same international human rights language to advocate for reform in the GDR.[136]

Lost in Translation

With the institutional churches either in retreat politically or co-opted on the problem of human rights, and thousands seeking to leave the GDR rather than change it, the question remains why those who stayed and did protest SED policy avoided the idea of human rights. Nowhere in the Eastern Bloc did human rights form the basis for a mass movement, but it did leave its mark on disillusioned intellectual and cultural elites in several other state socialist countries. In December 1975, 59 intellectuals in Poland sent an open letter to the government demanding the safeguarding of human rights based on the Polish constitution and the freshly signed Helsinki Accords.[137] In Czechoslovakia, the human rights organisation Charter 77 was founded by cultural luminaries such as playwrights Vaclav Havel and Pavel Kohout, intellectuals like Jan Patočka and disillusioned Communist Party elites such as Zdeněk Mlynář and Jiří Hájek. In the USSR, human rights dissidents (active since the 1960s) formed groups to monitor the implementation of the Helsinki Accords in Moscow, Tbilisi, Kiev and Yerevan.[138] Even in Romania, writer Paul Goma and historian Vlad Georgescu wrote a public letter denouncing human rights violations by Nicolae Ceaușescu and other socialist leaders.[139] Many of these intellectuals were disillusioned by socialism as it existed and aimed to democratise the system by increasing its respect for the individual, but without challenging state socialism's economic and social rights.[140]

---

[136] Hirschman argues that emigration (exit) undermined dissent (voice) in general, but I would argue that the particular discourses involved shaped this dynamic as it evolved. Albert Hirschman, "Exit, Voice, and the Fate of the GDR: An Essay in Conceptual History," *World Politics* 45, no. 2 (1993), 178.

[137] Wanda Jarzabek, "Lost Illusions? The Polish Government and Human Rights Issues from Helsinki to Belgrade, 1975–1978," in *From Helsinki to Belgrade*, 310.

[138] Wolfgang Eichwede, "'…But It Must Be a Détente with a Human Face,' Helsinki and the Human Rights Movements in Eastern Europe," in *From Helsinki to Belgrade*, 264–66.

[139] Paul Blokker, "The (Re-) Emergence of Constitutionalism in East-Central Europe," in *Thinking through Transition: Liberal Democracy, Authoritarian Pasts, and Intellectual History in East Central Europe after 1989*, ed. Michal Kopeček and Piotr Wcilik (New York: Central European University Press, 2015), 146.

[140] Benjamin Nathans, "The Disenchantment of Socialism: Soviet Dissidents, Human Rights, and the New Global Morality," in *The Breakthrough: Human Rights in the 1970s*.

As could be expected, the Stasi took credit for the comparative lack of human rights activism in East Germany, in contrast to its more restive socialist neighbours, but it must be remembered that these countries had their own effective secret police forces.[141] While the Ministry of State Security may have had to deal with a greater number of citizens seeking to exit the country, it was confronted with far fewer aiming to turn human rights into a movement for political reform. The vast majority of East German cultural and intellectual dissidents rejected human rights as overly liberal and too closely tied to belligerent anti-communism. The nascent peace and environmental movements emerging in East Germany at the time saw personal ethical change – not political democracy – as the crucial concern of modern times. Although women's demands for gender equality had expanded into a discourse of equal rights in the late 1960s, the SED successfully deflected such activism by increasing legal female autonomy and providing targeted material benefits over the course of the 1970s. For the average East German who was disgruntled enough to complain, but not sufficiently disillusioned to emigrate, the SED under Honecker increased state support for consumerism, as well as the number of legal venues where citizens could file grievances. Turning to the language of international human rights as a weapon against the state carried with it a high risk of both imprisonment and alienating possible allies, while other methods of protest appeared safer and more likely to effect change.

There was an outbreak of dissent among intellectuals in the 1970s, but little to indicate that human rights would eventually form an integral part of opposition to SED rule. Although some supported the "Eurocommunists" – the Communist Parties of Western Europe who aimed to democratise socialism – the human rights movement was too liberal for the cultural and intellectual elite of the GDR, some of whom had migrated to East Germany out of socialist conviction.[142] When the popular singer Wolf Biermann was stripped of his GDR citizenship for criticism of the SED in 1976, East German intellectuals asked the state to reconsider, citing his loyalty to socialism instead of positing any abstract

[141] Douglas Selvage examines the Stasi's self-promotion in response to defeating a nearly nonexistent human rights movement in "'Human Rights Demagoguery Hostile to Détente' the GDR and the Conference on Security and Cooperation in Europe, 1975–1989," in *Human Rights in Europe during the Cold War*, ed. Rasmus Mariager, Karl Molin and Kjersti Brathagen (London: Routledge, 2014), 142.

[142] Laura Fasanaro, "Eurocommunism: An East German Perspective," in *The Crisis of Détente in Europe: From Helsinki to Gorbachev 1975–1985*, ed. Leopoldo Nuti (London: Routledge, 2008), 244–45.

right to free expression.[143] Those East German intellectuals who did turn to dissident sought to reform the GDR from within, remaining convinced of the need for a system based on true antifascist socialism, divorced from the "bourgeois" liberal democracy of the West.[144]

A Stalinist turned dissident, Robert Havemann was one of East Germany's most influential dissidents, but his intellectual engagement with the problem of human rights remained conflicted.[145] A chemist by training, Havemann had been imprisoned during the Third Reich for his membership in the Communist Party and for his activism with the resistance organisation "European Union," of which he was a founding member. In the postwar period, he was initially an enthusiastic supporter of the SED, and in 1950 became a representative at the East German parliament, the *Volkskammer*, while also holding a professorship at the Humboldt University in Berlin. When, in 1963, he turned against the dogmatism of the state, he was expelled from the SED and fired from the university. Due to his continued dissent, regularly leaked to the Western media, he was placed under house arrest from 1976 to 1978.

Havemann advocated for greater freedom of expression and pluralism (supporting the creation of a socialist opposition party in the GDR and sympathising publicly with those seeking to leave East Germany), though he remained wary of what he saw as the destructive Cold War politics of human rights in the 1970s. In an exchange of letters with Joachim Steffen, a member of the radical Left of the West German Social Democrats, Havemann agreed that "generally, protection of human rights, both social and political, represents the essential foundation of a free and democratic society." But he asked, in turn, "where is there today a free and democratic society, in which individual human rights have been realized?"[146] Havemann argued that neither East nor West could claim to have totally realised these rights and that the use of the "human rights cudgel" in international affairs was simply counterproductive. As a dissident, Havemann rejected the idea that East Germany needed to go backwards to a system of bourgeois democracy or a market economy, but still believed that the communist revolution envisioned by Karl Marx, in which the state would wither away and all would exist harmoniously together in freedom, was still the endpoint of the state socialist

[143] Reprinted in Woods, *Opposition in the GDR under Honecker, 1971–85*, 139.
[144] Neubert, *Geschichte der Opposition in der DDR*, 97. Manfred Wilke "Warum gab es in der DDR keine Charta 77?," in *Annäherungen an Robert Havemann*, ed. Bernd Florath (Göttingen: Vandenhoeck & Ruprecht, 2016), 461–72.
[145] Robert Havemann, *Warum ich Stalinist war und Antistalinist wurde* (Berlin: Dietz, 1990).
[146] Jiří Pelikán and Manfred Wilke, *Menschenrechte: ein Jahrbuch zu Osteuropa* (Reinbek: Rowohlt, 1977), 474.

system. As such, he agreed, in theory, with Western human rights activists, that state socialism violated human rights, but rejected their solutions of a return to bourgeois democracy and capitalism as a treatment deadlier than the disease.

Havemann did at times clearly denounce certain SED actions as violations of human rights. In 1970, in *Fragen, Antworten, Fragen*, he supported the right of East Germans to travel freely and even to leave the country as one of the "most elementary human rights."[147] At the end of the decade, he also wrote that the judicial punishment of his wife and son for his actions "represents a blatant violation of human rights, that cannot be legitimized through the appearance of legality."[148] In terms of political rights, he argued that a socialist democracy would include "the rights and freedoms that were won in bourgeois democracy," but with the crucial difference that "the privilege that defines capitalism would be enjoyed by all through the true equality of all citizens."[149] For Havemann, the socialist revolution represented a transcendent event that eliminated class conflict and capitalist exploitation, and needed to progress further to achieve human rights, rather than to be dismantled.

As an alternative, Havemann argued that the East needed to make moves towards democracy while the West needed to advance towards socialism. Only through these mutually reinforcing processes could progress be made throughout the world. Politicians should go out and draw the world's attention to the failings of their own countries and learn how these could be addressed. This agenda would not result in a convergence of bourgeois and socialist systems but instead would represent the final success of the communist project.

While the implementation of political human rights in the lands of real existing socialism would be a revolutionary act with enormous and far-reaching effects, not just in our country, it would not be the beginning but rather the completion of a revolution, precisely the world-shaking October Revolution [of 1917].[150]

Although he rarely invoked the idea, in this passage Havemann presents human rights as the fundamental final act of the socialist revolution that would bring about his longed-for socialist utopia.

While Havemann sought to square the circle of imagining a discourse of human rights for a democratic socialism, other dissidents – such as

---

[147] Robert Havemann, *Fragen, Antworten, Fragen: aus der Biographie eines deutschen Marxisten* (Reinbek: Rowohlt, 1977), 72.
[148] Quoted from a declaration to Amnesty International in Clemens Vollnhals, *Der Fall Havemann: Ein Lehrstück politischer Justiz* (Berlin: Ch. Links, 2000), 220–21.
[149] Havemann, *Warum ich Stalinist war und Antistalinist wurde*, 209.
[150] Pelikán and Wilke, *Menschenrechte*, 475.

Rudolf Bahro – openly denounced the international human rights movement of the 1970s as a step backwards. A former SED functionary, Bahro
was imprisoned and then deported from the GDR following the publication of his 1977 eco-utopian treatise *The Alternative in Eastern Europe* in
West Germany. Bahro was openly contemptuous of the growing international human rights movement and bemoaned that, since the failure of
the Prague Spring,

> the bulk of the oppositional elements have seen themselves pushed back to a
> program of purely liberal democratic demands, a human rights campaign, which
> is the most general, platitudinous, and inane position possible. [...] Human rights
> and political democracy – of course! But what the Eastern European countries are
> missing, not least the Soviet Union itself, is an *organized, long-term struggle for
> another total system of politics.*

For Bahro, human rights were not inherently objectionable, but Eastern
Bloc dissidents' efforts to follow US President Jimmy Carter's human
rights agenda were "a disgrace."[151] Ironically enough, while imprisoned
in 1979, a West German NGO awarded Bahro the Carl-von-Ossietzky
Medal for his contributions to the cause of human rights.

  Others, such as intellectual Jürgen Kuczynski, looked to a revival of
traditional Marxism, rather than human rights as a means of overcoming
the shortcomings of real existing socialism. Kuczynski came from a
Jewish family of distinguished intellectuals, including his father Robert
René Kuczynski who was a prominent member of the Weimar-era
German League for Human Rights. In 1930, he joined the Communist
Party, spent much of the Nazi era in exile in Britain working for the US
military and leaking material to Soviet intelligence.[152] In the GDR, he
was a prolific scholar of Marxist economics and history and a self-
described "party-line dissident," staying loyal in public, but offering
criticism directly to SED leaders in private.[153] Although sympathetic to
Havemann's critiques of the SED, Kuczynski cut ties to him once he
broke with the Party publicly. Although Kuczynski was a member of the
GDR-Committee for Human Rights, he even disagreed with the idea
that socialists needed to adopt the language of human rights at all. In his
1977 book *Human Rights and Class Rights*, he attacked Western human
rights activism against the GDR, but also spurned socialist human rights,

---

[151] Rudolf Bahro, *Ich werde meinen Weg fortsetzen* (Frankfurt: Europäische Verlagsanstalt,
1977), 13.
[152] Guntolf Herzberg, *Anpassung und Aufbegehren: die Intelligenz der DDR in den Krisenjahren
1956/58* (Berlin: Ch. Links, 2006), 555.
[153] Jürgen Kuczynski, *Ein linientreuer Dissident: Memoiren, 1945–1989* (Berlin: Aufbau-
Verlag, 1992).

which he saw as a deviation from classical Marxism.[154] In a personal letter to Hermann Klenner, he wrote, "you know that on this point I do not agree: 'human rights are class rights,' it simply does not add up. It is either-or."[155] For Kuczynski, Marx had been correct to denounce human rights as a superfluous bourgeois concept that distracted from realising universal justice through class struggle.

There was one very public declaration of support for human rights, which claimed to represent a broad segment of the GDR elite, but this proved deceptive. In 1978, the West German magazine *Der Spiegel* published the manifesto of the "Union of Democratic Communists of Germany," which purported to represent a widespread movement from within the SED for liberalisation and human rights.[156] The Party was furious at the publication and it shuttered the East Berlin offices of *Der Spiegel*. A subsequent internal investigation into the article, however, found no traces of the "mass movement" for democratisation in their midst.[157] Although the manifesto was portrayed as the East German equivalent to Charter 77, it was a movement of one: the sole author turned out to be Hermann von Berg, a high-level SED functionary who eventually emigrated to West Germany in 1986.[158]

For the vast majority of East German intellectuals and cultural elites, demanding human rights equated too closely with rejecting socialism and siding with reactionary Western liberals and anti-communists. In West Germany, conservatives spoke of promoting "human rights in enslaved Europe," leaving little doubt that they saw the entirety of the communist system as a violation of human rights.[159] For those who remained sympathetic to the socialist cause, claiming the SED violated human rights meant comparing it to Chile under the Junta, Greece under the Colonels, or even the United States under Jimmy Carter. In a memoir written after the collapse of the GDR, American Victor Grossman, who defected to East Germany in 1952, recalled his frustration with those who advocated human rights under socialism while "turning a blind eye to human rights violations in the West," and ignoring the positive support provided by the

---

[154] Jürgen Kuczynski, *Menschenrechte und Klassenrechte* (Berlin: Akademie-Verlag, 1978).

[155] Akademie der Wissenschaften NL Jürgen Kuczynski 67 Kuczynski to Klenner (22.9.1978)

[156] The text of the Manifesto was printed over the course of two issues of *Der Spiegel*, 1–2 (2./9.1.1978).

[157] Dominik Geppert, *Störmanöver das "Manifest der Opposition" und die Schließung des Ost-Berliner "Spiegel"-Büros im Januar 1978* (Berlin: Ch. Links, 1996).

[158] Mike Dennis, *The Rise and Fall of the GDR, 1945–1990* (Harlow: Longman, 2000), 238. Jefferson Adams, *Historical Dictionary of German Intelligence* (Lanham, MD: Scarecrow Press, 2009), 29.

[159] Snyder, *Human Rights Activism and the End of the Cold War*, 10.

GDR for freedom fighters in South Africa, Central America and Chile.[160] As dissident Carlo Jordan later explained, the SED's conception of human rights still had some persuasive power among the GDR population: "In our socialist education, demands for equality always collided with demands for freedom, and this made the problem of human rights so sensitive. [...] Equality and freedom were always perceived as separate alternatives, especially in view of the USA, where freedom had been realized, but at the cost of equality."[161] As with other groups in the GDR, the intelligentsia chose the path of least resistance by engaging the SED on different and more favourable discursive ground rather than trying to formulate a middle path between the two conceptions of human rights.

The few that did turn to human rights as a form of dissent were rapidly intercepted by the Stasi. East German state security believed that outside groups sought members of the elite to act as "pacemakers" to jumpstart a local "human rights movement" within the GDR.[162] When anyone gained enough prominence to possibly fit that role, they were quickly dealt with. One such example was Bernd Eisenfeld, an economist who had served as a "construction soldier," the alternative to military service for conscientious objectors who performed manual labour on state projects. At a reunion of fellow "veterans," a Stasi informant reported that Eisenfeld accused the SED "of constant and deliberate violations of human rights.[...] He explained that the Constitution of the GDR was a farce [and] criticized the church for not acting against state power enough and he advocated for the establishment of democratic socialism."[163] Soon thereafter, he was banned from employment, subject to severe harassment and by the end of the year had emigrated to West Berlin. In another case, a young seminary student from East Berlin travelled to Czechoslovakia as part of a larger plan to create a "Committee for the Observation of Human Rights" in partnership with Charter 77; he was immediately arrested by the Stasi for

---

[160] Victor Grossman, *Crossing the River: A Memoir of the American Left, the Cold War, and Life in East Germany* (Amherst: University of Massachusetts Press, 2003), 224.

[161] Hoover Institution Archive, Joppke Collection, Box 1, Interview mit Carlo Jordan (16.6.1991), 4.

[162] Archiv der DDR-Opposition, AM 33 Analyse über die gegnerischen Aktivitäten zur Organisierung der politischen Untergrundtätigkeit, HA XX (10.1.1978), 17.

[163] Neubert, *Geschichte der Opposition in der DDR*, 302–3. Events organised by construction soldiers in the late 1970s sometimes focused on human rights, and like church events, were monitored by the Stasi and allowed within specific parameters. Bernd Eisenfeld and Peter Schicketanz, *Bausoldaten in der DDR: Die "Zusammenführung feindlich-negativer Kräfte" in der NVA* (Berlin: Ch. Links, 2012), 395.

"provocative conduct."[164] As activist Cornelia Matzke recalled, "In one way or another, our network was destroyed time and again; we never had the chance to build a stable oppositional structure."[165] The Stasi faced so few real threats that it was able to quickly contain these already marginalised individuals promoting reformist human rights politics before they could pose a serious threat.

The rise of new social movements for peace, feminism and environmentalism in the 1960s and 1970s was more muted in the GDR than in the West, but these groups also failed to turn towards human rights. In 1978, the SED introduced compulsory military education in schools, sparking the rise of an independent peace movement comprised mostly of Christians for whom this was a step too far.[166] Two years later, the NATO decision to deploy Pershing missiles in West Germany in response to Warsaw Pact intermediate range nuclear weapons stationed in Eastern Europe further fuelled this local impetus towards international peace. Environmentalism was rapidly becoming a source of dissent, as unrestricted industrial pollution from East Germany's chemical and heavy industry took an ecological toll across the country.[167] But for these emerging movements – primarily small groups based within the Protestant Church – the focus was not on political change, but individual improvement. Although these problems were global, they could only be solved through "spiritual-cultural activity, social engagement, and a lifestyle grounded in solidarity."[168] While the independent peace movement did challenge state policy on military training, the SED also launched its own mass peace initiative with orchestrated rallies and demonstrations to deflect enthusiasm away from alternative movements.[169]

---

[164] Bernd and Peter Eisenfeld, "Widerständiges Verhalten 1976–1982," in *Am Ende des realen Sozialismus 3. Opposition in der DDR von den 70er Jahren bis zum Zusammenbruch der SED-Herrschaft*, ed. Eberhard Kuhrt, Hannsjörg Buck and Gunter Holzweissig (Opladen: Leske & Budrich, 1999), 86–87. Connections to Charter 77 were particularly concerning to SED leadership and the Stasi, see Hanisch, *Die DDR im KSZE-Prozess*, 138–39.

[165] Quoted in Dirk Philipsen, *We Were the People: Voices from East Germany's Revolutionary Autumn of 1989* (Durham, NC: Duke University Press, 1993), 249.

[166] Neubert, *Geschichte der Opposition in der DDR*, 304–8.

[167] Merrill Jones, "Origins of the East German Environmental Movement," *German Studies Review* 16, no. 2 (1993), 236.

[168] Karsten Timmer, *Vom Aufbruch zum Umbruch: die Bürgerbewegung in der DDR 1989* (Göttingen: Vandenhoeck & Ruprecht, 2000), 54.

[169] Günther Wernicke, "The World Peace Council and the Antiwar Movement in East Germany," in *America, the Vietnam War, and the World: Comparative and International Perspectives*, ed. Andreas Daum, Lloyd Gardner and Wilfried Mausbach (Cambridge: Cambridge University Press, 2003), 299–302.

In this era, East German women turned to the language of rights to demand the state live up to its rhetoric on the equality of the sexes, but it too failed to translate into a movement for democratisation or human rights. Since the ban on abortion in the immediate postwar period, individual women had requested exemptions on the grounds of social necessity, but in 1967–68 – around the International Year for Human Rights – this shifted to an assertion of equal rights for women and the right to bodily self-determination.[170] In 1972, the SED responded to this criticism by liberalising abortion access as part of a larger package of welfare benefits specifically targeting women and working mothers.[171] Rather than forcing women to remain pregnant, the SED now crafted a set of pronatalist financial incentives and social programs including childcare and housework holidays.[172] These reforms were part of newly minted SED leader Erich Honecker's program for "Unity of Economic and Social Policy," which promised increased consumerism in stark contrast to previous leader Walter Ulbricht's calls for sacrifice on the path to building socialism. These benefits were heavily promoted as human rights successes – including in the first issue of the new international journal of the KMR, devoted entirely to the issue of women's rights.[173] In 1975, the GDR also hosted the World Congress of Women in East Berlin as the socialist answer to an official UN meeting in Mexico that commemorated the beginning of International Women's Year. In his opening speech to the Congress, Honecker touted the achievements of the GDR in providing for the rights and needs of women – two concepts he used interchangeably in reference to the welfare benefits implemented under his direction.[174] Gender equality was never fully achieved in the GDR (nor anywhere else), but the extensive public expenditure targeting women in the name of realising their equal rights in the 1970s was effective in securing increased loyalty to the system and diverting feminist activism from demanding radical political change.

Beyond increasing public propaganda and welfare benefits, the SED also provided new alternatives for all citizens to voice complaints within the official channels in the 1970s. The passage of a new Civil Code in 1975 created greater institutional opportunities for East Germans to

---

[170] Harsch, "Society, the State, and Abortion in East Germany, 1950–1972," 76.
[171] In response to Catholic protests invoking human rights, abortion liberalisation was the only free vote in the *Volkskammer* before 1989. There were 14 votes against and 8 abstentions. Ibid., 67 n. 63.
[172] Harsch, *Revenge of the Domestic*, 304–6.
[173] DDR-Komitee für Menschenrechte, *Schriften und Informationen* 1, no. 1 (1975).
[174] Celia Donert, "Whose Utopia? Gender, Ideology and Human Rights at the 1975 World Congress of Women in East Berlin," in *The Breakthrough*, 78.

assert their rights against fellow citizens in cases regarding private property.[175] Alongside petitioning the SED, citizens could now also access state-run Conflict Commissions and locally administered Dispute Commissions.[176] For disgruntled citizens frustrated by everyday matters ranging from defective consumer goods to housing problems to public disturbances, this social court system provided at least somewhat acceptable redress for grievances.[177] If citizens appealed to these courts in human rights terms, it is unlikely they would have received a charitable hearing, as training materials for lay judges in the late 1970s included material on socialist human rights theory.[178] A journal for the lay jurists who presided over the social courts and tribunals explained to its readers how the "socialist conception of human rights increasingly determines the nature of human rights at the United Nations." At the core of the socialist human rights concept was self-determination – not individual rights against the state – and one could observe how the absence of self-determination went hand in hand with oppression merely by observing the realities of life in Chile, South Africa, Rhodesia and Namibia.[179] So long as state-approved low-risk means of contesting specific SED policies existed, there was no incentive to invoke abstract international law in the face of openly hostile and incredulous state officials. Only when demands moved beyond the tenets of good socialist citizenship, by say, applying to leave the GDR, did human rights become a useful discourse of dissent.

Conclusion

Although human rights emerged as a language of protest and resistance in the 1970s, its appeal was limited to those seeking to exit the country and those trying to carve out a parallel space for Christianity within the larger socialist system (and to the very small number of dissidents who were soon imprisoned, suppressed or expelled). Most of the intelligentsia seeking reform disparaged international human rights politics as a distraction from bringing about a real socialist or ecological revolution. Without translators from the intelligentsia or the Church, the process

[175] Betts, *Within Walls*, 158–61.
[176] On conflict resolution systems available to East Germans, see Paul Betts, "Socialism, Social Rights, and Human Rights: The Case of East Germany," *Humanity* 3, no. 3 (2012), 416.
[177] On the experience of everyday legality in the GDR, see Inga Markovits, *Justice in Luritz: Experiencing Socialist Law in East Germany* (Princeton, NJ: Princeton University Press, 2010).
[178] Sperlich, *The East German Social Courts*, 40.
[179] "Sozialismus und Menschenrechte," *Der Schöffe: Zeitschrift für Schöffen und Schiedskommissionen* 12, no. 23 (1976), 312.

of transforming abstract international legal terms into a language for challenging SED abuses remained largely one of individual translation based on specific personal grievances. The problem for the development of human rights in East Germany was not the absence of privacy, but the lack of an unfettered public sphere in which citizens could organically link together their personal problems first with the concerns of others, and then, together, with the more abstract moral and legal principles of individualistic human rights. While East Germans may have increasingly engaged with the idea of rights in general, the SED's hold over the public sphere allowed the state to continue to instrumentalise the concept of human rights to legitimise and reinforce its own rule. From the vantage point of 1989, the growing demands to exit, the increasing interest of Christians in human rights and the rise of a very small number of dissident intellectuals were all important steps towards the eventual emergence of a human rights opposition, but in the 1970s these groups were fractured and divided in terms of ideologies, goals and actions.

By the early 1980s, the SED still maintained its hegemonic socialist human rights discourse within the GDR. But this would soon change: the ebb of the late 1970s in applications to leave would turn into a massive wave in 1984; the seemingly docile church organisations would become political; and the intelligentsia would become disillusioned with the SED to the point where they could no longer defend the status quo as the launch pad of the coming revolution. In the late 1970s, however, it appeared to SED leadership as though they had survived the torrent of international human rights activism. Unfortunately for the SED, "hypocrisy and illusion" could only delay the inevitable progress of human rights for so long – as Hermann Klenner had written. The people would see to it.[180]

---

[180] Hermann Klenner, "Human Rights–Hypocrisy and Truth," *Bulletin – GDR Committee for Human Rights* 3, no. 1 (1978), 15.

5 The Rise of Dissent and the Collapse of Socialist Human Rights, 1980–1989

At the beginning of the 1980s, a few hundred citizens at most were using human rights to demand exit visas; mere pockets of the church were speaking of human rights as a path to peace; and only a few lonely intellectuals clung to the idea of human rights as a means of demanding political reform. In no way was this scattered group capable of producing the organisation or shared vision necessary to revolutionise the GDR. By contrast, the SED and the East German intellectual establishment launched into the 1980s supremely confident in socialist human rights. As dissent hit a low point in 1981, the Ministry of Ideology set about drafting a "Socialist Declaration of Human Rights" – a symbolic retort to the European Convention on Human Rights of 1950.[1] The human rights activism of the Christian churches had been contained or co-opted and the burst of applications to exit the country in the wake of the Helsinki Accords had died down. Although some activists were causing trouble by agitating for peace outside of the state-approved movement protesting Western missile deployments, they too seemed to be under control.

By 1989, the world was a very different place: the SED found itself internationally isolated, with its own intellectuals admitting ideological defeat, and even other Eastern Bloc countries treating it as a pariah. From within, dozens of human rights groups were now active across East Germany and the number of GDR citizens applying to emigrate had grown to more than 100,000 per year. Those whose claims were rejected only became further radicalised, joining ever more vocal protest movements to demand their human rights.[2] Even the Protestant clergy, which

---

[1] The only mention of this project in any historical scholarship is a footnote in Heinz Mohnhaupt and Karl Mollnau, *Normdurchsetzung in Osteuropäischen Nachkriegsgesellschaften (1944–1989). Vol. 5.1, DDR 1958–1989* (Frankfurt: Klostermann, 1998), 567.

[2] Patrick Major, *Behind the Berlin Wall: East Germany and the Frontiers of Power* (Oxford: Oxford University Press, 2010), 215; Johannes Raschka, *Justizpolitik im SED-Staat: Anpassung und Wandel des Strafrechts während der Amtszeit Honeckers* (Cologne: Böhlau, 2000), 216–19.

had been seemingly pacified with the Church in Socialism agreement of the late 1970s, now openly called for political reforms through the implementation of human rights. At the beginning of the decade, the idea of human rights was marginal in dissident circles, but by 1989, it had become the lingua franca for a growing movement demanding the democratisation of the GDR.

A combination of local and global forces worked together to bring about an explosion in human rights activism from below and to sap confidence in socialist human rights amongst East German elites.[3] Within the GDR, the peace and environmental movements that had emerged in the 1970s reluctantly turned to the problem of human rights and political reform. After years of suppression by state security, many in these movements came to see democratisation and legally enforceable human rights as the only means forward towards realising their apolitical moral goals. New organisations such as the Initiative for Peace and Human Rights (*Initiative Frieden und Menschenrechte*, or IFM) acted as the translators for a broad array of dissident groups, connecting the idea of human rights to a variety of local problems ranging from draft resistance to environmental destruction to state-enforced military instruction for children. Rather than being inspired by Marxist utopianism or Western liberalism, this new generation of activists looked to pluralism, participatory democracy and legally guaranteed rights of civil society as the basis for reform towards a third way between socialism and capitalism.[4] SED antifascism, with its emphasis on the socialist triumph against the Nazis, failed to attract a younger generation that did not automatically associate parliamentary democracy with the fall of Weimar and the rise of the Nazis. As memories of the war and the power of antifascist rhetoric and ideology faded, so too did the legitimacy of a dictatorship for human rights.[5]

The decline of socialist human rights in East Germany stemmed from the growing economic and political crisis within the GDR, but it also was

---

[3] Konrad Jarausch, "Kollaps des Kommunismus oder Aufbruch der Zivilgesellschaft?," in Eckart Conze, *Die demokratische Revolution 1989 in der DDR* (Cologne: Böhlau, 2009), 45.

[4] Christof Geisel, *Auf der Suche nach einem dritten Weg: Das politische Selbstverständnis der DDR-Opposition in den 80er Jahren* (Berlin: Ch. Links, 2005), 49–51. Ehrhart Neubert, *Geschichte der Opposition in der DDR: 1949–1989* (Berlin: Ch. Links, 1998), 463; Karsten Timmer, *Vom Aufbruch zum Umbruch: die Bürgerbewegung in der DDR 1989* (Göttingen: Vandenhoeck & Ruprecht, 2000), 17; Siegfried Lokatis and Ingrid Sonntag, *Heimliche Leser in der DDR: Kontrolle und Verbreitung unerlaubter Literatur* (Berlin: Ch. Links, 2008), 72.

[5] On personal experience, generations, and ideology in the GDR, see Catherine Epstein, *The Last Revolutionaries: German Communists and Their Century* (Cambridge, MA: Harvard University Press, 2003).

entangled with global developments: The new Western-dominated human rights NGOs that emerged in the 1970s, focussed on individual freedoms, protection from arbitrary state power and cosmopolitan activism and displaced imperialism and self-determination from centre stage at the United Nations. The conflict over decolonisation had shifted from the problem of self-determination towards the terrain of international development and trade, while the problem of human rights was now being contested through the medium of ongoing East-West summits (stemming from the signing of the Helsinki Accords in 1975), which had the consequence of severing the Eastern Bloc from its Afro-Asian supporters at the United Nations. The SED's rhetoric of self-determination through state socialism, which once spoke to the most crucial issues of international politics, became increasingly dated and out of touch over the course of the 1980s. Incorporating human rights into state ideology in the late 1960s had helped to inoculate the SED against the initial wave of activism in the wake of the Helsinki Accords in the 1970s, but in the 1980s, the party's rigidity in holding on to its increasingly ineffective bromides about a global struggle against imperialism would signal its eventual downfall. As domestic economic conditions declined, migration skyrocketed and socialist allies began to abandon their human rights solidarity with the SED, even East German elites began to lose faith in the legitimacy of their ideology.

From Peace to Human Rights, 1982–1984

At the outset of the 1980s, East German elites presumed that the threat of human rights at home had been contained. In neighbouring Poland, martial law had been declared in 1981 to keep order after the rise of the Solidarność trade union movement and there was a restive dissident scene growing in Czechoslovakia and the USSR. By contrast, the GDR remained a relative beacon of state-socialist stability. East Germany lacked a single independent human rights organisation and the state-sponsored GDR-Committee for Human Rights (KMR) continued its work on the fight for justice and socialism in Southern Africa, the Middle East and Central America (though the situation in Afghanistan after the Soviet invasion was not a topic for discussion). Committee member and legal academic Hermann Klenner, whose 1964 *Studies in Basic Rights* had defined the field of thought in the GDR from the moment of its publication, wrote a new book, *Marxism and Human Rights*, that sought to update his earlier work and address contemporary political circumstances. Klenner wanted to demonstrate that Marxism and human rights were truly interconnected, pushing back against not only the new wave of

Western human rights activism (which paralleled US President Jimmy Carter's foreign policy) but also the work of the prolific East German academic Jürgen Kuczynski who argued for a return to the language of class rights.[6] Klenner's magnum opus concluded with a call for the continued fight for human rights, a "normative medium" in the transformation of the world: "The right to self-determination of peoples and individuals is based on their development, on progress, on evolutionary and revolutionary change."[7] In spite of scepticism from the Left and hostility from the West, Klenner maintained his total confidence in the capacity of the socialist revolution to realise human rights.

Klenner's was one of several works on the subject published in the GDR at the opening of the 1980s, but these texts were increasingly out of step with human rights politics in the rest of the world.[8] Western Marxists, including the Eurocommunist parties, were abandoning talk of revolutionary socialism and now saw individual rights and pluralistic democracy as core components of human rights.[9] The French socialist philosopher Claude Lefort remarked that while the Western Left had until recently seen human rights through the lens of Marx's critique, "these rights no longer seem to be formal, intended to conceal a system of domination; they are now seen to embody a real struggle against oppression."[10] In Yugoslavia, the Praxis group was developing arguments in favour of liberal democratic human rights as part of the revival of real socialism, in contrast to the bureaucratised shambles of Eastern Europe.[11] In Latin America, leftists who had been brutally suppressed and tortured by military regimes had turned to the language of individual

---

[6] On Kuczynski's writings on rights see Chapter 4. Klenner and Kuczynski extensively debated the meaning of human rights. Akademie der Wissenschaften (AdW) NL Jürgen Kuczynski 67, Korrespondenz Klenner.

[7] Hermann Klenner, *Marxismus und Menschenrechte: Studien zur Rechtsphilosophie* (Berlin: Akademie Verlag, 1982), 200–1.

[8] Werner Flach and Siegfried Ullrich, *"Menschenrechte": Entlarvung einer Demagogie* (Berlin: Dietz, 1980); Willi Büchner-Uhder, *Menschenrechte, eine Utopie?* (Leipzig: Urania-Verlag, 1981).

[9] Mark Bradley, "Human Rights and Communism," in *The Cambridge History of Communism: Volume 3, Endgames? Late Communism in Global Perspective, 1968 to the Present*, ed. Juliane Fürst, Silvio Pons and Mark Selden (Cambridge: Cambridge University Press, 2017), 162.

[10] Claude Lefort, "Politics and Human Rights," in *The Political Forms of Modern Society: Bureaucracy, Democracy, Totalitarianism*, ed. Claude Lefort (Boston: Massachusetts Institute of Technology Press, 1986), 240–41.

[11] Mihailo Markovic, "Philosophical Foundations of Human Rights," *Praxis International* 4 (1981), 386–400.

human rights as part of an international campaign against their own oppression.[12] While at the beginning of the 1980s, Polish émigré philosopher Leszek Kołakowski confidently declared human rights to be incompatible with Marxism, many were warming to the concept.[13]

Furthermore, the socialist world also lost its main partner at the United Nations, as the loose coalition of Afro-Asian states dedicated to self-determination fractured into separate African, Islamic and Asian human rights factions, each promoting their own discourse of tradition and cultural values.[14] Promulgated in 1980, the African Charter of Human Rights and People's Rights explicitly invoked the "traditional values" of Africa in a conscious effort to frame this new document as different but equivalent to Western conceptions of human rights. In parallel to this effort, Islamic scholars and eventually also majority-Muslim states were engaging in a similar process of reconciling traditional religious texts with modern international declarations and treaties. The first major effort to codify these claims came in 1981 with the "Universal Islamic Declaration of Human Rights" that declared, "Islam gave mankind an ideal code of human rights fourteen centuries ago." Here, religion was granted a privileged role as a means of understanding rights, rather than being understood as an alternative.[15] In the early 1980s, the People's Republic of China began to seriously engage with international human rights politics, but crafted an interpretation of rights based on the "different social and political systems, levels of economic and cultural development, and national customs and habits," not socialist human rights.[16] These initiatives legitimised their distance from Western liberal individualism through appeals to history, tradition and separate cultural values, rather than the universal principle of self-determination or inviolable state sovereignty.

As African and Islamic scholars sought to codify their human rights beliefs, so too did East Germans – on behalf of the entire socialist world. Without guidance or directive from the Soviet Union, the East German

---

[12] See Vania Markarian, *Left in Transformation: Uruguayan Exiles and the Latin American Human Rights Networks 1967–1984* (New York: Routledge, 2013).

[13] Leszek Kolakowski, "Marxism and Human Rights," *Daedalus* 112, no. 4 (1983), 81–92.

[14] On the decline of self-determination as a focal point in the late 1970s, see Adom Getachew, *Worldmaking after Empire: The Rise and Fall of Self-Determination* (Princeton, NJ: Princeton University Press, 2019).

[15] Ann Elizabeth Mayer, *Islam and Human Rights: Tradition and Politics* (Boulder, CO: Westview Press, 2012), 138. Other Islamic declarations followed, including Muammar Gaddhafi's Great Green Charter of Human Rights in the *Jamahiriya* Era (1988) and the Cairo Declaration of Islamic Human Rights (1991).

[16] Marina Svensson, *Debating Human Rights in China: A Conceptual and Political History* (Lanham, MD: Rowman & Littlefield, 2002), 262.

Ministry for Foreign Affairs launched an ambitious project to create a Socialist Declaration of Human Rights in near secrecy. Behind the scenes and with no public activity, a preliminary draft was written in 1981 by a team that included KMR veterans Hermann Klenner and Bernhard Graefrath.[17] The preamble began, "Whereas the abolition of the exploitation of man by man is the basic prerequisite for ensuring equal human rights without discrimination."[18] The text that followed represented human rights under socialism in its most idealised form. It proclaimed all citizens as equal, working together through self-determination towards the realisation of world peace. Under socialism, total gender equality meant that all citizens were able to fully take part in their workplaces, in the cultural life of the nation and in the political rule of the state. All citizens enjoyed the benefits of education, leisure and a healthy environment. Citizens were free to exchange views, to hold religious beliefs of their choosing and even to travel – on the condition that it did not threaten the "interests of national security or of public order and security or the protection of public health or morals or the protection of the rights and freedoms of others."[19] Party officials were pleased with the draft, but immediately removed all references to travel.[20]

The right to emigrate remained central for those speaking out against the SED in the name of human rights, but for East Germans hoping to change the GDR from within, the cause of peace and the environment aroused much greater enthusiasm. As mentioned in the previous chapter, East Germans had formed small peace groups, working under the protection of the Protestant Church, since the late 1970s. Rather than challenging the political structures of the state, GDR peace activists were more concerned with the military draft, the nuclear arms race and mandatory military education in public schools.[21] In 1982, this movement intensified from small-scale, private activism to public action, when longtime dissident scientist Robert Havemann and Protestant pastor Rainer Eppelmann published the *Berlin Appeal*, a one-page declaration calling for dialogue with the SED and the full demilitarisation of GDR

---

[17] BArch, DY30/24979 Süß to Sorgenicht (28.10.1981). The team also included legal academics Eberhard Poppe, Rudolf Hieblinger and Angelika Zschiedrich.
[18] BArch, DY30/24979 Entwurf einer Menschenrechtsdeklaration der sozialistischen Staaten (1981).
[19] Ibid., Article 16.   [20] BArch, DY30/24979 Heuer to Sorgenicht (4.11.1981).
[21] Steven Pfaff, "The Politics of Peace in the GDR: The Independent Peace Movement, the Church, and the Origins of the East German Opposition," *Peace & Change* 26, no. 3 (2001), 287.

society – from parades to education to mandatory service.[22] While the *Berlin Appeal* demanded greater political participation for East Germans, the language of human rights was noticeably absent. Several core ideals of other human rights movements – peace, dignity of the individual, free exchange of ideas – were present, but there remained a wariness of employing a discourse tainted by its association with Cold War propaganda. Despite Havemann's death (of natural causes) soon after the release of the *Appeal*, the document galvanised the peace movement, giving rise to many new organisations, including a GDR chapter of Women for Peace in 1982, and the nationwide Concrete Peace (*Frieden Konkret*) network of church organisations in 1983.[23] Women for Peace founders Ulrike Poppe and Bärbel Bohley would later be core members of the GDR human rights movement, but at this time, they too avoided the language of human rights so as to better focus on peace.[24]

The environmental movement also spread across East Germany in the early 1980s, in response to mass pollution and unrestricted industrial practices.[25] The waterways of the GDR were contaminated by the chemical industry's inveterate dumping mercury and other toxic waste; furthermore, the reliance on locally mined brown coal made East Germany the largest emitter of sulphur dioxide in Europe.[26] Like the peace movement, the greens had little initial interest in human rights. Activist Carlo Jordan later remembered, "Ecology as the destruction of the cultural and natural foundations of life [was] much more concrete than the abstract question of human rights."[27] The movement did not begin from theoretical foundations, but rather began with the environmental destruction that East Germans experienced in the everyday and it offered a tangible course of action such as taking part in tree plantings and writing letters to officials about specific problems.[28]

The SED regularly proclaimed its commitment to a clean environment, but in 1982 the responsible ministry decided to stop publishing data on pollution as it was becoming an embarrassment. This action

---

[22] Quoted in Woods, *Opposition in the GDR under Honecker, 1971–85*, 196.

[23] Neubert, *Geschichte der Opposition in der DDR*, 459–61 and 473–74.

[24] Pfaff, "The Politics of Peace in the GDR," 290. The first petition by Women for Peace only mentions the right to decline military service. Archiv der DDR-Opposition, RG/B 20/1-2 Frauen für Frieden Eingabe (12.10.1982).

[25] Neubert, *Geschichte der Opposition in der DDR*, 445.

[26] Merrill Jones, "Origins of the East German Environmental Movement," *German Studies Review* 16, no. 2 (1993), 236.

[27] Hoover Institution Archive, Joppke Collection, Box 1, Interview mit Carlo Jordan (16.7.1991), 4

[28] Wolfgang Rüddenklau, ed., *Störenfried: DDR-Opposition 1986–1989* (Berlin: BasisDruck, 1992), 45.

pushed activists to focus on access to information and the free exchange of ideas as a component crucial to their cause, and some activists began to see the absence of democratic rights and ecological catastrophe as interconnected problems.[29] As one wrote, "The struggle to improve the environment is only possible through the implementation of political rights and freedoms; it is only possible to guarantee more political rights and freedoms through the implementation of better environmental conditions."[30] In a similar vein, Horst Dienelt from East Berlin released the "95 Theses of the Green Manifesto" in 1983, which included a call for violence-free demonstrations for "general human rights and freedom of movement," and the "rejection of all dictatorships, including those of the Communist Party."[31] For this minority of activists, the solution to acid rain and toxic rivers was no longer planting trees, but political democratisation.

As a handful of grassroots activists began to embrace human rights and democratisation as a solution to their woes, a new generation of dissident intellectuals – Guntholf Herzberg and Peter Eisenfeld – also directly challenged SED human rights theory. An academic philosopher and party member, Herzberg had been kicked out of the SED in 1972 and subsequently lost his position at the prestigious Academy of Sciences due to his criticism of real existing socialism. Herzberg had taken part in the protests against singer Wolf Biermann's expulsion and became a good friend of ecological activist Rudolf Bahro.[32] When he turned to human rights in 1980, Herzberg encouraged his fellow citizens to appropriate the logic of the socialist human rights, not simply to take SED rhetoric literally. He told students to study officially sanctioned philosophy texts as a path to a better GDR and he specifically singled out Hermann Klenner's *Marxism and Human Rights* as an important source for ideas on how to engage with the state and demand change.[33] While East Germans were pessimistic that they could ever try to claim them against the state "because so many experiences speak against it," Herzberg argued that "every individual that sees himself as a responsible citizen should exploit every opportunity to realize his basic rights." In doing so,

[29] Jones, "Origins of the East German Environmental Movement," 236.
[30] Archiv der DDR-Opposition, RJ 11 Thesen zur Wechselbeziehung "Menschenrechte – Umweltverschmutzung in der DDR,"2.
[31] Archiv der DDR-Opposition, TH 02/ 01 Horst Dienelt, "95 Thesen des grünen Manifestes," (14.11.1983), Theses 38 and 47.
[32] Guntholf Herzberg, "Einen eigenen Weg gehen. Oder weggehen," in *"Freiheit ist immer Freiheit–": die Andersdenkenden in der DDR*, ed. Ferdinand Kroh (Frankfurt: Ullstein, 1988), 59–61.
[33] Ibid., 71.

however, he advised that one should always keep in mind that according to the SED, the "purpose of all rights is the development and protection of socialism," and be wary that the state was "allergic" to demands that appeared to be coordinated with "Western media, Amnesty International, or similar organizations."[34]

Peter Eisenfeld, by contrast, took a more direct approach in attacking the contradictions between socialist human rights doctrine and everyday life in the GDR. A longtime intellectual dissident, who would emigrate to the West in 1983, Eisenfeld first wrote a 40-page treatise on human rights in response to Jürgen Kuczynski's *Human Rights and Class Rights*.[35] Eisenfeld disputed Kuczynski's claim that the interests of the people and the state were unified in the socialist world following the revolution and detailed at length how recent history – including Stalinism, the crushing of the Prague Spring, martial law in Poland, the Cultural Revolution in China and the murderous purges by the Cambodian Khmer Rouge – had proven otherwise. In the GDR, there were the problems of "border fortifications, political prisoners, handling of dissidents, privileges like travel and information freedom for special citizens, the Intershops etc," which demonstrated that "the theoretical claims of the Marxist-Leninist Party do not, however, exist in reality."[36] He sent his text to Kuczynski and attempted to get it published in East Germany.[37] When this failed, Eisenfeld also submitted his ideas as a paper to the Philosophy Congress of the GDR – it was deemed "counter-revolutionary" and confiscated by state security.[38]

Although the vast majority of peace and environmental activists sought to avoid state repression by not engaging in political opposition or attacking SED legitimacy directly, this strategy did little to placate the Stasi. In the late 1970s, the Ministry of State Security had seen human rights and emigration as the primary vectors of Western imperialist subversion; by the early 1980s, however, the peace movement had

---

[34] Archiv der DDR-Opposition, RJ 04 Guntholf Herzberg: Bemerkungen zur Herausbildung der UNO-Menschenrechts-Konventionen und zum Grundrechte-Verständnis in der DDR, 30, 33.
[35] Jürgen Kuczynski, *Menschenrechte und Klassenrechte* (Berlin: Akademie-Verlag, 1978).
[36] "Menschenrechte und Klassenrechte," Brief von Eisenfeld an Kuczynski (1.5.1983), 37. Reprinted in Peter Eisenfeld, *"Rausschmeißen": zwanzig Jahre politische Gegnerschaft in der DDR* (Bremen: Edition Temmen, 2002), 430.
[37] Ibid., 203.
[38] Arno Polzin, *Fasse Dich kurz!: Der grenzüberschreitende Telefonverkehr der Opposition in den 1980er Jahren und das Ministerium für Staatssicherheit* (Göttingen: Vandenhoeck & Ruprecht, 2014), 240.

become enemy number one.[39] The SED rejected pacifism and viewed peace through an antifascist lens, wherein the socialist states had the duty to perform armed resistance against the forces of war. The independent peace movement was not seen as a class enemy, but "class indifferent," which threatened military readiness of the GDR by undermining the morale and ideological certainty of the armed forces.[40] While many in the Protestant Church sought to protect the fledgling groups devoted to peace, once activists began to demonstrate in public against military education, the Stasi swiftly intervened. In 1983–84, a campaign of suppression destroyed half the peace organisations in the country and the SED and the Stasi successfully pressured Churches to evict key activists from their community spaces. Important figures in the movement – such as Women for Peace founders Bärbel Bohley and Ulrike Poppe – were jailed. Rather than being imprisoned, the Stasi involuntarily deported Roland Jahn to West Germany in 1982 by locking him into the toilet of a Munich-bound train. Lower-level activists faced dismissal from work and educational institutions in retaliation for their public protests.[41]

Just as the Stasi seemed to succeed in suppressing the peace movement, the problem of emigration and human rights returned with a vengeance. In the early 1980s, the faltering economy was unable to keep up with the foreign debt payments that Erich Honecker had accrued to cover his consumer-oriented socialism.[42] The Soviet Union had unilaterally cut back on deliveries of subsidised oil to deal with its own financial difficulties creating a cascade effect throughout the GDR economy. Massive investments in the struggling East German microelectronic industry diverted funds from the rest of the economy. Consumer goods, including coffee and meat, became increasingly scarce, prompting a flood of angry petitions to all levels of the SED and state apparatus. In West Germany, a conservative-liberal government, now under Chancellor Helmut Kohl (CDU), took power, but the party veered from its earlier vehement anti-communism and began to seek increased economic ties with East Germany. On the one hand, the GDR was an

---

[39] A 1982 internal Stasi evaluation of domestic threats made no mention of human rights activism, see BStU, MfS, SED-KL 1088 Bericht des Leiters der HA XX über die "Bekämpfung des politischen Untergrundes, insbesondere der Versuche, unter dem Schutz der Kirche eine oppositionelle Bewegung mit konterrevolutionärer Zielstellung zu schaffen" (31.8.1982).

[40] BStU, MfS, SED-KL4862 Zu aktuellen feindlichen Bestrebungen, den politischen Pazifismus als Hauptform für die Schaffung einer politischen Opposition in der DDR zu missbrauchen (April 1982), 8.

[41] Pfaff, "The Politics of Peace in the GDR," 290.

[42] André Steiner, "The Globalisation Process and the Eastern Bloc Countries in the 1970s and 1980s," *European Review of History* 21, no. 2 (2014), 171–72.

important consumer of West German products; on the other, it was also a source of cheap agricultural goods, as well as inexpensive labour for major corporations including Volkswagen and a site for Western pharmaceutical companies to test new products.[43] Although Bavarian Minister-President Franz Joseph Strauß was once a staunch opponent of *Ostpolitik*, he now brokered a pair of billion mark loans with Honecker, saving the GDR from bankruptcy.[44]

Public anger about shortages, deteriorating housing stock and lack of political freedoms coalesced to set off a new wave of East Germans demanding to exit the country. In Madrid in 1983, at a Helsinki Accords follow-up meeting, the Soviet Union made a series of concessions on travel and emigration much to the horror of the SED leadership.[45] Rather than face the consequences of deteriorating domestic conditions and a growing dissident movement, the Stasi blamed a "campaign based on alleged violations of human rights," originating in West Germany.[46] Hoping to simply rid the country of its most dissatisfied, the SED decided in 1984 to allow the emigration of 37,000 "enemies, criminal elements, and incorrigibles."[47] Instead of quelling unrest, it set off a wave of petitions to emigrate – known as the *Ausreisewelle* – and first-time applicants quadrupled to more than 57,000.[48] Cultural luminaries had been departing the GDR since the late 1970s, but now politically connected citizens also sought to exit – including five relatives of Prime Minister Willi Stoph.[49] East Germans began to write to the KMR demanding assistance in emigrating: 150 in 1984 and 190 the following year.[50] Each of the letters was passed along (without reply) to the Ministry of the Interior for investigation. One bright spot for the SED

---

[43] On Western corporate ventures in the GDR, see Jonathan Zatlin, *The Currency of Socialism: Money and Political Culture in East Germany* (Cambridge: Cambridge University Press, 2007), 94–95. Rainer Erices, Andreas Frewer and Antje Gumz, "Testing Ground GDR: Western Pharmaceutical Firms Conducting Clinical Trials behind the Iron Curtain," *Journal of Medical Ethics* 41, no. 7 (2015), 529–33.

[44] Charles Maier, *Dissolution: The Crisis of Communism and the End of East Germany* (Princeton, NJ: Princeton University Press, 1997), 61–63.

[45] Hermann Klenner reported his own displeasure with the agreement in the third person as the anonymised informant "IM Klee" in a Stasi report on the reaction of East German intellectuals to the Madrid meeting. BStU, MfS, AIM 17340/89 Teil II Band 5. Hauptabteilung XVIII/5, Berlin (28.9.1983).

[46] Quoted in Anja Hanisch, *Die DDR im KSZE-Prozess 1972–1985* (Munich: Oldenbourg, 2012), 351.

[47] Major, *Behind the Berlin Wall*, 215.

[48] Ibid., 215; Raschka, *Justizpolitik im SED-Staat*, 216–19.

[49] Sabrina Ramet, *Social Currents in Eastern Europe: The Sources and Consequences of the Great Transformation* (Durham, NC: Duke University Press, 1995), 59.

[50] BArch, N 2535/2 Vorlage für die Leitungssitzung am 29.1.1985, 9; Vorlage für die Leitungssitzung am 20.12.1985, 8.

was the continued silence of the Catholic Church and the docility of most Protestant Church leaders: at a BEK conference in Eisenach in 1984, the primary theme was "Universal Human Rights and National Sovereignty: The Interdependence of Helsinki Principles VI and VII,"[51] in reference to the SED claims that the principle of sovereignty (VI) precluded intervention on the grounds of human rights (VII). Hermann Klenner of the KMR served as the keynote speaker and the Stasi reported that they were most pleased with the conference as the "socialist side was well represented," and no one made any "hostile-negative" statements during the proceedings.[52] Here too, the SED still maintained a hegemonic control over the language of human rights.

Human Rights for Pluralism and Dissent, 1985–1989

As with those trying to emigrate in the 1970s, the shift in the discourse of the peace movement towards human rights came from a position of desperation after efforts to campaign for apolitical moral goals had failed. Many feared that such a turn would be "political suicide," bringing with it greater Stasi repression, but for an increasingly vocal group of activists, it appeared that the only way to pursue their goals would be political reform through the embrace of human rights.[53] Frank Eigenfeld, a peace activist from Halle, later recalled: "We realized that we were not at all accepted by the powers that be, and that we had little opportunity to articulate ourselves in public ... the focus changed from the arms race towards human rights ... [but] only after we had begun to run into enormous organizing difficulties."[54] This shift generated significant resistance within the peace movement, both due to Stasi influence and from genuine fears and ideological objections. As feminist peace activist Ulrike Poppe later explained, "Democratic freedoms were always seen in a capitalist context. This made the debate about them problematic... I don't want to say that we used the theme of peace to work towards human rights and bourgeois freedoms. At the least, the people were, however, more open to the problem of human rights compared to just

---

[51] EZA 101/4830 Arbeitsgruppe Menschenrechte beim BEK 1984–1985 Universelle Menschenrechte und Nationale Souveränität: Die Interdependenz der Helsinki-Prinzipien VI und VII. Eisenach, DDR (September 1984).

[52] BStU, MfS, HA XX/4 1255. Bericht: Eisenach Menschenrechtskonferenz (November 1984).

[53] Marianne Schulz, *Von der Illegalität ins Parlament: Werdegang und Konzepte der neuen Bürgerbewegungen* (Berlin: Ch. Links, 1992), 150.

[54] Dirk Philipsen, *We Were the People: Voices from East Germany's Revolutionary Autumn of 1989* (Durham, NC: Duke University Press, 1993), 54.

working on the problem of our own democratic deficits."[55] The cause of peace was so important that it legitimised, at least for some, the venture from morally spotless demands for disarmament and demilitarisation into the grubby world of politics.

The first major human rights action by peace activists came in July 1985: a group of 34 dissidents mostly from organisations based in East Berlin wrote an open letter to the participants of the 12th World Games for Youth and Students held in Moscow. They argued that a "comprehensive development and realization of the person" – a standard slogan of socialist ideology – was only possible when "the fundamental rights laid down in the Universal Declaration of Human Rights have been fully realized." These rights included "freedom of expression, freedom of information, freedom of movement, unrestricted freedom to travel, the right to assembly and association, equal opportunities in education, regardless of religion and ideology."[56] This rhetoric broke from the cautious language of earlier dissidents by assuming that these rights were separable from socialism, rather than portraying them as the endpoint of the socialist revolution.

In January 1986, Ralf Hirsch, Wolfgang Templin and Peter Grimm, all longtime peace activists and signatories to the World Youth Games letter, issued a statement announcing the creation of the Initiative Frieden und Menschenrechte (Initiative for Peace and Human Rights, or IFM), the first dissident group to both work outside of the protection of the church and to focus on human rights within the GDR. In addition to the three signatories, the fledgling organisation was composed primarily of intellectuals, scientists and artists – many were part of the counter-culture scene centred in the East Berlin neighbourhood of Prenzlauer Berg – including Robert Havemann's widow Katja, Lotte Templin (wife of Wolfgang), Ulrike and Gerd Poppe, Bärbel Bohley and Werner Fischer. Having determined that the "goals of peace initiatives depended upon the implementation of basic democratic rights and freedoms," they called for assistance and cooperation from the various dissident communities as well the peace movement in developing the idea of human rights in relation to social justice, the right to work, the protection of the environment and the rejection of obligatory military service.[57] The freedom to choose a career path and a workplace was also an issue that united many of the members of the group with several having been forced

---

[55] Hoover Institution Archive, Joppke Collection, Box 1, Interview mit Ulrike Poppe (9.7.1991), 2.
[56] Quoted in Neubert, *Geschichte der Opposition in der DDR*, 596.
[57] Reprinted in Rüddenklau, *Störenfried*, 55–56.

out of educational programs or whose professional lives had been ruined due to state persecution.[58] Instead of focussing on a single issue or grievance in the name of human rights, the IFM's founding document pulled together the concerns of the many disaffected and disgruntled elements in East German society including the peace movement, religious believers, the environmental movement, draft resisters and workers, all under the collective umbrella of human rights.

Members of the IFM stressed the importance of human rights as a means of securing social well-being and harmony, not just the autonomy of the individual against the power of the state. In particular, they argued that the human right to peace, which had so long been the centrepiece of state propaganda, contradicted the SED's monopoly on power. IFM members sent a letter to the 11th SED Party Congress in 1986 stating: "Peace and security policy cannot only be a matter of party and government. Peace is a human right, and therefore every member of society must be able to discuss and take part in the decisions regarding anything relevant to this right." Crucial to this participation, the IFM also declared that "pluralism is an overarching value for the enforcement of fundamental human rights. [...] The essential tension between different approaches to human rights issues is productive and should not be destroyed by policy debates with the goal of unity."[59] The cause of human rights was about being open to all conceptions of human rights and working together through dialogue, not finding the one true path or correct theory.

Although IFM rhetoric was more confrontational than that of its predecessors, its members refused to side with Western anti-communists, and presented themselves as part of a "third way" between state socialism and capitalism. The group was not born of a total rejection of socialism, but from the frustrations of life under "real existing socialism" in the GDR. Even though many thought elements of parliamentary democracy were admirable, as Gerd Poppe put it, "when we use ideas like democracy and human rights, they are connected to quite a different conception than in the West."[60] The IFM rejected the opposition of socialist versus bourgeois rights presented by the SED and argued that greater political freedom need not come at the cost of

---

[58] Andreas Glaeser, *Political Epistemics: The Secret Police, the Opposition, and the End of East German Socialism* (Chicago: University of Chicago Press, 2011), 440.

[59] "Petition to the XI. SED Party Congress" (2.4.1986), in Kroh, *Freiheit ist immer Freiheit*, 226.

[60] Geisel, *Auf der Suche nach einem dritten Weg*, 50.

increased social equality. They were also careful to ascribe guilt to both sides of the Cold War when it came to the problem of peace.

Over the heads of those affected, there is a tense continuation of the arms build-up in both political blocs, negotiations are being held behind closed doors, and peace movement activists are being prosecuted and sometimes criminalized. As far as these practices are concerned, the "Western democracies" are right up there with our governing leaders.[61]

Human rights were universal, but also grounded in the realities of life in a state socialist country at the heart of the Cold War, which threatened all of humanity.

The birth of an independent East German human rights movement was complicated by organised resistance from within the peace movement in the form of the Counter-Voices (*Gegenstimmen*).[62] In contrast to the IFM's calls for individual civil rights and the introduction of political liberties, the Counter-Voices sought to advance human rights through the perfection of a moral or Marxist revolution.[63] Echoing Rudolf Bahro in the 1970s, they rejected liberal human rights activism, arguing that the focus on individual freedoms reinforced the problems of egoism and selfishness rather than contributing to the greater good. The Counter-Voices also rejected the demand for pluralism as a dead end, preferring to fight for the moral and economic revolution they thought was essential. Reinhard Schult, a draft resister, radical Marxist and cofounder of the group, dismissed the IFM's claim that political pluralism was necessary for the implementation of basic human rights: "That for me is no more than ideology or religion. It is on the same level as Lenin's line: Marxism is all-powerful because it is true."[64] For Schult and others, pluralistic human rights thinking was not a step along the way towards realising a socialist utopia, but a move backwards towards bourgeois liberalism.

In November 1986, under the auspices of Gottfried Gartenschläger, Reverend at a church in the East Berlin suburb of Friedrichsfelde (and a Stasi informant), the IFM and Counter-Voices held a joint human rights seminar attended by (depending on the source) between 25 and 125 activists.[65] Representatives of the Counter-Voices attacked the IFM's human rights proposals as pointless and counterproductive, and the

---

[61] Reprinted in Rüddenklau, *Störenfried*, 56.
[62] Neubert, *Geschichte der Opposition in der DDR*, 599.   [63] Rüddenklau, *Störenfried*, 52.
[64] Archiv der DDR-Opposition, RJ 02. Reinhard Schult to Roland Jahn (20.4.1987). Archiv der DDR-Opposition, RG/B 03 Stellungnahme zu einer Eingabe an den XI. Parteitag der SED 1986.
[65] On the low end of attendance estimates, see Jan Wielgohs, "Die Vereinigte Linke: Zwischen Tradition und Experiment," in Schulz, *Von der Illegalität ins Parlament*, 284–85; on the high end, Neubert, *Geschichte der Opposition in der DDR*, 604.

two groups left the meeting unreconciled.[66] Some historians have written off the Counter-Voice opposition to the nascent IFM as little more than a Stasi initiative to disrupt the creation of a human rights movement, but for some participants, it was a genuinely held position based on an ideological commitment to socialism and a rejection of liberal capitalism.[67] Several members had been harshly punished for their past political activities including Thomas Klein who had been imprisoned for a year and a half on the basis of manufactured evidence of conspiring with Western Trotskyites and Schult had been sentenced to eight months for illegal distribution of political material.[68] Although it is true that half of the members of the Counter-Voices were Stasi informants, the same was true of the IFM, which was also riddled with informants.[69] Even after the fall of the Berlin Wall, Schult maintained his stance.

[Human rights] were a type of ideological weapon against us. We were also against the state, but we didn't want unification with the West or the western system. Pure individual human rights stand in conflict with social human rights. [...] We rejected the bourgeois ideology of the human rights declarations. Naturally we were against the secret police. Nevertheless, we did not want to adopt the Western electoral system. "Free elections" were not our cause.[70]

Schult saw Western human rights criticism as an attack on his own political beliefs and he agreed with the SED that the West could only offer an inherently inferior version of human rights compared to those under a true system of socialism.

Despite the ongoing split in the nascent human rights movement, the creation of the IFM represented a breakthrough both in terms of ideas and organisation. As cofounder Ralf Hirsch later said, "[T]he IFM was a

---

[66] Environmental activist Wolfgang Rüddenklau frames the conflict around opposition to the innovations of the IFM, but Thomas Klein, a Counter-Voice, provides a more sympathetic interpretation that there was a genuine philosophical divide. Rüddenklau, *Störenfried*, 76–77; Thomas Klein, *"Frieden und Gerechtigkeit!": die Politisierung der Unabhängigen Friedensbewegung in Ost-Berlin während der 80er Jahre* (Cologne: Böhlau, 2007), 242–43.

[67] Christian Joppke, *East German Dissidents and the Revolution of 1989: Social Movement in a Leninist Regime* (Washington Square: New York University Press, 1995), 116–17. For the full argumentation of the Counter-Voices at the 1986 human rights seminar, see Rheinhard Schult, "Der Einzelne und die Gesellschaft: Menschenrechte im Neuen Testament und bei Marx," and Wolfgang Wolf (IMB Max) "Bürgerliche und sozialistische Demokratie in ihrer Beziehung zur Menschenrechtsfrage," Archiv der DDR-Opposition, WT 07 Menschenrechtsseminar 1986.

[68] Glaeser, *Political Epistemics*, 446.

[69] In the case of the IFM, 8 of the 16 founding members were Stasi informants, Hoover Institution Archive, Joppke Collection, Box 1, Interview mit Ralf Hirsch (10.7.1991), 5. Also see Neubert, *Geschichte der Opposition in der DDR*, 604.

[70] Hoover Institution Archive, Joppke Collection, Box 1, Interview mit Rheinhard Schult (1.7.1991), 3.

mixture of workers, intellectuals, and church members. It was also a melting pot for different groups – earlier the 'practitioners' and the 'theorists' were strictly separated. This mixing was something new."[71] Instead of a group of intellectuals trying to convince others of their ideas, the IFM was a forum in which people could more openly engage with one another on broad political issues.[72] Even if their individual grievances were not directly connected, single-issue activists could be introduced to one another and find common ground, creating a social dynamic wherein the IFM acted as a translator connecting local problems to the abstract language of human rights. The group remained on the margins of society, but the diversity of its membership and the combination of intellectuals interested in international human rights issues and local activists immersed in daily problems allowed for the development of a new kind of dissident human rights discourse from within East German society.

During the 1970s, the Stasi were able to suppress and imprison the few intellectuals who sought to start a human rights movement, but by the mid-1980s, there were far too many grassroots activists to contain through direct coercion.[73] In 1988, when the Stasi shuttered the Environmental Library (*Umweltbibliothek*) – a dissident East Berlin environmental organisation – in 1988 and seized its printing press (as punishment for providing assistance to the IFM), activists were able to put pressure on the SED. They held local solidarity vigils and generated negative publicity through Western media outlets, including through Roland Jahn, who acted as a bridge between East Germans and West German journalists and politicians, especially within the Green Party, after his expulsion from the GDR. Ultimately, critical coverage from the West and support from Church leaders, including the normally non-confrontational head of the BEK Manfred Stolpe, led the SED to return the printing press in a humiliating defeat. With West German loans

---

[71] Hoover Institution Archive, Joppke Collection, Box 1, Interview mit Ralf Hirsch (10.7.1991), 3.

[72] Helmut Fehr, "Von der Dissidenz zur Gegen-Elite: Ein Vergleich der politischen Opposition in Polen, der Tschechoslowakei, Ungarn und der DDR (1976 bis 1989)," in *Zwischen Selbstbehauptung und Anpassung: Formen des Widerstandes und der Opposition in der DDR*, ed. Ulrike Poppe, Rainer Eckert and Ilko-Sascha Kowalczuk (Berlin: Ch. Links, 1995), 315.

[73] The failure of the Stasi to suppress the IFM and other human rights groups in the 1980s supports Selvage's argument that the Stasi exaggerated its successes in the 1970s and was confronted with far less dissent than its Eastern Bloc counterparts. Douglas Selvage, "'Human Rights Demagoguery Hostile to Détente': The GDR and the Conference on Security and Cooperation in Europe, 1975–1989," in *Human Rights in Europe During the Cold War*, ed. Rasmus Mariager, Karl Molin and Kjersti Brathagen (London: Routledge, 2014), 142.

keeping the GDR economy afloat, the SED feared the political backlash that mass imprisonment would cause, so the Stasi was mandated with finding more creative alternatives.[74]

Rather than direct suppression, the Stasi targeted human rights activists through *Zersetzung* – a tactic of steady psychological pressure meant to distract and undermine the social life and mental well-being of dissidents. The Stasi had employed *Zersetzung* methods against those seeking to emigrate since the 1970s, and now tried to undermine the IFM through a variety of tactics, including ordering huge quantities of concrete to the home of one activist, sending postcards from a woman supposedly asking for child support to a married IFM member and even attempting to seduce Ulrike Poppe, to get to her husband and IFM cofounder Gerd.[75] One Stasi report on action against activist Wolfgang Rüddenklau of the Environmental Library argued "if we lock him up, we'll have everyone against us again," so they planned to have him alienate his own allies: "If we strengthen the nasty side of his character and subject him to more and more stress, to which he is clearly capable of reacting without consideration, then he will gain more enemies."[76] While Rüddenklau continued to organise, he described feeling as though he was in a "glass display case," always watched, with the Stasi often acting in plain sight to make clear he was under constant surveillance.[77]

Notwithstanding the Stasi's best efforts, human rights activism proliferated, and the church became increasingly politicised from within. In East Berlin, the creation of the IFM was soon followed in October 1986 by the church-based "Working Circle for a Church in Solidarity" (*Arbeitskreis Solidarische Kirche*). This group of theologians moved away from the church leadership-approved focus on morality, taking on the problem of "participation and democratization," within the GDR. In their founding declaration, they announced that "human rights are indivisible. We strive for a public dialogue with all social forces on how to implement human rights both at home and abroad."[78] While at the end of 1985, not a single human rights organisation existed in the GDR, by 1988, there were around 10 groups explicitly devoted to human rights activism, and numerous other peace and environment groups that now also addressed human rights issues.[79]

Protestant Church leaders initially opposed the turn to political human rights activism and sought to maintain comity with the SED. In 1985,

---

[74] Jones, "Origins of the East German Environmental Movement," 253–54.
[75] Joppke, *East German Dissidents and the Revolution of 1989*, 113.
[76] Jones, "Origins of the East German Environmental Movement," 256.
[77] Rüddenklau, *Störenfried*, 78–79.   [78] Quoted in Neubert, 620–21.   [79] Ibid., 724.

Manfred Stolpe gave a speech on "human rights deficits in the GDR," but his plea for greater dialogue and freedom of expression was still couched in praise for the GDR's extensive provision of social rights.[80] Similarly, Protestant Church leaders carefully policed events to forestall political human rights content – at a peace workshop in 1986, General Superintendent of East Berlin Günther Krusche personally removed posters from the IFM about human rights violations in Romania to keep the event on message.[81] But the careful balancing act of the "Church in Socialism" compromise proved unstable, as junior members began to dissent. When Christa Lewek, the chairwoman of the BEK's Human Rights Working Group, defended the GDR record on rights violations in an interview with a West German TV show, a group of younger clergy wrote an open letter accusing her of crossing a line and acting as though the BEK was a "Church of Socialism," by supporting the SED.[82]

Undeterred by pressure from the top, more Protestant clergy and church-based groups already involved in the environment and peace movements started to directly engage with human rights as well. In 1987, the Concrete Peace activism network first addressed human rights as one of the themes, with one participant's notes simply stating: "Human rights = advocacy = legitimization for existence of [activist] groups."[83] Heiko Lietz, a pastor who had been imprisoned as part of the draft resistance movement, organised a church meeting in the northern village of Warin on "Human Rights in the GDR: Claims and Reality." A far cry from the conciliatory events organised by the Church leadership that included KMR speakers, clergy such as Lietz were now reviving debate within the Church about human rights violations within East Germany.[84]

Independent and church-based human rights groups often emerged in pairs in this era. The Church could introduce new ideas and political concepts to their congregations, thereby bringing in more cautious East Germans who did not want to take on the risk of belonging to an explicitly dissident organisation. In Leipzig, for example, the young activist Uwe Schwab organised the independent Initiative Group for Life (IG Leben) bringing together democratic socialists and others from the

---

[80] BArch, DO4/1191 Manfred Stolpe, "Defizite bei den Menschenrechten in der DDR"(24.6.1985)

[81] Neubert, *Geschichte der Opposition in der DDR*, 578.   [82] Ibid., 593.

[83] Archiv der DDR-Opposition, ÜG 01/1-2 Frieden Konkret Gruppengespräch Notizen, 1. On the turn to human rights by Frieden Konkret, see Klein, *Frieden und Gerechtigkeit!*, 307.

[84] Archiv der DDR-Opposition, ÜG 01/1-2 Abschrift Nr. 2112.

alternative scene.[85] At the same time, the newly arrived dissident pastor Christoph Wonneberger made the city's Nikolai Church into a site of politicised activism. Wonneberger had experienced the Prague Spring firsthand and had been active in the peace movement in Dresden until he was forced to move to Leipzig.[86] In 1987, he also began organising regular peace prayers, which, by 1989, were attended by thousands of people. Dialogue between the two groups allowed for ideas to spread between different social classes and demographic groups that were otherwise isolated from each other in everyday life.

While BEK leaders opposed confrontation with the SED, human rights dissidents found allies in some senior Church figures such as Heino Falcke, the Provost of Erfurt, who had long supported the peace and environmental movements.[87] In 1988, Falcke organised the Ecumenical Assembly for Justice, Peace, and the Integrity of Creation that brought thousands of Christians of all denominations into a process of political engagement, which included the concept of human rights. Inspired by the World Council of Churches, the Ecumenical Assembly planned three mass gatherings over the course of 1988–89 in which the Christian communities of the GDR would discuss the problems of society.[88] East German Christians were once again critiquing the structure of the GDR in large groups, as they had during the mass consultations over the 1968 constitution, but now, rather than speaking deferentially to the state, they were doing so within their community on its own terms. The Assembly allowed participants to articulate why they were unhappy with the system and then collectively analyse what needed to be changed, providing another crucial step on the path towards the mass demonstrations to come.[89]

Assembly participants were asked to submit postcards with suggested discussion topics on the subjects of justice, peace and creation and East Germans responded by submitting more than 10,000. As in 1968 during the mass consultation on the new constitution, the issue of parental rights over their children's education and religious freedom remained contentious, but now, in the field of "justice and participation in our own

---

[85] Archiv der DDR-Opposition, RG/S 01/03 *Initiativgruppe Leben Leipzig.*
[86] Pfaff, "The Politics of Peace in the GDR," 292–93.
[87] Neubert, *Geschichte der Opposition in der DDR*, 251–52.
[88] These plans emerged from the 1983 WCC Assembly held in Vancouver. Heino Falcke, "The Ecumenical Assembly for Justice, Peace and the Integrity of Creation," *The Ecumenical Review* 56, no. 2 (2004), 184–91.
[89] Stephen Brown, *Von der Unzufriedenheit zum Widerspruch: der konziliare Prozess für Gerechtigkeit, Frieden und Bewahrung der Schöpfung als Wegbereiter der friedlichen Revolution in der DDR* (Frankfurt: Lembeck, 2010).

society," hundreds wrote in about human rights (173 postcards), freedom to travel (174), legal security (122), freedom of information (107),
democratisation (80) and an increased role for citizens and the church in
public life (78). For those writing about human rights, the main topics of
concern were civic equality and individual freedom, but also the freedom
to buy the texts of the Helsinki Accords and UN treaties from book-
stores.[90] The Assembly also gave Catholic clergy a chance to reconnect
with these issues because their church had not spoken out publicly on
human rights since the mid-1970s. One group of priests from Salzwedel
wrote in to say they believed that "every citizen of the GDR has the right
to freely choose the destination of their travel."[91] While global ecumenical support for antiracism through the 1970s had been used by the SED
to deflect human rights criticism at home, it now provided the catalyst to
mobilise East Germans for domestic reform.

The growing support from Christians for the right to travel represented
the narrowing gap between those seeking emigration and dissidents
trying to democratise the GDR.[92] As one human rights activist from
Leipzig later recalled about the conflict between the movements: "We
didn't care about that. There were also those trying to emigrate with us.
We didn't make the effort to think about it. That was a human right, so
what is this shit."[93] The increased support from dissidents for those
seeking to leave had a reciprocal effect, as some would-be emigrants
broadened the scope of their human rights concerns. In September
1987, Günter Jeschonnek, an artist who had been blacklisted following
his application to leave the GDR formed the "Working Group for Citizenship Rights" (*Arbeitsgruppe Staatsbürgerschaftsrecht*). This organisation
was the first formal effort to coordinate human rights demands by those
trying to emigrate. Wolfgang and Lotte Templin of the IFM assisted in
the creation of the group rather than simply asking them to remain and
fight for change. In return, the public statements of Jeschonnek and the
Working Group also addressed other human rights abuses in the GDR.
In a manifesto delivered to the KMR on 10 December 1987 – Human
Rights Day – the group declared: "The realization of human rights
cannot be solely a matter of the state. In our view, this includes equal
participation of all citizens, the unvarnished examination of existing
problems, open dialogue with dissenters and free space in society for

---

[90] Ibid., 216–21.
[91] Archiv der DDR-Opposition, HL 052/1-2 Copy of Card 9288 A 3058 (24.1.1988).
[92] Neubert, *Geschichte der Opposition in der DDR*, 672.
[93] "Das war für uns ein Menschenrecht, also was soll die Scheiße." Hoover Institution
Archive, Joppke Collection, Box 1, Interview mit Frank Sellentin (26.7.1991), 2.

the unrestricted work of independent peace and human rights groups."[94] Those who chose to leave were now also trying to change the system on their way out.[95]

On a mass scale, those seeking to emigrate were also moving from instrumentalising human rights language to exhibiting an internalised sense that they had an inherent right to leave. According to a report from the Ministry of the Interior, almost all applications to exit in 1988 included, "slander against the politics of the GDR, especially accusations of massive human rights violations. The assertion that conflicts exist between international agreements and the domestic policies of the GDR plays a dominant role."[96] Günter Jeschonnek recalled that he wanted to make clear that "we are not supplicants, but we have a right [to emigrate]," and that right was a "legitimate human right."[97] Gone were the polite reminders about international law or the subordinate language begging permission to leave. In its place, was a militant sense of entitlement grounded in the idea of human rights.

Across the GDR, individual human rights ceased to be a theoretical concept and became a way of life as rhetoric transformed into practice. Dissidents were not just demanding the right to speak, organise and participate in public life, but they were also acting as if they already had these rights. Activists arranged for interviews with foreign journalists and used Western television to transmit their message throughout the GDR and groups began to create newsletters and mass-produce mimeographed copies for underground distribution. Although these *samizdat* publications were intended for a broader audience, most were still stamped with the phrase "Only for Internal Church Distribution," as a fig leaf so that groups could try and claim that they were not trying to break into the SED-controlled public sphere. The most important of these publications for the human rights movement was the IFM's *Grenzfall*, a *samizdat* journal published irregularly beginning in 1986. While only a few hundred copies of these publications circulated and their impact on the public was limited, the process of writing and distributing

---

[94] Arbeitsgruppe Staatsbürgerschaftsrechte der DDR, Erklärung (10.12.1987), 4 (www.bstu.bund.de).

[95] Pfaff dubs these activists "noisy exiters," Steven Pfaff, *Exit-Voice Dynamics and the Collapse of East Germany: The Crisis of Leninism and the Revolution of 1989* (Durham, NC: Duke University Press, 2006), 80.

[96] BArch, DO 1/16491 Information über die Unterbindung und Zurückdrängung rechtswidriger Ersuchen auf Übersiedlung nach der BRD (June 1988), 4.

[97] Hoover Institution Archive, Joppke Collection, Box 4, Interview with Günter Jeschonnek (12.9.1991) (Q280), 2.

them provided the dissidents with a means of socially practicing rights instead of just talking about them.[98]

Human rights activists not only sought to create their own public sphere, they also tried to hijack existing state events and rituals. When the SED took part in the Olof Palme Peace March in 1987, a procession that ran from Sweden to Southern Europe in the name of a nuclear free corridor, East German activists joined holding signs that included Mikhail Gorbachev's slogan, "We need democracy like we need air to breathe."[99] In January 1988, a group from the IFM took part in the annual march to commemorate the German Communist Party cofounders Rosa Luxemburg and Karl Liebknecht with banners emblazoned with the Luxemburg quote, "Freedom is always freedom for those who think differently." The hijacking of parades, and the ensuing crackdown by the state also had a cyclical effect, inspiring others to dissent in similar ways.[100] After crossing the line into illegal public demonstrations, the Stasi reacted with a heavy hand and conducted mass arrests, including targeting the leadership of the IFM. Cofounder Bärbel Bohley was ejected from the GDR and landed in London with a six-month visa. Although the Stasi was able to silence much of the human rights movement in East Berlin, it came at the cost of bad international publicity, and only shifted the centre of the gravity in the movement south to Leipzig and Dresden, as well as into the smaller groups in small towns in the countryside.[101] Other groups started to hold their own public rallies: In Leipzig, IG Leben held a march in June 1988 to raise awareness about ecological problems in the city, and when denied a permit to do so, they "claimed for itself the right to have a demonstration."[102]

In December 1988, dissidents finally tried to publicly appropriate Human Rights Day for themselves. For the 40th Anniversary of the UDHR, activists organised numerous church events to discuss human rights problems and deficits in the GDR. The Stasi estimated that 800 people took part in a Human Rights Day service at a church in Berlin-Treptow, which included representatives from more than 200 groups and organisations. At another Berlin church, 120 people discussed Article 19 of the UDHR on freedom of speech. At a third

---

[98] Timmer, *Vom Aufbruch zum Umbruch*, 74.
[99] Jones, "Origins of the East German Environmental Movement," 252.
[100] For an example of contemporary impact, see Archiv der DDR-Opposition, Samizdat 338 PS 070/01 Merkwürdige Allgemeine Erklärung. The January 1989 issue featured a reprint of the UDHR and commentary on the importance of the Luxemburg-Liebknecht rally in inspiring further dissident activity.
[101] Neubert, *Geschichte der Opposition in der DDR*, 698–99.
[102] Quoted in Pfaff, *Exit-Voice Dynamics and the Collapse of East Germany*, 96.

Berlin church, 50 attendees interrogated the role of the church in over-coming human rights abuses within the GDR. Demonstrations by those seeking to leave also took place in Berlin, Halle and Erfurt.[103] In response to the SED's proclamation, several human rights groups issued their own declaration, pointing out the glaring contradictions between the regime's rhetoric and its reality.[104] In less than three years, human rights had moved from a language employed only on the fringes of the East German protest scene to a powerful shared discourse of dissent, linking together disparate movements for change across the GDR.

Inspirations and Influences for an East German Human Rights Movement

As East German dissidents turned to human rights, they borrowed from a diverse range of sources. Western media and the activism of NGOs certainly raised the issue of human rights, but the transmission of human rights ideas cannot be seen as a direct transfer from West to East. Western media was crucial in disseminating information on many of the abuses of SED rule, such as the shootings at the border, but (as mentioned in previous chapters) the emphasis on anti-communism in these reports was off-putting to peace activists and reform socialists. West German human rights activism was also directly incorporated into SED propaganda as "imperialist hypocrisy," deployed to stir up dissent and cover for the crimes of capitalism.[105] Informal networks connecting East and West emerged from the Helsinki process in the late 1970s and 1980s; but, in contrast to many other Eastern Bloc states, East Germany

---

[103] Information Nr. 535/88 über Aktivitäten feindlich-negativer Kräfte in der DDR anlässlich des 40. Jahrestages der Annahme der "Allgemeinen Erklärung der Menschenrechte" durch die UNO (12.12.1988) in Frank Joestel, ed., *Die DDR im Blick der Stasi 1988: die geheimen Berichte an die SED-Führung* (Göttingen: Vandenhoeck & Ruprecht, 2010), 295–96.

[104] Open letters in Archiv der DDR-Opposition, RG/Bra 02; RG/B 10; RHi 02; SaGem 18; GP 06 IFM (1) as well as *samizdat* publications, Archiv der DDR-Opposition, Samizdat PS 013/ 05; Samizdat PS 041/12 *Friedensnetz*; Samizdat PS 117/07 *Wendezeit*.

[105] Human rights themes continued to feature on *Der Schwarze Kanal* – the GDR show that commented on West German news – through the 1980s. Some examples: Episode Nr. 1121 Helsinki – Einmischung – Menschenrechte (11.1.1982) featuring non-intervention and human rights in the Helsinki Process; Nr. 1126 Frieden und Arbeit: Die beiden ersten Menschenrechte (15.2.1982) on the peace movement; Nr. 1316 El-Dorado der Menschenrechtler (2.12.1985) on human rights violations in Chile; Nr. 1326 Menschenrecht und Menschenwürde (10.2.1986) on West German social inequality; Nr. 1413 Das zweite Menschenrecht (12.10.1987) on unemployment in the West; and Nr. 1464 Wohnen: ein Menschenrecht (03.10.1988) on homelessness in West Germany.

did not have any Helsinki monitoring groups.[106] Organisations such as Amnesty International and the Society for the Protection of Human Rights (GfM) assisted in keeping activists out of prison and in helping them to emigrate to the West, but ideologically, they were not very influential.[107] A survey of those helped by Amnesty International in the 1980s showed that most of those assisted had heard of Amnesty before their own imprisonment, but that they thought of it primarily as a support group for political prisoners, rather than a human rights organisation. Some had only heard of Amnesty via state media, which depicted it as an "enemy organization"; and while most praised its work in helping them gain their personal prison release, the organisation was not seen as a source of inspiration for human rights activism at home.[108]

Eastern   Europe,   particularly   movements   in   Poland   and Czechoslovakia, proved to be a greater source of inspiration for ideas and tactics than Western activists.[109] Two leading dissidents in the human rights movement, Ludwig Mehlhorn and Wolfgang Templin, had both studied in Poland and worked with the pioneering human rights group KOR (The Worker's Defense Committee). The main lessons they took from the Polish experience was that dissent needed to take place in the open, and that pluralism rather than ideological purity was crucial for a movement's survival.[110] Charter 77 in Czechoslovakia was also a clear influence on the human rights movement and the Initiative for Peace and Human Rights in particular. In a letter from the IFM to Charter 77 printed in *Grenzfall*, the group declared, "for us, the existence of the Charter and other human rights movements in Eastern Europe was and is an encouragement and a source of inspiration. At the beginning, [...]

---

[106] Sarah Snyder, *Human Rights Activism and the End of the Cold War: A Transnational History of the Helsinki Network* (Cambridge: Cambridge University Press, 2011).

[107] Anja Mihr, *Amnesty International in der DDR* (Berlin: Ch. Links, 2002); Jürgen Wüst, *Menschenrechtsarbeit im Zwielicht: zwischen Staatssicherheit und Antifaschismus* (Bonn: Bouvier, 1999). Robert Brier, "Entangled Protest: Dissent and the Transnational History of the 1970s and 1980s," in *Entangled Protest: Transnational Approaches to the History of Dissent in Eastern Europe and the Soviet Union*, ed. Robert Brier (Osnabrück: Fibre, 2013), 21.

[108] Archiv der DDR-Opposition, AM 51 Fragebogen. The terms of archival access prevent the reprinting of further survey details.

[109] Klein, *Frieden und Gerechtigkeit!*, 78. Helmut Fehr, "Von der Dissidenz zur Gegen-Elite: Ein Vergleich der politischen Opposition in Polen, der Tchechoslowakei, Ungarn und der DDR (1976 bis 1989)," in Poppe, Eckert and Kowalczuk, *Zwischen Selbstbehauptung und Anpassung*, 317.

[110] Padraic Kenney, *A Carnival of Revolution: Central Europe 1989* (Princeton, NJ: Princeton University Press, 2003), 110–11. The early issues of *Grenzfall* included articles on events in Poland and protest letters to Polish officials. Lev Kopelev and Ralf Hirsch, *Grenzfall: Initiative Frieden und Menschenrechte: Vollständiger Nachdruck aller in der DDR erschienenen Ausgaben, 1986–87* (Self-pub., 1989), 1–13.

we were often accused of trying to copy Charter 77."[111] In addition to the importance of the group, the *samizdat* publication "Human Rights and the Political Revolution" by Peter Uhl, a far-left member of Charter 77, was also an important guiding text for how to reconcile revolutionary socialism with human rights.[112]

Global socialist solidarity was also an important site of inspiration for human rights activism. Dissident Thomas Rudolph would later note that the Working Group on Human Rights in Leipzig was initially more interested in Nicaragua and South Africa than the GDR.[113] The human rights problems highlighted by the SED and the KMR drew sympathy and interest, and eventually there was marked overlap between those fighting for rights in the developing world and those who took to the streets at home to demand democratisation.[114] In order not to alienate those who found the use of human rights language criticism for conditions in the GDR to be exaggerated in comparison with the repression of far-right military dictatorships or colonial racism, the IFM, in particular, took pains to emphasise that they did not consider violations within the Socialist Bloc "comparable with Chile and South Africa."[115] By making these distinctions, human rights activists could use enthusiasm for international human rights as a recruiting tool for their own movement.

Finally, socialist human rights theory (as produced by East German intellectuals) also provided an important source of rhetoric and argumentation. Early in the decade, Guntholf Herzberg and Peter Eisenfeld showed how socialist human rights could be used for dissent, and their ideas were picked up by later activists, including the founders of the IFM.[116] The personal papers of IFM cofounder Ulrike Poppe contain

---

[111] Kopelev and Hirsch, *Grenzfall*, 29. The letter to Charter 77 also aimed to demonstrate to the Counter-Voices that IFM positions had international support. Klein, *Frieden und Gerechtigkeit!*, 307.

[112] Mimeographed copies of Uhl's tract are in the personal papers of several dissidents at the Archiv der DDR-Opposition, as well as in the files of Archiv Bürgerbewegung-Leipzig (ABL) 03.33 Gruppe Frieden und Menschenrechte (Halle) and his work is mentioned in a Stasi report, Archiv der DDR-Opposition, AM 33 Analyse über die gegnerischen Aktivitäten zur Organisierung der politischen Untergrundtätigkeit, HA XX (10.1.1978), 25. On Uhl's activism, see Jonathan Bolton, *Worlds of Dissent: Charter 77, the Plastic People of the Universe, and Czech Culture under Communism* (Cambridge, MA: Harvard University Press, 2012), 144.

[113] Hoover Institution Archive, Joppke Collection, Box 1, Interview mit Thomas Rudolph (25.7.1991), 2. Neubert, *Geschichte der Opposition in der DDR*, 594–95.

[114] On independent Third World solidarity activism in the GDR, see Maria Magdalena Verburg, *Ostdeutsche Dritte-Welt-Gruppen vor und nach 1989/90* (Göttingen: V&R Unipress, 2012).

[115] Kopelev and Hirsch, *Grenzfall*, 132.

[116] Johannes Pohl, a pastor from Dresden in the peace movement sent a copy of Eisenfeld's treatise on human rights to Wolfgang Templin, one of the IFM's founders in Berlin.

articles and news clippings on human rights from East German academics such as Ernst Bloch, Hermann Klenner, Rolf Reissig and Polish legal scholar Adam Łopatka. She also corresponded with Professor Eberhard Poppe (no relation), who taught at the University of Halle and wrote extensively on human rights law.[117] The correspondence and personal papers of pastor and activist Heiko Lietz include notes on Hermann Klenner's writings, citations from socialist human rights scholar Bernhard Graefrath and a declaration from the GDR-Committee for Human Rights.[118] While many taking part in the human rights movement were possibly unaware of these connections, the key activists translating the idea of human rights into a workable program of grassroots activism were very conscious of socialist human rights ideology produced by the SED.

GDR human rights activists also adopted the heroes of German communism, especially Rosa Luxemburg, as their symbolic forebearers. Luxemburg's slogan "Freedom is always freedom for those who think differently," would become a mainstay of human rights activism, and her criticisms of Lenin and the Soviet Revolution were employed to legitimise calls for a new path for the GDR.[119] In a speech in 1986, on the interconnection of human rights and peace, Bärbel Bohley cited Luxemburg: "Socialist democracy means much more and in no way less than bourgeois democracy. It definitely does not mean the abolition of civil rights."[120] In January 1988, the effort by human rights protesters to infiltrate the Luxemburg-Liebknecht March represented a powerful symbolic claim to represent a more legitimate heir to the socialist past than the SED.

Although influenced by outside activists and movements, the human rights ideals of the IFM and others were indigenous to the GDR and clearly a product of its own unique history.[121] The KMR had acted as the primary "translator" of international human rights into local East German idiom since the late 1950s, but the dissident movement

---

Polzin, *Fasse Dich kurz!*, 240–41. Fellow IFM cofounder Ulrike Poppe had a copy of Gultholf Herzberg's human rights presentation in her personal papers, Archiv der DDR-Opposition, UP 044 Menschenrechtsproblematik.

[117] Clippings in Archiv der DDR-Opposition, UP 044 Menschenrechtsproblematik; and correspondence in UP 004/4.

[118] Clippings in Archiv der DDR-Opposition, RG/MV 01 and HL 177.

[119] In 1988, this phrase was the main slogan of dissidents at the Luxemburg/Liebknecht Protest and a book on the movement used it as a title, Kroh, *Freiheit ist immer Freiheit*.

[120] Archiv der DDR-Opposition, RJ 04 Bärbel Bohley: "Verknüpfung von Frieden und Menschenrechte" (2.8.1986), 3. Which Luxemburg text Bohley was quoting is unclear.

[121] As per Jarausch, the peace and human rights movements were "an authentic product of the GDR, the opposition developed from within socialism." Konrad Jarausch, *The Rush to German Unity* (Oxford: Oxford University Press, 1994), 44.

eventually displaced it from this role. The human rights discourse of the IFM was built on tangible local issues, such as the suppression of free speech, environmental destruction and draft resistance, but it also connected these issues together with the vocabulary of socialism, solidarity and popular antifascism. The IFM not only co-opted the rhetoric of the SED, it managed to hijack its claims to moral and political legitimacy.[122]

The Failed Declaration of Socialist Human Rights

Aside from specific negotiations at the United Nations and as part of the Helsinki process, cooperation in the field of human rights had never been a priority within the Eastern Bloc. While the various security services had increased their coordination, there had been very little formal ideological or intellectual cooperation. In March 1985, however, the problem of human rights took centre stage at a meeting of Eastern Bloc "Secretaries of Ideology and Propaganda" held in Moscow. In the midst of a discussion on economic issues, a young member of the Soviet Politburo, Mikhail Gorbachev, warned the attendees that the apologists for imperialism "make pretty speeches about 'bridging the gap' [between East and West], about freedom and human rights. They lie and dissemble with a single goal: to make us waver in our unity, to weaken us, and to eliminate us, the main obstacle to the realization of their imperialist plans."[123] Five days after that speech, Soviet General Secretary Konstantin Chernenko was dead, and Gorbachev was sworn in as his replacement.

Soon after, a Helsinki Accords follow-up meeting specifically for human rights experts, held in Ottawa, Canada, propelled the problem to the fore once again. Although the Soviets tried to limit the discussion to national implementation rather than critiquing the records of other nations, the meeting ground to a diplomatic standstill as East and West presented diametrically opposing visions of human rights.[124] As the stalemate in Canada was developing, the SED proposed a solution at a meeting of Eastern Bloc ideology and international affairs officials in Budapest.

---

[122] Szulecki argues that the opposition in Czechoslovakia and Poland "hijacked" human rights, peace, and the environment from the state. Kacper Szulecki, "Hijacked Ideas: Human Rights, Peace, and Environmentalism in Czechoslovak and Polish Dissident Discourses," *East European Politics and Societies* 25, no. 2 (2011), 272–95.

[123] BArch, DY30/IV2/1/630 Anlage 2 Rede auf dem Treffen der Sekretäre für Ideologie und Propaganda, 11.

[124] On Soviet tactics in Ottawa, see Elizabeth Kerley, "The Contest for Human Rights: Soviet Soft Power through Détente, Reform, and Collapse, 1973–1991" (Cambridge, MA: Harvard University, 2016).

It is important for us to counteract the strengthened campaign of the West on the issue of human rights. [...] We meet it head-on by demonstrating the humanistic values and achievements of real existing socialism in the everyday life of the people, above all in confronting [West German] propaganda and opposing the chronic crises, inhumanity, and lack of perspective of the capitalist world.[125]

The Ottawa meeting ended without an agreed-upon final statement – a first for the Helsinki process.[126] In October 1985, now General Secretary Gorbachev suggested that the next meeting of Eastern Bloc ideology officials (scheduled for Bucharest later that year) should be devoted entirely to the problem of human rights.[127]

While the Soviet Union had instigated the discussion on human rights in Bucharest, the GDR quickly took a leading role in shaping plans for the future. When it came time for SED Ideology Minister Kurt Hager to address the meeting, he made an ambitious proposal: the creation of a Declaration of Human Rights for the socialist states. An academic council of socialist experts would work through the ideological and theoretical problems and finally give the Socialist world its own version of the European Convention on Human Rights. Hager specifically praised the work of the KMR and noted its prescient founding back in 1959. Citing long experience in dealing with human rights propaganda from the West, Hager declared that the only option was to "raise the banner of human rights even more firmly in our hands" and to launch a counterattack.[128] As a first step, his office had prepared a series of briefing booklets on socialist human rights and Western propaganda, distributed to all delegates. Hager's ambition to take the fight to the West met with a favourable response and the SED was placed in charge of coordinating the ensuing effort.[129] It set to work on increasing the SED's institutional capacity for international human rights scholarship and propaganda by creating the "Interdisciplinary Academic Working Group for Questions on Human Rights" in June 1986.[130]

---

[125] BArch, DY30/11885 Bemerkungen zum Tagesordnungspunkt 1 auf dem Treffen stellvertretender Leiter der ideologischen und internationalen Abteilungen (18.5.1985), 8.

[126] Harm Hazewinkel, "Ottawa 1985 – The Half-Way Meeting Recollections of a Participant," *OSCE ODHR Bulletin* 3, no. 3 (1995), 41–47.

[127] This decision is referenced in BArch, DP1/21482 Neugebauer to Kern (2.12.1985), 1.

[128] BArch, DY30/11887 Auszug aus dem Referat des Genossen Kurt Hager (1985), 42–45.

[129] BArch, DY30/J IV2/2/2148 Anlage Nr. 5 zum Protokoll Nr. 1 vom 7.1.1986. Protokollniederschrift: Beratung der Sekretäre für internationale und ideologische Fragen (19./20.12.1985), 6.

[130] BArch, DY30/11891 Information der SED über die Tätigkeit in Verwirklichung der Vereinbarungen der Bukarester Beratung der Sekretäre für internationale und ideologische Fragen (05.11.1986), 7–8.

Based at the Academy for Social Sciences of the Central Committee, the so-called Red Think-Tank of the SED, this project was put into the hands of Rolf Reissig – a reform-minded intellectual who was only 46; relatively young in comparison to the more senior academics of the GDR-Committee for Human Rights.[131] While, at that time, Klenner was the GDR's representative at the United Nations on human rights matters and had risen to become the vice-chair of the UN Human Rights Commission, he was not only forced to withdraw his candidacy for a promotion to chair but also to resign from the commission entirely, when the Israeli delegation revealed that Klenner had been a member of the Nazi Party as a teenager in 1945.[132] The ensuing scandal undoubtedly damaged Klenner's position at home and explains why the much younger Reissig was given the position, to his own surprise and chagrin.[133]

Yet, just as Kurt Hager was holding up the GDR as an exemplar for the rest of the socialist world, East German elites were losing faith in the socialist human rights project. The KMR was rapidly being overwhelmed by citizens' complaints as East Germans now bombarded the Committee with requests for assistance in leaving the GDR, to complain about the absence of consumer goods (from cars to tropical fruit), and to register their distaste for ideological indoctrination, military education for youth and restrictions on basic freedoms, including the right to speak freely and travel.[134] Morale was already low due to this domestic engagement, but collaboration with other Warsaw Pact nations only served to further shake the resolve of the Committee. In 1986, a joint delegation of foreign affairs functionaries from the Soviet Union, Czechoslovakia and Bulgaria visited the Committee's office in East Berlin in preparation for the creation of similar human rights offices at home (an idea born of Hager's boasting of the GDR's long-standing expertise in the field). Once the visiting officials delved into the details of the operation, however, it was clear that they would not be replicating the East German model. The delegation asked how the Committee could handle communicating with the public with only Secretary Forberger and a handful of

---

[131] Lothar Mertens, *Rote Denkfabrik? die Akademie für Gesellschaftswissenschaften beim ZK der SED* (Münster: LIT, 2004).

[132] Klenner's past was revealed as part of the inquiry into the wartime career of Secretary General Kurt Waldheim. Henry Leide, *NS-Verbrecher und Staatssicherheit: Die geheime Vergangenheitspolitik der DDR* (Munich: Vandenhoeck & Ruprecht, 2007), 87.

[133] Rosa Luxemburg Stiftung, Archiv Demokratischer Sozialismus (AdS), Bestand Reissig Berg: Band 1 (Zweites) Gespräch mit Rolf Reissig (21.7.1998), 7–8.

[134] Copies of these letters have not survived, but Forberger recalls their contents in his memoir. Siegfried Forberger, *Das DDR-Komitee für Menschenrechte: Erinnerungen an den Sozialismus-Versuch im 20. Jahrhundert; Einsichten und Irrtümer des Siegfried Forberger, Sekretär des DDR-Komitees für Menschenrechte von 1959 bis 1989* (Self-pub., 2000), 477.

clerical staff working full-time. Forberger tried to explain that letters from dissidents or those seeking to leave the country were simply left unanswered before being transferred to the security services. The visiting officials "were not satisfied" with this answer and argued that they should at least have to officially respond and explain that the Committee was not authorised to assist in these requests.[135] For the visiting officials, a human rights office was meant to engage with disgruntled citizens; for the KMR, it existed to campaign for human rights abroad while maintaining the hegemonic discourse at home, sweeping domestic challenges under the carpet.

High-level cooperation among Eastern Bloc states fared no better. At a meeting of Warsaw Pact Foreign Ministers, the GDR delegation circulated a draft declaration entitled "Freedom and Human Rights under Socialism," but the other representatives shied away from any kind of formal commitment on its contents. The Romanian delegate simply stated that he had no mandate to agree to any specifics. All delegations involved demanded that the project be limited to a declaration on human rights rather than any kind of binding covenant or convention.[136] The only concrete decision of the meeting was to remove the term "self-governance" entirely from the draft presented by the GDR.[137] With everyone requesting revisions and time for further review, a new deadline was set for Spring 1987 to circulate a revised declaration, so that the "fraternal parties can decide on the concrete questions of adopting the document."[138]

While the project was launched to present a united front in the face of Western propaganda, in 1986, Mikhail Gorbachev had begun his reform program of Glasnost (openness) and Perestroika (restructuring) to deal with the actual structural problems of the Soviet political and economic systems.[139] Already by early 1987, a rift had opened between the socialist elites within the Eastern Bloc who supported Soviet reforms, and the hardliners, exemplified by East Germany's Erich Honecker, who completely rejected them: "When it comes to socialist democracy in the

---

[135] BArch, N2535/2 Vorlage für die Leitungssitzung am 21.1.87 (30.12.1986), 9.
[136] BArch, DY30/7470 Bericht über die Beratung von Vertretern der Außenministerien der Warschauer Vertragsstaaten zur Ausarbeitung einer sozialistischen Menschenrechtsdeklaration (15.10.1986), 1–2.
[137] BArch, DY30/7470 "Freiheit und Menschenrechte im Sozialismus," 1, 4.
[138] BArch, DY30/7470 Bericht über die Beratung von Vertretern der Außenministerien (15.10.1986), 3.
[139] On Gorbachev's reform program, see John Miller, *Mikhail Gorbachev and the End of Soviet Power* (Opladen: Springer, 2016).

GDR, there is nothing to improve," he announced at a meeting of SED officials, "we have always decisively rejected bourgeois liberalism."[140]

The conflict over the Soviet reforms quickly left its mark on the deliberations over the Socialist Declaration of Human Rights, as reformists began to see the project as a vehicle for the advancement of their agenda for change – rather than as a weapon for the defence of the status quo. In the first half of 1987, at a meeting in East Berlin, the divisions between the socialist states only grew.[141] The Polish delegate suggested that increased legal mechanisms for citizens to question state laws would be beneficial for human rights.[142] The Czechoslovak representative wanted to include rights to personal property in the draft. Non-European communists from Cuba, Laos, Vietnam and Mongolia – invited to prop up the claim that the declaration would represent the whole of the socialist world – wanted to shift the focus from presenting a united ideological front to including more cooperation with neutral and non-aligned states.[143] While everyone agreed that the creation of the Declaration was important, no one could agree on a concrete path forward.

In spite of these divisions, in June of that year, GDR experts managed to prepare a revised draft of the Declaration to be circulated at a meeting of Warsaw Pact Foreign Ministers. The declaration ran 20 pages of text, outlining 32 Articles, representing the mix of the socialist state constitutions and the human rights documents of the United Nations. The socialist world was on the cusp of presenting its own unified vision of human rights to rival the European Convention and counteract the slander and propaganda of the West. The first article outlined the broad principles that were to define socialist human rights on the world stage: "The peoples of the socialist states realize their right to self-determination through which they determine, free from exploitation and oppression, their economic, social and cultural development. They perfect the socialist system, the socialist state, and socialist democracy with the goal of building communism."[144]

---

[140] Honecker quoted in Hermann Wentker, *Außenpolitik in engen Grenzen: Die DDR im Internationalen System, 1949–1989* (Munich: Oldenbourg, 2007), 490.

[141] DY30/11891, Kurt Hager, Aktuelle Probleme der Theorie und Praxis des Sozialismus (22.1.1987), 17. BArch, DY30/7495 Bericht über das Treffen der stellvertretenden Abteilungsleiter der Zentralkomitees der Parteien der sozialistischen Länder zu Fragen der Menschenrechte in Berlin (26./27.3.1987).

[142] Poland had introduced a form of administrative judicial review in 1980. Inga Markovits, "'Law and Glasnost': Some Thoughts about the Future of Judicial Review under Socialism," *Law & Society Review* 23, no. 3 (1989), 402.

[143] BArch, DY30/7495 Bericht über das Treffen der stellvertretenden Abteilungsleiter.

[144] BArch, DP1/21481 "Freiheit und Menschenrechte im Sozialismus: Deklaration" (5.6.1987), 3–4.

After years of work, however, this was rejected, and the project stalled once again. Delegates from Czechoslovakia, Poland and Bulgaria remained positive, but the USSR, Hungary and Romania demanded to start over entirely. Citing the lack of constructive criticism from Soviet representatives, the East Germans concluded "there was no coordinated or coherent conception within the USSR on the further composition of the Declaration."[145] The Hungarian delegate announced that he had nothing against a general project on human rights, but it was simply not the time for a formal declaration.[146] The Romanians agreed that the timing was poor, reiterating, as they did at every meeting, that they lacked the mandate to agree on any specific plans.[147] Everyone involved agreed – in theory – that they championed human rights, but reconciling this heroic self-image with the actual norms of international human rights created too much internal conflict over the meaning of socialism at a time of deep ideological uncertainty. The Socialist Declaration of Human Rights was effectively dead.

Losing Faith in Socialist Human Rights

Throughout 1987, SED leaders made it clear that they saw Soviet reforms as a mistake. In an interview with West German media in April 1987, Kurt Hager ruled out the possibility that the GDR would follow in the footsteps of Gorbachev: "Would you, by the way, feel obligated to redo the wallpaper in your apartment just because your neighbour redid his?," he asked the reporter when reminded of the SED slogan "To learn from the Soviets is to learn how to win."[148] Although structural reform was off the table, Erich Honecker was scheduled to meet with West German Chancellor Helmut Kohl that year, the first such visit by an SED leader to the Federal Republic. As such, certain measures were taken to improve the human rights image of the GDR in advance: Honecker announced an amnesty for 25,000 prisoners, ostensibly to celebrate the 38th anniversary of the GDR, and the SED signed the UN anti-torture convention and abolished the death penalty, although this did not have a significant impact domestically. No civilian had been executed in the GDR since 1973, and after 1981, the SED declined to

---

[145] BArch, DP1/21481 Bericht über die 2. Runde der Beratung von Vertretern der Außenministerien der Warschauer Vertragsstaaten zur Ausarbeitung einer sozialistischen Menschenrechtsdeklaration (30.6.1987), 1–2.
[146] BStU, MfS, HA VII 508 Neugebauer to Süß, 92.
[147] BArch, DP1/21481 Bericht über die 2. Runde der Beratung (30.6.1987), 2.
[148] German History in Documents and Images, *No New Wallpaper* (10.4.1987) (http://ghdi.ghi-dc.org).

use the death penalty even in cases of espionage and treason.[149] In spite of these gestures, there would be no East German *perestroika*.[150]

At the lower levels of the state and party apparatus, the hardline approach to both the Soviets and the East German people on human rights was more difficult to sustain. At the KMR, pressure from East German citizens was mounting and the emerging split in the Socialist Bloc was once again felt at home. In 1987, the number of citizens writing to the Committee demanding help to leave the country more than doubled to 330. For the first time, citizens responded directly to the Committee's proclamations on Human Rights Day – 10 December – including protests and a joint letter from the emigration organisation, the Working Group for Citizenship Rights. Ignoring a few dozen letters from disgruntled citizens was one thing; being the direct target of an organised campaign from within the GDR was another. Dealing with an increasingly radicalised population outside of the shrinking bubble of loyal elites diminished KMR morale even further. Secretary Siegfried Forberger reported to the group's board: "We have taken notice that, unlike in previous years, a greater number of letter writers articulated an aggressive stand against the state." When East Germans wrote to the committee to ask for assistance, "Almost all letters contained misconceptions of UN documents and agreed upon international legal human rights standards in addition to the status and duties of the KMR." Failing to receive responses to their letters, East Germans now telephoned and appeared at the committee's office in person to demand answers: "Our brief but factual information and arguments did not receive a sympathetic hearing from these citizens because of their defiant attitude," reported Forberger. Not only were East Germans challenging the committee's human rights work, but in 1987, another visit from a Soviet Ministry of Justice official went just as poorly. Forberger noted "a lengthy dispute followed on the question of why the Committee as an NGO had no domestic function. In his view, a Soviet human rights committee that dealt only with foreign policy would not be sufficient to be approved by the Party."[151] From within and without, the certainties of SED human rights doctrine were besieged by dissent and doubt.

By early 1988, the Socialist Bloc had rapidly moved from gridlock on human rights to an open split between hardliners and reformers. In the Soviet Union, Mikhail Gorbachev shifted from conservative

---

[149] The abolition of the death penalty in the GDR had long been a priority for Amnesty International. Mihr, *Amnesty International in der DDR*, 137.
[150] On the 1987 Amnesty, see Raschka, *Justizpolitik im SED-Staat*, 234–48.
[151] BArch, N2535/2 Vorlage für die Leitungssitzung am 8.1.1988 (15.12.1987), 6–8.

modernisation to a program of radical reform; in the GDR, the SED leadership could do little but watch in horror as he seemed to dismantle the ideological basis of their rule.[152] Gorbachev formally integrated human rights reforms into his plans for *Perestroika* arguing that increased political freedoms of speech and democratic participation "will help to find optimal solutions with due considerations from all the diverse opinions and actual possibilities."[153] According to the General Secretary of the Communist Party, human rights remained an essential element of Soviet state socialism, but they were now to be reformed in the best interests of the system to forestall disaster. The realisation of human rights was no longer a given, accomplished years ago through revolution, but a very real contemporary problem that needed to be solved through reform.[154]

Gorbachev's speech and the ensuing academic work stemming from his pronouncement enabled reformers across the Eastern Bloc to follow suit in calling for a new position on human rights. Intellectuals who worked within the system were now turning towards reformist solutions under the cover of Gorbachev's speeches and the work of Soviet legal scholars, who elaborated a legal position to support the ongoing political reforms. Rolf Reissig, still officially leading the international socialist expert panel on human rights, published an article with fellow East German scholar Frank Berg in which they cautiously advocated for improving all forms of human rights, including political and civic freedoms: "the realization of human rights will strengthen socialism while making it more attractive to citizens, without weakening socialism."[155] In line with Gorbachev, Reissig and Berg spoke of human rights in the GDR as a project to be completed – contrary to decades of SED declarations that socialism had already accomplished this task.

Yet at the top, SED leaders did not accept that the meaning of human rights was changing beneath their feet, and they continued to seek in vain to keep the socialist bloc together on their terms. In May, a Politburo report noted with dismay that, in preparatory negotiations for a Helsinki

---

[152] V. M. Zubok, *A Failed Empire: The Soviet Union in the Cold War from Stalin to Gorbachev* (Chapel Hill: University of North Carolina Press, 2007), 308–9.

[153] Mikhail Gorbachev, *On Progress in Implementing the Decisions of the 27th CPSU Congress and the Tasks of Promoting Perestroika: Report by the General Secretary of the CPSU Central Committee to the 19th All-Union Party Conference, June 28, 1988* (Moscow: Novosti Press Agency, 1988), 44–45.

[154] On Gorbachev's human rights politics, see Daniel Thomas, "Human Rights Ideas, the Demise of Communism, and the End of the Cold War," *Journal of Cold War Studies* 7, no. 2 (2005), 110–41.

[155] Frank Berg and Rolf Reissig, "Menschenrechte in der Politik des Sozialismus," *Deutsche Zeitschrift für Philosophie* 36, no.7 (1988), 606 and 601 n. 7.

follow-up meeting to take place in Vienna, every other socialist state, aside from the GDR, was beginning to accept the idea of legally binding agreements regarding the implementation of human rights. It noted that "multiple attempts to induce the USSR and other fraternal states to take up the same position have had no effect."[156] In November, at a UN-sponsored conference in Moscow, the GDR delegates frantically reported that the East Germans were the only representatives to say that they did not have serious human rights deficits in their own country, and, along with the Polish and Czechoslovakian delegations, the only ones to connect the realisation of human rights to socialism.[157]

As socialist allies and intellectuals began to defect from the party orthodoxy on human rights, the SED made the mistake of alienating mid-level party members and civil servants through two incidents of heavy-handed state censorship. In September 1988, a group of students at the Carl-von-Ossietzky high school were expelled for criticising martial law in Poland and questioning the militarisation of the GDR.[158] Such a punishment for students advocating peace – at an elite high school in Pankow (a district of East Berlin, home to many of the leading members of the SED), then attended by the son of Deputy Secretary Egon Krenz – was unnerving for those who wanted to work within the system. Then in November, the SED censored an issue of the popular Soviet press digest *Sputnik* because it contained an article that criticised the German Communist Party's failure to work with Social Democrats to prevent Hitler's rise to power in 1933. Banning *Sputnik* set off what one Stasi report described as a "massive wave of critical opinion," particularly from party members and teachers, many of whom used the publication in class to address contemporary issues.[159] One complained, "I have been in the party a long time and cannot remember a time when I was so helpless and clueless."[160] For normally loyal East Germans, such actions transformed freedom of expression into an issue of everyday life and work. As a result,

---

[156] BArch, DY30J IV2/2/2251 Anlage 1 Information, 2. Erhard Crome and Jochen Franzke, "Die SED-Führung und die Wiener KSZE-Konferenz 1986–1989," *Deutschland Archiv* 26 (1993).
[157] BArch, DP 1/ 21440 Information über das [...] Seminar mit europäischen sozialistischen Ländern zum Thema: "Rechtspflege und Menschenrechte," 5.
[158] BStU collection "Rausgeschmissen" Die Relegation von Schülern der Carl-von-Ossietzky-Schule (www.bstu.bund.de/).
[159] Pfaff, *Exit-Voice Dynamics and the Collapse of East Germany*, 54 and 57.
[160] Major, *Behind the Berlin Wall*, 233.

many from within the middle tier of the state and party system began to link these actions to an absence of human rights.[161]

At the moment of the GDR's sudden isolation, the Stasi began to heavily indoctrinate its own agents on the subject of human rights.[162] In the late 1970s, the SED only thought it necessary to flood the public media with stories on human rights achievements in the socialist world and human rights abuses under capitalist imperialism; in the summer of 1988, it was finally deemed necessary to reinforce the ideological backbone of the secret police. The Stasi issued two separate internal training manuals on the subject, in which the contemporary human rights movement in the GDR was portrayed in near apocalyptic terms.[163] One described the ultimate goal of the dissidents as "destroying the leading role of the party, the end of the socialist planned economy and means of production, and a return to capitalist economic relationships."[164] But the texts also sought to reassure Stasi officers of the superiority and successes of the GDR. Socialist human rights continued to be "of a higher quality than those brought about by capitalism," and "political and personal rights did not simply remain declarations," but rather were guaranteed by basic social conditions and institutions. One manual concluded,

On the theme of human rights, we have nothing to dread [... we] must also continue to work steadfastly to ensure that the human rights situation in the GDR is a highly visible part of the growing appeal of socialism.[165]

The message was contradictory: If socialism had nothing to fear, why did it have to work so hard to ensure that human rights were maintained, particularly because they were supposedly emanating from all officials, institutions and the basic conditions of society? Did the "growing appeal of socialism" imply that the cause was ever strengthening or that support had collapsed and was once again recovering? Here again, overcoming the friction between rhetoric and reality caused problems even among the most loyal members of the regime.

---

[161] As an example, the petition of Gersten Lühr of Merseburg (11.4.1989) in Archiv der DDR-Opposition, TH 04, who linked his complaints over the censorship of *Sputnik* to the UDHR and the 1966 UN Human Rights Covenants.

[162] This educational effort presaged the increased fears of an ideological breakdown within the Stasi at the end of 1988. Walter Süss, *Staatssicherheit am Ende: warum es den Mächtigen nicht gelang, 1989 eine Revolution zu verhindern* (Berlin: Ch. Links, 1999), 105–14.

[163] One focused on legal issues and one on ideology: BStU Rechtsstelle 1108 "Menschenrechte in den Kämpfen unserer Zeit" (August 1988) and BStU ZOS 2894 "Menschenrechte: Grundlegende Aussagen und politisch-ideologische Fragen zur Menschenrechtsproblematik und zur Menschenrechtsdemagogie in unserer Zeit" (June 1988).

[164] BStU ZOS 2894 "Menschenrechte," 33.   [165] Ibid., 55.

In December 1988, the SED put on a brave face for the 40th Anniversary of the UDHR, issuing an official proclamation boasting of the human rights achievements of the GDR, and touting fidelity to the universal norms of civilisation outlined by the United Nations.[166] Four days later, despite his claims that the GDR would not be redecorating, Kurt Hager introduced a program of judicial reform meant to recapture the loyalty of GDR citizens. In the 1970s, the social court system effectively diverted many citizens from moving into illegal dissent by giving them an outlet to air grievances, but by the 1980s, the futility of filing complaints through formal channels had become apparent and participation declined.[167] To revive faith in socialist legality, a cautious system of judicial review was introduced that allowed judges to determine if state officials were violating the constitutional rights of East German citizens.[168] Hager assured the SED Central Committee that this reform represented the progress of the GDR as a "socialist state under the rule of law" (*sozialistischer Rechtsstaat*), which guaranteed citizens "their fundamental human rights."[169] With state finances spiralling out of control, the only reforms that the Politburo would authorise were superficial changes to the justice system.[170]

Elite confidence in the SED's capacity to uphold human rights now began to openly fall apart. In a letter to the head of the SED's International Relations Section, the leading members of the KMR admitted that they could no longer successfully propagate socialist human rights doctrine when it appeared as though no such thing existed: "Recent events in the socialist bloc itself have shown that [...] there is no longer a unified conception of socialist human rights."[171] Of particular concern was the decision by Hungary and Poland to adopt "bourgeois attitudes"

---

[166] BArch, DY30/J IV2/2/2304 Anlage 2. There were, however, no commemorative stamps.

[167] Paul Betts, *Within Walls: Private Life in the GDR* (Oxford: Oxford University Press, 2010), 167–68.

[168] *Gesetz über die Nachprüfung von Verwaltungsentscheidungen* (14.12.1988) (GB1. I. 327). Markovits, "Law and Glasnost," 402.

[169] The *sozialistischer Rechtsstaat* was not Hager's invention, but originated at the GDR Supreme Court, having been first floated as a concept by Karl Polak before his death in 1963 and used on occasion by Walter Ulbricht. Raschka, *Justizpolitik im SED-Staat*, 255–57. On the failure of the law to produce significant judicial review, see Inga Markovits, *Gerechtigkeit in Lüritz: eine ostdeutsche Rechtsgeschichte* (Berlin: C. H. Beck, 2006), 232–33.

[170] In 1988, the GDR faced a 2 billion mark export shortfall and needed to stop the growth of its foreign debt. Jeffrey Kopstein, *The Politics of Economic Decline in East Germany, 1945–1989* (Chapel Hill: University of North Carolina Press, 2000), 101–2.

[171] BArch, N2535/2 Letter from Chairwoman Malter, Deputy Chairs Graefrath and Thun to Sieber (20.12.1988).

towards human rights and to consider talks with the West over the creation of a pan-European human rights declaration. The letter writers were not young reform communists, but rather old party stalwarts, including Chairwoman Friedel Malter, a Communist Party activist since the Weimar era who had led the committee since its founding in 1959. The failure of Eastern Bloc unity and SED paralysis was now breaking the morale of even lifelong socialists.

To avoid total isolation and a complete loss of international credibility, committee leaders recommended that they should begin engaging with internal human rights complaints – as had been suggested to (and rejected by) the SED in 1969. The KMR argued that it could assist in domestic governance by dealing with citizen complaints directly, and by advising the government on reforms needed to ensure that the GDR was in line with international agreements: "In this way, the credibility and effectiveness of the work of the Committee internally and externally could be substantially increased. The Committee could help citizens see that their rights and obligations are realized through the human rights policy of the GDR."[172] While the letter spoke reassuringly that such moves would help stabilise the situation at home and abroad, such a decision would make official that human rights could exist outside of socialism, and that there could be, as the SPD claimed back in the 1940s, "No Socialism without Human Rights!" Faced with a proposal for difficult reform with the potential to fatally undermine the ideological legitimacy of the entire system, the Central Committee chose to simply ignore the letter.[173]

In the first months of 1989, the demolition of the SED's carefully constructed human rights politics by its socialist allies and domestic translators accelerated. In January, the Helsinki process follow-up meeting in Vienna concluded with a fresh round of compromises on human rights by the rest of the Eastern Bloc. The Soviet concessions were so dramatic as to practically erase the theoretical distinction between East and West on the problem of human rights.[174] When Stasi Chief Erich Mielke met with his KGB counterpart following the meeting, he railed against Soviet rhetoric, which "accused and defamed individual socialist states (the GDR and Czechoslovakia) as hostile to the Helsinki process, hostile to reform and as states that violate human rights."[175] Mielke also wrote to the leaders of regional SED and Stasi offices warning that

---

[172] Ibid., 3.   [173] Forberger, *Das DDR-Komitee für Menschenrechte*, 481.
[174] Snyder, *Human Rights Activism and the End of the Cold War*, 2.
[175] Quoted in Süss, *Staatssicherheit am Ende*, 97.

"those who think 'we must change our politics' no longer belong in our party."[176] For the hardline leadership of the SED, in the conflict over human rights, the reformers of the Eastern Bloc had become the real enemy.

As Eastern Bloc allies abandoned the long-standing line on human rights, Western rivals struck an unexpectedly conciliatory tone. As part of a series of meetings (that had begun in the mid-1980s) held between the SED and the West German SPD in April 1989, representatives from the two parties met to talk about human rights.[177] Rather than follow the standard script of listing accusations against each other, the SPD delegation opened instead by discussing the failings of the Federal Republic – including xenophobia and employment restrictions for members of the Far Left – and asked that the SED reciprocate.[178] After more than 40 years of conflict with the SPD over human rights, dating back to the first postwar elections in 1946, SED representatives were blindsided when the SPD spoke of common ground, dialogue and reconciliation.[179] Rather than the SPD declaring "No Socialism without Human Rights," this sentiment now came from within: the groups of human rights experts from across the socialist world, originally called upon to write the Socialist Declaration of Human Rights, now issued a report advocating democratising reforms. The group, still led by the East German academic Rolf Reissig, identified a series of key errors in the thinking of the socialist bloc, including that "social property and production methods and the political power of the working class meant that the problem of human rights had 'automatically' been solved in a qualitatively superior way." Such a misconception led to the "undervaluation of personal and political rights versus economic, social and cultural rights and the undervaluation of the legal guarantees of personal rights of the citizen against state and society."[180] The report was circulated to leaders of the participating countries, and the KMR began to publish cautious discussions of human rights reforms in its quarterly journal for the first time.[181]

---

[176] Quoted in Mary Elise Sarotte, *The Collapse: The Accidental Opening of the Berlin Wall* (New York: Basic Books, 2014), 18.

[177] Rolf Reissig, *Dialog durch die Mauer: die umstrittene Annäherung von SPD und SED* (Frankfurt: Campus Verlag, 2002), 64–69.

[178] AdS Bestand Reißig Berg: Band 1 Gespräch mit Rolf Reißig (20.11.1995), 11.

[179] Briefing notes, BArch, DY30/IV2/2.035/81.

[180] AdS Bestand Reissig Berg: Band 1. Multilateraler Wissenschaftlicher Problemrat von Bruderparteien sozialistischer Länder zu Fragen der Menschenrechte: Konzeptionelle Grundlagen der gegenwärtigen Politik auf dem Gebiet der Menschenrechte (April 1989), 13.

[181] Frank Berg "Sozialistische Menschenrechtskonzeption in der Diskussion," DDR-Komitee für Menschenrechte, *Schriften und Informationen* 15, no. 2 (1989), 87–99.

By early 1989, the hardliners were completely overwhelmed not only by actions on the ground by dissidents and protestors, but also internally by the reformists who had become less cautious about their rhetoric. On 5 February, East German border guards shot 20-year-old Chris Gueffroy to death as he tried to cross the Berlin Wall – its 139th victim since 1961 and the second last person to die in the attempt. Coming so soon after the compromises at Vienna, an international outcry forced the SED to retreat from asserting its right to protect the sovereignty of the border with lethal force. To avoid a deepening pariah status as a violator of human rights, Honecker rescinded the order to shoot those trying to cross the Berlin Wall – an order that originally legitimised killing illegal border-crossers as a defence of human rights.[182]

Conclusion

In a matter of only a few years, the scattered dissident groups of the GDR had turned towards human rights as a means of politicising a movement that – until then – had focused on moral goals rather than democratic reform. The activists who took up the cause of human rights did not have the luxury of either a mass moral epiphany on the part of the East German people or a population that already agreed with their message (and simply needed to be roused out of their passivity). Before a human rights movement could be created, the founders of the IFM and other dissident groups needed to overcome not only the disruptive activities of the Stasi, and the concerns of activists who feared that the politicisation of their cause could dilute the pure moral message of peace, but also the hegemonic discourse of socialist human rights that led some dissidents to reject pluralism and human rights as tools of bourgeois capitalism and a distraction from realising true socialism. A growing sense that the political system of the GDR needed to be changed before moral goals could be fought for – let alone achieved – altered the calculus of dissent and helped bring about a shift in the use of human rights language on the ground.

At the same time, socialist human rights rapidly crumbled as a convincing ideological viewpoint for loyal intellectuals and officials working for the SED. As long as East German elites were able to situate themselves in a global politics in which the Socialist Bloc was united for human rights, in partnership with the Afro-Asian states, against the imperialist forces of the West, the contradictions of domestic politics could be rationalised.

---

[182] Sarotte, *The Collapse*, 16. On human rights and the "shooting order" see Chapter 2.

But by the 1980s, the fragile alliance for self-determination between the Socialist and Afro-Asian Blocs had fractured. Even within the Eastern Bloc, solidarity on human rights had fallen apart with the advent of Gorbachev's plans for *Glasnost* and *Perestroika*. While the leadership of the SED held a hard line against Soviet reforms, increased domestic pressure and the loss of external support broke the morale of those tasked with maintaining the hegemony of socialist human rights within the GDR.

Human rights now acted as a unifying concept bringing together diverse constituencies of East Germans whether they sought to change the system from within or simply to escape from it. Party *apparatchiks* and the intelligentsia still believed that human rights were an essential aspect of socialism, but they no longer believed in the SED's capacity to realise human rights through democratic centralism. Dissidents presented an alternative to the status quo as a fulfilment of both the ideals of socialism and human rights, right at the very moment when many in the establishment faced a crisis of faith about SED rule. As East Germany careened into perpetual crisis in 1989, the linkage between human rights reforms and socialism would be crucial in ensuring a peaceful transition to democracy.

6   Revolutions Won and Lost, 1989–1990

On 7 October 1989, the SED celebrated the 40th anniversary of the founding of the GDR with massive parades and a visit from Soviet leader Mikhail Gorbachev. In contrast to earlier celebrations, the angry hecklers in the crowd cheering on Gorbachev and booing the SED presaged the massive demonstrations that would take place two days later in the city of Leipzig, bringing more than 120,000 people into the streets. Unwilling to use deadly force to disperse the protestors, the People's Police and the military retreated from the protesters and the SED effectively lost control of the public spaces in its major cities. Little more than a month later, on 9 November, a clumsily announced change to travel regulations caused crowds to gather at the border checkpoints around the Berlin Wall. Rather than use force, border guards chose to open the gates and abandoned efforts to control cross-border traffic. By December, the SED had abolished its monopoly on power, and a new generation had taken control of the party, guiding East Germany towards its first competitive elections since those held in Berlin in 1946. The demands of human rights dissidents for democratisation and freedom of movement had helped to create this moment: SED power crumbling in the face of massive crowds carrying the slogan *Wir sind das Volk* – We Are the People.

The idea of human rights did not bring down the SED, but it did shape East Germany's transition to democracy in 1989. SED rule was fatally undermined by long-term economic decline, the accelerating crisis of mass emigration and the Soviet decision to no longer guarantee its predominance with military force.[1] These factors alone did not, however, make the peaceful opening of the Berlin Wall inevitable. Human rights

---

[1] Jeffrey Kopstein, *The Politics of Economic Decline in East Germany, 1945–1989* (Chapel Hill: University of North Carolina Press, 2000); Charles Maier, *Dissolution: The Crisis of Communism and the End of East Germany* (Princeton, NJ: Princeton University Press, 1997); Konrad Jarausch, *The Rush to German Unity* (Oxford: Oxford University Press, 1994).

provided a language that mobilised a divided population around a simple set of political goals. As this discourse helped to bind together a diverse protest movement and legitimise mass emigration, large swaths of the power structure – within the SED, the state bureaucracy and the security services – lost faith in the idea that the system they worked to protect was in line with the ideals of human rights. While the language of human rights had contributed to the legitimacy and stability of the GDR for decades, once the SED lost control of this discourse in the late 1980s, it began to act as a powerful tool for democratisation.[2] After years of internalised propaganda, the message of human rights appealed to disaffected mid-tier SED members and civil servants who were not ready to fully abandon socialism, but who were willing to fight for change.[3] The language of human rights also effectively demoralised members of the state security forces, enough of whom refused to see the crowds as "counterrevolutionaries" that needed to be suppressed by lethal force to make mass protests possible.[4] For many loyal to the idea of socialism, but disaffected by the status quo, defecting to the side of the protestors became a way to stay true to one's own ideals.

This intersection of grassroots mobilisation in the streets and the implosion of elite power led to the opening of the Berlin Wall on 9 November 1989, and soon thereafter to the end of SED monopoly rule.[5] But without

---

[2] Detlef Pollack, "Modernization and Modernization Blockages in GDR Society," in *Dictatorship as Experience: Towards a Socio-Cultural History of the GDR*, ed. Konrad Jarausch (New York: Berghahn, 1999), 40–41.

[3] Dieter Segert, "The GDR Intelligentsia and Its Forgotten Political Role during the Wende of 1989," *Debatte: Journal of Contemporary Central and Eastern Europe* 17, no. 2 (2009), 145. Detlef Pollack, "Mass Pressures, Elite Responses – Roots of Democratization: The Case of the GDR," *Communist and Post-Communist Studies* 35, no. 3 (2002), 27–46. Thomas argues that human rights language provided a discourse for reformist elites but presents human rights as something foreign to state socialism. Daniel Thomas, "Human Rights Ideas, the Demise of Communism, and the End of the Cold War," *Journal of Cold War Studies* 7, no. 2 (2005), 110–41.

[4] On the demoralisation of security services in fall 1989, see Walter Süss, *Staatssicherheit am Ende: warum es den Mächtigen nicht gelang, 1989 eine Revolution zu verhindern* (Berlin: Ch. Links, 1999), 301–10; Daniel Niemetz, "Einen neuen '17. Juni' verhindern. Volkspolizei-Bereitschaften und 'Kampfgruppen der Arbeiterklasse' im Herbst 1989," in *"Damit hatten wir die Initiative verloren": zur Rolle der bewaffneten Kräfte in der DDR 1989/90*, ed. Heiner Bröckermann (Berlin: Ch. Links, 2014), 91–136.

[5] Konrad Jarausch, "Implosion oder Selbstbefreiung," in Konrad Jarausch and Martin Sabrow, *Weg in den Untergang* (Göttingen: Vandenhoeck & Ruprecht, 1999), 15–40. On the implosion side, Kotkin exaggerates the determinism of economic factors, arguing "the GDR was a Ponzi scheme that fell in a bank run," while Mitter and Wolle reduce East Germany to an artificial creation propped up by the support of "Soviet bayonets," making its collapse inevitable once the guarantee of violent suppression disappeared. Both interpretations are overly mechanistic and do not consider how popular mobilisation combined with elite loss of faith. Stephen Kotkin, *Uncivil Society:*

the unity forged in opposition to SED hardliners, the opposition fractured as the first free elections of March 1990 approached. Although rapid unification with West Germany had appeared far-fetched at the beginning of 1989, a majority of East Germans soured on reforming the GDR as revelations of SED corruption and Stasi abuses poured out in the newly liberalised media. As unification with West Germany became seemingly inevitable, many human rights dissidents joined together with the fallen GDR elites, including reformers from the SED, to try to rescue a democratised, yet still socialist and independent, East Germany. Yet the human rights dissidents who had helped to spark the revolution of 1989, along with their ex-SED allies, now found themselves outmanoeuvred and marginalised. The very triumph of GDR human rights activists led to their marginalisation in the newly unified Germany, where human rights were defined according to the norms of the Federal Republic rather than those of East German dissidents.

From Dissent to Demonstrations

East Germany had been careening towards an economic crisis since the early 1980s as it struggled to pay its foreign debt and migration steadily rose. By 1989, the SED provoked a political crisis through a botched effort at half-hearted democratic reform. It would be the first of several such episodes in which the SED tried to halt the downward spiral of its legitimacy, but only managed to stir up further dissent. The first act began with local elections on 7 May 1989: they would not be competitive, but civic organisations would be allowed to monitor the polling stations to show that citizens could vote against the pre-approved National Front lists and that their votes would nonetheless be fairly counted.[6] Compared to neighbouring Poland where the Round Table talks between the state socialist leadership and the opposition had led to a parliamentary-approved law that formally abandoned the monopoly on power held by the Polish United Worker's Party, it was a rather tiny gesture.[7] The SED leadership had no intention of negotiating with

---

1989 and the Implosion of the Communist Establishment (New York: Random House, 2009), 61. Armin Mitter and Stefan Wolle, *Untergang auf Raten: unbekannte Kapitel der DDR-Geschichte* (Munich: Bertelsmann, 1993), 162. On contingency in 1989, see Mary Elise Sarotte, *The Collapse: The Accidental Opening of the Berlin Wall* (New York: Basic Books, 2014).

[6] Hans Michael Kloth, *Vom "Zettelfalten" zum freien Wählen: die Demokratisierung der DDR 1989/90 und die "Wahlfrage"* (Berlin: Ch. Links, 2000), 114–16.

[7] Wiktor Osiatynski, "The Round Table Talks in Poland," in *The Roundtable Talks and the Breakdown of Communism*, ed. Jon Elster (Chicago: University of Chicago Press, 1996).

dissidents or planning for a transition of power, but election monitors appeared to be a safe concession to gain some credibility on the international stage because the Politburo still expected to get more than 90 percent approval. However, when some districts registered less than 50 percent approval, local officials took it upon themselves to improve National Front support during the count. The published results claimed 98.5 percent voting in favour of the official slate and the fraud was immediately apparent, even to senior members of the SED.[8]

While many human rights groups had tried to organise a boycott of the elections to protest the continued absence of secret ballots, the obvious fraud perpetrated by the SED had a far more damaging effect.[9] Observers had been able to see that the numbers were clearly off after watching so many publicly vote no, and now they demanded recounts in the presence of non-party members to gain concrete evidence. When people took to the streets to protest the rigging of the election, the People's Police responded with violence, creating new grounds for further protest. Human rights groups justified their public demonstrations by citing the GDR constitution's right to free expression (Article 27) and accused the SED of "violating the inner peace" of the country and declared that the police "must ask themselves whether the GDR is truly under the rule of law and if their actions are appropriate."[10] In response to evidence of the fraud produced by human rights groups, several church pastors were convinced to move protests out to the streets; on the seventh of every month afterwards there were demonstrations to commemorate the event.[11] Other citizens tried (unsuccessfully) to use the legal system to punish officials involved in the fraud, alleging that they had violated their right to take part in the political system of the GDR.[12]

As with the ban on the Soviet magazine *Sputnik* the year before, the fraudulent elections drove many of the remaining activist church groups to demand political change and human rights. If even a symbolic vote against the SED was impossible, what reforms could be achieved under the status quo? According to a Stasi report on every known underground and dissident group in the GDR, "'human rights groups' are among the

---

[8] Maier, *Dissolution*, 132–33.

[9] On the impact of the fraudulent elections on dissidents, see Karsten Timmer, *Vom Aufbruch zum Umbruch: die Bürgerbewegung in der DDR 1989* (Göttingen: Vandenhoeck & Ruprecht, 2000), 79–82.

[10] Archiv der DDR-Opposition, Samizdat PS 018/05 Ausblick Arbeitsgruppe Menschenrechte Leipzig. Offener Brief von AG MR und AK Gerechtigkeit in Leipzig (6.7.1989).

[11] Jarausch, *The Rush to German Unity*, 38.

[12] Patrick Major, *Behind the Berlin Wall: East Germany and the Frontiers of Power* (Oxford: Oxford University Press, 2010), 238.

youngest and, as a type, the most complex in structure and differentiated in terms of membership."[13] The Protestant Church had failed to sufficiently crack down on human rights groups within its walls and numerous "provocations" could be attributed to the movement, such as the commandeered 1988 Luxemburg-Liebknecht March. These groups focused on "failures to grant human rights and fundamental freedoms in the GDR," including attacks on "the principle of democratic centralism, and the organization of socialist democracy." The protestors demanded the "'democratization of society,' 'change of authorities,' reforms to socialist law, the elimination of 'exclusion, and the absence of legal protection' for citizens in addition to the 'full' realization of human rights for everyone."[14]

At the top of the Stasi's list of human rights groups was the Initiative for Peace and Human Rights (IFM), along with a number of groups in Leipzig, almost all of which had some connection to Pastor Christoph Wonneberger of the Nikolai Church. The report also noted diverse organisations and groups in smaller communities across the GDR. The "Eisenach Women's Peace Circle" wrote protest letters to the GDR-Committee for Human Rights (KMR).[15] The "Church from Below" community in Halle discussed "socialist democracy, freedom of speech, freedom of belief, constitutional legality, travel practices and environmentalism," and had organised a public rally to support the imprisoned Luxemburg-Liebknecht human rights activists.[16] In Karl-Marx-Stadt, the "Discussion Group Auerbach" dealt with problems of current events, ecology, peace, human rights and medical ethics. Its membership included "artists, doctors, church representatives and workers."[17] In Rostock on the Baltic coast, the "Schalom Society," one of many groups organised by the dissident pastor Heiko Lietz, met to talk about peace, civil alternatives to the draft, and "the implementation of human rights in the GDR." The eight-person group was composed of Catholics, Protestants and those seeking to emigrate, and included a printer, a chemist from the regional Academy of Science and an electronics specialist from a local fisheries plant.[18]

Human rights acted as the rhetorical, moral and tactical glue holding these disparate groups together. As Lietz later explained, human rights appealed to a broad range of people looking for change: "Without free access to data (freedom of information) any environmental work was a waste, without the right to belief and freedom of conscience, alternative

[13] Archiv Bürgerbewegung Leipzig, Stasi Bericht – Überblick der Opposition: Anlage zur Information Nr. 150/89, 10.
[14] Ibid., 11.   [15] Ibid., 147.   [16] Ibid., 195.   [17] Ibid., 243.   [18] Ibid., 297.

peace services were impracticable, without the freedom to travel, it was impossible to establish contacts with the 2/3rds world[19] and conduct projects internationally." In addition to these logistical problems, "because the curtailing of basic human rights was becoming stronger, the question of a fundamental change in the political system turned increasingly urgent."[20] Human rights, as a discourse of dissent and civic engagement, appealed to the disaffected intellectuals and artists in Prenzlauer Berg – East Berlin's countercultural enclave – but also to factory workers on the Baltic coast, and retirees in small towns in the hinterlands of Thuringia. Human rights provided a discourse that could be used to demand basic rights within the system or to call for the end of the system.

As the May election fraud radicalised and mobilised demonstrators in the GDR, on 4 June 1989, events in Poland and the People's Republic of China presented two diametrically opposing paths forward for the SED in the face of brewing unrest. Although the Polish opposition party Solidarność (until recently banned) was limited in how many seats it could run for, virtually every one of its candidates won. In a compromise deal, the old guard of the Polish United Worker's Party was able to keep the position of president, while Solidarność was able to form a government and name the prime minister.[21] By working with dissidents through Round Table talks, the state socialist elite had negotiated a transition to democracy. On the same day, Chinese leaders decided to end the student occupation of Beijing's Tiananmen Square with force. Horrified by Gorbachev's reforms and his lack of determination to stand against counterrevolution in Europe, Chinese leaders chose to use mass violence to maintain their hold on power and the army was sent to disperse the protestors, killing hundreds.[22] Eastern Bloc reactions were divided: the Soviets, Poles, and Hungarians condemned the killings, but East Germany along with the hardline leaders of Czechoslovakia and Romania publicly supported China.

In the Soviet Union, Gorbachev had already decided to hold back on a violent response to public unrest after security forces killed protestors in

---

[19] A GDR opposition term for Global South, which comprised two-thirds of the world's population.

[20] Heiko Lietz, "Die Entwicklung der Opposition im Norden," in *Am Ende des realen Sozialismus 3. Opposition in der DDR von den 70er Jahren bis zum Zusammenbruch der SED-Herrschaft*, ed. Eberhard Kuhrt, Hannsjörg Buck and Gunter Holzweissig (Opladen: Leske & Budrich, 1999), 284.

[21] Kotkin, *Uncivil Society*, 129–31.

[22] Bernd Schäfer, "Die DDR und die 'chinesische Lösung': Gewalt in der Volksrepublik China im Sommer 1989," in *1989 und die Rolle der Gewalt*, ed. Martin Sabrow (Göttingen: Wallstein-Verlag, 2012), 153–72.

Tbilisi, and the events in China only strengthened his resolve.[23] Less than two weeks after Tiananmen, Gorbachev flew to Bonn to meet with West German Chancellor Kohl and the two issued a joint statement on the importance of shared European values, including human rights and self-determination.[24] Gorbachev ally Alexander Yakovlev marked the 200th anniversary of the French Revolution by promising reforms to guarantee Soviet citizens the "inviolable and natural rights of man" proclaimed in 1789.[25] By contrast, after the East German parliament passed a resolution praising China for ending the "counterrevolutionary riots" at Tiananmen Square, high-level SED members participated in a series of visits to Beijing over the summer of 1989, that were intended to secure support for the increasingly isolated GDR.[26] By casting their lot in with China, the SED alienated many of its own members, who saw the massacre as a barbaric attack on peaceful demonstrators rather than a necessary measure to protect socialism.[27] The question had now been asked: if push came to shove, was the SED prepared to implement a "Chinese solution" to deal with the dissidents?

Rather than waiting for reforms at home, East Germans continued to emigrate in growing numbers. Aside from those leaving illegally, between January and September 1989, the SED received 160,785 applications to leave the GDR. A total of 59,725 were first-time applicants, while the remainder had been applying for several years without success.[28] One out of every five arrested at demonstrations over the summer had an outstanding application to exit.[29] The Ministry of the Interior reported that most petitions included the claim, "Since the application is supported by a variety of applicable laws, we rule out the possibility that it will be

---

[23] On the Soviet turn away from violence, see Jan Behrends, "Oktroyierte Zivilisierung: Genese und Grenzen des sowjetischen Gewaltverzichts 1989," in *1989 und die Rolle der Gewalt*, 401–24.

[24] Marie-Pierre Rey, "'Europe Is Our Common Home': A Study of Gorbachev's Diplomatic Concept," *Cold War History* 4, no. 2 (2004), 33–65.

[25] Jonathan Harris, *Subverting the System: Gorbachev's Reform of the Party's Apparat, 1986–1991* (Lanham, MD: Rowman & Littlefield, 2005), 73.

[26] Zhong Zhong Chen, "Defying Moscow, Engaging Beijing: The GDR's Relations with the People's Republic of China, 1980–1989" (PhD diss., London School of Economics, 2014), 200–12. Visitors to China included Egon Krenz and Hans Modrow, both of whom would succeed Honecker within the year. Schäfer, "Die DDR und die 'chinesische Lösung.'"

[27] Quinn Slobodian, "China Is Not Far! Alternative Internationalism and the Tiananmen Square Massacre in 1989 East Germany" (forthcoming).

[28] BArch, DO1/16491 Information über die Unterbindung und Zurückdrängung rechtswidriger Ersuchen auf Übersiedlung nach der BRD (1.1.1989-30.09.1989), 1.

[29] Steven Pfaff, *Exit-Voice Dynamics and the Collapse of East Germany: The Crisis of Leninism and the Revolution of 1989* (Durham, NC: Duke University Press, 2006), 101.

rejected from the outset. Whosoever rejects this application will be rejecting human rights."[30]

In summer 1989, the number of civic movement organisations was estimated at around 350, with an active membership of 5,000 – but dissatisfaction was widespread among the rest of East Germany's 17 million citizens.[31] In August, a report on why so many East Germans sought to leave found citizens complaining about long-standing issues such as declining economic benefits and the shortages of consumer goods, but now there were also widespread demands that the GDR "catch up" to the level of human rights achieved in the West with an emphasis on "the discredited recent elections."[32] One leaflet being passed around that summer categorised the increasingly glaring contradictions of "real existing socialism" through *The Seven World Wonders of the GDR*.

1. There is no unemployment, but half of us have nothing to do.
2. Even though half of us have nothing to do, there is a shortage of manpower.
3. Even though there is a shortage of manpower, we fulfil the plan.
4. Even though we fulfil the plan, there is nothing to buy.
5. Even though there is nothing to buy, the people have almost everything.
6. Even though the people have almost everything, more than half always complain.
7. Even though half of us complain, we still vote 99.9 percent in favour of the candidates for the National Front.[33]

The objective realities of life – political, economic and social – were worsening and the population was becoming less tolerant of the SED's failings, thus creating a receptive audience for the message of the human rights movement.

Such sentiments were common not just in the general public but also among those who were until recently highly supportive of the system. An internal Party report from Leipzig, one of the epicentres of dissent, found that among the mid-tier of SED officials and state functionaries, "the policies of the party are said to be dogmatic and conservative and

---

[30] BArch, DO1/16491 Information über die Unterbindung und Zurückdrängung rechtswidriger Ersuchen auf Übersiedlung, 8.
[31] Christof Geisel, *Auf der Suche nach einem dritten Weg: Das politische Selbstverständnis der DDR-Opposition in den 80er Jahren* (Berlin: Ch. Links, 2005), 14–15.
[32] BArch, DY30/IV 2/2.039/309, Vorlage für das Politbüro des Zentralkomitees der SED, Abteilung Sicherheitsfragen (August 1989), 6.
[33] Archiv der DDR-Opposition, EP 11/01-05 Kommunalwahl 1989. Die sieben Weltwunder der DDR.

incapable of change [...] more democracy is supported, and in this context the protection of human rights in the GDR is placed under criticism."[34] One teacher wrote to her local SED district office saying,

The state leadership of the GDR has proclaimed its recognition of human rights for all citizens for years and years. In dealing with those who think differently politically it appears as though, in my humble opinion, this principle has been repealed or how else would you explain and justify the many actions of the police in front of the Nikolai Church in Leipzig? Students have been eyewitnesses and they have questions![35]

Activists rhetorically challenged the human rights doctrine of the SED but the response of the state to their demonstrations also undermined public conviction that human rights could exist under the status quo. Once this negative cycle had begun, it was self-reinforcing as more joined to protest, resulting in more open state brutality.

Among young people, a loss of faith in the legitimacy of the state grew rapidly: by spring 1989, more than half of SED members under 25 surveyed by the Leipzig Institute for Youth Research were willing to admit that they had lost confidence in the Party's leadership.[36] In Leipzig, one such example was Katrin Walter, who quit her position as a secretary of her local Free German Youth chapter to become a human rights activist in 1989. She was from a loyal socialist family, raised with the stories of the "horrors of the evil imperialists," and had joined the Free German Youth to make her family proud: "But that quickly disillusioned me. My desire for justice and democracy could not be achieved there."[37] To live up to ideals they had been raised with, some East Germans were now abandoning the SED and fighting for human rights with the opposition instead.

In spite of the ideological defections within the Party, no reform faction emerged from the senior ranks of the SED. There were reform-minded members in the higher echelons of the Party, but they were initially as hostile to the human rights activists as the Party leaders. They sought to ascend to leadership and had the "ultimate goal [of] the establishment of a 'better' or 'more beautiful' socialism in the GDR."[38] Much like Robert Havemann and Rudolf Bahro in the 1970s, these

---

[34] Quoted in Pfaff, *Exit-Voice Dynamics and the Collapse of East Germany*, 181.
[35] BArch, DY 30/5908 Dr. Micaela K. an der Bezirksleitung der SED Leipzig. (30.8.1989), 2.
[36] Walter Friedrich, Peter Förster and Kurt Starke, *Das Zentralinstitut für Jugendforschung Leipzig 1966–1990* (Berlin: Edition Ost, 1999), 152.
[37] HIA Joppke Collection, Box 1, Interview mit Katrin Walter (25.7.1991), 1.
[38] Dietrich Orlow, *Socialist Reformers and the Collapse of the GDR* (London: Palgrave Macmillan, 2015), 11.

reformers advocated for the perfection of the socialist revolution, in contrast to the new generation of dissidents who sought a third path between "real existing socialism" and Western liberal democracy. Even then, most of the reformers within the SED were kept from reaching the Politburo: the most prominent was Hans Modrow, who led the SED's Dresden regional office, but was not given a national position because of his reformist tendencies.[39]

Although the KMR had broken from its earlier stance of total deference to the SED, it struggled to find an independent voice. At the 30th anniversary of its founding in May 1989, Secretary Siegfried Forberger offered cautious criticism of the status quo by calling for more research into the "dialectical contradictions of our development" and their implications for the practice of socialist human rights, socialist democracy and the "state-citizen-relationship."[40] A speech by Frank Berg argued that the crimes of "Stalinism" in the GDR needed to be laid bare, but he warned the audience of going too far in critiquing socialism, which could "be turned upside down if it was represented as a history of human rights violations."[41] Where and when the crimes of Stalinism ended remained unclear. Earlier anniversaries of the committee had received extensive press coverage, but in 1989, the East German media barely covered the event, prompting Forberger to send a complaint letter to the central news agency demanding an explanation.[42] After three decades of loyal support, even mild criticism excluded the committee from the official public sphere.

Although Hermann Klenner maintained a lower profile after withdrawing from his position at the United Nations in 1985 (having been exposed as a former Nazi Party member), he continued to reject Western human rights initiatives as a form of imperialist aggression. In an article from mid-1989, he argued "human rights have become a central foreign policy initiative for the conscious rejection of a peaceful coexistence, disarmament, and the politics of Détente." As his colleagues from across the Eastern Bloc appeared to be intellectually defecting to the West, Klenner wanted to remind them that the American president approached the world "with the neutron bomb in one hand and human rights in the other."[43] Against the dissidents calling for a third way, he maintained that bourgeois conceptions of human rights could not be reconciled

---

[39] Ibid., 18.   [40] BArch, DZ7/25 Rede von Sekretär Forberger (23.5.1989), 11–12.
[41] Frank Berg, "Socialist Conception of Human Rights under Discussion," *Bulletin – GDR Committee for Human Rights* 15, no. 2 (1989), 17.
[42] BArch, DZ7/25 Forberger to ADN Redaktion (26.5.1989).
[43] Hermann Klenner, "Die Menschenrechte im ideologischen Klassenkampf der Gegenwart," *Deutsche Zeitschrift für Philosophie* 37, no. 7 (1989), 652.

with the Marxist understanding of human rights, which remained rooted in the principle of class struggle. Klenner had always seen a place for more legality within the socialist system, but he could not abide by the idea of renouncing the Marxist basis for human rights and siding with the United States against the cause of socialism.

At the top of the SED, Erich Honecker was unmoved by the demands of the dissidents and genuinely could not imagine that criticism from his own citizens was sincere, rather than just an expression of Western subversion. Otto Reinhold, rector of the Central Committee's Academy of Social Sciences, later said, "Honecker always remained the Saarland Communist Youth Functionary of 1932. [For him] the highest that could be achieved was that everyone had enough to eat at cheap prices, that everyone had work, and that everyone had a good and cheap apartment....He thought that everyone was happy. Everyone had cheap bread, a cheap apartment, and work."[44] On 5 September, little more than two months before the opening of the Berlin Wall, the SED theory journal *Einheit* published a comment from Honecker assuring readers that East Germany is a "state with a functioning, effective, socialist social system which will, with its fully realized human rights, manage the challenges of the 1990s."[45]

Mass Movements for Human Rights

After months of radicalisation, two very different forms of movement threatened the existence of the GDR: the mass emigration of East German citizens to the West and the start of regular street demonstrations numbering first in the hundreds and then rapidly growing into thousands. On 11 September 1989, Hungary announced that it would open its border with Austria, and within three days more than 15,000 East Germans crossed over with no intention of returning. Six thousand more – including one newborn infant – intent on leaving, but unable to make it to Hungary, took refuge in the West German embassy in Prague. Thousands took to the streets in Leipzig, joining weekly Monday peace marches organised by the Nikolai Church. Although there had been conflicts between those seeking to exit and those who wanted to stay, by 1989, "emigration was a precondition for mass movement," as the

---

[44] Catherine Epstein, *The Last Revolutionaries: German Communists and Their Century* (Cambridge, MA: Harvard University Press, 2003), 219.
[45] Quoted in Karl-Dieter Opp, *Origins of a Spontaneous Revolution: East Germany, 1989* (Ann Arbor: University of Michigan Press, 1995), 188.

mass exodus of East Germans to the West sparked the formation of new groups and encouraged street demonstrations.[46]

Many in the dissident movement were wary of moving from protesting the SED to openly organising a political opposition, but the migration crisis drove many to accept the need for mass organisations and parties.[47] The SED continued to hold a constitutionally mandated right to lead the GDR, but pluralism returned unofficially from below. Some new groups, like Neues Forum (New Forum), were concerned with generating dialogue and creating a participatory society. New Forum was to be a mass movement that could engage directly with the SED as a democratic representative of the people in contrast to the earlier groups such as the IFM which were more oriented around leading protests and direct action. Others, such as the Sozialdemokratische Partei (Social Democratic Party, SDP, not to be confused with homonymous SPD in West Germany), were organisations with definite policy objectives that sought to create a political opposition from within the GDR.

Human rights appeared across the spectrum as both an end goal and as a means for how to get there. The SDP program included the duty for all members to work towards the "protection of human rights and civil rights as contained in the Universal Declaration of Human Rights and the two human rights covenants (1966)."[48] At the same time, a splinter group of disillusioned officials from the SED and the FDGB, the state trade union organisation, formed the Vereinigte Linke (United Left). Its platform in early September 1989 demanded "political democracy, the rule of law, consistent implementation of the indivisible human rights and free expression of the individuality of each member of society."[49] Demokratischer Aufbruch (Democratic Awakening), a group of Protestants, officially focused on the creation of a "socialist society on a democratic basis," called for the rule of law and argued that they did not expect "the state to grant human rights, but rather to respect them."[50] This meant splitting apart party and state, developing a free and open public sphere and the introduction of market mechanisms into the economy while maintaining a "society of solidarity."[51] In fighting for these causes,

---

[46] Hans-Hermann Hertle, *Der Fall der Mauer: Die unbeabsichtigte Selbstauflösung des SED-Staates* (Opladen: Westdeutscher Verlag, 1999), 243.
[47] Pollack, "Mass Pressures, Elite Responses: Roots of Democratization," 310.
[48] "Das vorläufige Statut der SDP," in Rein and Böhme, *Die Opposition in der DDR*, 90.
[49] "Mindestanforderung für die Gestaltung einer freien sozialistischen Gesellschaft in der DDR," in *Die Opposition in der DDR*, 109.
[50] Quoted in Jarausch, *The Rush to German Unity*, 41.
[51] Aufruf zum "Demokratischen Aufbruch – sozial, ökologisch," in *Die Opposition in der DDR*, 34.

Democratic Awakening portrayed its cause as the outcome of "the realization of guaranteed human rights as found in the constitution and international agreements."[52] In early October 1989, most of the new opposition organisations, alongside many of the smaller dissident groups, came together to issue a joint declaration demanding free elections and democratisation. At a minimum, they could agree that their overall goal was "to end the situation in which citizens of this society lack the opportunity to enjoy political rights, as guaranteed in the human rights covenants of the United Nations and the [Helsinki Accords]."[53] In spite of the ideological and political differences of these groups, human rights and the restoration of democratic pluralism acted as a common point of reference for all.

The Catholic Church had avoided political engagement in the GDR since the 1970s, but in autumn 1989 it once again took up the mantle of human rights. In September, the Church made an official statement endorsing the right to travel and to emigrate. In October, this statement was expanded to include the right to free elections, the right to free speech, peaceful assembly, and free association. In a notice to all priests and deacons, the bishops implored them to remember these rights "as contained in the UN Human Rights Declaration."[54] As the Catholic leadership cautiously re-entered the world of politics, Catholics in general were outpacing them. For many, a sense of Christian duty compelled them to speak out on the problem of human rights and democratisation, whether the church hierarchy agreed or not. On 12 October, 71 employees of the East Berlin office of the Catholic charity Caritas signed on to a letter to Prime Minister Willi Stoph calling for the "acknowledgement and maintenance of all human rights," by means of "an open and general societal dialogue about the foundational democratization of the state." The writers did not seek permission to speak out on the subject and did not notify their superiors until after the letter was sent. They noted that while they were "accustomed to remaining silent about the current situation in our country [as] Catholic Christians and church employees, we want to speak up and no longer wait for what church authorities negotiate non-publicly with the state."[55]

---

[52] *Flugblatt für die Demokratie* in *Die Opposition in der DDR*, 46.
[53] "Joint Declaration of the Civic Movement," in *Uniting Germany: Documents and Debates, 1944–1993*, ed. Konrad Jarausch (New York: Berghahn, 1994), 50.
[54] Ute Haese, *Katholische Kirche in der DDR: Geschichte einer politischen Abstinenz* (Düsseldorf: Patmos Verlag, 1998), 93–94; Gerhard Lange, *Katholische Kirche – sozialistischer Staat DDR* (Berlin: Bischöfliches Ordinariat, 1993), 362–68.
[55] Bernd Schäfer, *The East German State and the Catholic Church, 1945–1989* (New York: Berghahn, 2010), 254.

As human rights became a unifying rallying cry of peace marchers, church groups and the organised dissident movement, the SED lost its ideological grip on its own members and its own slogans. One Stasi evaluation of public opinion from 11 September 1989, determined that the level of discontent of SED members was essentially the same as that of the general public.[56] Out in the streets, as protests grew to more than 100,000 by October, the language of human rights provided a unifying theme. Historian and demonstration participant, Hartmut Zwahr, described the atmosphere in Leipzig, the epicentre of the street protests:

Singing, the demonstrators encouraged each other. They began with the *Internationale* – learned in 7th and 8th grade music class at the polytechnic high schools of the GDR. Memorized, sullenly performed, never to be sung again, until this moment, when a chunk of the refrain suddenly fit, to sing out the protest with all the power of their voices: "people hear the signal/ on to the last fight/ the Internationale/ wins the human right!" Human rights. How they had been distorted! Now we all felt the same. To go into the streets was a human right.

According to Zwahr: "Some only understood in this instant, in the pincer of state power, the loss of human rights, and that [they were] absolutely prepared to win them back."[57]

The use of the human rights message from the *Internationale* was just one of the means protestors used to appropriate SED human rights discourse as a language of protest. As with the Luxemburg-Liebknecht march in 1988, human rights activists promoted freedom of speech with Rosa Luxemburg's quote: "Freedom is only the freedom of those who think differently." Protesters also picked up on the phrase "Practice Solidarity!," which had been a slogan of the communist group Red Aid during the Weimar era and of the KMR in its campaigns for prisoners in the 1950s and 1960s.[58] While the SED rejected foreign human rights criticism as it "intervened in the internal affairs" of a sovereign GDR, the protesters turned the phrase around, declaring that they had a "right to intervene in our own affairs."[59] If the East German people had the right to self-determination, they demanded to exercise it themselves.

---

[56] Bernd Florath, "Die SED im Untergang," in *Das Revolutionsjahr 1989: Die demokratische Revolution in Osteuropa als transnationale Zäsur*, ed. Bernd Florath (Göttingen: Vandenhoeck & Ruprecht, 2011), 79.

[57] Hartmut Zwahr, *Ende einer Selbstzerstörung: Leipzig und die Revolution in der DDR* (Göttingen: Vandenhoeck & Ruprecht, 1993), 42–43.

[58] Michael Richter, *Die Friedliche Revolution: Aufbruch zur Demokratie in Sachsen 1989/90* (Vandenhoeck & Ruprecht, 2010), 445. On the slogan "Übt Solidarität," see Chapter 2.

[59] Ibid., 230. The phrase appears to have been coined by Heiko Lietz in early 1989. Archiv der DDR-Opposition, Samizdat PS 041/17 Friedensnetz.

The process of embodying the freedoms they were denied led to a collective internalisation of an inherent right to speak, assemble and leave. As dissident physicist Sebastian Pflugbeil remembered it, only after change had begun, did "the dimensions of what they had done to us, [become clear] how many rights we had given up, even though most had been guaranteed constitutionally. It's very strange."[60] In taking to the streets, previously well-behaved East Germans were now victims of violent repression by the very state security organs they had assiduously avoided antagonising their whole lives. When subjected to physical abuse or detention for demonstrating – or seeing this occur to friends and loved ones – East Germans were outraged, and their perspective radically shifted.[61]

The practice of exercising rights fed into a growing discourse of demanding rights: according to one Ministry of the Interior study of all documented protests on October 4th, the most common sentiment expressed on large banners at demonstrations was anti-SED and anti-Stasi, but the most common positive agenda was that of realising human rights.[62] In the town of Schmölln, signs demanded the resignation of Erich Honecker alongside posters for "Comply with Human Rights" and "Helsinki-Human Rights."[63] In Leipzig, protestors carried banners demanding "Freedom of Assembly – Freedom of Association" and "Freedom to Travel Instead of Mass Flight."[64] When Mikhail Gorbachev came to visit the GDR in early October, slogans and banners had the same mix of anti-SED and pro-human rights messages. In Pirna, protestors carried posters saying, "Out with the Reds," alongside those demanding "Human Rights" and "Freedom to Travel Instead of Mass Flight."[65] In Berlin on 7 October – the 40th anniversary of the founding of the GDR – handouts at a demonstration called for "Democracy – Establish a Dictatorship of the People, Down with the Dictatorship of the SED," along with demands for human rights, reform and "real socialism."[66]

Crucially for the opposition groups, reformers within the SED did not view the demands of the human rights activists as antisocialist or anti-

---

[60] Dirk Philipsen, *We Were the People: Voices from East Germany's Revolutionary Autumn of 1989* (Durham, NC: Duke University Press, 1993), 155.
[61] Major, *Behind the Berlin Wall*, 246.
[62] Of 76 banners: 37 attacked the SED, party corruption or the Stasi; 16 demanded human rights; 9 promoted different organisations; 4 environmental causes; 2 peace and disarmament; 9 miscellaneous. Pfaff, *Exit-Voice Dynamics and the Collapse of East Germany*, 295.
[63] Richter, *Die Friedliche Revolution*, 194.   [64] Ibid., 199.   [65] Ibid., 263.
[66] Ibid., 283.

GDR. Hans Modrow entered into negotiations with the dissidents in Dresden, reporting to East Berlin that "these groups recognize in their language the GDR and socialism, but demand changes and reforms. [...] Participants explained that they are going into the streets because otherwise nothing about the acute problems in our development will be discussed."[67] In agreeing to talk with these groups specifically as representatives of the people, senior elements in the SED effectively admitted that the Party was failing, and that it was now reduced to negotiating with representatives of the population.

Reformers were sympathetic to human rights demands, but the Politburo was still led by Erich Honecker, who continued to refuse all compromise. When protestors sought to disrupt the 40th anniversary celebrations, they were met with a non-lethal but violent crackdown and the police and Stasi wielded batons and water cannons to disperse the hostile crowds. As East Germans marched in the streets for change rather than to honour the founding of the GDR, Honecker deflected this criticism by pointing to the failings of the West: "Mass unemployment, homelessness, lack of social protection – all of which accompany modern technology in the FRG – do not exist here now and will not in the future. It is a perversion of human rights when one-third, one-fourth, or whatever proportion of the population is shunned and excluded."[68] While Mikhail Gorbachev reiterated to Honecker that he would not deploy the Soviet military to secure his rule in the event of open rebellion, the GDR did still have the support of China: Honecker assured the visiting Chinese vice premier that he would "never give up the leading role" of the SED.[69] But a report from the Stasi the following day found that the hardliners continued to lose ground: "Many working people, including many members and officials of the party, openly say that the party and state leadership is no longer able to assess the situation in real terms," and many were positively inclined towards the goals of New Forum and other mass protest organisations.[70]

The demonstrations held in Leipzig on 9 October proved to be a turning point, as state security services chose to tacitly accept a right to publicly protest, rather than enforcing control through lethal violence.[71]

---

[67] Quoted in Pfaff, *Exit-Voice Dynamics and the Collapse of East Germany*, 185.
[68] Erich Honecker Defends the Achievements of Socialism on the 40th Anniversary of the GDR (6.10.1989) (http://germanhistorydocs.ghi-dc.org).
[69] James Miles, *The Legacy of Tiananmen: China in Disarray* (Ann Arbor: University of Michigan Press, 1997), 45. Quoted in Chen, "Defying Moscow, Engaging Beijing," 208.
[70] Florath, "Die SED im Untergang," 79.
[71] Walter Süss, "Der friedliche Ausgang des 9. Oktober in Leipzig," in *1989 und die Rolle der Gewalt*.

In the days before, the head of the Stasi Erich Mielke promised "I will now once and for all deploy my special troops, and will show that our authority still has teeth."[72] Individual officers tried to rally their troops by framing the current conflict as the struggle for the soul of socialism: "Today, once and for all, we will end the counter-revolution in Leipzig [...] today it is decided, it is us against them."[73] But within the worker militias (*Kampfgruppen*) – formed after the 17 June 1953 Uprising in preparation for just such an event – morale had already plummeted and most units could barely muster half their official numbers.[74] For those who did remain, there was a deep reluctance to employ violence against the wider population, with one militia commander later saying "we were not there to start shooting, we were there to dissolve counter-revolutionary groups."[75]

On 9 October, however, the 8,000 members of the various security services encountered the weekly Monday peace march in Leipzig, which had swelled to 130,000 demonstrators, rather than a band of counterrevolutionaries.[76] Instead of reclaiming the streets, the police, military and militias simply withdrew. The demands from the crowds for human rights undermined – rather than supported – the Stasi's claims that the protestors were nothing more than imperialist provocateurs.[77] A group of six local elites – a cabaret performer, a theologian, famed Leipzig Gewandhaus conductor Kurt Masur, and three senior SED officials – issued a joint appeal for nonviolence pleading for "a free exchange of views on the continuation of socialism in our country."[78] Having heard the crowds singing the *Internationale* and demanding reform, General Major Raimund Kokott, an army officer sent to help restore order in Dresden, reported that the demonstration "was no counterrevolution. The people wanted a better GDR."[79] When

---

[72] Kotkin, *Uncivil Society*, 58.

[73] Niemetz, "Einen neuen '17. Juni' verhindern. Volkspolizei-Bereitschaften und 'Kampfgruppen der Arbeiterklasse' im Herbst 1989," 133.

[74] Hertle, *Der Fall der Mauer*, 117; Niemetz, "Einen neuen '17. Juni' verhindern. Volkspolizei-Bereitschaften und 'Kampfgruppen der Arbeiterklasse' im Herbst 1989," 131–32.

[75] Pfaff, *Exit-Voice Dynamics and the Collapse of East Germany*, 174–75.

[76] Opp demonstrates that while the total number of demonstrators is traditionally cited at 70,000, the actual number was likely between 124,500 and 166,000 (around 26 percent of the city). Karl-Dieter Opp, "The Production of Historical 'Facts': How the Wrong Number of Participants in the Leipzig Monday Demonstration on October 9, 1989 Became a Convention," *Journal of Economics and Statistics* 231, no. 5–6 (2011): 598–607.

[77] Pfaff, *Exit-Voice Dynamics and the Collapse of East Germany*, 117.

[78] Quoted in Süss, *Staatssicherheit am Ende*, 310.

[79] Richter, *Die Friedliche Revolution*, 281.

confronted with such crowds in their own country, police and militia units were unwilling to do "the dirty work" of the Party to stop them.[80] While many in the lower ranks of the security apparatus could justify attacking counterrevolutionaries to themselves in the defence of socialism, they did not want to shoot peaceful demonstrators, many of whom were neighbours or relatives, just to prop up the SED. The mass mobilisation of the population had shifted the narrative lines, and symbolically placed the hardliners as the antagonists of socialist citizens that only sought human rights.

After the retreat on 9 October, the SED abandoned plans to suppress the protests by force and abandoned control of the streets. As Hartmut Zwahr noted, "Something deep within broke that evening and in the end it all fell down like a house of cards."[81] In spite of this, the Politburo still tried to put a positive spin on events. On 11 October, with hundreds of thousands now protesting freely in Leipzig, Dresden and Berlin, the Politburo issued a statement saying "Once again, the imperialists of the FRG have confirmed that they will never come to terms with a socialist state on German soil; agreements have been broken and human rights have been violated."[82] In spite of the Politburo's protestations, East Germans maintained their demands: the Stasi documented a stonemason in the town of Bad Lausick who hung a sign in his storefront window on the main street saying "More Democracy and Human Rights."[83] In Dresden, a protest of several thousand sang the *Internationale* and marched with the slogans "We Want New Forum,""We Want Out" and "Human Rights and Freedom," as the local playhouse staged its own protest and declared "We Have a Right to Dialogue."[84] In Karl-Marx-Stadt, dissidents organised a discussion session between citizens and local officials at a church, ending with a final declaration that, "we will not be silenced again and we will practice solidarity with those who are threatened and we must protect our human rights."[85]

On 18 October, Honecker's long-standing right-hand man Egon Krenz finally decided to take action. At a Politburo meeting, Krenz made a motion calling on Honecker to resign, and in keeping with the tradition of unanimous voting, Honecker voted with the rest of his colleagues to end his 18-year tenure as leader of the GDR. Appearing on the evening television broadcast, Krenz announced a program of reform, which he

[80] Pfaff, *Exit-Voice Dynamics and the Collapse of East Germany*, 178.
[81] Zwahr, *Ende einer Selbstzerstörung*, 99.
[82] "Politburo Declaration," (11.10.1989) in Jarausch, *Uniting Germany*, 60.
[83] Richter, *Die Friedliche Revolution*, 371.   [84] Ibid., 279.   [85] Ibid., 445.

called a turnaround – *Wende* – that would include elections, the release of those imprisoned for "fleeing the republic" and immediate measures to stabilise the faltering economy. As a harbinger of reform, Krenz had little credibility with the public, as he had overseen the fraudulent local elections in May and had publicly expressed support for the Chinese government following the Tiananmen Square massacre.[86] His proposed elections, which did not include "bourgeois pluralism," were not planned to take place until 1991, and his comments about how he could imagine a vote where the SED "were to win with only eighty percent of the popular vote," did nothing to reassure the population that this would be a fair contest.[87] Although Krenz reopened the border to Czechoslovakia, this only provoked protesters who demanded total freedom of movement and an end to the Berlin Wall.[88] Like Honecker and Ulbricht before him, Krenz tried to paper over these problems with rhetoric: on 8 November, the Central Committee announced that its program of reform was rooted in "the socialist rule of law emanating from fundamental and human rights."[89] This would mean more freedom and legal security within the existing political structure of the GDR, rather than any kind of radical transition negotiated through Round Table talks between various party and opposition factions, as in Poland or Hungary.[90]

In spite of the *Wende*, the crowds were not placated and protests demanding peace, democratisation and freedom in the name of human rights continued. The Ministry of the Interior documented a peace rally organised by the churches of Friedrichsroda, Gotha and Erfurt where they sang the *Internationale* in protest. Two days later in Plauen and Karl-Marx-Stadt, demonstrators carried posters stating, "We Have a Right to Democracy."[91] At the end of October, demos in Greifswald and Rostock in the north called for "human rights and peace," while in the southern town of Olbernhau, 800 people chanted for "Human Rights – Reform – We Want Freedom," and in East Berlin, 2,000 protestors rallied to

---

[86] Pfaff, *Exit-Voice Dynamics and the Collapse of East Germany*, 225.
[87] Major, *Behind the Berlin Wall*, 251; Gareth Dale, *Popular Protest in East Germany* (London: Routledge, 2004), 160.
[88] Jarausch, *The Rush to German Unity*, 61.
[89] Karl Wilhelm Fricke, *Der Wahrheit verpflichtet: Texte aus fünf Jahrzehnten zur Geschichte der DDR* (Berlin: Ch. Links, 2000), 168.
[90] In Hungary, Round Table talks ran from March to September 1989. András Bozáki, *The Roundtable Talks of 1989: The Genesis of Hungarian Democracy* (Budapest: Central European University Press, 2002).
[91] BArch, DO1/8/41781 Information (20.10.1989) Betreff Gewährleistung der öffentlichen Ordnung und Sicherheit, 3; Information vom 22.10.1989, 2.

support human rights activists in neighbouring Czechoslovakia.[92] On
4 November, a massive rally was held in the heart of East Berlin, Alexanderplatz, attended by more than half a million people who heard
speeches from dissidents like Bärbel Bohley, cultural icons like authors
Christa Wolf and Stefan Heym and elite reformers including Politburo
member Günter Schabowski and recently retired Stasi foreign intelligence chief Markus Wolf (no relation to Christa). At the rally placards
included the slogans: "Visa-free to Hawaii" and "Waiting Times: Car 15
Years, Telephone 20 Years, Democratic Elections 40 Years."[93]

While Krenz and the Politburo were fumbling the *Wende*, socialist
reformers promoting human rights were still timid in instigating real
change. The GDR-Committee for Human Rights finally launched its
first public campaign on domestic issues – including open criticism of the
SED. The committee issued a declaration calling for equality before the
law, an independent judiciary, the legal presumption of innocence,
improved access to lawyers, an overhaul of the criminal code and modi-
fications to domestic laws concerning the right to free speech, assembly
and association. Such reforms were "urgently necessary, so that in the
future any arbitrariness in dealing with citizens is precluded to the best of
human ability."[94] The committee's declaration (devoid of any mention
of the freedom of movement!) was made public on 9 November – only
hours before the Berlin Wall opened.

The ultimate opening of the Berlin Wall came about due to a myriad of
factors: the incompetence of the SED, a wilful optimism on the part of
the crowds and the border guards' loss of faith in the right of the state to
use deadly force against civilians.[95] In announcing that East Germans
could begin travelling to the Federal Republic (with the appropriate visa)
Politburo member Günter Schabowski accidently conveyed that the
liberalisation of travel would take effect "immediately," rather than
the following day. Rumours that the border was now open spread – the
subtleties of Schabowski's announcement ignored entirely – and crowds
gathered at border crossings around East Berlin. Without a near-
universal belief in a human right to travel, Schabowski's announcement
could very well have been dismissed as one more incremental reform

---

[92] BArch, DO1/8/41781 Information (26.10.1989), 4; Richter, *Die Friedliche Revolution*,
487. Archiv der DDR-Opposition, Samizdat TK 009/01 Depesche IFM.
[93] Losungen der Wende (04.11.1989) in Matthias Judt, ed., *DDR-Geschichte in
Dokumenten: Beschlüsse, Berichte, interne Materialien und Alltagszeugnisse* (Berlin: Ch.
Links, 2013).
[94] BArch, DP1/9093 Erklärung des DDR-Komitees für Menschenrechte (8.11.1989).
[95] On the optimism of the crowds, see Gareth Dale, *The East German Revolution of 1989*
(Manchester: Manchester University Press, 2006), 95.

instead of the dissolution of the border between East and West Germany.[96] After several tense hours, as the crowds grew larger and louder, the guards finally stepped aside and let the people pass – first by stamping their identity cards to invalidate them, but soon giving up on even that. By acting as though the border had been opened, the crowds made the right to free movement a reality.[97] For nearly three decades, the border guards of the Berlin Wall stood at their posts, willing to use deadly force against their fellow citizens – in the name of protecting state sovereignty and human rights – and then, on 9 November, when confronted by crowds demanding to pass, they stood down.

Self-Determination for the GDR or for Germans?

The opening of the Berlin Wall was not, however, the end of the SED, nor did it mark the demise of socialism in the GDR. Many reformers saw this as their chance to finally remake East Germany into the socialist state that it was always meant to be. In an interview published in the journal of the KMR, Jürgen Kuczynski confidently declared "this country is having a revolution at last!"[98] The public discourse in East Germany radically transformed as the SED and state organs changed gears to trumpet the forward march of human rights in the GDR. While the national newspaper *Neues Deutschland* had been filled with articles on human rights abuses across the capitalist world, ranging from hunger-striking Roma in Hamburg to racial oppression in South Africa, after 9 November, human rights suddenly became a domestic problem that the SED was diligently seeking to solve. The "Proposed Program for a Fundamental Transformation," presented by the SED in the *Volkskammer* announced a new focus on "the development of the socialist rule of law and the guarantee of human rights," including free and secret elections, freedom of expression and a total overhaul of the criminal code.[99]

But after only a month in office, General Secretary Egon Krenz's credibility was completely spent and the SED sidelined him by appointing the reformer Hans Modrow as the prime minister on 13 November. Krenz would hold onto his position as General Secretary until December, but the centre of power shifted from party leadership to the SED-led government and its Bloc Party allies. Modrow assured the population

---

[96] Hertle, *Der Fall der Mauer*, 205.
[97] On the role of the internalisation of a right to travel, see ibid., 304–5.
[98] Jürgen Kuczynski, "This Country Is Having a Revolution at Last," *Bulletin – GDR Committee for Human Rights* 15, no. 3 (1989), 6.
[99] Werner Jarolinsky, "Aktionsprogramm Angebot für eine tiefe Umgestaltung," *Neues Deutschland* (14.11.1989), 3.

that "the intended political reform already under way has provided a new foundation to preserve and implement a policy of self-determination for the people of the GDR. This gives new strength to the GDR's legitimacy as a socialist state, as a sovereign German state."[100]

The SED reformers hoped that this program of democratic socialism could restore stability, but the opening of the Berlin Wall completely upended the political calculus. With East Germans migrating to the West in droves the question of unification came to the fore.[101] Before the opening of the Wall there were some vociferous advocates for reunification, but such talk remained subdued on both sides of the Wall. In the East, New Forum, the largest civil society group in the GDR, tied their demands for rights and democratisation to the reform of the GDR, not its abolition. The chapter of New Forum in the city of Hoyerswerda agreed on a platform for reforming the electoral system, defending all basic rights, freedom of movement, press freedom and the right to assemble, but clarified that reunification was "not a theme we are pursuing, since we are starting from the position that there are two Germanies and we are not striving for a capitalist social order."[102] Ludwig Mehlhorn of the group Demokratie Jetzt (Democracy Now) echoed these statements, lamenting "in the West it is unfortunately the case that self-determination for the Germans of the GDR is automatically identified with reunification."[103]

Yet even in the FRG, this equation of self-determination with unification was tempered by fears that such rhetoric could disrupt the ongoing revolution in the GDR and reopen old conflicts over the German-Polish border. In September, Dorothee Wilms, the CDU Minister for All-German Questions, argued that the realisation of human rights and self-determination in East Germany "should result in a process at the end of which lies German unity."[104] But Bavarian Minister-President Max Streibl (CSU) disagreed, reasoning that, "for East German citizens, the first priority are freedoms and human rights, and after that comes the question of the nation."[105] The West German Free Democrats and the SPD saw the possibility of two Germanies continuing into the future – if East Germans chose that path based on their free self-determination. Theo Sommer, editor of *Die Zeit*, captured the concerns of many when

---

[100] Jarausch, *Uniting Germany*, 83.
[101] On 9 November as a caesura, see Andreas Apelt, *Die Opposition in der DDR und die deutsche Frage 1989/90* (Berlin: Ch. Links, 2009), 189–97.
[102] Richter, *Die Friedliche Revolution*, 711.
[103] Ludwig Mehlhorn, "Wir brauchen eine vom Staat unabhängige Gesellschaft," in *Die Opposition in der DDR*, 82.
[104] Richter, *Die Friedliche Revolution*, 130.   [105] Ibid.

he said that "nobody nowadays has the right to thump on a powder keg with the burning torch of human rights."[106] In such a precarious situation, loud pronouncements connecting human rights to reunification could backfire badly, and even ardent nationalists held back.

Hoping to forestall calls for reunification, representatives from the East German cultural elite, reform communists, dissident groups and some church leaders came together to stand for the continued existence of an independent GDR. On 26 November, they produced a joint appeal titled "For Our Country," calling on the East German people to resist the siren call of the West. For this group, which included Stefan Heym, Christa Wolf, IFM cofounder Ulrike Poppe, Sebastian Pflugbeil of New Forum and Protestant leader Günter Krusche, the establishment of human rights and self-determination in the GDR was only a first step. The choice was clear: "Either we can insist on GDR independence [and] develop a society of solidarity, offering peace, social justice, individual liberty, free movement, and ecological conservation," or there would be "a sell-out of our material and moral values and [we will] have the GDR eventually taken over by the FRG."[107] Over the next two weeks, more than 200,000 East Germans signed on, stating their support for a program to reinforce the "anti-fascist and humanistic" ideals of the German Democratic Republic. This movement represented the dream of realising a "Third Way" between state socialism and Western liberal democracy echoing the early pronouncements of the IFM and other dissident groups.[108]

Two days later, however, West German Chancellor Helmut Kohl released his own Ten-Point Plan for German Unity. Kohl spoke of a "new epoch in European and German history," which had come about due to "the work of the people, who demand freedom, respect for their human rights, and their right to be master of their own future."[109] Point Six of his plan included "unqualified respect for the principles and rules of international law, especially respect for the people's right of self-determination," and "the realization of human rights."[110] According to Kohl, human rights were deeply intertwined with liberal democracy and Christian values. The GDR was an anomaly of history that had artificially divided the nation; only democratic elections could put East Germans on the path to self-determination, which would then finally allow them their

[106] Ibid., 857.   [107] Quoted in Jarausch, *The Rush to German Unity*, 67.
[108] Geisel, *Auf der Suche nach einem dritten Weg*, 62.
[109] Harold James and Marla Stone, eds., *When the Wall Came Down: Reactions to German Unification* (London: Routledge, 1992), 35.
[110] Jarausch, *Uniting Germany*, 87–88.

long-denied human rights. The choice was clear: human rights according to a West German model by way of reunification or a new kind of democratic socialist human rights through continued independence.

Although more than a million East Germans had chosen to quit the SED over the course of 1989, Hans Modrow believed that the popularity of the "For Our Country" manifesto demonstrated that "the overwhelming majority of GDR citizens" wanted the country to remain socialist and under the leadership of a democratised SED.[111] On 1 December, the SED formally abolished its right to lead the country in perpetuity – Section 1 of the Constitution since 1968 – but Modrow resisted calls for a negotiated transition through Round Table talks with the opposition, as was underway even in Czechoslovakia where the hardliner regime had rapidly imploded in late November.[112] In a conversation with West German Chancellor Helmut Kohl, Modrow said he wanted to accelerate reforms, "but following the Moscow model, not Warsaw's or Budapest's."[113] Rather than relinquish power, he aimed to usher in reforms from above as Gorbachev was still attempting in the USSR.

In the end, however, Modrow faced the same problems that plagued the short tenure of Egon Krenz: rapid economic decline, mass emigration and plunging political legitimacy. While elections were still planned for 1990, mass protests continued in the streets and the weekly Monday Demonstrations in Leipzig proceeded as they had before the Wall opened. Patience with the unelected Modrow government ran low and protestors demanded "no more experiments – reunification now!" The crowds shifted from chanting "we are *the* people" to "we are *one* people."[114] While the dissidents did not want to seize power directly, they did want to increase the speed of reforms and ensure that when elections came, there would be a credible democratic alternative to rapid reunification.[115] Modrow finally relented and a German Round Table met on 7 December with 30 members, 15 from the SED and the other Bloc parties (which now dropped their unconditional support for the

---

[111] Orlow, *Socialist Reformers*, 42–45.

[112] Jon Elster, ed., "The Round Table Talks in Czechoslovakia," in *The Roundtable Talks and the Breakdown of Communism* (Chicago: University of Chicago Press, 1996).

[113] Conversation between Helmut Kohl and Lech Walesa (9.11.1989), Svetlana Savranskaya, Thomas Blanton and Vladislav Zubok, eds., *Masterpieces of History: The Peaceful End of the Cold War in Eastern Europe, 1989* (Budapest: Central European University Press, 2010), 581.

[114] On the rise of pro-unification sentiment in public demonstrations between late-November and mid-December 1989, see Timmer, *Vom Aufbruch zum Umbruch*, 345–46. Jarausch, *The Rush to German Unity*, 87.

[115] Geisel, *Auf der Suche nach einem dritten Weg*, 104.

SED) and 15 representatives from civic organisations including New Forum and the Initiative for Peace and Human Rights.[116]

Hoping to transform his transitional government into a democratically elected one, Modrow and his fellow reformers sought to use the language of human rights to present themselves as democratic socialists and to distance themselves from the past 40 years of what they now called the "Stalinism" practiced by the old leadership of the SED. In late December 1989, he assured the declining readership of the Free German Youth newspaper, *Junge Welt*, that reforms would demonstrate "strict respect for human rights without exception, which demands – in contrast to the time before November 1989 – a new attitude of the state towards the individual."[117] On 16 December, in anticipation of the planned elections, the SED added "Party of Democratic Socialism" to its name to become the SED-PDS. The party chose Gregor Gysi – a lawyer who had acted as defence counsel for prominent dissidents including Robert Havemann and Rudolf Bahro – to be its new chairman. Gysi was quickly dispatched to France to meet with President François Mitterrand to convince him of the party's democratic bona fides and to lobby against West German plans for rapid reunification. He told the French socialist that his party offered "unqualified support for democracy and human rights," and pledged that they would "overcome and abolish Stalinism" in the GDR.[118] Frank Berg, one of the academics who had worked on the Socialist Declaration of Human Rights project, argued that while the SED had only used human rights as a propaganda tool, it was now the real watchword of its successor party. When asked, "Does the SED-PDS have the moral right to speak about human rights?," Berg replied, "The SED – no. The PDS – yes."[119] According to these reformers, the transition to the PDS was to be the beginning of a truly democratic socialism based on the principle of human rights for all.

But the credibility of the SED-PDS as democratic reformers was undermined by the continuing existence of the Stasi – the institutional embodiment of the abuses of state socialism. The SED had abolished its monopoly on power, but the secret police had been largely untouched by the revolution, aside from a name change from the Ministry for State

[116] Ulrich Preuss, "The Roundtable Talks in the GDR," in *The Roundtable Talks and the Breakdown of Communism*, ed. Jon Elster (Chicago: University of Chicago Press, 1996), 105.

[117] Quoted in Frank Berg, *Menschenrechte: der Autor im Gespräch mit Jürgen Weidlich* (Berlin: Dietz, 1990), 8.

[118] Horst Möller et al., eds., *Die Einheit: Das Auswärtige Amt, das DDR-Außenministerium und der Zwei-plus-Vier-Prozess* (Göttingen: Vandenhoeck & Ruprecht, 2015), 202.

[119] Berg, *Menschenrechte*, 4.

Security to the Office for National Security (*Amt für Nationale Sicherheit*), which had the unfortunate acronym of NaSi. Popular anger towards the agency exploded as revelations of abuses streamed across the newly free East German media and in the early morning of 4 December protestors stormed the Stasi office in the city of Erfurt when they suspected that incriminating files were being burned. On 10 December, a pastor in Suhl dedicated his Human Rights Day address entirely to the problem of eliminating the Stasi as an agency, but also imploring the audience not to take revenge upon Stasi agents or their collaborators through vigilante violence.[120] Finally on 15 January 1990, during a protest outside Stasi headquarters in East Berlin, when it became clear that agents inside were destroying incriminating files, the crowd occupied the building and looted it. Members of New Forum called for calm; the crowds ignored them.

While the end of the Stasi came through the dramatic occupation of its central headquarters, the KMR disappeared with a whimper not a bang. Hermann Klenner and Bernhard Graefrath sought to transform the group into a democratic organisation for the post-SED era, but they were haemorrhaging members, in many cases due to poor health and old age: Chairwoman Friedel Malter resigned her position in December 1989 – aged 87 – her unsteady signature barely recognisable.[121] At a meeting of the remaining members on 4 January 1990, other human rights groups were invited to take part in the hope that the committee could become an umbrella organisation. Just as in its founding documents from 1959, members spoke idealistically of acting in the tradition of the League for Human Rights and its leading member Carl von Ossietzky, the Nobel Peace prize winner murdered by the Nazis. But even at that meeting, a representative from the Initiative for Peace and Human Rights made clear that he was not impressed, neither by their plans nor by the assumption that dissident groups would automatically be interested in working under their auspices.[122] By February, Graefrath wrote to Secretary Siegfried Forberger to inform him that 39 longtime members – more than half the total – had resigned from the organisation and that none of the new civil society groups had agreed to join with them. With Party funding ending soon, the organisation was broke and would be forced to fire its employees within the next two months.

---

[120] Erhard Kretschmann, Rede zur Demo am Tag der Menschenrechte (10.12.1989), Suhl. Daniel Weißbrodt, *Die Wende in Suhl: das Umbruchjahr 1989/90 in der Bezirkshauptstadt Suhl* (Zella-Mehlis: Bürgerkomitee des Landes Thüringen, 2002), 128–29.

[121] BArch, DZ7/25 Malter Letter of Resignation (27.12.1989).

[122] BArch, DZ7/25 Protokoll (4.1.1990).

Graefrath, who had first begun working on human rights in 1956, asked Forberger: "What did we do wrong?"[123] Forberger, hired straight out of law school in 1959, retired in May 1990 after a more than 30-year career with the committee.[124] While it limped along under new leadership until the end of the year, the initiative to remake the committee for a democratic GDR was a failure.[125]

As the former representatives of the GDR were met with a chilly reception from civil society organisations, left-wing and third-way dissidents were being sidelined by the growing popularity of reunification over the democratisation of an independent GDR. The first competitive elections, planned for May 1990, were moved up to 18 March and those seeking to maintain GDR independence were quickly marginalised. The pro-unification Christian Democrats (CDU-Ost), Social Democrats (SDP) and Liberals (LDPD) were all able to draw upon material support from their sister parties in the Federal Republic – in contrast to the PDS (which had fully dropped the acronym SED from its name by February) and many of the independent dissident groups. The IFM sought to prevent guest speakers from West Germany from participating in public election events for all parties in the interests of preventing unfair advantages – already public speeches by Helmut Kohl and former Chancellor Willy Brandt had drawn crowds in the hundreds of thousands – but this initiative was voted down at the Round Table, 22 to 10 with six abstentions.[126] The GDR's first openly competitive election would not be fought only on a national level, but it would already be intertwined with the party politics of the FRG.

As a result, ex-SED officials, socialist reformers and third-way dissidents now found themselves working together at the Round Table in a last-ditch effort to realise a vision of human rights that preserved the often unrealised social and economic promises of state socialism alongside the political and civil rights for which dissidents had fought. Together, this alliance produced three key documents in the months leading up to the election: the Social Charter, the Essential Features for the Equality of Women and Men and a draft constitution of the GDR. The Social Charter called for the right to work, to strike and to collective bargaining, as well as a ban on lockouts. Workplaces would be expected to provide meals and medical care for employees and maintain the

---

[123] BArch, N 2535/2 Forberger to Graefrath (18.2.1990).
[124] Siegfried Forberger, *Das DDR-Komitee für Menschenrechte: Erinnerungen an den Sozialismus-Versuch im 20. Jahrhundert; Einsichten und Irrtümer des Siegfried Forberger, Sekretär des DDR-Komitees für Menschenrechte von 1959 bis 1989* (Self-pub., 2000), 516.
[125] Ibid., 513–15.   [126] Kloth, *Vom "Zettelfalten" zum freien Wählen*, 708–10.

existing childcare system for working mothers.[127] The Equality of Women and Men called for the achievement of social equality rather than just legal equality. This entailed a broad program of active state measures to support women economically, and the realisation of full self-determination for women, in terms of their capacity to make independent choices about their lives, their careers, and their bodies.[128]

After lengthy deliberations, the Round Table finally released its draft Constitution in March 1990 shortly before the elections – to stand as an alternative against the simple absorption of the GDR into the legal and political structures of West Germany. The draft contained extensive guarantees for political and civil liberties, as negative freedoms from the state, but also as positive mechanisms to allow for greater participation through direct forms of democracy. Social rights for the elderly, for those with disabilities, and for the unemployed, alongside measures to ensure substantial gender equality through equal pay, state-sponsored childcare and the protection of bodily self-determination also featured prominently. Many of these provisions echoed the promises of earlier socialist constitutions, including restrictions on free speech in the case of "war propaganda" and limitations on the amount of farmland that could be privately held.[129] It was also a GDR-specific document including specific rights for the Sorbian minority population that was not present in the West. As a whole, the constitution promised the social and economic rights inherent to an idealised form of socialism, guaranteed through a new commitment to individual rights and freedoms inherent to an idealised form of liberal democracy. As Inga Markovits has argued, it was not a rebuke of the West German Basic Law, but rather an attempt to surpass it by "moving towards a more participatory, more culturally diverse, more inclusive and more tolerant democracy."[130]

While the actual content of the Round Table Constitution reflected the broad demands of the demonstrators from the autumn of 1989, its political appeal was limited in part by the problematic history of many of

---

[127] On the Social Charter, see Gerhard Ritter, *The Price of German Unity: Reunification and the Crisis of the Welfare State* (Oxford: Oxford University Press, 2011), 141–43.

[128] Brigitte Young, *Triumph of the Fatherland: German Unification and the Marginalization of Women* (Ann Arbor: University of Michigan Press, 1999), 106–8. "The Essential Features for the Equality of Women and Men" drew from the Lila Manifesto, produced by a group affiliated with the Autonomous Women's Association. Lisa DiCaprio, "East German Feminists: The Lila Manifesto," *Feminist Studies* 16, no. 3 (1990), 621–26.

[129] Peter Quint, *The Imperfect Union: Constitutional Structures of German Unification* (Princeton, NJ: Princeton University Press, 2012), 31.

[130] Inga Markovits, "Constitution Making after National Catastrophes: Germany in 1949 and 1990," *William and Mary Law Review* 49, no. 4 (2008), 1327.

its drafters, SED stalwarts turned reformers: Hermann Klenner and Bernhard Graefrath, of the now defunct KMR, were two of the experts responsible for drafting the section on rights.[131] Internal discussions still revolved around SED slogans, such as "abolishing the exploitation of man by man," and the document's emphasis on "revolutionary renewal" made it unclear if the Constitution represented a reformed version of "real existing socialism" or the foundational text for an entirely new GDR.[132]

Many of the intellectual dissidents associated with the project also alienated possible supporters by acknowledging that this path would involve financial hardship. Author Christa Wolf told audiences that there would be "no quick prosperity but participation in a great transformation," and artist Bärbel Bohley promised "we will be poor for a long time, but we don't want to have a society in which profiteers elbow their way to the front."[133] Emerging political leaders – facing collapsing infrastructure and shortages of basic goods – had little time for such utopianism. For much of the East German population, the continued appeal of socialism was not anti-capitalism or a new social order, but rather guaranteed economic benefits and the possibility for consumerism unseen by previous generations of the working class.[134] For these GDR citizens, an essential aspect of the revolution in 1989 was also securing the right to economic prosperity and equal access to consumer goods (including the much clichéd blue jeans and bananas).[135]

While many of the human rights dissidents had previously shied away from electoral politics, several activist groups, including New Forum, Democracy Now and the Initiative for Peace and Human Rights formed a joint political party – Bündnis '90 (Alliance 1990), promising to realise

---

[131] Archiv der DDR-Opposition GP 32 Gerd Poppe Notes from AG Neue Verfassung (12.1.1990).

[132] BArch, DA3/36 Grundsätze für eine neue Verfassung der DDR. 6. On internal deliberations on the human rights sections, see Uwe Thaysen, ed., *Der Zentrale Runde Tisch der DDR: Wortprotokoll und Dokumente. Band 4* (Wiesbaden: Westdeutscher Verlag, 2000), 1098–1100.

[133] Dale, *The East German Revolution of 1989*, 88; Maier, *Dissolution*, 198.

[134] Ina Merkel, "Consumer Culture in the GDR, or How the Struggle for Anti-Modernity Was Lost on the Battleground of Consumer Culture," in *Getting and Spending: European and American Consumer Societies in the Twentieth Century*, ed. Susan Strasser, Charles McGovern and Matthias Judt (Cambridge: Cambridge University Press, 1998), 282.

[135] On popular conceptions of consumer rights as equal rights, see Daphne Berdahl, "Re-Presenting the Socialist Modern: Museums and Memory in the Former GDR," in *Socialist Modern: East German Everyday Culture and Politics*, ed. Katherine Pence and Paul Betts (Ann Arbor: University of Michigan Press, 2008), 361.

"human rights and humanity in all sectors of society."[136] But this hardly set it apart in a crowded field: the liberal German Forum Party promised to fully implement the tenets of the UDHR and the UN Human Rights Covenants;[137] the Greens portrayed their agenda of improving the health and well-being of the GDR as contribution to "fundamental human rights;"[138] the SDP promised, "the creation of social and democratic relations in our country to provide a legal foundation for fundamental human rights in order to participate in a pluralistic society in which everyone has the right to take part in decision-making processes;"[139] and finally, the PDS program, entitled "Democratic Freedoms and Social Security for All" pledged "an unrestricted guarantee of human rights" through constitutional measures to protect democratic freedoms and workers' rights.[140]

Many of the human rights promises made by the left-wing parties were also made by the conservative Allianz für Deutschland (Alliance for Germany).[141] A coalition of the Christian Democrats (CDU), the Protestant Church–oriented Democratic Awakening (which had taken a conservative turn in early 1990), and the populist Deutsche Soziale Union (German Social Union), the Alliance ran on a platform of rapid unification and was directly supported by Helmut Kohl's government in Bonn. Under the slogan "Never Again Socialism," the first point of its platform emphasised German unity and the restoration of human rights. Despite blistering rhetoric against both the PDS and socialism in general, it promised that privatisation would spread wealth to the "employees" of the community, that it would protect people from massive rent increases, and ensure co-responsibility at workplaces through unions, as well as increase pensions for the elderly and maintain the state system of day cares and child benefits.[142] The Alliance offered most of the benefits contained in the dissent/PDS platforms, but stripped out the Marxist

---

[136] "Initiative Frieden und Menschenrechte Wahlprogramm" (www.ddr89.de/ddr89/ifm/IFM16.html).

[137] "Programm der Deutschen Forumpartei" (www.freiheit.org/files/288/1990_DFP-Programm.pdf).

[138] "Grüne Partei: Die Ziele der Grünen Partei in unserem Bezirk" (www.ddr89.de/ddr89/gp/GP31.html).

[139] "Sozialdemokratische Partei in der DDR (SDP) – wer ist und was will unsere Partei?" (www.ddr89.de/ddr89/sdp/SDP22.html).

[140] "Demokratische Freiheiten für alle Soziale Sicherheit für Jeden," *Neues Deutschland* (10.2.1990), 3.

[141] Not to be confused with the Far Right *Alternative für Deutschland* (AfD), founded in 2013.

[142] Allianz für Deutschland, "Nie wieder Sozialismus." Konrad-Adenauer-Stiftung (www.kas.de).

jargon, the taint of dictatorship, and offered the prospect of having it all funded by West Germany.

When elections were held on 18 March 1990, the results were a resounding victory for the Alliance for Germany, which won nearly 50 percent of the vote. The Social Democrats, who many had expected to win, took slightly less than 22 percent. In spite of Modrow's hopes back in December that the SED would retain power by democratising, the PDS did not even clear 17 percent. The dissidents of Bündnis '90 trailed far behind with only a paltry 2.9 percent of the final vote. The language of human rights had become ubiquitous in East German political discourse and the parties were now largely distinguished by how they planned to achieve these lofty goals. Promises of a new kind of democratic human rights on paper, promoted by dissident intellectuals, were not as appealing as concrete plans for realising mass prosperity through reunification with West Germany. Bündnis '90 had the vote of the intelligentsia, but the Alliance had gained the support of the "workers and farmers" of the GDR, most of whom were tired of experiments and uninterested in exploring new forms of democratic politics if that meant continued economic sacrifice.[143]

On 19 April, newly minted Prime Minister Lothar de Maizière (CDU) presented the government's program to the first democratically elected East German parliament. In his address to the *Volkskammer*, he proposed "as much market as possible and as much state as necessary" by converting the "previous state-controlled command economy into an ecologically-oriented social market economy." On the subject of German unity, he declared that citizens of the GDR had much to contribute to the process,

[including] our identity and our dignity. Our identity: that is our history and culture, our failures and our achievements, our ideals and our suffering. Our dignity: that is our freedom and our human right to self-determination.[144]

As de Maizière presented it, East Germans were entering into the reunification process as equal partners – not supplicants. Joining together with the Federal Republic was not "selling-out" as left-wing critics claimed, but a conscious and democratic choice to realise self-determination. Reunification would bring the experiences of East Germans together with those of their Western counterparts. Just as the IFM and other dissident groups had appropriated the language of human rights from

[143] Ritter, *The Price of German Unity*, 21.
[144] Lothar de Maizière's Government Program (19.4.1990) (http://germanhistorydocs.ghi-dc.org).

the SED, through the course of the election campaign, the Alliance had done the same, by wresting human rights from the third-way activists and connecting it directly to German reunification. Far from having simply failed, the dissidents were victims of their own success, as human rights became the universal language for radical change in the GDR.

Efforts to ensure that the GDR was an equal partner in constitutional terms were, however, rapidly subdued. In the *Volkskammer*, Gerd Poppe of the IFM proposed a national referendum on adopting the draft Constitution of the Round Table, but the Alliance voted this down, with the support of the Liberals and Social Democrats. The new Ministry of Justice worked behind the scenes to create its own East German constitution, but this too was abandoned.[145] At the end of this process, plans for creating a new joint-German constitution never came to fruition, and the GDR was simply absorbed into the FRG, according to provisions of the West German Basic Law of 1949.[146] The human rights alternative offered by the reform socialists and the third-way activists through the Round Table had been thoroughly defeated. In the Unification Treaty signed by the two Germanies on 31 August 1990, the preamble emphasised the need to be "aware of the continuity of German history and bearing in mind the special responsibility arising from our past for a democratic development in Germany committed to respect for human rights and peace."[147] On 9 November, 1989, SED reformers had seen the fall of the Berlin Wall as an opening to salvage real socialism in East Germany. On 3 October 1990, mere days before the GDR's 41st anniversary, East Germany ceased to exist, and its territory was absorbed as the five "new" *Bundesländer* of the FRG – all under the banner of human rights.

Conclusion

The peaceful revolution of 1989 has been mythologised as the final triumph of human rights over the forces of socialist totalitarianism, ushering in a new age of individual freedom.[148] Rejecting mere economic benefits offered by the state in lieu of democratic freedoms, the people of East Germany rose up to claim their political and civil human rights and abolished the ruling dictatorship through mass demonstrations of

---

[145] Ritter, *The Price of German Unity*, 59.   [146] Quint, *The Imperfect Union*, 29.
[147] Jarausch, *Uniting Germany*, 189.
[148] On this phenomenon see Mark et al., "1989 after 1989: Remembering the End of State Socialism in East-Central Europe," in *Thinking through Transition: Liberal Democracy, Authoritarian Pasts, and Intellectual History in East Central Europe after 1989*, ed. Michal Kopeček and Piotr Wcilik (New York: Central European University Press, 2015), 463–504.

popular will. There are elements of truth in this narrative: the language of human rights was crucial in mobilising hundreds of thousands of individuals against the SED, and they did demand democratisation through the implementation of political and civil freedoms. But competitive elections revealed a broad variety of interpretations of human rights, held across the population, from those who wanted a new form of democratic socialism, to those who wanted to put an end socialism altogether. Although the revolution centred on democratisation, the focus of the first elections of 1990 was the question of precisely how a democratised GDR would cope with its economic decline and create a prosperous future for all.

Human rights were powerful no because they represented a singular logic of change leading inexorably to liberal democracy and peaceful German unification, but because human rights could mean almost anything – from radical market liberalisation to a more humane and democratic socialism.[149] Since the 1940s, the SED had erected a complex ideology of human rights to defend the status quo, which stabilised the system to a point, but ultimately contributed to its rapid collapse. Once the SED lost control of the discourse in the 1980s this precipitated a radical shift in the meaning of these ideas.[150] For East German citizens hoping to leave or just make a better future for themselves and their communities, human rights ceased to be one more phrase in the canon of state propaganda or Western television documentaries, and became a vital and pressing cause, that could bring about revolutionary change. By 1989, SED officials did not need to be convinced to believe in human rights, they just needed to change their minds about what they meant in practice. Once this subjective shift had occurred, the possibility of saving socialism by realising human rights proved, however, to be an illusion. The incited reforms facilitated continued mass protests against the SED and led to a popular vote to abandon independence and unify with West Germany. The SED's long-standing embrace of human rights discourse was fundamental to the peaceful revolution because it created the shared language between those in power and those without. Ultimately, it would lead to a state apparatus that abolished itself to realise its own ideals.

[149] On singular logic, Lynn Hunt, *Inventing Human Rights* (London: W.W. Norton, 2008), 160.
[150] On the radical reimagining of meaning within official discourses of late socialism, see Alexei Yurchak, *Everything Was Forever, Until It Was No More: The Last Soviet Generation* (Princeton, NJ: Princeton University Press, 2006).

Conclusion
Erasures and Rediscoveries

The reunification of Germany in October 1990 realised one form of human rights in the former GDR, but it also erased the alternative visions of human rights for which so many East Germans had fought. Human rights are supposed to be timeless, universal, natural – rooted in the self-evident equal moral worth of all individuals based on their shared humanity.[1] Much of the rhetorical power of human rights originates from these assertions because, without them, human rights would be merely one moral argument among many. As a result, however, historicising fallen conceptions of human rights becomes problematic as it calls into question their self-evident nature: complex social, intellectual and political struggles over the meaning of human rights are thus often replaced by a superficial morality tale of good triumphing over evil.[2] With SED rule so thoroughly discredited – even among its own members – it rapidly became common wisdom that human rights had always been anathema to state socialism. The fall of the Berlin Wall has become such a powerful symbol of the triumph of Western liberal democracy, that it has become difficult to imagine it as anything other than the logical endpoint of the struggle for human rights.

After the fall of the Berlin Wall, the collapse of SED legitimacy in the field of human rights was so complete that many East German elites simply erased socialist human rights from their past: Ideology Minister Kurt Hager omitted his role in spearheading the Socialist Declaration of Human Rights from his recollections of the 1980s, which in his retelling focused on socialist cooperation on the problem of international peace.[3]

---

[1] On the naturalisation of human rights, see András Sajó, "Ambiguities and Boundaries in Human Rights Knowledge Systems," in *Global Justice and the Bulwarks of Localism: Human Rights in Context,* ed. Christopher Eisgruber and Andras Sajó (Leiden: M. Nijhoff, 2005), 20.

[2] Ned Richardson-Little, "Human Rights as Myth and History: Between the Revolutions of 1989 and the Arab Spring," *Journal of Contemporary Central and Eastern Europe (Debatte)* 23, no. 2–3 (2015), 151–66.

[3] Kurt Hager, *Erinnerungen* (Leipzig: Faber & Faber, 1996), 375–80.

One East German legal scholar claimed that Hermann Klenner's 1982 work *Marxism and Human Rights* represented a courageous over-coming of state censorship, on the grounds that it cited the UN Human Rights Covenants.[4] Because the SED self-evidently opposed human rights, to write on such a topic under this dictatorship could be nothing but an act of audacious nonconformity. Others were now confronted with dissonant memories: Siegfried Forberger, secretary of the KMR, was puzzled by his past inability to see the contradictions in the system in which he worked for 30 years, when they seemed so clear with only a decade of hindsight after the fall of the Berlin Wall. In his memoirs he wrote, "Yes, the free development of the person [through socialist human rights] – that sounded full of promise and was also what socialists had held up to us as the ideal. But did we not notice that we were light-years away from this in the GDR?"[5] Forberger remained proud of East Germany's contributions to the cause of anti-imperialism and its support for the anti-apartheid movement, but he could no longer fathom his own blindness to the human rights violations in the GDR. Until the end, however, Erich Honecker believed that there could be no human rights without socialism. While awaiting trial in Moabit Prison, charged with the manslaughter of Berlin Wall victims, Honecker remained resolute that the SED had simply been too passive and failed to make clear the human rights violations of the West. In his memoirs, he admitted that it was possible that he could have – perhaps – liberalised travel rights, but aside from that he maintained that the GDR had an exemplary record of championing human rights at home and around the world.[6]

The vigorous forgetting of socialist human rights has also conveniently erased the ideological collaboration and accommodation of the SED by senior members of the Protestant Church. In the memoirs of leading Church figures, the very idea of human rights is described as a taboo, implying that the act of publicly saying it aloud was a form of resistance.[7] Günther Krusche who was as a steadfast opponent of the independent human rights movement in the 1980s (as well as being a Stasi informant), later claimed that all Church activity on the subject was inherently

---

[4] Karl Mollnau in Inga Markovits, *Die Abwicklung: ein Tagebuch zum Ende der DDR-Justiz* (Munich: Beck, 1993), 178–80.

[5] Siegfried Forberger, *Das DDR-Komitee für Menschenrechte: Erinnerungen an den Sozialismus-Versuch im 20. Jahrhundert; Einsichten und Irrtümer des Siegfried Forberger, Sekretär des DDR-Komitees für Menschenrechte von 1959 bis 1989* (Self-pub., 2000), 198–99.

[6] Erich Honecker, *Moabiter Notizen* (Berlin: Edition Ost, 1994), 60.

[7] Albrecht Schönherr, *Gratwanderung: Gedanken über den Weg des Bundes der Evangelischen Kirchen in der DDR* (Leipzig: Evangelische Verlagsanstalt, 1992), 28.

transgressive while omitting the Church's institutional support for the SED's human rights politics.[8] Manfred Stolpe successfully wielded his record of promoting human rights as a church leader to launch a career in politics after reunification, becoming minister-president of Brandenburg from 1990 to 2002. His post-GDR writing on the subject, however, leaves out his personal praise for SED compliance with international human rights norms through the 1970s and early 1980s.[9] Rather than confront the complexity and moral ambiguity of Church relations with the SED, the erasure of socialist human rights has also allowed Church officials to present themselves as inherently oppositional figures.

As those East Germans most connected to the socialist human rights project were putting it out of their minds, FRG officials also contributed to this erasure through a Western-centric memory of East-West relations in the late Cold War. Twenty years after the collapse of SED rule, West German Foreign Minister Hans-Dietrich Genscher claimed that "the final Helsinki Act, in 1975, opened a completely new chapter in that it introduced Western values such as the right to self-determination of peoples, human rights, the solving of humanitarian questions in the East-West dialogue, indeed, obligated the other side to base itself on these ideas. [...] This was an especially politically astonishing development because the idea of this conference actually came from Moscow."[10] In Genscher's memory (and forgetfulness), there was neither a connection between anti-colonial activism and self-determination, nor an alternative vision of human rights advanced by the Eastern Bloc. These concepts were self-evidently Western, liberal and democratic; their realisation part of the long path towards the inevitable, if ironic, reunification of Germany.

Post-1989 legal institutions have also been crucial in shaping public memory of GDR human rights abuses, as the courts enshrined the status of the SED as structural violators of human rights into law.[11] When Erich Honecker along with other SED leaders, senior Stasi officials and several former border guards were charged with manslaughter, they were ultimately prosecuted on the basis of the International Human Rights

---

[8] Günter Krusche "Menschenrechte in christlicher Verantwortung. Die Kirchen in der DDR und die Menschenrechte," *Ökumenische Rundschau* 49 (2000), 26–42.

[9] Manfred Stolpe and Iring Fetscher, *Demokratie wagen: Aufbruch in Brandenburg: Reden, Beiträge, Interviews 1990–1993* (Berlin: Schüren, 1994), 193.

[10] Quoted in Alexander von Plato, *The End of the Cold War? Bush, Kohl, Gorbachev, and the Reunification of Germany* (New York: Palgrave Macmillan, 2015), 18.

[11] Raluca Grosescu, "Criminal Justice and Historical Master Narratives in Post-1989 Bulgaria and Germany," *European Politics and Society* 18, no. 1 (2017), 66–80.

Covenants of 1966 signed by the GDR.[12] While the courts initially sought to bring charges based on the violation of East German law, this fundamentally disregarded the nature of socialist legality in the GDR: After all, the so-called order to shoot at the border had ostensibly been put into place to defend human rights.[13] In the end (and lacking a suitable juridical alternative), the Constitutional Court of the Federal Republic found that the human rights abuses committed by the border guards, and by those issuing their orders, were so great as to legitimise a degree of retroactive punishment, even if those responsible were acting in accordance with the laws of the state in which they lived.[14] At one point, the courts invoked the UDHR, specifically the section on the right to life – despite its legal unenforceability – to justify the prosecution of those who gave the orders and those who obeyed them.[15] For some, this did not go nearly far enough, with one former regional high court justice arguing that the similarities between the crimes of the SED equalled those of the Nazis: "The one group disregarded human rights from the standpoint of race while the other did it from the class standpoint."[16] The SED had always presented itself as the antithesis to fascist rule; after the collapse of the GDR, the courts of reunified Germany portrayed it as little more than an ideologically inverted Third Reich.

Public discourse in the media in reunified Germany also depicted West German conceptions of human rights as objectively correct, with any deviations from these norms understood as politically suspect.[17] In 1995, the director of the influential Allensbach Institute for Public Opinion Research, Elisabeth Noelle-Neumann, published an article in the *Frankfurter Allgemeine Zeitung* (*FAZ*) arguing that West Germans believed in individual freedoms, but East Germans were only concerned with rights provided by a paternalistic state: "Among the East Germans resounds a conception of freedom held by totalitarian states: the state secures the freedom of the citizen from want. The conception of freedom

---

[12] James Sweeney, *The European Court of Human Rights in the Post-Cold War Era: Universality in Transition* (London: Routledge, 2013), 52–56.

[13] Peter Quint, "Judging the Past: The Prosecution of East German Border Guards and the GDR Chain of Command," *The Review of Politics* 61, no. 2 (1999), 313. On the "order to shoot" and human rights, see Chapter 2.

[14] Ibid., 321.

[15] Rudolf Geiger, "The German Border Guard Cases and International Human Rights," *European Journal of International Law* 9, no. 3 (1998), 545.

[16] A. James McAdams, *Judging the Past in Unified Germany* (Cambridge: Cambridge University Press, 2001), 26.

[17] On the delegitimisation of East German perspectives, see Paul Cooke, *Representing East Germany since Unification: From Colonization to Nostalgia* (New York: Berg, 2005).

held by Western democracies is completely antithetical to this."[18] The failure of East Germans to match the opinions of the West was pathologised as both a rejection of democracy and a nostalgic longing for totalitarianism. Yet the survey evidence cited to support this East-West dichotomy was flimsy at best: the right to free expression was deemed an important human right by 30 percent in the West, and 19 percent in the East; the right to life and the prohibition on torture by 15 percent in the West, and by 9 percent in the East. West German support for these rights was not terribly high, but it was held up as the natural and correct result of postwar democratisation. Crucial data points from the survey, were however, selectively omitted from the version published in the *FAZ*: East German support for the right to housing used to show a preference for state benefits over democracy did not mention that respondents included the inviolability of the privacy of the home within their understanding of that right. Also absent was the fact that more East than West Germans associated the idea of human rights with the "freedom of the individual – absence of arbitrary detention" and with the right to free movement – both freedoms limiting state power.[19] Despite painting all former GDR citizens as permanently tainted by their associations with totalitarianism, Noelle-Neumann had recently been engulfed in her own controversy over her antisemitic writings as a journalist in the Nazi era.[20]

The meaning of human rights in post-unification German politics was also intertwined with the ongoing delegitimisation of the GDR. While the FRG supposedly stood for human rights rooted in the freedom from state control over the private sphere, one of the first conflicts of post-unification was the imposition of West German abortion law on the new *Bundesländer* – a notable (and new) restriction on abortion access for the citizens of the former GDR. For many abortion opponents, reunification represented an opening to reverse the much more limited West German liberalisation of the 1970s by using reunification and its attendant reforms to East German law as cover for a more sweeping rollback: as one CDU (West) representative stated, "The Unification Treaty provides us with a unique opportunity that cannot be missed to realize human rights across Germany. The Treaty must be used to give a clear

[18] Elisabeth Noelle-Neumann, "Kein Schutz, keine Gleichheit, keine Gerechtigkeit," (*FAZ*, 8.3.1995).

[19] Elisabeth Noelle-Neumann, "Rechtsbewußtsein im wiedervereinigten Deutschland," *Zeitschrift für Rechtssoziologie* 16 (1995), 127.

[20] "Professor Is Criticized for Anti-Semitic Past," *The New York Times* (28 November 1991).

signal in favour of life and to bring about the end of current abortion practices."[21] Conservatives within the CDU/CSU caucus went even further, putting forward a proposal that would increase the criminal punishment both for doctors who were too lenient in their interpretation of "exceptional circumstances" and for women who sought to evade existing regulations on abortion access. They justified these measures on the grounds that "the unborn child is murdered through an abortion and thus its basic and human rights are violated."[22] Here, the attack on abortion access was tied to the broader delegitimisation of East Germany and "the GDR abortion law was cast as the last remnant of a 'failed system' that was both economically and morally 'bankrupt.'" For East German feminists, "self-determination with respect to abortion paralleled self-determination with respect to democracy; it was considered an individual's fundamental political right."[23] This linkage between human rights and bodily self-determination was already apparent in the first open GDR election in March 1990: the Independent Women's Association argued that "elementary human rights include the possibility of women's self-determination over their bodies," including "the right to free, self-decided pregnancy and abortion."[24] Support for these rights went beyond feminist activists and had broad cross-party support. The PDS election program directly quoted the Round Table Constitution: "Women have the right to a self-determined pregnancy. The state protects unborn life through the offer of social assistance."[25] The East German Christian Democrats and the Liberals (LDPD) did not endorse this line of argumentation on self-determination during the election campaign, but they both opposed the introduction of West German abortion law.

Women's groups from the former East Germany scrambled to organise a national campaign to preserve their rights but found it difficult to gain the support of their Western counterparts. Fearful of being associated with the crimes of the GDR, West German feminist groups rejected the link between self-determination, abortion access and the cause of human rights; instead, they framed the issue around "helping rather than

[21] Quoted in *Auf dem Weg zur deutschen Einheit: Deutschlandpolitische Debatten im Deutschen Bundestag vom 5. bis zum 20. September 1990* (Bonn: Der Bundestag, 1990), 597.

[22] Elizabeth Boa and Janet Wharton, eds., *Women and the Wende: Social Effects and Cultural Reflections of the German Unification Process* (Amsterdam: Rodopi, 1994), 42.

[23] Susan Gal and Gail Kligman, *Reproducing Gender: Politics, Publics, and Everyday Life after Socialism* (Princeton, NJ: Princeton University Press, 2000), 99.

[24] Berndt Musiolek, Jürgen Eichler and Carola Wuttke, *Parteien und politische Bewegungen im letzten Jahr der DDR* (Berlin: BasisDruck, 1991), 166.

[25] Margrit Gerste, "Gesetz Gut, Praxis Mies," *Die Zeit* (11.5.1990) and "Wahlprogramm der Partei des Demokratischen Sozialismus," *Neues Deutschland* (27.2.1990).

punishing" women.[26] In the *Bundestag*, a majority of West German representatives along with support from an East German minority were able to push through legislation to dramatically restrict access to abortion. For many East German women, the loss of legal bodily autonomy was traumatising, especially in concert with the loss of other social and economic rights, such as state-provided child care, that had previously facilitated their independence through participation in the workforce. One study in the mid-1990s noted, "In every interview, women made the point that the new law can only be understood as a conservative and/or aggressive response to women's claim for autonomy, bringing them once again under the supervision and control of the state."[27] The supposedly ingrained illiberalism of East Germans had successfully been used to delegitimise a campaign for the preservation of individual autonomy against state interference. While West Germany was held up as the paragon of liberal human rights, when it came to women's bodies, state power trumped the rights of the individual.

Conversely, former members of the East German elite – professors in particular, but also ex-Stasi officials – now found themselves practically unemployable in reunified Germany and scrambled to adapt their discourse of human rights to a hostile new political environment. Groups such as the Gesellschaft zum Schutz von Bürgerrecht und Menschenwürde (Society for the Protection of Civil Rights and Human Dignity, or GBM) and the Society for Human Rights in Saxony emerged as the champions of East Germans now persecuted (and prosecuted) by the Federal Republic.[28] In one 1994 GBM report on the impact of unification on human rights, they acknowledged that although certain areas of rights had improved, including improved political rights, civil liberties and freedom of movement,

the [Unification] Treaty and its extensive annexes have imposed on East Germany a special legal regime. [...] Because of the limitations on their rights, a majority of ex-GDR citizens are now in a legally inferior position, with the unequal status of a minority.[29]

While these organisations sought to challenge mass privatisation of the former GDR economy and the legal mechanisms employed against former East German citizens, their association with the abuses of the

[26] Gal and Kligman, *Reproducing Gender*, 100.
[27] Brigitte Young, *Triumph of the Fatherland: German Unification and the Marginalization of Women* (Ann Arbor: University of Michigan Press, 1999), 184.
[28] Roland Brauckmann, *Amnesty International als Feindobjekt der DDR* (Berlin: Berliner LStU, 1996), 93.
[29] GBM, *Human Rights in East Germany* (Berlin: GBM, 1994), 3–4.

SED and the Stasi undermined the acceptance of such campaigns with the broader public. One such human rights group – the Society for Legal and Humanitarian Support – elected a former Stasi general to act as honorary chairman, causing a seemingly predictable backlash in the media.[30]

Some ex-GDR intellectuals were able to push for a different kind of human rights post-unification through the Party for Democratic Socialism in the 1990s, and through its successor party The Left (Die Linke), to the present day. Hermann Klenner continued to publish prolifically for more than 20 years after the fall of the Berlin Wall, criticising the inequalities and hypocrisies of bourgeois liberal democracy, and promoting a socialist – though now democratic – vision of human rights.[31] He was even awarded a human rights prize from the GBM in 2005, a year after it had been awarded to Angela Davis, the African-American feminist and Communist activist whose release from prison had once been a cause of the KMR. Some sought to use their own experiences under dictatorship to bolster their own authority as human rights experts. In an article, Uwe-Jens Heuer, a reformist Marxist legal scholar and PDS representative at the Bundestag in the 1990s, and former SED member Georg Schirmer wrote,

Political and civil rights are unconditionally necessary and [cannot] be compensated through economic and social rights. This we had to learn painfully in our country, the GDR. But now we are having the no less painful experience that these (political and civil) rights exist primarily in the space of pious imagination; and are experienced by the former citizens of the GDR as a welcome, but very limited increase in freedom, because these political rights are not sufficiently supported by the realization of social rights.[32]

Rather than speaking of themselves as individual victims of reunification, they argued from a position of those who could truly see the failings of both systems.

Although the activism of former SED and Stasi elites was self-interested (and self-centred), their criticisms were not unfounded. While unification represented the realisation of pluralistic elections and of guaranteed rights to free speech and assembly, as well as other political and civil liberties that had been denied to East Germans for 40 years, the rapid transition to a private economy impoverished, dislocated and

---

[30] Brauckmann, Amnesty International als Feindobjekt der DDR, 94.
[31] Sebastian Prinz, Die programmatische Entwicklung der PDS: Kontinuität und Wandel der Politik einer sozialistischen Partei (Paderborn: Springer-Verlag, 2010), 143.
[32] Uwe-Jens Heuer and Gregor Schirmer, "Human Rights Imperialism," Monthly Review (blog), 1.3.1998 (https://monthlyreview.org).

alienated many. Although Chancellor Helmut Kohl had promised that "No one will be worse off than before – and many will be better off," privatisation gutted many sectors of the East German economy.[33] Rather than bringing universal prosperity, the transition to a market economy caused unemployment to skyrocket to nearly 30 percent, and compelled the migration of more than two million ex-East Germans to the West.[34] For many, the political and civil freedoms offered by a union with the Federal Republic stood in contrast to the economic devastation of many communities and the rollback of social services, particularly for working women.

For the GDR dissidents who had fought for human rights in the 1980s, reunification brought mixed emotions: Bärbel Bohley famously lamented that the dissidents sought justice, but all they got was the *Rechtsstaat* – a state under the rule of law. This has been interpreted by some as nostalgia for dictatorship, but in fact, it spoke to the sadness over lost opportunities after the revolution of 1989 for a more egalitarian and democratic society.[35] The dissidents won their revolution against the SED, but the fight to imagine and establish a better form of human rights – more than just what was on offer from West Germany – was lost. Bohley's concerns were not universal among former dissidents, however, and many were satisfied that the establishment of pluralism had realised the human rights they had fought for. Martin Böttger, one of the earliest members of the IFM and New Forum and later a Bündnis '90/Green Party representative, saw participatory democracy and the establishment of a free public sphere as the primary victory of the human rights movement, and did not see demands for socioeconomic rights in the 2000s as an equivalent and morally necessary cause.[36] Others, such as Vera Lengsfeld, who would eventually find a home with the Christian Democrats, took a conservative turn after the fall of the Berlin Wall and advocated for the "right to a homeland" – echoing the demands of postwar nationalists in West Germany.[37] Just as the mass movement of 1989 fractured after the fall of the Berlin Wall, so too has the judgement

---

[33] Helmut Kohl, "Blooming Landscapes Address" (1.7.1990) (http://ghdi.ghi-dc.org).

[34] For an overview of the economic collapse in the 1990s, see Philipp Ther, *Europe since 1989* (Princeton, NJ: Princeton University Press, 2016), 88–89.

[35] Charles Maier, *Dissolution: The Crisis of Communism and the End of East Germany* (Princeton, NJ: Princeton University Press, 1997), 319.

[36] Martin Böttger, *Friedliche Revolution und deutsche Einheit: sächsische Bürgerrechtler ziehen Bilanz* (Berlin: Ch. Links, 2006), 28.

[37] Eckhard Jesse, ed., *Eine Revolution und ihre Folgen: 14 Bürgerrechtler ziehen Bilanz* (Berlin: Ch. Links, 2000), 88.

of former dissidents on the relative merits of reunification and its impact on human rights.

First in the Soviet Zone of Occupation and later in the GDR, the idea of human rights acted as an icon of legitimacy, and the language was adopted and instrumentalised by almost every faction and group imaginable. For the SED, human rights provided a rhetorical means to push back against Social Democratic attacks, to campaign against West German persecution of Communists, to appeal to anti-imperial solidarity and to negotiate global diplomatic recognition. For East German citizens, it was a tool with which to demand greater religious freedoms, the right to leave the country, the introduction of a pluralistic and democratic socialism and, finally, the dissolution of the GDR. At each of these points, such claims were ostensibly self-evident to those who held them, yet the transitions from one set of ideas to another came about through social and political conflict, rather than the seamless unfolding of an idea towards the natural endpoint that was German unification. This multiplicity of conceptions of human rights that saturated the history of East Germany reinforces Samuel Moyn's argument that "what is self-evident about human rights turns out not to be very much."[38]

The collapse of socialist human rights and the rapid transformation of the discourse surrounding human rights towards pluralism and democratisation came about as the result of complex changes in global politics, local social dynamics, and the declining capacity of the SED to project an image of legitimacy rooted in antifascist struggle and economic achievement. Although the GDR had long been closely attuned to international debates about human rights politics, East Germany was steadily isolated from the international community, including fellow socialist states. While the postcolonial world was never as allied to the socialist position as the SED portrayed in its propaganda, the abundance of "development dictatorships" and other authoritarian states demanding self-determination at first prevented the East Germans from becoming a pariah in the field of human rights in the 1960s and 1970s. By the 1980s, however, the turn throughout the Western world towards individual rights, liberal democracy and the rule of law as basic prerequisites for human rights steadily reduced the number of East German allies and sympathisers. As Afro-Asian countries turned to discourses of tradition and culture to deflect from Western human rights criticism, the SED and the rest of the Eastern Bloc continued to invoke an outdated ideological

---

[38] Samuel Moyn, "Afterword: The Self-Evidence of Human Rights," in *Self-Evident Truths? Human Rights and the Enlightenment*, ed. Kate Tunstall (New Haven, CT: Yale University Press, 2012), 261.

conception that now had little intellectual purchase in the rest of the world. Once Eastern Bloc solidarity on the matter of human rights fell apart completely (as East Germany's neighbours began to introduce limited "bourgeois" political and civil rights), the basis for the SED's claims of superiority in the field of human rights collapsed with it.

The capacity of SED elites and the GDR-Committee for Human Rights to reconcile reality with theory also began to falter in the 1980s. Growing economic problems undercut even the hope for modest egalitarian prosperity and the explosion of official requests to exit the GDR shook the faith of loyal intellectuals who now came to believe that reform was imperative if the cause of socialism was to survive. As a human rights movement emerged from the independent peace movement, groups like the Initiative for Peace and Human Rights translated the hegemonic discourse of the SED into a new vocabulary that addressed everyday problems and called for the democratisation of the socialist system, and further undermined the resolve of wavering intellectuals and mid-tier Party officials and functionaries. From the perspective of the East German people, there was a steady collapse in the regime's legitimacy as the cultural potency of antifascism faded along with the memory of the Weimar and Nazi eras, and the benefits of accepting the "welfare dictatorship" of the SED dwindled.[39] Once joining the demonstrations in the street (and fighting for human rights) seemed more likely to help individuals realise their interests, East Germans moved in huge numbers from apathy to open revolt. The dissident movement fashioned a discourse of opposition that was broad and inclusive enough to allow for a coalition with diverse interests and goals, thus creating a new space for East Germans to demand their rights as citizens.

The realisation of human rights in East Germany was not a linear movement from a universal bequest of self-evident moral values to a clear program of liberal democratic revolution: for some, it was about rescuing the old utopias; for others, about creating an altogether new utopia; and for others still, human rights were just another strategy for survival. The initial spread of the language of human rights alone did little to spur on democratisation in the GDR and helped to reinforce the SED dictatorship for decades. As human rights were codified in the postwar era through international treaties and turned into law, it remained a highly malleable discourse capable of serving a diverse array of social, economic and political arrangements, rather than simply acting

---

[39] Konrad Jarausch, "Care and Coercion: The GDR as Welfare Dictatorship," in *Dictatorship as Experience: Towards a Socio-cultural History of the GDR*, ed. Konrad Jarausch (New York: Berghahn, 1999), 47–69.

as the basis for a Western model of liberal democracy and market economics. When a human rights movement for democratisation arose in the 1980s, it encompassed communist reformers, Christian socialists, feminists, revolutionary Marxists, environmental activists and others whose main priority was simply the fulfilment of basic material needs or the desire to see distant family members.

The endpoint of German reunification ultimately resulted in the privatisation of the former GDR, but demands for human rights in East Germany were not merely a vehicle for promoting rapacious capitalism under the guise of universal values.[40] Human rights in the West may have been intertwined with a depoliticised liberal politics of fear or a new quest for a minimal utopia for those disillusioned by socialism, but in the GDR this was not the case.[41] While some who demanded human rights in East Germany were making depoliticised demands to exit the country, for most, the language of human rights was a vehicle for domestic and international political engagement. For the SED, human rights were part of a machinery for politicising the population to promote a socialist agenda at home and around the world.[42] For the Church and for many dissidents, human rights acted as a vehicle to also address socioeconomic problems, global inequality and solidarity with the Global South. Rather than depoliticise its subjects, human rights dissent in the 1980s specifically aimed to have East Germans engage in a moribund political process to foster a reinvigorated democratic community. The fact that a vision of human rights focused on negative liberties from state power eventually triumphed does not erase the myriad alternatives – fought for by so many East Germans, albeit unsuccessfully – that promoted a vision of democratic values in tandem with strong provisions for positive social and economic rights. In short, it was never just about (freedom through) blue jeans.

Histories of human rights have often focused on the search for origins, be it in the Code of Hammurabi, the American and French Revolutions, the creation of the UDHR in 1948, the rise of transnational NGO activism in the 1970s or the liberal interventionism of the 1990s. This orientation towards finding the source of the present-day hegemony of

---

[40] Samuel Moyn, "A Powerless Companion: Human Rights in the Age of Neoliberalism," *Law and Contemporary Problems* 77, no. 4 (2014), 147–69.

[41] On human rights as a minimalist utopia, see Wendy Brown, "'The Most We Can Hope For...': Human Rights and the Politics of Fatalism," *The South Atlantic Quarterly* 103, no. 2 (2004), 451–63.

[42] On solidarity as a "politics machine," see Toni Weis, "The Politics Machine: On the Concept of 'Solidarity' in East German Support for SWAPO," *Journal of Southern African Studies* 37, no. 2 (2011), 351–67.

the liberal democratic human rights movement, however, creates a bias towards those past movements that connect directly to the present day as a natural endpoint. As an alternative, Upendra Baxi has argued that "the originary narratives that trace the birth of human rights in the Declarations of the Rights of Man need replacement by a history of human rights struggles for human rights futures."[43] Although the human rights movement hit a high point of international legitimacy and influence in the 1990s, for the past 20 years its claims to represent a universal and undeniable good has been steadily challenged. Critics charge that international human rights NGOs have become a force for Western imperialism, acting to legitimise global neoliberal hegemony and military interventionism, while trampling on cultural diversity and ignoring skyrocketing economic inequality.[44] For that, and many other reasons, it is important to return to the historical alternatives that were pushed aside and forgotten over the course of the late 20th century. The authoritarian human rights politics of the SED stands as a warning sign, illuminating how individual rights and freedoms can be sacrificed on the altar of human rights. At the same time, however, the human rights activists and dissidents of the GDR present us with an alternative conception of human rights that goes beyond freedom from state oppression and from basic want to offer a vision of how both liberty and equality can be achieved together. The example of the GDR shows the extremes to which human rights can be reinvented and reimagined: for dictatorship or dissent, for reform or revolution.

---

[43] Upendra Baxi, *The Future of Human Rights* (New Delhi: Oxford University Press India, 2012), 109.

[44] On recent criticism of the international human rights system, see Stephen Hopgood, *The Endtimes of Human Rights* (Ithaca, NY: Cornell University Press, 2013); Lori Allen, *The Rise and Fall of Human Rights: Cynicism and Politics in Occupied Palestine* (Stanford, CA: Stanford University Press, 2013); Samuel Moyn, *Not Enough: Human Rights in an Unequal World* (Cambridge, MA: Harvard University Press, 2018).

Archival Sources

Archiv Bürgerbewegung Leipzig (ABL)

Archiv der Akademie der Künste, Berlin (AdK)

Archiv der sozialen Demokratie, Bonn (AdsD)

Archiv der Berlin-Brandenburgischen Akademie der Wissenschaften, Berlin (AdW)

Archiv der DDR-Opposition, Robert Havemann Gesellschaft, Berlin

Bundesarchiv, Berlin and Koblenz (BArch)

Bundesbeauftragte für die Unterlagen des Staatssicherheitsdienstes der ehemaligen DDR, Berlin, Berlin (BStU)

Deutsches Rundfunkarchiv, Potsdam-Babelsberg (DRA)

Evangelisches Zentralarchiv, Berlin (EZA)

Hoover Institution Library and Archives, Palo Alto, CA

Mecklenburgisches Landeshauptarchiv-Schwerin (MLHA-Schwerin)

Politisches Archiv des Auswärtigen Amts, Berlin (PA AA)

Sächsisches Staatsarchiv, Hauptstaatsarchiv (Dresden) and Staatsarchiv (Leipzig)

Thüringisches Staatsarchiv-Rudolstadt (ThSA)

Index

For EU product safety concerns, contact us at Calle de José Abascal, 56–1°,
28003 Madrid, Spain or eugpsr@cambridge.org.

www.ingramcontent.com/pod-product-compliance
Ingram Content Group UK Ltd.
Pitfield, Milton Keynes, MK11 3LW, UK
UKHW020431240426
470322UK00017B/450